Philip the Bold

Philip the Bold

THE FORMATION OF THE BURGUNDIAN STATE

RICHARD VAUGHAN

LONGMAN
London and New York

Longman Group Limited London

Associated companies, branches and representatives
throughout the world

Published in the United States of America
by Longman Inc., New York

First published 1962
First published in paperback 1979

British Library Cataloguing in Publication Data
Vaughan, Richard, b.1927
Philip the Bold.
1. Burgundy – History
944'.4'026   DC611.B776

ISBN 0-582-49048-0

Printed in Great Britain by
Richard Clay (The Chaucer Press) Ltd
Bungay, Suffolk

Contents

List of Maps and Genealogical table

Maps

Genealogical table

Abbreviations

AB	*Annales de Bourgogne*
ABSHF	*Annuaire-bulletin de la Société de l'histoire de France*
ACFF	*Annales du Comité flamand de France*
ACO	Archives départementales de la Côte-d'Or, Dijon
AD	Archives communales, Dijon
ADN	Archives départementales du Nord, Lille
AFAHB	*Annales de la Fédération archéologique et historique de Belgique*
AGR	Archives générales du royaume, Brussels
AHR	*American Historical Review*
AN	Archives nationales, Paris
APAE	*Ancien pays et assemblées d'États*
ASEB	*Annales de la Société d'émulation de Bruges*
ASHAG	*Annales de la Société d'histoire et d'archéologie de Gand*
ASRAB	*Annales de la Société royale d'archéologie de Bruxelles*
BAB	*Bulletin de l'Académie des sciences, belles-lettres et arts de Besançon*
BARB	*Bulletin de l'Académie royale de Belgique*
BARBL	*Bulletin de l'Académie royale de Belgique. Lettres*
BBB	*Bulletin du bibliophile belge*
BCHDN	*Bulletin de la Commission historique du département du Nord*
BCRH	*Bulletin de la Commission royale d'histoire*
BD	Bibliothèque publique, Dijon
BEC	*Bibliothèque de l'École des chartes*
BEFAR	Bibliothèque des Écoles françaises d'Athènes et de Rome
BEHE	Bibliothèque de l'École des hautes études
BIHR	*Bulletin of the Institute of historical research*
BM	*Bulletin monumental*
BMHGU	*Bijdragen en mededeelingen van het historisch gezelschap te Utrecht*
BN	Bibliothèque nationale, Paris
BR	Bibliothèque royale, Brussels

BSEC	Bulletin de la Société d'études de la province de Cambrai
BSHAF	Bulletin de la Société de l'histoire de l'art français
BSHAG	Bulletin de la Société d'histoire et d'archéologie de Gand
CABSS	Comptes rendus des congrès de l'Association bourguignonne des sociétés savantes
CDIHF	Collection de documents inédits sur l'histoire de France
CRH	Commission royale d'histoire
GBA	Gazette des beaux-arts
GBK	Gentsche bijdragen tot de kunstgeschiedenis
GWU	Geschichte in Wissenschaft und Unterricht
HG	Hansische Geschichtsblätter
HV	Historische Vierteljahrsschrift
IAB, etc.	Printed inventories of archives, see below, pp. 249–50, for full titles
JGVV	Jahrbuch für Gesetzgebung, Verwaltung und Volkwirtschaft
MA	Le Moyen Âge
MAD	Mémoires de l'Académie des sciences, arts et belles-lettres de Dijon
MAH	Mélanges d'archéologie et d'histoire
MARBL	Mémoires de l'Académie royale de Belgique. Lettres
MAS	Mémoires de l'Académie des sciences, belles-lettres et arts de Savoie
MCACO	Mémoires de la Commission des antiquités du département de la Côte-d'Or
MCMP	Mémoires de la Commission départementale des monuments historiques du Pas-de-Calais
MSA	Mémoires de la Société académique du département de l'Aube
MSAN	Mémoires de la Société académique du Nivernais
MSBGH	Mémoires de la Société bourguignonne de géographie et d'histoire
MSE	Mémoires de la Société éduenne
MSED	Mémoires de la Société d'émulation du Doubs
MSHAB	Mémoires de la Société d'histoire et d'archéologie de Bretagne
MSHAC	Mémoires de la Société d'histoire et d'archéologie de Chalon-sur-Saône
MSHAL	Mémoires de la Société historique et archéologique de Langres
MSHDB	Mémoires de la Société pour l'histoire du droit et des institutions des anciens pays bourguignons, comtois et romands
MSHP	Mémoires de la Société de l'histoire de Paris et de l'Île-de-France
PSHIL	Publications de la section historique de l'Institut grand-ducal de Luxembourg
PTSEC	Positions des thèses soutenues à l'École des chartes
RAAM	Revue de l'art ancien et moderne

RAG	Rijksarchief, Ghent
RB	*Revue bourguignonne*
RBAHA	*Revue belge d'archéologie et d'histoire de l'art*
RBPH	*Revue belge de philologie et d'histoire*
RCB	*Revue champenoise et bourguignonne*
RCC	*Revue des cours et conférences*
REH	*Revue des études historiques*
RH	*Revue historique*
RHD	*Revue d'histoire diplomatique*
RHDFE	*Revue historique de droit français et étranger*
RHE	*Revue d'histoire ecclésiastique*
RN	*Revue du Nord*
RNHB	*Revue nobiliaire, héraldique et biographique*
RV	*Rheinische Vierteljahrsblätter*
SHDPF	Société d'histoire du droit des pays flamands, picards et wallons
SHF	Société de l'histoire de France
ZK	*Zeitschrift für Kirchengeschichte*

Introduction

The region of modern France known as Burgundy has its name from the Burgundians, a people of East Germanic origin who settled there in the fifth century. From 1032 onwards part of this area, the duchy of Burgundy, which broadly speaking lay between Troyes and Lyons to the north and south, and was bounded on the east by the river Saône, was ruled in unbroken succession by descendants of Hugh Capet, the first Capetian king of France. It was one of the largest and wealthiest fiefs of the French crown and, on the whole, its dukes, though intent on consolidating their own authority and enlarging their own territories, were staunch supporters of the Capetian rulers of France. When the Capetian dynasty of Burgundy died out in 1361 it was replaced by a Valois dynasty, which ruled the duchy from 1363 to 1477. The Valois dukes, in spite of their membership of the royal house of France, proceeded to set up a state of their own which, during most of the fifteenth century, constituted a major European power on the eastern boundaries of France. They were able to do this because they possessed, not only the duchy, but also the county, of Burgundy, lying on the eastern side of the duchy, and, ultimately, the whole of the Low Countries as well. The subject of this study is the first of the Valois dukes of Burgundy, Philip the Bold; its theme, the emergence of a Burgundian state under his aegis in the years 1384–1404. The name Burgundy has been used by historians simply because the history of this new political entity began when Philip the Bold was invested with the duchy in 1363; they continue to use it, for want of a better word, when, in the fifteenth century, the centre of gravity of the state shifted to the Low Countries, and even after the loss of the duchy of Burgundy in 1477.

Although many books have been written about the Valois dukes of Burgundy, the attention of historians has centred on the last two dukes, Philip the Good and Charles the Rash, both of whom have recently been the subject of excellent studies.[1] Interest in Valois Burgundy as a whole has tended, too, to be secondary to interest in certain parts of it. Thus to the Belgian historians, not unnaturally, the Low Countries are of paramount importance, and the two Burgundies recede into such insignificance that they may even be dismissed as not forming part of the Burgundian state.[2] In France, Valois Burgundy was treated in great detail in the eighteenth century by Dom Plancher, but, because he was writing the history of geographical Burgundy, the Low Countries were largely ignored by him. More recently, Burgundian studies in France have concentrated on the Capetian dukes, whose history was ably traced in Petit's exhaustive work, and who have lately been the subject of a brilliant study by Richard.[3] This century still awaits a history of Valois Burgundy which might serve as a modern version of de Barante's *Histoire des ducs de Bourgogne de la Maison de Valois*. Two historians, one French and the other German, made the attempt at the beginning of the century, and their first volumes were published in 1909–10, but Petit's work was cut short by death, and Cartellieri's by the First World War.[4]

The present work is a study of the formation of the Burgundian state under Philip the Bold and, as such, it embraces all his principal territories. Its limitations will be apparent: it is not a biography of Philip the Bold, nor does it extend to an examination of the religious, cultural and economic life of the lands over which he ruled. But it does attempt to describe his policies, his administration, his court and his finances, and to depict Burgundy as a European power. In all this, it presents an interpretation of Burgundian history which might be described as controversial, for, according to received notions among historians, the formation of the Burgundian state is linked with the unification of the Low Countries under Philip the Good, and Philip the Bold, far from being acclaimed as the founder of a new state, has been relegated to the position of an ambitious French prince.

I extend my grateful thanks to all those who have helped with the writing of this book: Mr. C. A. J. Armstrong, Professor C. R. Cheney and Professor Bruce Dickins have kindly read it through in type-

---

[1] Bonenfant, *P. le Bon*, and Bartier, *Charles le Téméraire*. On the Valois dukes as a whole there are two recent short works of little value: Colin, *Ducs de Bourgogne*, and Calmette, *Grands ducs de Bourgogne*.

[2] Thus Pirenne, *AHR* xiv (1908–9), 477.

[3] Petit, *Ducs de Bourgogne de la race capétienne*, and Richard, *Ducs de Bourgogne et la formation du duché*.

[4] Cartellieri, *Geschichte der Herzöge von Burgund*, i. *P. der Kühne*, and Petit, *Ducs de Bourgogne de la Maison de Valois*, i. *P. le Hardi, 1363–1380*.

script and made many valuable suggestions; I have drawn heavily, with her generous permission, on Mlle A. van Nieuwenhuysen's unpublished thesis on Philip the Bold's receipt-general; Professor Dr. H. Heimpel, Professor J. Richard and Professor M. Mollat have sent me copies of their papers; Mr. P. Rycraft has furnished me with transcripts from the Aragonese archives; Mr. P. Grierson has given me advice on monetary matters; and Mr. W. Prevenier has taken a great deal of trouble on my behalf in many different ways. I have to thank the Directors of the departmental archives at Lille and Dijon and the Assistant Librarian of the Dijon public library for answering queries about documents in their repositories; and I also gratefully acknowledge the help and kindness which has invariably been extended to me by the authorities of the libraries and record offices which I have visited or from which I have requested photographs: the Bibliothèque nationale and the Archives nationales at Paris; the Bibliothèque royale and the Archives générales du royaume at Brussels; the departmental archives at Lille and Dijon; the public library and the Archives communales at Dijon; and the Rijksarchief at Ghent. For their help with, and permission for, the illustrations, I am indebted to the authorities of the museum and public library at Dijon (especially MM. P. Quarré and J. C. Garreta), the Bibliothèque nationale at Paris and the Rijksmuseum at Amsterdam, and I also thank the numerous other persons who have helped me to find suitable illustrations for this book. Finally, I am much indebted to the authorities of the National Central Library for borrowing numerous works from abroad for my use at Cambridge.

RICHARD VAUGHAN

Corpus Christi College, Cambridge
November 1961

Author's note to the paperback reprint

The only changes from the original edition made in this reprint are the omission of the seven illustrations and the references to them, and the correction of minor errors. Important corrections and revisions, which have not been incorporated into the text of the reprint, have been made or suggested in the following works:

Prevenier, W. 'Financiën en boekhouding in de Bourgondische periode. Nieuwe bronnen en resultaten'. *Tijdschrift voor Geschiedenis* lxxxii (1969), 469–81 (especially on Philip the Bold's revenues).

Prevenier, W. *De Leden en de Staten van Vlaanderen, 1384–1405*. Verhandelingen van der Koninklijke Vlaamse Academie, xliii. Brussels, 1961 (especially on the Members and Estates of Flanders, pp. 138–9).

Richard, J. 'Un nouveau "Philippe le Hardi" '. *AB* xxxv (1963), 54–7 (corrects several factual errors).

Stengers, J. 'Philippe le Hardi et les Etats de Brabant'. *Hommage au Professeur Paul Bonenfant*, 383–408. Brussels, 1965 (shows that the meeting was in 1401, not as stated on p. 101 below, in 1403, and makes other corrections).

One major collection of source material has appeared since the original edition: *Ordonnances de Philippe le Hardi, de Marguerite de Male et de Jean sans Peur, 1381–1419*: vol. i, *1381–1393*, ed. P. Bonenfant, J. Bartier and A. van Nieuwenhuysen. Recueil des ordonnances des Pays-Bas, Brussels, 1964; vol. ii, *Ordonnances de Philippe le Hardi et de Marguerite de Male du 17 janvier 1394 au 25 février 1405*, ed. A. van Nieuwenhuysen, Ministry of Justice, Brussels, 1974.

Other relevant works published since *Philip the Bold* or inadvertently not noted therein are:

Buchet, A. 'La saisie du château et de la terre de Bolland par Philippe le Hardi, duc de Bourgogne, 1389–1402'. *Bulletin de la Société verviétoise d'archéologie et d'histoire* xliii (1956), 43–55.

Cockshaw, P. 'A propos de la circulation monétaire entre la Flandre et le Brabant de 1384 a 1390'. *Contributions à l'histoire économique et sociale* vi (1970–71), 105–42.

Cockshaw, P. 'Le fonctionnement des ateliers monétaires sous Philippe le Hardi'. *Cercle d'études numismatiques, Bulletin trimestriel* vii, 2 (1970), 24–37.

Cockshaw, P. 'Mentions d'auteurs, de copistes, d'enlumineurs et de librairies dans les comptes généraux de l'État bourguignon (1384–1419)'. *Scriptorium* xxiii (1969), 122–44.

Debersée, M. 'Une dépense à la charge du duc de Bourgogne à la fin du XIVe siècle: les travaux et réparations effectués à Lille et dans sa châtellenie'. *RN* liii (1971), 409–31.

Graffart, A. and Uyttebrouck, A. 'Quelques documents inédits concernant l'accession de la maison de Bourgogne au duché de Brabant, 1395–1404'. *BCRH* cxxxvii (1971), 57–137.

Hinkey, D. M. 'The Dijon altar piece by Melchior Broederlam and Jacques de Baerze: a study of its iconographical integrity'. *Dissertation abstracts international A* xxxvii (1976): 1897.

Hommerich, L. van. 'Philippe le Hardi et les États du duché de Limbourg et des autres pays d'Outre-Meuse, 1387–1404'. *RN* xlix (1967), 193–4.

Hughes, M. J. 'The library of Philip the Bold and Margaret of Flanders, first Valois duke and duchess of Burgundy'. *Journal of medieval history* iv (1978), 145–88.

Leman, A. 'La politique religieuse de Philippe le Hardi en Flandre'. *AFAHB* xvi (1903), 437–49.

Marchal-Verdoodt, M. *Table des noms de personnes et des lieux mentionnés dans les plus anciens comptes de la recette générale de Philippe le Hardi, duc de Bourgogne (1383–1389)*. CRH. Brussels, 1971.

Muynck, R. de. 'De Gentse oorlog (1379–1385) Oorzaken en karakter'. *ASHAG* (n.s.), v (1951), 305–18.

Nieuwenhuysen, A. van. 'La comptabilité d'un receveur de Philippe le Hardi'. *Hommage au Professeur Paul Bonenfant*, 409–19. Brussels, 1965.

Nieuwenhuysen, A. van. 'L'organisation financière des États du duc de Bourgogne Philippe le Hardi', *Acta historica bruxellensia*, i, *Recherches sur l'histoire des finances publiques en Belgique*, 215–47. Brussels, 1967.

Nieuwenhuysen, A. van. 'Les ordonnances de Philippe le Hardi'. *Bulletin de la Commission royale des anciennes Lois et Ordonnances de Belgique* xxv (1971–2), 75–138.

Pistono, S. P. 'Flanders and the Hundred Years War: the quest for the *trêve marchande*'. *BIHR* xlix (1976), 185–97.

Pistono, S. P. 'Henry IV and the Vier Leden: conflict in Anglo-Flemish relations, 1402–3'. *RBPH* liv (1976), 458–73.

Pistono, S. P. 'The accession of Henry IV: effects on Anglo-Flemish relations 1399–1402'. *Tijdschrift voor Geschiedenis* 89 (1976), 465–73.

Prevenier, W. 'Les perturbations dans les relations commerciales anglo-flamandes entre 1379 et 1407'. *Economies et sociétés du Moyen Âge: Mélanges Edouard Perroy*, 477–97. Paris, 1972.

Proot, H. 'Filips de Stoute en de stad Kortrijk'. *De Leigouw* xii (1970), 131–9.

Rey, M. 'Philippe le Hardi et la Franche-Comté'. *Publications du Centre européen d'études burgundo-medianes* viii (1966), 55–62.

Rey, M. 'La politique financière de Philippe le Hardi en Franche-Comté'. *MSHDB* xxvi (1965), 7–50.

Salet, F. 'Histoire et héraldique: La succession de Bourgogne de 1361'. *Mélanges offerts à René Crozet*, 1307–16. Poitiers, 1966.

Sapin, C. 'Claus de Werve imagier des ducs de Bourgogne. Musée des Beaux-Arts, Dijon, du 26 juin au 19 septembre 1976'. *Archeologia* xcvii (1976), 58–61.

Sterling, C. 'Œuvres retrouvées de Jean de Beaumetz, peintre de Phillippe le Hardi'. *Bulletin Musées Royaux des Beaux-Arts: Miscellanea Erwin Panofsky*, 57–82. Brussels, 1955.

Toth-Ubbens, M. 'Een dubbelvorstenhuwelijk in het jaar 1385'. *Bijdragen voor de Geschiedenis der Nederlanden* xix (1964), 107–10.

Vignier, F. 'Réunion du Charolais au duché de Bourgogne'. *MSHDB* xxii (1961), 191–5.

Winter, P. M. de. 'The patronage of Philippe le Hardi, duke of Burgundy (1364–1404)', *Dissertation abstracts international A* xxxvii (1977), 5409–10.

RICHARD VAUGHAN

University of Hull
September 1978

CHAPTER ONE

Philip the Bold and the Recovery of France under Charles V

France had for long enjoyed an unchallenged, apparently unshakeable, supremacy in European affairs when Philip the Bold, fourth son of King John the Good and Bonne of Luxembourg, was born at Pontoise on 17 January 1342. She had played the leading part in almost all those movements and activities which had occupied and transformed medieval Christendom in the previous two hundred years. Her culture, language and political influence had been diffused or extended over much of Europe; her material resources were second to none. While the house of Valois, in the person of King Philip VI, had in 1328 succeeded the Capets on her throne, descendants of the latter now occupied those of Naples and Hungary. In the half-century before Philip the Bold's birth France had first defied and then domesticated the papacy; she had extended her boundaries to the east at the expense of the Holy Roman Empire and reduced Navarre and Flanders to puppet states. At the same time the political authority of her rulers had been reinforced by the emergence of two central bureaucratic institutions, the *Parlement* and the *chambre des comptes*. But a series of fateful and decisive events now intervened to upset the fortunes of France and undermine her hegemony: on 7 October 1337 King Edward III of England publicly laid claim to her throne[1] and thus provoked a war which was in fact only an episode in medieval Anglo-French rivalry, but which historians, by throwing in with it for good measure a succession of later struggles, have been able to call the Hundred Years War.

The defeat of France and her allies, the kings of Majorca and Bohemia and the counts of Flanders and Savoy, on the field of Crécy in 1346 was decisive but not disastrous, for Edward III, too exhausted

---

[1] *Foedera*, ii (3), 192.

to follow up his success, had to content himself with the siege and conquest of Calais. Soon after this the hideous visitation of the Black Death intervened and put an effective stop to any French plans of retaliation across the Channel. In 1350 Philip VI was succeeded on the throne by his son John the Good whose promising nickname and reputation for chivalry have not dissuaded posterity from reckoning him among the worst of medieval French kings. On 19 September 1356, in spite of the presence of nineteen others dressed exactly like him, and the efforts of his fourteen-year-old son Philip the Bold, who is reputed to have stood by his father through the thick of the fight shouting warnings and encouragement and who was wounded in the struggle,[1] King John was captured and his army overwhelmed on the field of Poitiers. Deprived of her king, France was now convulsed by a struggle for power between the Dauphin Charles, regent in his father's absence, on the one hand, and Estienne Marcel, master of Paris and acknowledged leader of the Estates, allied with King Charles the Bad of Navarre, aspirant and claimant to the crown of France, on the other. A peasants' revolt in 1358 and Edward III's prolonged raid in the winter of 1359–60 added to her miseries. In these years of crisis and tragedy the king of France found some relief from the rigours of his captivity in England in hunting excursions at Windsor and other diversions, while his son Philip played chess with the Black Prince and was instructed in the intricate art of falconry by the French royal chaplain, Gace de la Buigne, who had voluntarily followed his master into captivity.[2] When finally, in 1360, their release was effected by the treaty of Brétigny, which guaranteed the payment to Edward III of the enormous ransom of three million *écus*, Philip was given the duchy of Touraine by a grateful and generous father. Thus, and in these testing circumstances, he entered on his career as a vassal of the French crown, as a holder of land, and, ultimately, as a ruler.

The diminutive and relatively insignificant duchy of Touraine could not for long have satisfied the ambitions of a prince of the blood, nor have been accepted by John the Good as an adequate expression of his gratitude to Philip. Greater things were in store for him. On 21 November 1361 died the youthful Philip of Rouvres, last Capetian duke of Burgundy. King John at once laid claim to and took possession of this important fief which, if it could have been incorporated

---

[1] Plancher, ii. no. 315.
[2] La Marche, *Mémoires*, i. 61–2; *Comptes de l'argenterie*, 195–284; *Notes et documents relatifs à Jean, roi de France*.

into the royal domain, would have greatly increased the power and the income of the crown. But the local particularism of the inhabitants, coupled with King John's generous feelings towards his youngest son, made this impossible.[1] On 27 June 1363 he appointed Philip his lieutenant-general in the duchy of Burgundy, and on 6 September secretly invested him and his heirs with it, creating him First Peer of France as well as first Valois duke of Burgundy. This handsome gift was accompanied by the transference to Philip of all royal rights there save only fealty and homage, and was made without the condition normally stated in similar grants, that the fief should return to the crown in the absence at any time of male heirs. Touraine Philip had to surrender, but his claim to the county of Burgundy, an imperial fief with which he had already been invested by the Emperor Charles IV, was now strengthened by the transference to him of his father's claims to its succession. On the death of John the Good, Philip's eldest brother succeeded to the throne as Charles V, and, after lengthy conversations in May 1364, these arrangements were confirmed and published in a series of letters exchanged between the two brothers and dated 2 June 1364. Philip's lieutenancy was now extended to include the dioceses of Lyons, Mâcon, Autun, Chalon and Langres. At the same time he agreed to surrender to his brother the imperial diploma investing him with the county of Burgundy, and to permit him to levy the same taxes in Burgundy as in the rest of France. But neither of these amounted to a serious concession: the county, ruled as it was by a princess of the French royal house, Margaret of Artois, could not in any case have fallen to Philip until after her death, and the royal taxes levied in the duchy were in the event made over to him by his brother. Philip the Bold was thus assured, at the start of Charles V's reign, of a position of pre-eminence and authority in France, both as a brother of the king and as First Peer of the realm. He ruled one of the largest and richest fiefs of the crown and participated, as royal lieutenant, in its sovereignty over a much wider area.

During many centuries of her recent history the political destinies of Europe have depended in a large measure on the matrimonial alliances of her ruling houses. In all the marriage schemes which were set on foot for Philip the Bold political interest was inextricably mixed, as motive and guiding principle, with his own personal ambitions. As early as 1362 his father had planned to marry him to Joanna,

[1] For what follows, see Plancher, ii. no. 315, and Petot, *MSHDB* ii (1935), 5–13 and iii (1936), 125–37.

the widowed ruler of Naples, and so extend and strengthen French influences in Italy. In spite of his earlier support of a quite different scheme the compliant Pope Urban V responded to a personal visit at Avignon from John the Good by writing to Joanna on Philip's behalf, but that princess, unwilling to jeopardize her independence in this way, firmly refused, and a few months later married instead King James III of Majorca, who had recently escaped from fourteen years' imprisonment in an iron cage at the hands of his uncle the king of Aragon.[1] After this rebuff a scheme for marrying Philip to Elizabeth, a niece of the king of Hungary, was put forward in 1365 by the Emperor Charles IV, but fell through in the same year.[2] Yet a third project was privately devised in 1367 by a French knight, Jehan de Beaumont. This ingenious adventurer relieved the ruler of Pavia, Galeazzo Visconti, of 20,000 florins by successfully posing as a French royal ambassador and offering the hand of Philip the Bold to Galeazzo's daughter Violante in return for a loan.

The events and negotiations which led to Philip's marriage had begun in the year before the earliest of these projects.[3] Philip of Rouvres' death on 21 November 1361 not only left the duchy of Burgundy without a ruler; it also released on to the European marriage market his twelve-year-old widow, Margaret of Flanders, daughter of the count of Flanders, Louis of Male, and heiress of the five counties of Flanders, Burgundy, Artois, Nevers and Rethel. As early as 8 February 1362 Edward III had empowered two emissaries to negotiate a marriage between her and his son Edmund Langley, earl of Cambridge. Margaret's father was favourable to this alliance, but in France it was regarded with pardonable hostility, for it would probably have led to the establishment on her north-eastern frontier of a branch of the English royal house ruling territories as wide and as useful a base for military operations against France as those on her south-western frontier already ruled by another of Edward III's sons, the Black Prince. Charles V was thus faced, at the beginning of his reign, with a delicate and critical situation. On 19 October 1364 a marriage treaty was finally signed between the parents of Edmund and Margaret: Edward agreed to hand over Calais and Ponthieu to

---

[1] Léonard, *Angevins de Naples*, 402–4; Prou, *Urbain V*, 8–14.

[2] Quicke, *Pays-bas*, 133, who says, wrongly, a daughter of the king of Hungary. See *Lettres secrètes . . . Urbain V*, no. 1798. For what follows, see *Inventaires mobiliers* i. 175 n. 1.

[3] For what follows, see especially Vernier, *BCHDN* xxii (1900), 89–133; Cartellieri, *Philipp der Kühne*, 115–19; and Quicke, *Pays-bas*, 140–57.

his son and pay 175,000 *livres*[1] to Louis of Male, in return for an increase of English political influence on the Continent which would probably have decisively tipped the Anglo-French balance of power in England's favour. All details, including the date of the marriage, were settled in this treaty, but one loophole was left to France: since Edmund and Margaret were related within the fourth degree of consanguinity, a papal dispensation was required for their marriage, and Pope Urban V was a patriotic Frenchman who almost invariably acted in the interests of France. On this occasion he acted at the behest of the French crown: on 16 January 1365 he wrote to Edward III categorically refusing to issue the dispensation, and he remained firm in spite of Edward's repeated requests for it in the ensuing months, going so far, on 30 October, as to order the archbishops of Rheims and Canterbury to forbid the marriage. Thus did the Avignon papacy make use of the instruments of its spiritual jurisdiction in the political interest of France, and Urban's issue, on 17 April 1367, of a dispensation to allow Philip the Bold to marry any of his relatives within the third or fourth degree of consanguinity, thus permitting in his case what had been denied in Edmund's, is a further striking example of this, for it enabled Philip to marry Margaret in spite of the fact that he was almost as closely related to her as was Edmund.

Philip had come forward as the French candidate for Margaret's hand in 1365. He was strongly supported by Charles V, who saw in his brother's union with the heiress of Flanders a triumphant and successful conclusion to the repeated attempts of his predecessors to bring that turbulent and powerful fief finally into the French political fold. Louis of Male's aversion to this French alliance, which endangered the very independence he had struggled to achieve for Flanders, was overcome largely by his mother, Margaret of Artois, whose sentiments as a princess of the royal blood of France caused her to intervene decisively in Philip's favour. Louis, however, struck a hard bargain, and it was Charles V's hesitation in accepting his harsh terms which prolonged the negotiations for so long. Only on 12 and 13 April 1369 were the conditions finally settled and incorporated in two treaties, the second of which was the formal contract of marriage. Charles V ceded to Louis the towns and dependencies of Lille,

[1] Here, and throughout this book, *livres* (*l.*) = *livres tournois* (of Tours) unless otherwise stated. The *livre tournois* was a money of account equivalent to 240 *deniers tournois*. It was four-fifths of the *livre parisis* (of Paris), these two being the chief systems of account employed at this time in France and the southern Netherlands.

Douai and Orchies, which had been annexed by the French crown early in the century, and promised to pay him 200,000 *livres*. Half of this was to be paid over before the wedding and the rest within the two following years, and Philip the Bold in fact contributed half the total, for both the initial sum and the succeeding payments were equally shared between him and his brother.[1] Charles V reserved to the French crown the right to buy back Lille, Douai and Orchies in the event of Philip being without male heir, but this clause, as well as an oath which he had secretly extracted from Philip, to return these three towns on Louis of Male's death, were nullified by written guarantees made to Louis of Male by both Philip and Margaret, that they would never be alienated from Flanders. The Anglo-French struggle for the succession to Flanders had been won by France, but at considerable cost; moreover, Philip's guarantee to Louis showed that he was prepared to put the interests of his own house before those of the French crown, even at the cost of perjury.

The wedding took place at Ghent on 19 June 1369.[2] To the pomp and magnificence customary on these occasions Philip seems to have added a certain panache, and we may consider his wedding as the first of that series of glittering and elaborate ceremonies which punctuated the history of Valois Burgundy and enhanced the prestige of its rulers. Philip's baggage-wagons rumbled into Ghent stuffed with plate and jewels and accompanied by all the paraphernalia of chivalry, including jousting-horses, musicians and heralds lent for the occasion by Charles V—one of the first examples of Philip's exploitation for his own ends of the immense resources of the French monarchy. His eye was already fixed on the future. A shower of gifts descended on the Flemish nobles and, more particularly, on the councillors and officers of the court, and sumptuous banquets were given for the princes and nobles who had assisted at the wedding, for the knights of Flanders, and for the citizens of Bruges. Although fifteen years were to elapse before he became ruler of Flanders, Philip had already on his first visit established by his generosity and magnificence a claim to the loyalty and respect of his future subjects.

Historians have rightly regarded the reign of Charles V as one of recovery for France, for between 1364 and 1380 the worst effects of

[1] Vernier, *BCHDN* xxii (1900), 99; AN J571/17; and BN Coll. de Bourg. 53, f. 41.
[2] See Plancher, iii. 30; Vernier, *BCHDN* xxii (1900), 89–133; Bazin, *MSE* (n.s.) xxix (1901), 60; *Inventaires mobiliers*, i. nos. 972–1017 and Quicke, *Pays-bas*, 158.

the disasters of King John's reign were palliated or removed, and royal authority was firmly re-established. At the start of the reign the king was threatened by the claims to the throne of Charles the Bad, king of Navarre, supported as he was by numerous French partisans; the country was overrun and everywhere pillaged by the so-called companies—bands of soldiers of various nationalities under their free-lance captains who had either been released from their military duties by the treaty of Brétigny in 1360 or had been attracted to France by hopes of plunder; and important areas had been annexed by the English. It was in these circumstances that Charles was induced to confirm his father's donation of the duchy of Burgundy to Philip the Bold, and, by establishing and maintaining law and order there Philip contributed in an important way to the internal recovery of France, just as his wedding in 1369 was a step in the recovery of her position in Europe as a whole. Philip, however, contributed in a much more direct way to the restoration of effective monarchy in France, for throughout his brother's reign he co-operated in French wars and French diplomacy. In these years he had the opportunity to study at close quarters, to participate in, and to grasp the technique of these operations, and it was surely at this time that he learnt to eschew the former and developed his flair for the latter, while his possession of Burgundy taught him the importance and the intricacies of adminis-tration.

Charles V was one of the few medieval rulers who never took the field of battle in person, although he directed the military operations which occupied his entire reign.[1] In the early years these were aimed at the destruction of the companies and the Navarrois or supporters of Charles the Bad, and the conquest of some castles held by English captains and adventurers in defiance of the treaty of Brétigny. Open war with England was not resumed until Charles's formal confiscation of Aquitaine in 1369, and from then on a systematic reconquest of that area was undertaken, while at the same time a series of English raids or *chevauchées* were parried, rather than destroyed, for the lesson of Crécy and Poitiers was not lost on the king: there were to be no more pitched battles. The most famous and able of Charles's military leaders was the constable, Bertrand du Guesclin, but his brothers also played a part, particularly Louis, duke of Anjou, the eldest. The other two, John, duke of Berry, and Philip, were much less prominent in this respect. Indeed Philip the Bold's record as a military leader is an

[1] For what follows I have used, especially, Delachenal, *Charles V*, and Petit, *Philippe le Hardi*.

uninspiring one, though his bravery in battle is unquestioned. During his very first campaign under his brother Charles's orders, in the late summer of 1364, when he besieged and captured a group of castles near Chartres, the chronicler tells us that he was often the first in an assault 'et moult hardiement se contenoit'.[1] Shortly after these successes he was summoned by Charles, at the end of August 1364, to capture a Navarrois castle near Rouen, but this enterprise was abandoned in September in favour of the recapture of La Charité-sur-Loire, north of Nevers, which had been seized a year before by a party of Navarrois in league with some English adventurers, and used as a base for pillaging excursions in the neighbourhood. The direction of this series of rather minor sieges occupied Philip from early July until late September 1364. They were followed, in January 1365, by the siege and capture of Nogent-sur-Seine, one of the strongholds of the companies in Champagne, but after this Philip for some time took little or no part in French military operations, though he was active against the companies in his own duchy. These years were, in fact, the quietest of the reign, but when the war with England flared up openly again in 1369 Philip became involved in operations of some importance.

Early in July 1369 Charles V, having elaborated and carefully prepared a plan for the invasion of England, appointed Philip to command it with a personal company of one thousand lances, to be paid for by the royal treasury. In the same month Philip sent to Dijon for a confessor to accompany him on this hazardous enterprise, but it was forestalled early in August by an English counter-attack launched from Calais by John of Gaunt. In this emergency Charles had no option but to send his brother, with the forces already gathered for the invasion, to ward off or destroy the English army. Philip marched towards Calais and on 25 August halted on a low eminence near Ardres called 'le mont de Tournehem', within a league of John of Gaunt's fortified encampment. In spite of his superior numbers Philip the Bold made no attempt to attack the English position. Instead he chose to indulge in those futile and unrealistic, though chivalrous, negotiations, which characterize the annals of feudal warfare. He challenged John of Gaunt to a pitched battle. John accepted the challenge provided the battlefield was chosen four days in advance, and, after further discussion, a committee of six knights from each side was appointed to decide its whereabouts. But agreement on this vital point was not achieved, and on 12 September Philip retired, leaving John of Gaunt to continue unchecked across Normandy on his career

[1] *Chron. 4 premiers Valois*, 151.

of devastation and pillage. Although it seems possible, as a chronicler reports,[1] that Philip's brusque withdrawal was partly due to a lack of funds to pay his troops, and possible too that Charles V had ordered him to avoid a pitched battle, one cannot escape the conclusion that the pitiful ineptitude of the Tournehem episode was due in part at least to his failings as a military leader.[2]

In the last decade of the reign Philip took the field in France on at least six occasions. Between 1370 and 1372 he participated, though in a small way, in the reconquest of Poitou from the English, a success which was almost entirely due to the efforts and ability of the constable, Bertrand du Guesclin, and to a lesser degree, of Louis, duke of Anjou. The role of Philip and his brother John of Berry seems to have been limited to the provision of troops, though they often led these in person. It must not be imagined that their services were rendered gratis: Philip for instance received four thousand *livres* per month from Louis of Anjou while campaigning against the English early in 1371,[3] and was paid six thousand *livres* by Charles V for his services in Aquitaine in 1372, when he took part with du Guesclin and others in the siege and capture of several English castles. In the following year he made a brief appearance in Brittany. It was in this year, 1373, that John of Gaunt made his famous *grande chevauchée* right across France from Calais to Bordeaux, covering a distance of well over six hundred miles in five months. Philip was successful in harassing John of Gaunt's army and in deflecting it from Paris and the fertile regions to the south, but his military services were not again enlisted by Charles V until 1377, when between 4 and 13 September he wrested several castles near Calais from their English garrisons. The captains of two of them were afterwards condemned to death by the English Parliament for dereliction of duty in their defence. One of them had only thirty-eight men to defend his castle against Philip's army of several thousand, and it is clear that the capture of these castles was a military success of a very minor kind. In its main object, the conquest of Calais itself, the expedition failed, but this time no blame attaches to Philip, for he was compelled to abandon the campaign by the deterioration of the weather and the failure of the French fleet to co-operate with his forces.

---

[1] *Chron. 4 premiers Valois*, 205.
[2] See Delachenal, *Charles V*, iv. 209–14 and Ramsay, *Genesis of Lancaster*, ii. 5–6.
[3] ACO B319, f. 3b. For the 1372 campaign, see Petit, *MSBGH* ii (1885), 421–40.

Philip the Bold was a diplomat rather than a soldier, and Charles V gave him important opportunities to develop his skill and knowledge in this art. Here again he acted, whenever his services were required, as a loyal and useful servant of the French crown. It may have been his first-hand experience of England as a prisoner of war there which caused Charles to put him in charge of the French embassy appointed in 1375 to negotiate a peace with that country.[1] Ever since 1371, within a few months of his accession, Pope Gregory XI had been actively pursuing the policy of his predecessors at Avignon in trying to mediate between England and France; but neither side wanted peace, and at first the papal efforts met with no success, in spite of conferences near Calais in March 1372 and at Bruges early in the following year. In January 1375, however, a further conference was agreed to which held out rather more hope of success, since each embassy was to be headed by a prince of the royal blood: that of England by Edward III's son John of Gaunt, duke of Lancaster, and that of France by Philip the Bold. The latter had already in December been retained by Charles V to remain near his person on a monthly salary of one thousand *livres*, and this was now increased to five thousand *livres* to help cover his expenses at the conference. In January Philip arranged for the transport to Bruges of a quantity of fine Burgundian wine; and in March fifteen horses dragged three cartloads of tapestry and robes there from Paris.[2] Philip evidently spared no pains to appear in a state commensurate with his position as brother of the king of France, and he took with him a large retinue fitted out in a livery specially designed for the occasion. The usual dinners and jousts accompanied the negotiations, which continued intermittently from late March until 27 June. Instead of a firm peace, however, the parties could only agree to a truce, which was to last until dawn on 30 June 1376. In the north of France and England it was to run from 27 June, elsewhere in France, to allow time for it to be proclaimed in more distant parts, only from 22 July. The proceedings were finally closed on 1 July with a banquet given by Philip for all those who had taken part. It had been agreed that a further conference should be opened in the autumn, and this time Philip's brother, Louis of Anjou, accompanied him, while John of Gaunt was supported by his brother Edmund, earl of Cambridge. After some delay,

---

[1] For these negotiations, see Petit, *P. le Hardi*, 303–6 and 312–15; Delachenal, *Charles V*, iv. 553–87; and *Anglo-French negotiations*.
[2] *Inventaires mobiliers*, i. nos. 2238 and 2286, and for the next sentence, no. 2304.

they met at Bruges on 28 December and a series of negotiations followed which ended with a prolongation of the truce until 1 April
1377 and a tournament given at Ghent by Philip the Bold and his
father-in-law the count of Flanders, in honour of the dukes of Anjou,
Lancaster and Brittany. The failure of these conferences, which were
ineffectually continued in 1377 without him, reflect no discredit
on Philip's skill as a diplomat. The positions of the two kings were at
this time quite irreconcilable. Charles V was unwilling to make
any important concessions now that France's military situation
was favourable, while Edward III, in spite of the fact that by this
time he held firmly only Calais and a coastal strip from Bordeaux
to Bayonne, still maintained his claim to most of Aquitaine in full
sovereignty.

It is hardly surprising that Philip the Bold played an important part
in French diplomacy in the Low Countries. This area had for long
been a diplomatic battle-ground between France and England, but
Philip's position as heir to Flanders gave him additional motives for
exerting himself to extend French influence there.[1] Early in 1375,
after lengthy negotiations, the success of which seems to have been
largely due to Philip, a marriage was agreed to between a daughter of
Charles V and William, the heir of the united counties of Hainault,
Holland and Zeeland, whose father was perceptibly drawn, by this
alliance, away from his neutrality in the Hundred Years War towards the side of France. Philip played a part, too, as was only natural, in Charles V's relations with his father-in-law Louis of Male,
who was led by his own sentiments and the commercial advantage of
his subjects to actions and policies which were by no means always in
the best interest of France. One other diplomatic mission of Philip the
Bold, undertaken on his brother's orders, deserves mention. Ever
since they had taken up their residence at Avignon, in 1309, the
French popes of the fourteenth century had declared their enthusiasm
for the return of the papacy to Rome. But circumstances, and, in
some cases, their own secret intentions, had conspired against this
plan. In 1367 Urban V succeeded in transporting himself there with
part of his court, but he returned to Avignon three years later. His
successor, Gregory XI, was made of sterner stuff, and in 1376 he
left Avignon for Italy, never to return. It was clearly in the interests of
France to keep the papacy at Avignon and Charles V made several
attempts to delay Gregory's departure. In August 1376 Philip the
Bold sailed down the Rhône with a fleet of boats to support his

[1] See Quicke, *Pays-bas*, especially 272–80.

customary splendour, to make the last of these attempts on his brother's behalf, but the intransigent pope left for Italy a few months later.

When Charles V died in September 1380 Philip was thirty-eight. He had enhanced his natural position as brother of the king by his manifold activities in the service of the crown. His powers as royal lieutenant, at first confined to the ecclesiastical province of Lyons, were extended in 1366 to include the whole of Champagne.[1] In 1369 he was royal lieutenant in Picardy, and, from 1378, in Normandy; and a month before the king's death he was appointed captain-general of all the troops and castles in the realm, and invested with wide powers. His influence and reputation in France had also been furthered in a more direct and self-interested manner. As early as 1367 he had begun to install his own men in the king's service, for Charles V's powerful and notorious provost of Paris, Hugues Aubriot, was transferred there in that year on Philip's advice from the relatively humble post of ducal bailiff at Dijon.[2] Philip took care to include among the recipients of his New Year's gifts a number of influential royal councillors and household officers, and to these regular blandishments he added sporadic distributions of Burgundian wines.[3] He even went so far as to offer a pension or annual allowance to several of Charles's leading officers, one of whom was the king's right-hand man, Bureau de la Rivière.[4] The grant of such an allowance in return for homage, a device often called a money fief or fief-rent, was a common means of acquiring friends and influence, but two of these royal officers, Bureau de la Rivière and Jehan le Mercier, found it impossible to divide their loyalties by doing homage to Philip, with the result that their allowances were stopped, although some years later Bureau, in need of cash, relented, and did homage in return for the capitalization of his allowance. Philip, of course, had been able during his brother's reign to make intimate acquaintance with most of the great men of the land. He had campaigned with military leaders like Bertrand du Guesclin and Olivier de Clisson and diced and played tennis with them, and his frequent and often prolonged stays at court had familiarized him with the personnel of the royal administration and household. In all this we can discern, clearly and not surprisingly, an element of self-

---

[1] Plancher, iii. no. 27, and, for the next sentence, *Mandements de Charles V*, no. 564; BN fr. 20458, p. 103; *Mandements*, no. 1921; and Plancher, iii. no. 69. [2] Perier, *Aubriot*, 57–8.
[3] *Inventaires mobiliers*, i. no. 648 and p. 347 n. 3.
[4] Moranvillé, *le Mercier*, 36–8 and Plancher, iii. 39.

interest. Evidently, Philip the Bold missed no opportunity to exert his influence and extend his popularity in the ruling circles of France.

Although Philip was intent, during his brother's reign, on upholding and strengthening the authority of the French crown, he was never averse from acting on his own. His private affairs in this period, in Burgundy and Flanders, and elsewhere in his inheritance, will concern us in later chapters, but we may note here the origins and genesis of foreign contacts and diplomatic activities specifically his own, by means of which he had begun, before Charles's death, to present himself in the eyes of Europe as a ruler in his own right as well as a French prince. He could scarcely avoid contacts with his duchy's southern neighbour, the county of Savoy, which was closely linked to France by geographical proximity, language and dynastic marriage.[1] Its counts had participated on France's side in the Hundred Years War and even possessed residences in Paris. In 1365 a tournament was planned between the united chivalry of Burgundy and Savoy and the companies, but this was forbidden by Urban V.[2] In 1368 a private war broke out between vassals of Savoy and Burgundy which led in the following year to a mutual defence treaty between Philip, Margaret of Artois, countess of Burgundy, Amadeus VI, count of Savoy, and Hugues de Chalon, lord of Arlay. In the years after this at least one dispute between Savoy and Burgundy was settled amicably at the conference table, and in 1379 Philip and Amadeus VI signed another treaty, this time promising each other military aid in the event of either being involved in war. With Lorraine, his neighbour to the north, Philip also had diplomatic contacts of his own, and early in 1377 he sent military aid to the duke of Lorraine in a war he was engaged in with the archbishop of Trier.[3]

Philip was likewise bound to keep in close touch with the papal court at Avignon, where from 1372 at least he had one or more resident agents to look after his interests, and to which, from time to time, he dispatched consignments of wine.[4] Early in 1371, as soon as he heard of the election of Pope Gregory XI, he decided to ensure his good relations with the new pope by means of a personal visit, conceived in the usual elaborate manner. A parchment roll surviving among the departmental archives at Dijon and written at Villeneuve-

---

[1] On this and what follows, see Cordey, *Comtes de Savoie*, especially 207–9, and Vernier, *MAS* (4) iv (1893), 493–507.
[2] *Lettres secrètes . . . Urbain V*, nos. 2069 and 2070.
[3] Plancher, iii. 49.
[4] *Inventaires mobiliers*, i. nos. 1549 and 2739, and p. 518 n. 3; *Itinéraires*, 501.

lès-Avignon on 18 January 1371 records the wages of Philip's house-hold and retinue on this occasion.[1] The five-day journey down the Saône and Rhône from Chalon to Avignon was undertaken in six boats, one each for Philip himself, his chancellor, the ducal kitchen, the wardrobe, the bread and wine pantries (*paneterie* and *échansonnerie*) and the choice fish designed to grace the tables of pope and cardinals as well as of the duke himself. Thirty-six casks of wine were sent separately to the papal court[2] and a supply of jewellery was taken, in accordance with the practice of the times, as a kind of travellers' cheque to raise cash *en route* from the pawnbrokers whenever this was required. The ostentatious generosity and extravagant mode of travel in which Philip indulged on this, as on almost every other, occasion only shows that he shared, or perhaps consciously pandered to, the mentality and the tastes of his contemporaries.

Philip's contacts at this time with Italy remain obscure, but he was certainly in touch with Galeazzo Visconti's son Giangaleazzo who later, by purchasing the title from an impecunious king of the Romans, became the first duke of Milan. We learn, for instance, that in 1375 Giangaleazzo had given Philip a leopard which accompanied the duke on his journeys under the charge of a special keeper, and in 1376 he sent a gift of fourteen horses.[3] It is not surprising to find Philip developing and maintaining contacts with Avignon and north Italy, as well as with neighbours like Savoy and Lorraine, but towards the end of Charles V's reign he was involved in a more distant and unusual episode. A Polish prince, Ladislas, had sought and found refuge in the Benedictine abbey of St. Bénigne at Dijon, but in 1376 a revolt occurred in his home country and the rebels offered him the crown. Although Philip embraced the cause of Ladislas and even sent a military escort with him to help place him securely on the throne, the revolt was a failure and a number of the Burgundian knights who had undertaken this enterprise had to be ransomed by their duke.[4] In spite, then, of his activities on behalf of the French crown, as well as constant pre-occupations with his own inheritance, Philip had found time, while still only duke of Burgundy and no more than a vassal of the French crown, to make contacts with other rulers. In thus extending his activities on to the European scene he was, it is true, acting

[1] ACO B11934.

[2] *Inventaires mobiliers*, i. no. 1356, and, for what follows, see ibid., no. 1361.

[3] *Inventaires mobiliers*, i. no. 2436 and p. 463 n. 7, and p. 466 n. 2; *Itinéraires*, 504.   [4] Petit, *P. le Hardi*, 354–6.

as a French prince, but he was also acting for himself—and for Burgundy.

A study of Philip the Bold's itinerary enables us to ascertain approximately how he divided his time in the years of his brother's reign. Until his marriage in 1369 an average of over seven months in each year was spent in France, but after this his annual visits to the Low Countries and longer sojourns in the duchy of Burgundy allowed him much less time there. During the five years 1374-8, for instance, he was in France for only thirteen months, and in no later period of his life was he there so seldom. It must therefore in conclusion be emphasized that, although his contribution to the recovery of France under Charles V was real and important, in the years after 1369, in spite of the renewal of war with England, Philip was devoting the greater part of his time and energies to his own inheritance.

CHAPTER TWO

The Acquisition of Flanders:
1369-85

When, on 19 June 1369, Philip the Bold married Margaret, daughter
of the count of Flanders, Louis of Male, his succession to the five
counties of which she was heiress was virtually assured. At that time
her father ruled the counties of Flanders and Rethel, as well as the
towns of Malines and Antwerp, while her grandmother Margaret of
Artois was countess of Artois and Burgundy. The county of Nevers,
with its dependent barony of Donzy, was shared between Louis and
his mother. In 1382, on the death of Margaret of Artois, Louis of
Male added her possessions to his, and the combined inheritance
passed, on his death early in 1384, to Philip and Margaret. But the
smooth and detached succession of inheritances was modified by
brutal facts, for between 1379 and 1385 the count was faced with a
revolt against his authority inspired and led by the city of Ghent.
Thus, although Philip's succession to Flanders was technically complete early in 1384, it was not finally consummated until the peace of
Tournai at the end of 1385, when Ghent at last submitted to him.
Furthermore, because of its wealth, as well as because of the turbulent proletariat and particularist ambitions of its great cities of Ghent,
Bruges and Ypres, Flanders was of incalculably greater concern to
Philip than the rest of his matrimonial inheritance, and his activities
there, long before his succession in 1384, reflect his growing appreciation of this. Because of these complications, both before and after
1384, the history of Philip the Bold's acquisition of Flanders assumes
sufficient importance to demand separate and detailed treatment. In
discussing this, however, we must not forget the lands contiguous to
Flanders which were acquired with it: on its south-western border,
the county of Artois stretching between Calais and Cambrai but
including neither; and, at its north-eastern extremity, the towns of

Antwerp and Malines. The towns and castellanies of Lille, Douai and Orchies, which Charles V had ceded to Louis of Male in 1369 as part of the price of marrying his daughter to Philip the Bold, were thenceforth, unlike Malines and Antwerp, part of Flanders.

Philip's first visit to Flanders took place in 1369: he was married at Ghent, and his cultivation on that occasion of the friendship of the citizens and knights of Flanders by means of banquets, and of Louis of Male's officers by gifts, has already been noted.[1] In the decade that followed, Philip pursued a consistent policy of ingratiating himself with the rulers and people of the lands that were to become his. He visited Flanders every year except in 1373, and it is instructive to compare the nine visits in these ten years with his eight visits in the twenty years which followed his succession to Flanders in 1384;[2] for this comparison shows that it was in the period before he became count that Philip was in closest personal touch with Flanders. In 1370 he spent most of March in Ghent; in 1371 he was there, with Louis of Male, for a month at the end of the summer, and in 1372 he took his wife there for a week early in the spring. During a three-week stay with his father-in-law in 1374 Philip paid his first visit to Antwerp and Malines, but it was only in 1375 and 1376 that his visits to the Low Countries began to take the form of regular tours. In both these years Philip was engaged at Bruges for long periods in negotiations with the English on behalf of his brother Charles V, but he found time in 1375 to visit Ghent, Damme, Sluis, Ypres and Male, and in 1376 he visited some of these again, and also Aardenburg, Courtrai and Oudenaarde. By 1379 he must have been well known in the principal Flemish towns, and had had ample opportunities to acquaint himself with the condition and political aspirations of his future subjects. Moreover, on almost every visit to Flanders he had stopped for a few days at least in Artois, usually at Arras, and thus maintained contact with its ruler, Countess Margaret, and at the same time became familiar with another portion of his inheritance.

Although in France at this time the new year was reckoned to begin at Easter, the custom of exchanging gifts—called *étrennes*—on 1 January was widespread, and the annual exchange of these *étrennes* between Philip and Louis of Male cannot be cited as evidence of any especially close contact or friendship between them. On the other

---

[1] Above, p. 6. Our knowledge of Philip's movements comes from Petit's *Itinéraires*, with additions and corrections in Petit, *P. le Hardi* and Prost, *Inventaires mobiliers*.

[2] I here exclude visits to Lille, Artois and Brabant. See below, p. 172.

hand, there was also a constant exchange of gifts during the year, which perhaps does point to a rather special and close relationship.[1] Thus, in 1372, Philip sent thirty-one barrels of wine to his father-in-law, and further consignments were sent in 1373 and 1374. Margaret frequently sent him millet and, at least once, truffles. Louis of Male returned these compliments with the special products of his own territories, sturgeon, goslings, or salted whale, as well as imported luxury goods like gyrfalcons and saker falcons. A similar gift-exchange took place between Margaret of Artois and Philip and Margaret. Louis of Male evidently took an affectionate interest in family events: in April 1373 couriers were sent off from Dijon to inform him and others of the birth of a second son, Charles, to Philip and Margaret; and in 1377 he stood godfather to another son, who, according to the custom at that time, was named Louis after him.[2] The cordial relations existing in these years between Philip and his father-in-law are further attested by a letter of Philip to Louis construed in the most affectionate terms and ending with the words: 'se aucune chose vouléz que je puisse, faites le me savoir, et par ma foi je le feray de bon cuer et à tout mon povoir.'

Philip took care, too, in the years after his marriage, to ingratiate himself with the Flemish townspeople. At both Ghent and Bruges he organized tournaments, partly as a spectacle for the urban populace, but also to attract and impress the chivalry of Europe. Perhaps the most famous of these tournaments was that held at Ghent in the spring of 1376, at which the dukes of Lancaster, Brittany, Anjou and Brabant were present, as well as Count Louis of Male and Albert of Bavaria, the ruler of Hainault-Holland.[3] It was, in fact, a gathering of the ruling houses and nobility of the Low Countries under Burgundian auspices, and no doubt the citizens of Ghent were flattered and pleased that their town had been chosen by Philip for such a splendid gathering. Philip the Bold soon came to be well known as a customer among the merchants, especially of Bruges and Arras, and was able, in 1376, to raise a loan of 12,000 francs[4] from the former. When he

[1] For these gifts, see *Inventaires mobiliers*, i. 248 n. 2, 250 n. 1, 259 n. 1, 284 n. 6, and 347 n. 3; and nos. 1389, 1448, 1454, 2301, etc.
[2] Petit, *P. le Hardi*, 291 and 320–1, and, for what follows, ibid., 17–18. This letter, dated 1 June, is placed by Petit in 1381, but seems in fact to have been written in 1377.
[3] Above, p. 11. Quicke, *Pays-bas*, 259, following Froissart, Kervyn, viii. 372–3 and SHF, viii. 217–18, wrongly dates it November 1375. See Petit, *P. le Hardi*, 315 and Froissart, SHF, viii. p. cxxxiv n. 8.
[4] The franc was a gold coin weighing 3·9 grams introduced by King John

was at Bruges in 1375 he clothed some of the burgesses in his livery; was entertained to dinner and lodged by one of the leading citizens; and went to Sluis and conversed with the captains and owners of some newly arrived vessels. He seems to have delighted in cross-bow shooting, for there was a special case containing 'les arbelestres de monseigneur', and he engaged in this sport with the crossbowmen of Ghent in 1371 and with those of Bruges in 1375. On this latter occasion the practice target was a popinjay set on a pole, and the thirst of the competitors was assuaged with a barrel of Beaune provided by Philip the Bold, who in the same year was invested by the *arbalétriers* of Ypres with their livery hood.[1]

In 1379, quiet and prosperous Flanders, visited annually by its future ruler, who had made himself equally popular with the count and people, was shattered and torn by the last of those prolonged and ferocious civil wars which punctuated its history in the fourteenth century. The reign of Louis of Male had begun—in 1348-9—with such a war, and with such a war it ended, for the struggle continued during the whole of the last five years of his reign and into that of his successor Philip. This war, which was in effect a revolt against the authority of the count, brought about Philip's first interventions in the affairs of Flanders, first as arbitrator, then as victor of the blood-stained field of Roosebeke. It irreparably damaged the most prosperous territories of Philip's inheritance and transformed his succession to Flanders from a mere automatic transference of power to a formidable, dangerous and prolonged politico-military undertaking.

The causes of the revolt of Ghent, as this civil war is more or less aptly called by historians, were both social and political.[2] In its three great towns of Ghent, Bruges and Ypres Flanders possessed some of Europe's largest concentrations of industrial workers. This urban proletariat had been in a more or less permanently turbulent condition since the early years of the fourteenth century, and during Louis of Male's reign the attempts of the poorer artisans in the cloth industry—weavers and fullers—to better themselves had taken the form of tumult, riot and even revolt. At Ypres they seized control and organized a reign of terror in 1359-61; and they rose again in 1367, 1370, 1371 and 1377. Even Bruges was shaken by disturbances in

the Good in December 1360 with the value of 1 *livre tournois*. It subsequently became a money of account having this value.

[1] For this and what precedes, see *Inventaires mobiliers*, ii. nos. 1447, 2304, 2345, 2350, 2356, 2357, 2363 and 2656.

[2] See Demuynck, *ASHAG* (n.s.) v (1951), 305-18.

1351, 1367 and 1369. Although the situation at Ghent had remained fairly stable since the revolt of 1359–60, the atmosphere there was tense. Such attempts by artisans or peasants to improve their situation by revolutionary means were, of course, common enough in the fourteenth and fifteenth centuries, and there was in fact something of an epidemic of them in the years 1378–85, coinciding more or less exactly with the revolt of Ghent. On 20 July 1378 the workers of the Florentine cloth-industry, led by the *ciompi* (wool-combers), overturned the government and seized control of the state; there were popular risings in many of the principal French towns, including Paris, Rouen and Montpellier, between 1379 and 1382; and in June 1381 London fell for a moment into the hands of Wat Tyler and the English peasantry. In Flanders, this social struggle was purely urban; it was accentuated by the failure of wages to rise in proportion to the rising cost of living consequent on the devaluation of the *gros*; and it was modified by inter-town rivalries and civic particularism, especially between commercial, patrician Bruges and industrial Ghent. Moreover, in 1379–85 it was modified, and indeed in some respects dominated, by political considerations, for, above all, the revolt of Ghent was a revolt against the comital government. Its principal cause was Louis of Male's policy of centralization and his consequent attempts to increase his own authority at the expense of the towns, which had, during the previous century, acquired a large degree of autonomy. Louis of Male had systematically tried to subject the municipal tribunals to the comital courts and to interpret or misinterpret municipal privileges, whenever disputes arose, in his own favour. In the interests of centralization and therefore of his own power, he had created a new office, that of sovereign-bailiff of Flanders, and augmented the jurisdiction and authority of the central court of justice or *audience*. The sparks that touched off the fire in 1379 were two arbitrary acts of comital authority, both prejudicial to Ghent: her privileges of *bourgeoisie* were infringed by the arrest of one of her burgesses, and Louis permitted the city of Bruges to construct a canal from Bruges to the Lys, which would destroy Ghent's monopoly of that waterway and its traffic. In the first week of September the people of Ghent, led by the weavers, rose in open revolt, assassinated the local officer of the count, the bailiff of Ghent, and on 8 September burnt down Louis' newly built castle of Wondelgem on the outskirts of the city.[1]

[1] For this and what follows in the rest of the chapter I have used especially Froissart; *Istore et croniques de Flandres*, ii; *Chron. comitum Flandrensium;*

During the next six years Ghent conducted and led a determined and often ferocious opposition to the count of Flanders. Her leadership was maintained not only because she had initiated the revolt, but also because she was the largest and most independent of the three great towns of Flanders, and the traditional leader of revolts there. Ypres, which possessed an almost equally numerous industrial proletariat, had succumbed to a much greater extent to Louis's centralizing activities, while Bruges was dominated by a merchant patriciate which had important interests in common with the count and was consistently favoured by him. The immediate aim of the popular government now installed at Ghent was to rally the rest of Flanders to its cause, and armed expeditions were at once dispatched which had succeeded, by the end of September, and with little bloodshed, in gaining both Ypres and Bruges. Everywhere the lower classes rose in sympathy with Ghent. By early October almost the whole of Flanders had been persuaded or compelled to support the revolt, and on 7 October a combined army laid siege to one of the two important towns which still held for the count: Oudenaarde. The other, Termonde, in which Louis himself had taken refuge, was assaulted in vain on 10 November. Although it successfully repulsed a whole series of assaults, the garrison of Oudenaarde was extremely hard-pressed, for the besiegers were able to cut off its supplies by closing the river Scheldt above and below the town. The unfortunate defenders had to submit to a sustained artillery bombardment which caused the inhabitants to cover the roofs of their houses with earth against the risk of fire from incendiary missiles. In these straits and with winter approaching, Louis of Male had no option but to sue for peace, and in this Philip the Bold acted as his principal agent. According to Froissart, Philip's intervention was due to Louis of Male's mother, Margaret of Artois, who invited him to undertake the office of mediator.[1] A preliminary conference planned for 2 November 1379 did not take place, because Louis of Male's envoys failed to arrive. On 12 November, however, Philip arrived at Tournai, and on 15 November opened direct negotiations with the Flemish army besieging Oudenaarde. The first meeting took place at Pont-à-Rosne, half-way between Tournai and Oudenaarde, on 19 November, and

Cron. de Tournay; Chron. rimée; Chron. de Jean II et Charles V; van Dixmude, Merkwaerdige gebeurtenissen; Rekeningen der stad Gent; and, among modern works, Vandenpeereboom, Ypriana, vii; Pirenne, Belgique, ii; Quicke, Pays-Bas; and Demuynck, ASHAG (n.s.) v (1951), 305–18.
[1] Kervyn, ix. 204–5 and SHF, ix. 201.

others followed daily during the rest of the month, Philip returning each night to his lodgings in Tournai accompanied by an escort of some two hundred men-at-arms under the command of Guy de Pontailler, the marshal of Burgundy.[1] These negotiations were eventually brought to a successful conclusion on 30 November with a banquet given by Philip for the deputies of the towns with which he had been negotiating, and with the drawing up of a treaty which imposed such exceedingly harsh terms on the count that it is hard to believe he meant to honour them, though he ratified it on 1 December. A general pardon was issued; existing privileges were confirmed; a leading councillor of Louis was deprived of his office and banished; and the count's officials as well as the people of Flanders were to be subjected to exhaustive and permanent scrutiny at the hands of special commissions, on which the three principal towns were represented, and which were empowered to investigate and punish infringements of their privileges. Thus Philip the Bold, by his skilful diplomacy, saved his father-in-law from disaster and at the same time ingratiated himself with the representatives and probably the populace of the principal Flemish towns, of which he would one day be the ruler.

In fact the peace of Pont-à-Rosne caused only a brief interruption of hostilities, which took the form, in 1380, of a struggle between the count, supported by the aristocratic elements in the population both rural and urban, on the one hand, and the artisans, and especially the weavers of Ghent, on the other, for control of the chief towns. In May Louis of Male secured Bruges; in August he regained Ypres, which he had held for a time in the spring; and early in September, after Albert of Bavaria, ruler of Hainault-Holland, had made an abortive attempt to negotiate a peace, his troops occupied Courtrai. Ghent now stood alone against him, and he determined to crush the revolt by forcing her to submit. But the siege of Ghent in the autumn of 1380 was a failure: the town was too large to invest completely, so that the besieging army could neither cut off its supplies nor even hinder the inhabitants from raiding the surrounding countryside. Early in November, when his own supplies were endangered, Louis of Male was forced to raise the siege, and on 11 November once again made an

---

[1] La Chauvelays, *MAD* (3) vi (1880), 97–100 and *Cron. de Tournay*, 225. There is no evidence that these troops, enumerated by la Chauvelays and referred to in the ducal letters of 19 October (la Chauvelays, 97–8) as being sent against the Flemish rebels, did anything but act as an escort for Philip the Bold. He and they were together at Troyes on 19 October; the Tournai chronicler says that Philip had some 250 men-at-arms with him there on 19 November; and they were reviewed at Tournai at the end of the month.

unwilling and unfavourable peace with his redoubtable adversaries. During the brief truce that followed he consolidated his authority over Bruges and Ypres, and the latter's political autonomy was more or less entirely suppressed by the peace of Dixmude, imposed on it in January 1381, together with a fine of 50,000 *livres* of Paris. By March 1381 the war had broken out again, and this time Philip the Bold sent a contingent to Louis' aid, which was ordered to report armed, at Bruges, on 23 July 1381, and for the upkeep of which the Estates of Burgundy voted in May the unusually large sum of 60,000 francs.[1] Again, in summer 1381, a siege of Ghent was attempted by Louis of Male, and failed; and he now resolved to starve the great city into submission by applying a wider blockade, which was maintained during the winter of 1381–2 with help from the rulers of the neighbouring states of Brabant and Hainault-Holland, though the city of Liége refused to co-operate. Further attempts at negotiating a peace had been made in the second half of 1381, and Philip and his wife seem to have been concerned in them, for the town accounts of Ghent record the arrival of a letter from them about 1 August 1381.[2] In the spring of 1382 Ghent had been reduced by this blockade to near starvation, and we read in Froissart of an armed party from the city, 12,000 strong, entering Brabant and spending three weeks outside Brussels to recuperate their strength with the ample supplies furnished them by its sympathetic citizens, and then returning to Ghent with six hundred cart-loads of provisions from Liége.

Philip the Bold seems to have played no part in the peace conference held at Tournai in April 1382 which failed completely. Soon after it the recently elected captain of Ghent and self-styled *rewaert* or regent of Flanders, Philip van Artevelde, son of the James who had united the Flemish communes in defiance of France at the beginning of the Hundred Years War, and been captain-general of Ghent and virtual ruler of Flanders from 1338 to 1345, led the army of Ghent on a desperate bid to take Bruges. They arrived outside the town on 3 May 1382, and were met by a confused and happy-go-lucky militia whose celebration of an important religious festival had been interrupted by their enemy's arrival, and many of whom were either openly in sympathy with Ghent, or else under the influence of alcohol. These unprepared and undisciplined troops were soon put to flight and so hotly pursued that the men of Ghent were able to cross

---

[1] Plancher, iii. 60–1.
[2] Quicke, *Pays-Bas*, 316 and n. 81. For what follows, see Kervyn, x. 4–6 and SHF, x. 203–5.

the bridges over the moats with them, and so enter and capture the town. Louis of Male was lucky to escape, during the following night, by swimming the moat. Everywhere the artisans now returned to the allegiance of Ghent, and in a few weeks almost the whole of Flanders had once again slipped from Louis' grasp and recognized the authority of the regent Philip van Artevelde. The count was no better off in May 1382 than he had been in October 1379: once more, the only towns of significance which still held out for him were Termonde and Oudenaarde, and he himself was compelled to retire to Lille, while his birthplace, the castle of Male near Bruges, was sacked, and his bathtub and cradle broken in pieces. After destroying a considerable part of the fortifications of Bruges, Philip van Artevelde laid siege to Oudenaarde on 9 June and, in spite of the timely flight into the town of five hundred pigs which had inadvertently been pastured too near the walls,[1] soon reduced its garrison to desperate straits. He did not, however, succeed in capturing it—a failure which Froissart attributes to his lack of skill in military matters, occasioned by a youth misspent angling in the Scheldt and Lys.[2]

It was at this point in the long and complicated history of the revolt of Ghent that it took on a new importance in the eyes of Europe through the military intervention first of France and then, in the following year, of England. The first three years of the struggle had shown that neither Ghent nor Louis of Male could achieve decisive results unaided, and so, in the summer of 1382, both appealed for outside help: Louis to Paris, and Philip van Artevelde to London. The former was successful. The king of France, after all, was his suzerain, and could hardly refuse to come to his distressed vassal's aid against the populace of Ghent, whose victory at Bruges had been saluted with dangerous enthusiasm by the urban proletariat of Paris, Rouen, Amiens and other French towns. Moreover, the populace of Paris, which had itself raised the standard of revolt in March 1382, was certainly in touch with the Flemish rebels in the summer of that year. It was known in France, too, that Ghent had made diplomatic contacts with England; and her troops had actually violated French territory and burnt down several villages near Tournai. There were thus reasons enough to persuade or justify the French government in following its traditional policy of armed intervention in Flanders. At this time Philip the Bold was in control both of the French government and of the youthful and pliable king, and there could have been no nicer and more exact coincidence of interests than those of France

[1] Rel. de Saint-Denys, i. 186–8.   [2] Kervyn, x. 71 and SHF, x. 259.

and those of Philip himself; no better opportunity for Philip to make use of his position in France and of French military and financial resources for the benefit of his own inheritance of Flanders. A massive blow at the Flemish rebels was thus delivered at his request and in his interests, just as much as in those of Charles VI and Louis of Male, though he was unscrupulous enough to see to it that he was handsomely rewarded by them: the former paid him 103,100 *livres* for his services, and the latter 100,000 *écus*.[1] This campaign also gave Philip an excuse to require an *aide* from the inhabitants of the duchy of Burgundy, which, he was careful to point out, was needed 'pour le fait de la guerre de mons. le roy'.[2]

After an abortive exchange of letters in October 1382 between Charles VI and Philip van Artevelde, the king left Paris for Arras, where he arrived on 3 November. At Seclin, about six miles south of Lille, a council of war was held, and a decision taken which showed some strategic insight. Three courses were open to the French army. It might advance directly by the shortest route towards the centre of Flanders, which would entail forcing the passage of the river Lys between Menin and Armentières; or it could swing round to the west to avoid the Lys and enter West Flanders from St. Omer; or it might march north-eastwards along the borders of the county in order to relieve the beleaguered garrison of Oudenaarde. The first of these three possibilities was chosen. In the face of determined opposition the Lys was crossed at Comines, partly with boats and partly over the half-destroyed bridge, and the whole army crossed into Flanders. By 21 November Ypres had surrendered and detachments had either burnt down or captured the neighbouring towns of Poperinghe, Messines and Wervicq. The weather was cold and the autumn rains had already set in, but the French army pressed slowly on with its horses sinking up to their bellies in the Flanders mud. The Flemish rebels now faced a dangerous situation. The whole of West Flanders had capitulated to the French, who seemed to be making straight for Bruges—a city which was wavering in its allegiance to Ghent and part of whose defences Philip van Artevelde had recently destroyed. Philip took the only possible course, collected an army and marched out to do battle. On the night of 26 November the two armies were encamped a mile or two apart, the Flemish a short distance east of West Roosebeke and the French probably half-way between Poelkapelle and Passchendale. The Flemish army, which included

---

[1] Plancher, iii. 67, who says erroneously 100,000 *livres*.
[2] ACO B2293, fos. 1–2b.

contingents from many parts of Flanders, with the Ghent militia forming a solid nucleus, is said to have been about 40,000 strong, but this is almost certainly a wild exaggeration. The French may have mustered as many as 10,000 men-at-arms, of which at least 1,500 had been provided by Philip the Bold.[1] Many of the principal French lords were in the army, including Charles VI himself and his other two uncles the dukes of Bourbon and Berry. The exact course of events on

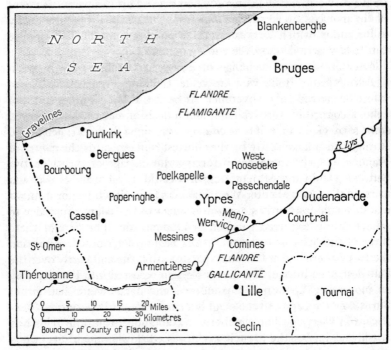

1. Map illustrating the Roosebeke campaign of 1382 and the English campaign in Flanders of 1383

27 November is difficult to determine, although a number of eyewitness accounts of the battle of West Roosebeke have survived, including those of the Florentine diplomat Buonaccorso Pitti and the Spanish chronicler Pedro Lopez de Ayala. Both armies were at first enveloped in a thick fog which only cleared—miraculously, it was claimed by some—when the French royal banner or *oriflamme* was unfurled. Battle was joined by the Flemish, who attacked the French centre in a single massed formation which drove it back in some dis-

[1] Plancher, iii. 565-7.

order; but the situation was saved by the two wings of the French army, which more or less encircled the Flemish and caused such confusion in their ranks by this manœuvre that many of them, including Philip van Artevelde, were suffocated in the press. Before two hours had elapsed the French had achieved a decisive victory. In spite of a measure of agreement among the sources that the Flemish lost about 25,000 men, and the statements of Lopez de Ayala, who says that, in the French army, only twenty-six knights and squires were killed, and of the monk of St. Denis, who mentions by name seven Frenchmen killed and adds that forty-four others perished on the battlefield,[1] we can hardly permit ourselves a more definite conclusion than that the Flemish losses were far more numerous than the French.

Although the battle of Roosebeke itself was decisive enough, its effects were limited. Apparently on account of the lateness of the season and the unfavourable weather, as well as because of an illusory hope that this single resounding defeat would bring Ghent to her knees, the campaign was broken off immediately after the battle. In the first half of December negotiations were set on foot at Courtrai, but, with the weather deteriorating and the royal army rapidly dispersing, the deputies of Ghent could well afford to be defiant. It was scarcely credible that the king of France would dare to attempt, with diminished forces and in the dead of winter, the formidable task of a siege of their city, and they therefore refused to purchase the conditional pardon offered them for the sum of 300,000 francs. But if the battle of Roosebeke did not end the revolt of Ghent, at least the whole of the rest of Flanders now submitted to the count and his suzerain the king of France. Bruges had surrendered on 30 November, and escaped pillage by the payment of 120,000 francs; the siege of Oudenaarde had been raised as soon as the besiegers heard of the defeat of their comrades at Roosebeke, probably in the night of 27 November; and, as a parting gesture, Charles VI had Courtrai burnt down when he left it on 18 December. In this respect the Roosebeke campaign does mark a turning-point in the war, for never again was Ghent able to coerce or persuade her neighbours to join her cause. Henceforth she was alone. Louis of Male's position was thus significantly improved through the timely action of Philip the Bold, although it is

[1] Lopez de Ayala, *Cronicas*, ii. 165; Rel. de Saint-Denys, i. 220. For the Roosebeke campaign, besides these and the sources already mentioned (above p. 20 n. 1), I have used *Analectes belgiques*, i. 169–73; Pitti, *Cronica*, 60–2; and *Chron. regum Francorum*, iii. 41–6; as well as Mohr, *Rosebeke* and de Maere d'Aertrycke, *Recherches*, 150–60.

hard to see the latter acting here as a dutiful son-in-law. He appears, rather, as a man of vision, who was prepared to make use of others or render them services—for a consideration—as his own interests and those of his house demanded.

The French invasion of Flanders in 1382 was followed by an English invasion in 1383. Both expeditions were complicated by religious considerations, for at this time, owing to the Great Schism, there were two rival popes: France supported Clement VII, England and Flanders backed Urban VI. After Roosebeke the French had imposed their pope on the citizens of Bruges and Ypres, and had tried to persuade Ghent to accept him, in spite of the fact that Louis of Male, on whose behalf the French were ostensibly acting, was himself responsible for guiding these towns, and indeed the whole of Flanders, into the obedience of Urban VI. A similar anomaly was brought about in 1383, for the English campaign of that year was preached as an Urbanist crusade against the supporters of Clement VII, yet it was directed against Flanders, whose count and populace were Urbanist,[1] though a part of the latter had nominally abandoned Urban at the end of the previous year in order to escape destruction at the hands of the French. The truth is that the religious aspect of the English expedition to Flanders was only a veneer which concealed an underlying economic motive. During the winter of 1381-2, as part of his blockade of Ghent, Louis of Male had indirectly dealt a severe blow at the English economy by stopping the movement of wool through the great Flemish entrepôt of Bruges to the principal centre of the cloth industry at Ghent. Although this embargo was lifted when Bruges fell to Ghent on 3 May 1382, it was applied again after Roosebeke, and it was the urgent need to reopen the Calais–Bruges–Ghent export route of English wool which caused her Parliament, in autumn 1382, to agree to launch an expedition to Flanders in support of Ghent in the following year; an expedition, like so many others in the late Middle Ages, which was successfully disguised as a crusade.

The English army which disembarked at Calais on 17 May 1383 was commanded by Henry Despenser, bishop of Norwich, an egocentric adventurer who had already made a mark on history in incidents not normally connected with the duties of a bishop: in 1377 he had caused a serious riot at King's Lynn by insisting on having the mace carried before him in a procession, though this civic honour had

---

[1] At first, however, the invasion was confined to the lands of Yolande of Bar, who, though a vassal of Louis of Male, was in fact a supporter of Clement.

hitherto been reserved for the mayor alone, and in 1381 he had taken arms against the rebellious peasants and personally led a force which carried by assault a fortified position at North Walsham and over-powered the defenders in a hand-to-hand struggle. At first his cru-sade, which was dispatched from England on a wave of religious en-thusiasm and blessed with public prayers ordered by the archbishop of Canterbury, was crowned with success.[1] Gravelines and Bourbourg surrendered, and a counter-attack on 25 May was driven off with losses which the English chronicler Thomas Walsingham improbably assessed at seven men, as against enemy losses of 12,000! Dunkirk fell that day, and very soon the whole of the Flemish coast as far as Blan-kenberghe was in the bishop's hands. On 10 June, at the request, apparently, of his ally Ghent, which sent a contingent to help, siege was laid to Ypres, at that time one of the largest cities of Europe, second only to Ghent as a Flemish cloth-manufacturing centre and much larger than the small country town whose defenders earned immortal renown in 1914–18. Here, in 1383, fortune turned against the English. True, new recruits arrived in numbers, but many were unarmed and most only interested in loot, while dysentery soon began to take its toll among the besiegers—'percussitque eos Deus in posteriora', says an English chronicler.[2] In vain Despenser summoned the citizens of Ypres to surrender, and, when they refused, asserting that they too were loyal supporters of Urban VI, he had the effrontery to excommunicate them. After a two-month siege and a final unsuc-cessful assault, he withdrew towards the coast on 10 August.

In the meantime Louis of Male had by no means remained inactive. After the failure of his initial counter-attack on 25 May he had tried to make peace with Despenser by pointing out his own Urbanist sympathies and even, if we may believe Froissart, by offering him five hundred lances for three months to fight with him wherever he wished against the supporters of Clement VII.[3] But these advances were rebuffed, and he now turned to France once more for help. As in the previous year, Philip the Bold, who had already contributed to the garrisoning of some of the Flemish towns, was the instrument of his father-in-law's salvation. Since he still enjoyed control of the

---

[1] To the sources cited above (p. 20, n. 1) should be added, for what follows, Rel. de Saint-Denys, i. 256–94, and Walsingham, *Hist. anglicana*, ii. 84–104. See too Monteuuis, *ACFF* xxii (1895), 259–313; Wrong, *Crusade of 1383*; Coulborn, *BIHR* x (1932–3), 40–4; Perroy, *Angleterre et Schisme*, 166–209 and Quicke, *Pays-bas*, 341–55. I have not seen Skalweit, *Kreuzzug des Bischofs Heinrich von Norwich*.

[2] *Eulogium hist.*, iii. 357.   [3] Kervyn, x. 235, and SHF, xi. 115–16.

French government and king, he was able once again to make use of France to help secure his own inheritance, this time from the threat of English conquest. Part of the royal war-taxes in Artois, Boulogne and St. Pol were made over to Louis of Male; in an effort to win or maintain their support the citizens of Bruges were excused the rest of the 120,000 francs fine imposed on them after Roosebeke; and a new invasion of Flanders was resolved on which, like its predecessor, was to be accompanied by Charles VI in person, though the actual command was given to Philip. Because of the resounding victory of Roosebeke the year before, this expedition attracted much attention and support, and the French army which took the field at the end of August probably numbered some 15,000–20,000 men-at-arms, possibly more. The monk of St. Denis says that nothing like it had been seen before in France: he was told that it was big enough to overrun many barbaric nations 'multas barbaricas naciones'; and the Flemish chronicler Olivier van Dixmude claims that it was larger than any other army assembled by a king in the previous hundred years.[1] Another chronicler states that when the army was encamped near Thérouanne on 1 September the king was unable to review the whole of it owing to the fog and smoke from innumerable camp-fires and the mass of transport which cluttered the place. He did, however, inspect the duke of Burgundy's contingent, which was 6,000–7,000 strong. Long before this powerful threat materialized, the English crusade had suffered a kind of internal disintegration. What exactly happened between the raising of the siege of Ypres on 10 August and the end of the month is obscure, but when the French blow was struck in early September the English forces were dispersed and already demoralized. Cassel was abandoned in the night of 1–2 September; Bergues fell at midnight on 7 September to the French advance-guard; and Bourbourg, after withstanding an assault on 12 September, surrendered a few days later, along with Gravelines. Henry Despenser returned ignominiously to England to be impeached in Parliament for his incompetence and deprived in consequence for two years of the temporalities of his see, while the captains of some of the garrisons were accused of treasonably surrendering to the enemy, and sentenced to varying terms of imprisonment. 'Benedictus Deus qui confundit insolentes' was an English chronicler's comment on this sad history.[2] England certainly had gained nothing from her

---

[1] Rel. de Saint-Denys, i. 262, and van Dixmude, *Maerkwerdige gebeurtenissen*, 19. For the next sentence, see *Chron. de Jean II et Charles V*, iii. 55–6.　　　　[2] *Eulogium hist.*, iii. 357.

intervention in Flanders, although her ally Ghent had been able to strengthen its position by the brilliant night seizure of Oudenaarde, and remained as determined as ever to carry on the struggle. Ypres had suffered irreparable damage from the siege and from the destruction of the suburbs at the hands of the inhabitants themselves which had necessarily preceded it. Louis of Male had once again been extricated from a dangerous situation, but it was Philip the Bold who profited most from the events of 1383, for they enabled him to increase still further that influence in Flanders which had been greatly extended after the battle of Roosebeke. Much of it, indeed, was ostensibly French, but it was in fact wielded and developed by Philip the Bold in his own interests.

On 30 January 1384 Louis of Male died at St. Omer and Philip the Bold, now forty-two years old, became count of Flanders. In spite of his intimate knowledge of the country, his contacts with its government and administration, and his untiring and repeated efforts to support the authority of his father-in-law, his position there remained critical, and the implementation of his succession in terms of the submission of the whole county to his authority was to occupy his attention and test his ability during the greater part of the next two years. His first task, which was to bury the remains of his predecessor, gave him an opportunity to parade his wealth, and the love of elaborate ceremony which he shared with most of his contemporaries, before the admiring chivalry of Europe, and at the same time to demonstrate his power and prestige to his new subjects. In the bizarre pomp of this splendid funeral we may detect not only a solemn tribute from the new dynasty to the old, from the house of Valois to that of Dampierre, but also the formal act of inauguration of a new political entity which now combined Flanders and Burgundy for the first time under a single ruler, and which was carried out by their joint nobility. After lying in state for nineteen days in the abbey of St. Bertin, the body of Louis of Male was removed to the abbey of Loos, near Lille, where it was joined by the remains of his wife, who had died four years before. On 28 February 1384 Philip and the members of his household, dressed in black, escorted the hearses, on which the coffins lay under black palls with crimson crosses, to the gates of Lille. There the procession continued to the church of St. Peter, augmented by sixteen fully armed mounted knights with their attendant squires and some four hundred torch-bearers, dressed in black, drawn from Louis of Male's household and the civic magistrates of Flanders. After an all-night vigil in the church, mass was celebrated the next morning by the archbishop of Rheims, assisted by the bishops of Paris, Tournai, Cambrai and Arras, and five abbots. Above the catafalque, which was illuminated with seven hundred candles, hung the banners of the five counties of Philip's superb inheritance: Flanders, Artois, Burgundy, Nevers and Rethel. At the offertory the new count and a succession of Burgundian and Flemish knights presented the shields, gauntlets, helms, swords and even the fully caparisoned chargers of the dead count. The proceedings were closed with the inevitable banquet, and an official description of them seems to have been circulated, perhaps more for purposes of propaganda than for the benefit of posterity.

Instead of journeying on from Lille after the funeral to visit the other principal towns of his new inheritance, Philip, after a brief visit to Arras, set out for Brussels, the capital of Brabant, in order to establish his claims to the succession of that duchy. Flanders was thus kept waiting while the future was cared for, though time was found to visit Malines and Antwerp between 21 and 26 March, from Brussels. Only in the last week of April, after assembling an escort of three hundred men-at-arms and fifty mounted crossbowmen, did Philip and his wife Margaret penetrate beyond Lille to make their ceremonial entry into Bruges and Ypres, where they received the gifts and oaths of fidelity of the magistrates, and swore to respect the municipal privileges.[1] After brief visits to Messines, Dixmude and Damme they returned to Lille, which had become the seat of the comital administration in the last years of the reign of Louis of Male, and remained the capital of Flanders under his successor. There was no question of a visit to rebellious Ghent, but the possibility that she might soon submit to the new ruler was by no means remote, for she had been included in the Anglo-French truce signed at Leulinghen on 26 January 1384 and published in February. When he left Lille, on 11 May, Philip might well have congratulated himself on the course of events in Flanders. Everywhere, he had been made welcome: Ghent was at least no longer in arms against him, and he had received the formal submission of Sluis, Cassel, Gravelines, Bergues, Bourbourg and some other towns, besides the places already mentioned.[2] Moreover, on 10 May he had put the finishing touches to this initial work and made provision for the future by the issue of a general

[1] La Chauvelays, MAD (3) vi (1880), 102–5; IAB, iii. 1–2; and Vandenpeereboom, Ypriana, ii. 324–34.
[2] Cartellieri, P. der Kühne, 25 n. 3 and IADNB, i (1863), 187. The general pardon is analysed by Gachard, Rapport . . . Lille, 66–7.

pardon to all those now faithful to him, which was conditional on the levy of a monthly tax or *aide* on the Flemish towns for their own defence against the rebels of Ghent and their supporters. Finally, the government and defence of Flanders had been fittingly entrusted to a leading Burgundian and a leading Flemish noble: Guy de Pontailler, marshal of Burgundy, and Jehan de Ghistelles.[1] The former had led the contingents of Burgundian troops in Flanders since 1379; the latter had been prominent among the councillors of Louis of Male.

Although his reign in Flanders had begun peacefully, Philip the Bold was not the man to ignore his military security there. He maintained or strengthened his father-in-law's garrisons: Termonde, for instance, was guarded in March 1384 by a force some two hundred strong.[2] In Artois his officials were busy, within a fortnight of Louis of Male's death, carefully inventorying the contents of a group of castles in the Pas-de-Calais.[3] It is remarkable, too, that the great programme of castle-building and repair, which was later carried out by Philip in Flanders, was begun at this time. Repair or rebuilding of some kind was in progress on Lille castle as early as April 1384. In the same month Philip paid the expenses of two *pionniers* (engineers) brought from Paris to Lille to advise about 'certain works' at Sluis; in May we hear of masons searching in Holland, Hainault and elsewhere for suitable stone for 'la forteresse' there; and on 15 June 1384 Philip appointed his secretary, Gilles le Foulon, whom he had taken over from Louis of Male, and the maritime bailiff of Sluis, to administer the funds for the construction of the new castle.[4] Thus, within four months of his accession to Flanders he had begun the work which was to be among the most elaborate and expensive of all his architectural and military enterprises. This castle was in a position of the utmost strategic importance, for, besides possessing a flourishing harbour of its own, Sluis controlled the mouth of the Zwin, the estuary up which to Bruges flowed at this time a considerable proportion of the world's commerce. Furthermore, a castle there would serve equally well to dominate the towns and fertile plain of Flanders.

As count of Flanders Philip entered into a new relationship not only

[1] *IADNB*, i (2), 318 and ADN B4073, fos. 72 and 73 and 4074, fos. 57b and 58. For the next sentence, see Dumay, *MSBGH* xxiii (1907), 1–222 and Limburg-Stirum, *Cour des comtes de Flandre*, 148–52.
[2] La Chauvelays, *MAD* (3) vi (1880), 105. See too, ADN B4073, fos. 72 ff.
[3] For this and what follows, see *Inventaires mobiliers*, ii. pp. 141–56 and nos. 1071, 1069 and 1084.
[4] *IADNB*, i (2), 352–3. Gilles himself became maritime bailiff of Sluis in 1396, *IAB*, iii. 358. For this office, see below, p. 137.

with the people of Flanders, but also with the king of France, who became his suzerain for most of the county. He did not scruple to make use of his control over this suzerain, who was also his nephew, in his own interests, and one of his first acts, after his father-in-law's death, was to apply to the royal treasury for help to pay his expenses in taking over his new lands. On 7 February 1384 Charles VI signed an order making a free gift to his uncle of 100,000 francs. Two years later Philip helped himself to a further 120,000 francs, a sum which was described in the royal grant as compensation for the expenses he had incurred in defending and pacifying Flanders.[1] Thus were the financial resources of France exploited on the flimsiest of pretexts for the private advantage of Philip the Bold, just as her military resources had been exploited in 1382 and 1383, and were to be again in 1385. The Burgundian state was founded on the wealth and military might of France.

The general situation in Flanders seems to have changed little during the summer of 1384.[2] One event stands out. On 25 May Arnould de Gavre, the lord of Escornay, whose estates had been extensively damaged by the garrison which the rebels of Ghent had placed in neighbouring Oudenaarde after its capture by them in the previous autumn, took the law into his own hands. He managed to introduce some wagons, ostensibly provision-wagons from Hainault, into the main gateway of Oudenaarde, and, while the armed men concealed in them overpowered the unsuspecting guard, his main detachment was able to enter and seize the town. In spite of Philip the Bold's disclaimers, Ghent regarded this hostile act as an infringement of the truce, and arms were taken up on both sides. The warfare that followed was, however, sporadic and inconclusive. Philip tried, with the help of Joan of Brabant and Albert of Bavaria, to establish an effective blockade of Ghent, and he succeeded in getting control of the fertile area north of the city called the *pays des Quatre-Métiers*. But supplies, particularly from Zeeland and England, still trickled through; Ghent showed no sign of surrender; and when at the end of August the truce of Leulinghen was extended for a further nine months, until 1 May 1385, she was once more included in it.[3] Her situation, however, was both dangerous and difficult. She was more or less isolated, both from the rest of Flanders and, because of the en-

---

[1] Plancher, iii. 73–4 and BN Coll. de Bourg. 53, f. 226b.
[2] For the events of 1384–5, see *Geschiedenis van Vlaanderen*, iii. 13–20 and Kervyn, *Flandre*, iv. 5–49, as well as the sources already cited.
[3] Dubosc, *Voyage*, 342.

tente which was nurtured and maintained by Philip between the rulers of the Low Countries, from Brabant and Hainault-Holland. Moreover, in the summer of 1384 she suffered from serious internal dissensions. It was this combination of circumstances which induced her to alter her relationship with England from an association of equals into one of virtual subjection. On 18 November 1384 Richard II, pointing out that since, as king of France, he was also suzerain of Flanders, and that he had not yet received the homage of Louis of Male's successor, appointed a *rewaert* or regent of Flanders, and of Ghent in particular.[1] This regent, John Bourchier, arrived at Ghent in the winter of 1384–5 with a contingent of one hundred men-at-arms and three hundred archers,[2] and thereafter seems to have shared the military governorship of Ghent with one of its citizen leaders, Francis Ackerman.

The presence of an English garrison and the protection and support of Richard II must have considerably emboldened the inhabitants of Ghent, and in the spring of 1385 they began a series of acts of aggression which ultimately led to a third French expedition against them. Their strategy was dictated by their commercial needs: it was imperative for them to secure communication with England to ensure a continued supply of raw material for the cloth-workers. But their efforts in this direction were at first unsuccessful. They reoccupied the *pays des Quatre-Métiers*, which was their nearest and most important source of provisions, and successfully beat off a counter-attack led by Guy de Pontailler from the fortified town of Aardenburg. This town, whose garrison was strengthened by Philip immediately after this discomfiture, commanded, with Sluis and Damme, the approaches to the Zwin on the side of Ghent, and control of it, or of Sluis or Damme, by Ghent, would have made an effective blockade of that city virtually impossible. Late on 30 May Francis Ackerman led an army some 7,000 strong out of Ghent. In the early hours of 31 May scaling-ladders had already been fixed to the walls of Aardenburg and the intrepid militia of Ghent had begun to mount them, when the alarm was tardily given by a sleepy guard; but the foremost assailants were successfully held back by a handful of defenders until the garrison had scrambled out of their beds to join in the fray. It was a near thing, and Ackerman's army managed to draw off without loss, ready to pounce again. The next blow was struck, not at Aardenburg, but at Damme. During the night of 14–15 July

[1] *Foedera*, iii (3), 174.
[2] Froissart, SHF, xi. p. lx n. 6, and Perroy, *Angleterre et Schisme*, 206 n. 4.

Ackerman's troops marched stealthily to Bruges, but discovered that there was no hope of their entering and surprising the town. They learnt, however, that the captain of Damme, Rogier de Ghistelles, had temporarily left his post, and, marching thither during the night, they made themselves masters of the place without a blow being struck while the citizens and garrison were still asleep.

News of Ghent's brilliant success in thus reopening and securing her communications with the Zwin and therefore with England reached Philip the Bold at Amiens the day after the king's wedding to Isabel of Bavaria. At this moment France and England were about to drift into open war. The negotiations for a general truce had broken down, and even the local truce in Picardy and West Flanders had not been prolonged beyond 15 July.[1] Meanwhile, France had resolved to take the offensive. On 20 May an expeditionary force had left for Scotland to provide a diversion in the north, while the real blow against England was being prepared in the south. Already, before his wedding, the king had fixed 1 August as the departure date of the latter, and at the time of his wedding on 17 July the fleet was already assembled in the harbour of Sluis. The capture of Damme, half-way between Bruges and Sluis, by Ghent, the ally of England, was thus as great a disaster for France as for the count of Flanders, for the projected French invasion of England could certainly not take place with this key point in enemy hands. The royal army was at once diverted from Sluis to Damme, and Philip the Bold and the king, leaving Amiens on 21 July, arrived there to begin the siege ten days later. It is perhaps a measure of Ghent's isolation at this time that contingents from the other Flemish towns, including Bruges and Ypres, took part in the siege of Damme: indeed it seems likely than an unsuccessful assault on the town had already been made by a mixed army from Bruges, Sluis and Aardenburg before the arrival of the king of France and his army.[2] Francis Ackerman held on firmly at first, confident of the arrival of reinforcements and supplies from England, but these, though preparations to send them were set on foot,[3] were not forthcoming, and, in the last days of August, Damme was skilfully evacuated by night. The length of the siege had caused the abandonment of the French expedition to England, but before the army dispersed, the *pays des Quatre-Métiers* was systematically devastated. The monk of St. Denis records the execution of prisoners during this

---

[1] Dubosc, *Voyage*, 348–9. For what follows, see Moranvillé, *le Mercier*, 102–4. [2] D'Oudegherst, *Flandres*, 308.
[3] Froissart, SHF, xi. p. lx n. 6.

operation, and the desperate courage of the rebels is reflected in his story of the statement made by one of them to the king, that even if all the Flemish were put to the sword, their desiccated bones would carry on the struggle—'adhuc ipsa ossa arida prelium suscitarent'.[1]

In fact, Ghent was by now finding it increasingly difficult to maintain her solitary resistance to the count. Her nourishment during the coming winter had been jeopardized by the devastation of the *pays des Quatre-Métiers* and England's failure to assist her in her hour of need at Damme cast some doubt on the future possibilities of help from that direction. On top of all this, indeed partly because of it, a peace party had sprung up within her walls. Philip the Bold, for his part, after the failure of this third attempt to crush the rebels with the aid of France, was now willing to abandon the policy of force for that of conciliation, which he had already applied with success to the rest of Flanders. Furthermore, events had shown that the projected invasion of England, which had been deferred till 1386, could hardly be launched until Flanders had been pacified. The first moves came from the French side: already in August, during the siege of Damme, Charles VI and Philip had appealed to Ghent to surrender, and this appeal was repeated during the ravaging of the *pays des Quatre-Métiers* in a royal letter of 7 September.[2] Throughout the preliminary negotiations Philip made skilful use of the king. On 12 October, for instance, his own letter to Ghent offering pardon, confirmation of privileges and safe-conducts for her negotiators valid till Christmas, was reinforced by a similar one from Charles VI, inviting the city to recognize Philip as its lawful ruler. On these terms, Ghent was ready to negotiate, and on 6 November letters written in Flemish were sent by Charles VI granting a truce until 1 January and fixing the peace conference for 7 December at Tournai. Philip himself arrived there on the appointed day with his chancellor Jehan Canard; Ghent sent an embassy numbering 150 persons; and, after lengthy discussions, a treaty was drawn up and signed on 18 December 1385. Ghent was pardoned and her privileges fully confirmed, and similar treatment was promised to those towns which had at one time or another supported her, and which had not yet come to terms with Philip. Free commerce was granted, the banished were to be allowed to return, and the absence of any clause to the contrary implied, what Philip had already verbally promised, that no one was to be constrained against his will to

---

[1] Rel. de Saint-Denys, i. 382.
[2] Besides the chroniclers already mentioned see, for what follows, Cartellieri's list of documents, with references, *P. der Kühne*, 120–3.

abandon his allegiance to Pope Urban VI. For these concessions on the part of her ruler, Ghent offered a solitary *quid pro quo*: she formally renounced her alliance with England. On the whole, however, Philip's concessions were unimportant, and they did not seriously undermine his authority in Flanders. On the other hand it must be recognized that Ghent had held out to the last, in spite of three Franco-Burgundian expeditions to Flanders, two of them against her alone, and that in so far as Philip had aimed, like his father-in-law, to crush her, he had failed. Although the peace of Tournai gave her no opportunity for extending her autonomy at the expense of the count, it left Ghent powerful and unsubdued. She remained, indeed, a source of trouble and a centre of criticism. She preserved a sensitivity to absolutist measures, to maladministration, to infringements of her privileges, which prompted her from time to time openly to oppose her ruler, though without again, in Philip's reign, having recourse to arms.

Soon after the conclusion of the peace of Tournai, Philip paid the first of his three visits to Ghent as count of Flanders.[1] On 4 January 1386, after a short stay in Oudenaarde, he and Margaret were received outside the walls by the clergy, magistrates and citizens, and escorted by them to the cathedral, where they solemnly swore to respect the privileges of the town and received in return the loyal oaths of the municipality. According to Froissart, Philip wore on this occasion a scarlet robe sewn with pearls, worth 50,000 francs. Later he entertained the magistrates and officials to dinner, and a week or more elapsed before he continued on his travels to visit Sluis, Aardenburg and then Bruges, Ypres and Lille. At last, nearly two years since his formal accession, Philip had actually taken possession of the whole of Flanders and made his 'joyous entry' into all its principal towns. At last conditions could return to normal and the reign of the new count really begin.

[1] For what follows, see Kervyn, x. 447–51 and *Cron. regum Francorum*, iii. 77.

CHAPTER THREE

The First Peer of France: 1380-1404

Although in reality Philip the Bold's position as a French prince was inextricably bound up with and scarcely distinguishable from his position as count of Flanders and duke of Burgundy, it is difficult for the historian to respect this unity. He is tempted to look at Philip first from one angle and then from the other: to treat his activities in France separately from those in his own lands. This method is well nigh essential for the historian of Burgundy, however abhorrent it might be to the biographer of Philip the Bold, and since our aim is to throw light on the formation of the Burgundian state, it is inevitable that Philip's activities in France should be discussed apart and more or less briefly. Nor should we lay too much emphasis on the fact that Philip, from 1380 onwards, spent about half of every year in France, and in the last ten years of his life was there, on average, more than eight months in each year, for his scattered territories could be ruled from Paris more easily than from anywhere else. Paris, after all, was equidistant from Flanders and Burgundy, and although it was not on the direct route between them it had the advantages of excellent communications in all directions. Here Philip inherited or acquired a group of residences, the most favoured of which were the *hôtel d'Artois* in the city itself and the *hôtel de Conflans* just outside it, both of them inherited from the Capetian dukes of Burgundy. A third, the *hôtel de Bourgogne*, which Philip bought in 1363 and subsequently enlarged, was used very little after 1380. The *hôtel d'Artois* was apparently the largest and most elaborate: it was surrounded by gardens and some at least of the officers of the ducal household could be lodged there with their families in separate buildings.[1]

When Charles V died on 16 September 1380 his son, successor

[1] Petit, *P. le Hardi*, 26–39, describes these *hôtels*.

and namesake was a boy of eleven, but his father had already provided for the regency which would be necessary in this contingency: Louis, duke of Anjou, was to be regent, while the dukes of Burgundy and Bourbon were to have the care and personal guardianship of the young king.[1] In spite of these arrangements the new reign opened with quarrels between the dukes which caused the hurried coronation of Charles VI on 4 November and even disturbed the accompanying festivities. On 30 November, however, a *modus vivendi* was worked out which preserved the broad lines of Charles V's arrangement but reduced the powers of Louis of Anjou, who had to be content thenceforth with the presidency of the council.[2] That prince was meditating a military expedition to Italy, with the aim of securing the kingdom of Naples for himself, but until he left for Provence in February 1382 to prepare for it, he seems to have held the reins of power in France. His rule was disturbed by a series of popular movements of protest against taxation which came to a head soon after his departure in the insurrection of the *maillets* at Paris. This affair took its name from a nasty but useful weapon, a two-handed leaden hammer. A supply of these had been stored in the *hôtel de Ville* against the next English raid and were now seized and used by the Paris mob. Philip the Bold was largely responsible for the successful suppression of this revolt,[3] as well as the contemporary one at Rouen, and, in spite of continuing protest and unrest, he was subsequently able to reestablish the royal taxes.

After Louis of Anjou's departure in February 1382 Philip the Bold's authority in France was unquestioned. In these years his only potential rivals in power were his brother John, duke of Berry, and the constable, Olivier de Clisson, but neither was in a position to challenge him effectively. In spite of his seniority in years, John of Berry seems usually to have deferred to Philip, who was much his superior in political energy and acumen. By mutual agreement, each had his own sphere of influence: Philip, who was royal lieutenant in Normandy, Flanders and Picardy, was allotted the whole of the north of France, while the south was made over to John.[4] When they quarrelled, as they did briefly in November 1383, it was because John had dared to

---

[1] The queen having died in the interval. See Delachenal, *Charles V*, iv. 536–9, and, for what follows, Rel. de Saint-Denys, i, Mirot, *Insurrections urbaines*, and Cartellieri, *P. der Kühne*, 15–16. The Religieux de Saint-Denys has been used throughout this chapter.   [2] Plancher, iii. no. 70.

[3] See, for example, *Istore et croniques de Flandres*, ii. 279.

[4] ADN B1846/11746 (1388); Froissart, Kervyn, xi. 75, SHF, xii. 66; and le Petit, *Grande chron.*, i. 311.

act on his own authority.[1] The constable, Olivier de Clisson, who was a personal enemy of John of Berry, was at first unable to make serious headway against the two brothers united against him, for both regarded him as a possible rival in power, and in February 1384 they signed a mutual defence treaty with his enemy John IV of Montfort, the duke of Brittany.[2] His turn was to come.

It is not difficult to find evidence of Philip's authority in France in the years 1382–8, an authority in which his brother of Berry was a docile and co-operative partner. Early in 1383 'having the government of the king and his kingdom', they deprived the chancellor of his office.[3] In 1385 it was Philip the Bold who was mainly responsible for King Charles VI's marriage to Isabel of Bavaria. Her father, Duke Stephen of Bavaria, was at first unfavourable to this alliance. Froissart tells us that it was customary for the lady destined to be married to the king of France to be examined, quite naked, by a panel of court ladies, with a view to ascertaining her suitability for the royal embraces, and explains Stephen's reticence by hinting that he was unwilling to expose his daughter to this formidable interview.[4] Be this as it may, his scruples were overcome or the examination dispensed with, and the wedding brought to a successful conclusion on 17 July 1385 at Amiens. Froissart, who had first-hand knowledge of French affairs at this time, makes it abundantly clear that the government was firmly in the hands of Philip the Bold and John of Berry: with reference to a decision of theirs in 1384, for instance, he says that they 'avoient le gouvernement dou roiaulme'.[5] This is confirmed by Jehan le Fèvre, bishop of Chartres and chancellor of the duke of Anjou, who tells us that in December 1384 certain important matters concerning the duchess of Anjou and the duke of Brittany could not be dealt with without the two brothers:

> les genz du Roy à Paris Orgemont, Corbie et l'autre conseil ne ont osé ce conseiller à faire jusques monsegneur de Berri et de Bourgongne soient devers le Roy. Et lors ce qui sera à faire soit fait par leur ordenance.[6]

It is even admitted by King Charles VI himself in his letter to the magistrature of Cologne, written on 1 April 1385, in reply to a request of theirs, in which he explains that he can do nothing at the moment

---

[1] Le Fèvre, *Journal*, i. 50–3.
[2] *Choix de pièces inédites*, i. no. 27. For Clisson, see Lefranc, *Olivier de Clisson*. [3] *Chron. de Jean II et Charles V*, iii. 38–9.
[4] Kervyn, x. 345, SHF, xi. 224.   [5] Kervyn, x. 299 and SHF, xi. 179.
[6] Le Fèvre, *Journal*, i. 75.

since the dukes of Berry and Burgundy are both away from court 'sine quorum aut eorum alterius presencia nil concludendo deliberare intendimus'—but he will deal with it on their return.[1]

The regency of the royal uncles, which Philip had so well exploited in 1382 and 1383 in the interests of his Flemish inheritance, came to a sudden end early in November 1388 at Rheims, when Charles VI officially took charge of the government and dismissed them with rewards and thanks. In spite of their entreaties and efforts, they were forced during the next four years to yield their place in the control of affairs, and of the weak and pliable king, to veteran councillors and officers of Charles V like Jehan de Montagu, Bureau de la Rivière and Olivier de Clisson. It seems unlikely that the king's brother, Louis of Orleans, had anything to do with this affair, for he was only sixteen at the time. The ringleader was evidently Olivier de Clisson. By good fortune, the instructions have survived which were drawn up at this time by John of Berry for his secretary Gontier Col to convey certain statements to Philip. From this curious document we learn that the constable, Olivier de Clisson, had boasted to Richard Abberbury that it was he who had made Charles VI 'roy et seigneur de son royaume et mis hors du gouvernement et des mains de ses oncles'.[2] But, if the political control of Philip and John was bitterly resented and now for a time effectively removed, Philip was content to undertake diplomatic missions on behalf of the French crown to Italy in 1391 and to Amiens in 1392 to negotiate with the English, and both he and his brother continued to take part in the elaborate and frequent festivities of the court. Only a few days after his dismissal at Rheims, on 10 November 1388, Philip entertained the king, Louis of Orleans and others to dinner in his *hôtel* at Conflans.[3] At the celebrations which followed the knighting of Louis of Anjou's sons in early May 1389, which the monk of St. Denis was persuaded to describe in his chronicle in spite of his disapproval of the four nights of drunkenness, gluttony and debauchery that attended them, Philip appeared with his eldest son and a retinue of eighty knights and fifty squires dressed in green embroidered with the ducal arms and devices, and with their

---

[1] *Hans. Urkundenbuch*, iv. no. 825.

[2] *Analectes historiques*, 157–60 and Coville, *Col*, 24–9. The 'Messire Richart Alberbery' of the original document (ADN B655/14460) described there as John of Gaunt's chamberlain, is to be identified with Sir Richard Abberbury, chamberlain and councillor of Queen Anne of Bohemia (Tout, *Chapters*, vi, index, *s.v.*). For his connection with John of Gaunt, see Gaunt, *Register*, i. 7 and 199; ii. 407 and 409. [3] *Itinéraires*, 527–8.

saddles and horses' foreheads covered with green velvet.[1] Thomas, marquis of Saluzzo and author of *Le chevalier errant*, who was present, tells us that Philip the Bold bore a marguerite on his helm in honour of his wife, while John of Berry chose a white swan.[2] Later in the summer a more elaborate series of festivities in which Philip and John both participated was held in Paris to mark the coronation of the queen and the marriage of Charles VI's brother Louis to Valentina Visconti. Philip, who took special pride in matters of dress, had four velvet doublets specially made for this occasion, one of which was decorated with forty sheep and forty swans each with a bell round its neck or in its beak, all made of pearls.[3] Again, on 1 May 1390, he was present at a banquet and tournament given by the king at Paris. In these years, moreover, he on several occasions returned the compliment by acting as host to the king, either at Dijon, Paris, or Amiens.

In 1392 an event occurred which enabled Philip the Bold to regain control of the government of France. On a hot August day, just after setting out on a punitive expedition against the duke of Brittany, Charles VI, then in his twenty-fourth year, was seized with a maniacal fit. Surprised by a stranger who called out to him as he rode along, and further startled by the noise caused by a careless page letting fall his lance on to a neighbour's casque, he drew his sword, fell on his retinue, and is said to have killed more than one member of it before he was seized and disarmed. From this time on the unfortunate king suffered from periodic fits of madness, during which he would at times caper to and fro along the corridors of the royal palace howling like a wolf, or labour under delusions as to his identity, believing himself to be called George, or even that he was made of glass. Philip, supported as always by his brother of Berry, acted at once and firmly assumed control of affairs. The principal councillors and royal officers who had enjoyed power since 1388 were thrown into prison and were at one time so near to execution that a crowd assembled on several successive days in the *place de Grève*, where public executions usually took place, in the hopes of a spectacle. Among these unfortunates were Bureau de la Rivière and Jehan le Mercier, to whom Philip had offered pensions in Charles V's reign. Olivier de Clisson fled from court and sought refuge in his native Brittany, where he was soon engaged in warfare with his suzerain and enemy Duke John IV of Montfort.

[1] Rel. de Saint-Denys, i. 584–98; Plancher, iii. 115.
[2] Jorga, *Thomas III*, 177.
[3] *Inventaires mobiliers*, ii. nos. 3253 and 3254, and, for the next sentence, nos. 3506 and 3507.

From 1392 until his death in 1404 Philip the Bold was able, though with increasing difficulty, to maintain power in France. He continued to enjoy the support of his brother, and found another powerful ally in the queen, Isabel of Bavaria, who is said to have been for ever grateful to him for providing her with a royal husband, and whom patriotic Bavarian chroniclers with some exaggeration regarded as virtually ruling France, during the king's 'absences', with the help of her brother Louis of Bavaria, who was certainly a frequent visitor at the French court.[1] Philip's rivals for power had been scattered in the autumn of 1392: all save one, the king's brother, Louis. In 1389 he had married Valentina Visconti, daughter of Giangaleazzo the famous tyrant and first duke of Milan, and accepted the north Italian county of Asti and 450,000 florins as a dowry. Soon after his twentieth birthday, in April 1392, he was given the extensive and wealthy duchy of Orleans in apanage, and from about this time he embarked on a career of aggrandizement which in the last few years of Philip's life enabled him to threaten and even jeopardize his uncle's authority in France. Louis of Orleans, though he was handicapped in the struggle for power in France by his frivolity and impetuosity and was constantly forced to defer to the superior political and administrative experience of his uncle, had one advantage: he was the brother of the king. This gave him considerable influence over Charles VI during his lucid periods, and at all times an unassailable position at the French court. Thus when, early in 1393, plans were drawn up and published of the arrangements which would be necessary if Charles VI succumbed to his illness, there could be no question of excluding him —indeed he was to be regent, while his uncle Philip had to be content with sharing the guardianship of the young king with John of Berry and others.[2] Between 1392 and 1400, however, scarcely a murmur was heard against Philip the Bold's rule. Creatures of his and of John of Berry were introduced into the royal service. After 1392 there were three ex-chancellors of John's in the royal council: Philippe de Moulins, Simon de Cramaud and Pierre de Giac;[3] while Philip had, by 1403, introduced three of his financial officers into the topmost ranks of the royal financial administration: Pierre de Montbertaut, Hervé de Neauville and Jehan Despoullettes.[4] He had other methods

---

[1] Thibault, *Isabeau de Bavière*, 275 and 320.   [2] *Ordonnances*, vii. 530–38.
[3] Valois, *Conseil du roi*, 98 and 101; Lacour, *Jean de Berry*, index, *s.v.*
[4] Van Nieuwenhuysen, *Recette générale*, 46–7 and 76–7. The two former had originally been recruited by Philip from the lower ranks of the royal financial service.

of consolidating his control over the royal secretariat. Regular distributions of wine were made to councillors and others, pensions and gifts were liberally bestowed, and, while protégés were inserted, undesirables were sometimes removed. Concerning gifts, there are some telling entries in the accounts of Philip the Bold's receiver-general of all finances. In 1396, for instance, one Guillaume Barberi, described as 'varlet de chambre et garde des coffres' of the king, was given money to buy a fur-lined silk robe like the one which Philip had given to the king's *trésoriers des guerres*, as well as a wedding-present of 500 francs.[1]

In spite of her ever-increasing internal weaknesses, France was extremely active, in the last twenty years of the fourteenth century, in European affairs, and, from the early years of Charles VI's reign, her diplomacy and foreign relations were more or less under Philip's control. In her policy towards the papacy he played a preponderant role.[2]

In April 1378 sixteen cardinals had met in conclave at Rome and, amidst scenes of popular tumult, elected an Italian, the archbishop of Bari, as pope, who took the name of Urban VI. Six months later, partly because of the rude treatment meted out to them by Urban, who was an irascible and abusive Neapolitan, the cardinals entered into another conclave at Fondi where they denounced the earlier election as invalid because carried out under the pressure and threats of the Roman mob, and elected a Frenchman, Clement VII. The Great Schism had begun. While the rival popes excommunicated each other and each created his own new cardinals, Europe divided into two obediences: France, followed by the Spanish kingdoms and Scotland, opted for Clement VII, who in 1379 installed himself at Avignon, while England, Flanders and much of Germany and Italy supported Urban VI. Political differences were now exacerbated by religious ones and military campaigns between France and England were promoted to the status of religious wars. Politics and religion were inextricably mixed.

Between 1378 and 1392 the French court, encouraged by public opinion, lent all its support to Clement VII. Louis of Anjou's

---

[1] ACO B1511, f. 55. Perhaps to be identified with the G. Barbery who was appointed 'général sur le fait de la finance des aides' in 1398, see Dupont-Ferrier, *Études*, index, *s.v.*

[2] The principal authorities for what follows are Müller, *Frankreichs Unionversuche*; Valois, *France et le Grand Schisme;* Bess, *ZK* xxv (1904), 48–89; and Cartellieri, *P. der Kühne*.

ill-starred expedition of 1382-4 to conquer the kingdom of Naples took
on the aura of a religious war designed to put Clement in possession
of Rome and restore Italy to his obedience, while Philip the Bold's
expeditions to Flanders in 1382 and 1383, though not actually
preached as crusades, were given the appearance of holy wars against
the Urbanists of Flanders and England. After 1385, when Flanders
was his and peace had been made with the Flemish rebels, Philip's
position became more difficult, for his lands were divided between the
two obediences, and the allegiance of his Flemish subjects could only
be preserved by tolerating their devotion to Urban VI. Because of this
Philip, more than most other European princes, found it in his interests to try to end the Schism as quickly as possible, and when, in 1391
and 1392, at about the time of his resumption of power in France, the
University of Paris began to agitate for more effective measures in
this direction, he extended to it his protection and sympathy. One of
the favourite methods now put forward for ending the Schism was the
via cessionis: the voluntary abdication of both popes, to be followed
by the co-operation of the two colleges of cardinals in electing a new
one. There were many in France, however, who were prepared to go
much further than this, and Philip himself is credited with bluntly
informing Clement's legate in Paris that, if his master refused to abdicate, France might well withdraw herself and the administration of
her church from his jurisdiction and obedience.[1]

When Clement VII died on 16 September 1394, the French
government vainly requested the cardinals at Avignon to defer the
election of a new pope. Their choice fell on the Aragonese Peter of
Luna, who took the name of Benedict XIII. Although he had been a
prominent supporter of measures to end the Schism, and soon after
he became pope is said to have affirmed that he would abdicate the
papal office as readily as he took off his cloak, it soon became clear
that he was inspired by an unflagging resolve to maintain possession
of the throne of St. Peter, or at least his share of it. In May 1395
Philip sailed down the Rhône with the usual flotilla of boats, accompanied by the dukes of Berry and Orleans, in an attempt to
persuade Benedict to resign. We are told by a curious historian that,
during the weeks of discussion that followed, Philip the Bold took up
his residence in the royal town of Villeneuve-lès-Avignon, used a pair
of embroidered scarlet leather slippers in his room, hung his portable
clock on the wall and slept in a woollen night-cap.[2] But neither the

[1] *Ampl. coll.*, vii. col. 498.
[2] David, *Philippe le Hardi, train somptuaire*, 24.

traditional display of generosity and splendour, nor the powers of persuasion, nor even the threats, of Philip and his colleagues, made any impression on Benedict. After seven weeks of fruitless talk, the three princes returned to the French court with nothing gained save a first-hand knowledge of his obstinacy. Philip now prepared to implement the threat of withdrawing France from the obedience of Avignon. John of Berry supported him and, in spite of active opposition to this drastic step from Louis of Orleans and a section of the French clergy, in the summer of 1398 it was carried into effect. From this moment until 1403 France owed allegiance to neither pope: her Church was independent of all papal jurisdiction. Some time later Castile followed her example, but, although Philip was able to persuade the duchess of Brabant, the archbishop of Besançon and both Cambrai and Liége to renounce their allegiance to the Roman pope, the efforts of the French government to induce the kings of England and Germany to follow suit met with no success.

The stubborn Benedict was now deserted even by his cardinals, who joined with the citizens of Avignon to lay siege to the papal palace. At the age of seventy he took active command of the garrison of Spanish soldiers and summoned the able-bodied members of his household to man the walls. He had the dubious distinction of joining the select band of popes wounded in battle. On one desperate occasion a party of assailants crawled along a drain and had almost forced an entry into the papal kitchens when a chimney, dexterously overturned on their heads, crushed and dispersed them. For more than four years Benedict remained a virtual prisoner in his own palace until, on 11 March 1403, he escaped under the guise of a simple monk and was at last able to shave off the enormous beard which, against all the customs of the Latin Church, he had allowed to grow as a result of a sombre resolution not to shave until he was free. By this time French opinion had swung in his favour and Philip's influence at court was being challenged by his nephew Louis of Orleans. While the rebellious cardinals returned to their pope with tearful apologies, Louis, taking advantage of the absence from court of both his uncles and of a temporary alleviation of the king's insanity, was able, on 28 May 1403, to proclaim the restitution of France to the obedience of Benedict XIII. Thus, in the last year of his life, Philip lost that control over the ecclesiastical policy of France which he had exercised, in varying measure, for more than a decade.

Philip the Bold had already become the acknowledged expert on English affairs in the reign of Charles V, and from the early years of

Charles VI's reign until the last year of his life he exercised a controlling influence over French policy towards England. Neither government wished to continue the war, but neither was prepared to make concessions. In particular, no prospects of permanent peace existed while the English insisted on the retention of Calais and the return of most of the territories conquered from them in Charles V's reign. Because of this, the history of Anglo-French relations between 1376 and 1405 is a history of continual negotiation and truce, interrupted by occasional campaigns. The negotiations of 1376–7 were taken up again in 1379 and continued in 1381 at Leulinghen on the Anglo-French frontier between Calais and Boulogne. They were interrupted by the so-called crusade of Henry Despenser, bishop of Norwich, in Flanders in 1383, but early in 1384 a truce was once more agreed on which was prolonged as a result of further negotiations in the late summer of 1384 conducted by Philip himself with the formidable liveried retinue of 314 persons.[1] Nicolas Dubosc, bishop of Bayeux, who led the French deputation at many of these conferences, has left us a detailed account of them in his journal, and among the numerous documents which he inserted in it there is a letter of Philip the Bold to the French negotiators at the renewed conferences in the spring of 1385 which clearly demonstrates his command of French diplomacy at this time.[2] These negotiations did not interrupt or even delay the dispatch in the summer of 1385 of a military force to Scotland under the command of Jehan de Vienne, admiral of France, with the object of invading England from the north, nor the assembly in the harbour of Sluis at the same time of an invasion fleet destined to attack her from the south. Although this latter project had to be cancelled, a new invasion attempt was planned for 1386 which, it was hoped, would end the war once and for all with the total submission of England.

There is no reason to disbelieve the assertion of Froissart that Philip the Bold was one of the leading exponents and supporters of this plan:[3] indeed he was probably its author. His aim throughout these years was peace with England, for the prosperity of Flanders depended on free commercial intercourse across and through the Channel, and this was quite impossible when a state of war existed between the powers on either side of it. Moreover, until the peace of

---

[1] *Inventaires mobiliers*, ii. no. 1100.   [2] Dubosc, *Voyage*, 344–6.
[3] Kervyn, xi. 356–7 and xii. 23 n. 7–8; SHF, xiii. 1–2 and 97. See, too, Cabaret d'Orville, *Chronique*, 180–2. For what follows, I have principally used Mirot, *REH* lxxxi (1915), 249–87 and 417–66.

Tournai in 1385 the English had been actively supporting the rebel city of Ghent, and Richard II had publicly refused to recognize Philip as lawful count of Flanders. The intermittent negotiations between 1379 and 1385—which were even renewed early in 1386—had proved ineffectual, and it must have seemed to Philip that a better prospect of permanent peace with England, which would set the seal on his successful pacification of Flanders, lay in its enforcement at the point of the sword. Every care was taken in the preparation of this expedition, which over-enthusiastic Frenchmen compared to the siege of Troy.[1] Philip's spies were active across the Channel; the whole summer of 1386 was employed, Froissart tells us, in grinding flour and making biscuit, and supplies of every kind were assembled at Sluis from all parts. Philip's own provisions were purveyed by a special officer, Pierre Varopel—'maistre des garnisons monseigneur le duc de Bour-goingne'—and included several hundred cheeses, a hundred or more oxen, 447 sheep, 457 fowls and some 500 barrels of wine.[2] The ducal painter, the renowned Flemish artist Melchior Broederlam, was employed decorating banners with the coats of arms of Philip's different possessions and inscribing the ducal motto in gold letters all over the mainsail of his ship. An immense wooden fort, constructed in sections at Rouen, and consisting of a twenty-foot-high curtain wall several miles in circumference with towers at intervals, was to be shipped across the Channel and set up as soon as the army landed in England; but disaster overtook this elaborate armament, for part of it was intercepted by the English squadron based on Calais while it was being transported to the embarkation port of Sluis, and the rest was later given by Charles VI to Philip the Bold.

By September 1386 the French army was gathered in the neighbourhood of Sluis, and a well-equipped fleet of over a thousand vessels had been assembled in the harbour. In England parts of the suburbs of London were destroyed to facilitate its defence, military contingents were posted along the south coast, and look-outs placed on every prominence overlooking the sea scrutinized the horizon for the first sight of hostile sails. On Sunday 28 October the French king and princes were ready to embark and the final plans for the departure were made.[3] What exactly happened during the following fortnight is uncertain, but it seems that it was contrary winds and bad weather, rather than John of Berry's hostility to the project, enlarged

[1] Cabaret d'Orville, Chron., 184–5.
[2] IADNB, vii. 207–11 and Finot, Comptes et pièces comptables, pp. lxxix-lxxxiv.　　　[3] Cron. de Tournay, 359–60.

on by Froissart, which delayed the fleet's departure.[1] The well-informed contemporary chronicler of Tournai provides a detailed account of the final abandonment of the expedition. Towards the middle of November the royal council received a report, drawn up by the captains of some hundred and fifty vessels, which concluded that the invasion was now impossible. Their reasons, which read more like excuses and demonstrate a marked lack of enthusiasm for the whole affair, are summarized by the chronicler as follows:

> Très redoubtez Sires et puissans, véritez est que le mer est maulditte; item sont les nuis trop longhes; item sont trop noires; item sont trop froides; item sont trop en pleuves; item sont trop fresques. Item nous fault viveyave. Item nous faut avoir plaine lune. Item nous faut avoir vent pour nous. Item les terres d'Engleterre sont préilleuses. Item tous les havènes d'Engleterre sont préilleux. Item il ly a en ce la rive chy trop de viez fassiaux; item il y a trop de petis vassiaux; item mettons doubte en ces vassiaux que li grans vassiaux ne les noice. . . .

The force of these objections was recognized and the advice of the captains accepted. On 16 November, in spite of keen disappointment, the king left Sluis for Lille through mud and continuous rain, and at Amiens, at the end of the month, it was agreed to gather again at Sluis in the following autumn for yet another attempt on England.

In the event, circumstances intervened during the winter of 1386–7 to cause the complete abandonment of further preparations against England, and the French government, acting on the initiative of Philip the Bold,[2] resorted once more to the arrangement and periodic renewal of a truce, while intermittent negotiations kept open the possibility of a permanent peace. These negotiations were continued each year between 1388 and 1393.[3] In 1392 and 1393 the conferences at Amiens and Boulogne were attended by the dukes of Berry and Burgundy in person, and Philip's desire for a firm peace, evidently reflected in his extravagant gifts of tapestries to the English negotiators on the latter occasion, is attested by Froissart.[4] On 10 June

---

[1] Kervyn, xii. 23–7 and SHF, xiii. 96–100. ACO B2299, f.1a–b (letter of Philip the Bold of 6 May 1387); Lopez de Ayala, *Cronicas*, ii. 261; Deschamps, *Œuvres*, xi. 49–51 and references; Minerbetti, *Cronica*, cols. 103–4; *Memorieboek der stad Ghent*, i. 119, and the English chroniclers all attribute the delay to the weather. For what follows, see *Cron. de Tournay*, 289–91.
[2] Perroy, *Angleterre et Schisme*, 354.
[3] Moranvillé, *BEC* l (1889), 355–80 and Mirot and Deprez, *Ambassades anglaises*, 61–3.
[4] David, *P. le Hardi, train somptuaire*, 28; Froissart, Kervyn, xiv. 385; xv. 109–10, 185.

1394 Richard II's first wife, Anne of Bohemia, died, and in the following year the first suggestions were made by the English for his marriage to Charles VI's six-year-old daughter Isabel. The discussions which followed, though they made little or no progress towards a peace, ended with the publication of a truce of record though absurd length, for it was to last for twenty-eight years; with a meeting of the two kings in October 1396 at which Isabel was handed over by her father; and, finally, with her solemn marriage to Richard II on 4 November, at Calais.[1] In all this, Philip the Bold had played a leading part and might well have congratulated himself, as the English court sailed back to Dover with over three thousand *livres* worth of his liberality in jewels alone,[2] that at last he had solved the English problem. Where negotiation and force had failed, a judicious wedding seemed to have succeeded in ensuring peace in the Channel and, with it, the prosperity of Flanders. But this was not to be.

The deposition of Richard II and the accession of Henry IV on 30 September 1399 introduced new and difficult problems into Anglo-French relations, the most immediate of which was the future of Isabel.[3] Her return to France was not finally settled until 27 May 1401, and Philip the Bold, who had exerted himself during the previous eighteen months to avoid a rupture and bring the negotiations to a successful conclusion, travelled in state to Leulinghen in the late summer to welcome her and escort her back to her father in Paris. The twenty-eight-year truce, though precariously maintained in the ensuing years, chiefly by the efforts of Philip, was now threatened by challenges, the most famous of which was that issued to Henry IV by Louis of Orleans in 1402 and repeated in 1403, and eventually broken by military operations. These were initiated by France, and for the first time for many years the war was carried across the Channel. But the sack of Plymouth in August 1403 and the landing on the Isle of Wight in December of that year did not deter the patient negotiators from continuing their meetings at Leulinghen, for neither of these was in fact an official French expedition, the former having been undertaken by the Bretons, and the latter by Waleran of Luxembourg, count of St. Pol, acting as a private individual. In October and November 1403 rumours of war were current on both sides of the

---

[1] See Mirot, *RHD* xviii (1904), 544–73 and xix (1905), 60–95.
[2] David, *P. le Hardi, train somptuaire*, 32 n. 7.
[3] For what follows, see Mirot, *RHD* xix (1905), 481–522; Wylie, *Henry IV*, i. 379–91 and Jarry, *Orléans*, 285–7.

Channel; and, while Louis of Orleans actually embarked on an invasion of Guienne with the aim of blockading Bordeaux, Philip of Burgundy was credited with designs on Calais. Still, Anglo-French negotiations continued, although the two countries remained on the verge of open war.

During the years of his ascendancy in France, apart from attempts to cut the Gordian knot in 1385 and 1386 by invading England, Philip had consistently aimed at avoiding hostilities: a policy in the best interests both of France and Flanders. If the activities of certain elements in France—and perhaps his own too—in the last year of his life threatened the truces he had so sedulously maintained, this was probably not due to a change in Philip's inclinations or policy, but to the increasing influence of the bellicose Louis of Orleans in the counsels of the realm.

In directing France's policy towards the papacy and England, Philip the Bold was acting in the interests of the religious and commercial needs of his Flemish subjects, as well as in those of France. In other spheres of French diplomatic activity his role was equally important and equally in the interests of France, but here again his own private advantage was involved. His interference in Brittany was the result of his political ambitions inside France; his activities in Savoy were linked to dynastic considerations.

The year 1364 marked the formal accession to the ducal thrones of Brittany and Burgundy of two new dynasties, those of Montfort and Valois. The first Montfort duke of Brittany, John IV, was connected by personal inclinations and political interests with England, and by blood with Philip's wife Margaret.[1] At the end of Charles V's reign he was in open revolt against his suzerain the king of France, and the reconciliation which was effected in 1381 between him and the French government was probably the work of Philip the Bold, as was certainly the alliance of the three dukes of Burgundy, Berry and Brittany which followed early in 1384. At this time the personal animosity between John IV and the constable of France, Olivier de Clisson, who was one of his principal vassals, grew in intensity until it broke out into an open quarrel which seriously disturbed the peace of Brittany between 1387 and 1395. That this quarrel did not deteriorate into civil war was due to Philip the Bold, who was responsible for arbitrating between the parties in 1388 and 1392, and who in 1394–5 finally succeeded in reconciling them. This friendly and bene-

[1] For what follows, see Pocquet, *RCC* xxxv (2) (1933–4), 481–93 and 595–612 and idem, *MSHAB* xvi (1935), 1–62.

ficent interest in the internal affairs of Brittany bore fruit for Philip after John's death, for in October 1402 he travelled to Nantes and, amid the customary distribution of gifts, received the guardianship of the duchy on behalf of John's ten-year-old son, John V. The latter reached his majority in December 1403, so that Philip was regent of Brittany for only a year. Although his last act was to lay down detailed regulations for the government of Brittany, which kept the nominations to important offices in his hands, this element of control was shaken off by John V within a few months of Philip's death in April 1404, so that his guardianship of the duchy remained an isolated episode with no sequel in the history of Burgundy.

Unlike Brittany, which was a fief of the French crown, Savoy was technically part of the Holy Roman Empire. During Charles V's reign, Philip had forged links of his own with his neighbour on the south-east. After 1380, although his personal interests were so nicely combined with those of France that it is difficult to treat them separately, his interventions in the affairs of Savoy were the actions of a French prince pursuing the traditional French policy of influence, infiltration and even control, and it is for this reason that they find their place in this chapter.[1] Count Amadeus VII of Savoy had always been attached to the French. He had married Bonne, daughter of John of Berry, and had hoped to lead his troops to England with the French army in 1386. After the abandonment of this expedition his friendship with France was cemented by a prolonged visit to the French court and by a dynastic alliance with Philip the Bold: it was agreed that Philip's daughter Mary should wed Amadeus's son and heir. A few years later, in 1391, Amadeus VII died suddenly when his son was still only eight years old. The regency was hotly disputed between the mother and grandmother of the young prince, and when one party appealed to France, Philip and his brother of Berry made the most of their opportunity. On 2 November 1393, three days after the celebration of the marriage of Amadeus VIII and Mary of Burgundy, a document was drawn up by Philip and John which entrusted the government of Savoy to a council whose members were to tender their oaths of office to them, and in which it was explicitly stated that important affairs of state were not to be settled without their advice and consent. Philip the Bold thus became virtual ruler of Savoy, though his other commitments made his intervention there rather sporadic. He took an active part in the complex relations of Savoy

[1] For what follows, see especially Cognasso, *MAH* xxxv (1915), 257–326; Marie José, *Maison de Savoie*, 373–83 and the references given there.

with her Italian neighbours;[1] he supervised and controlled the movements of Amadeus VIII; and he kept a watchful eye on the finances of the state. In 1398 a new arrangement was made during Amadeus's stay in Paris in that year, which maintained the right of Philip and John to be consulted on all important matters and even allowed them to send their own representatives to sit on the council. The latter provision was made use of by Philip, for one of his own councillors, Jehan de Saulx, was deputed by him to the council of Savoy, and remained for some years a regular and influential member of it. As late as 1401 the two dukes were still intimately concerned with the affairs of Savoy, for in that year they sent Guillaume de Vienne to the duke of Milan 'pour le fait de monseigneur le conte de Savoie'.[2]

Little need be said here of Philip the Bold's part in French relations with the Empire and French schemes in Italy. In both the question of the Schism was of paramount importance. French policy towards the Empire was based on the maintenance of good relations, while attempts were made from time to time to persuade its ruler to transfer his allegiance to the French pope or, after 1398, to emulate France by a withdrawal of obedience. In the spring of 1398 conferences took place at Rheims between Charles VI and the king of the Romans, Wenzel, the chief object of which was to persuade Wenzel to act in concert with France to end the Schism, but they were interrupted by the periodic drunkenness of Wenzel and cut short by a recurrence of Charles VI's insanity.[3] In 1400 German exasperation with Wenzel reached such a pitch that a group of Electoral Princes met together, deposed him, and elected Rupert of Wittelsbach, the Elector-Palatine of the Rhine, in his place. To the charges of political incompetence and cruelty brought against him by the Electors, the chronicler adds a colourful touch: Wenzel, it was said, had had a negligent cook turned and roasted on the spit; he had casually shot an unfortunate monk whom he had come across while hunting, and justified his action with the assertion that monks should stay in their monasteries and not wander about in the woods; and, when he found the words 'Wenceslaus alter Nero' chalked up on a wall he had at once added after them: 'si non fui adhuc, ero.'[4] After 1400 it was Philip the Bold who ensured that France would not commit herself too far in the support of either Wenzel or Rupert, though his influence was wielded on behalf of the latter rather than the former, partly because his rival, Louis of Orleans, actively aided Wenzel, and

[1] See Gabotto, *Ultimi principi d'Acaia*. [2] ACO B1526, f. 87b.
[3] Rel. de Saint-Denys, ii. 564–70. [4] De Dynter, iii. 74–5.

partly because of Rupert's dynastic relationship with his ally in France, Queen Isabel.[1]

In Italy, French policy was more vigorous and forceful, and a series of projects were initiated by means of which, it was hoped, the Schism would be ended in favour of the Avignon pope and French hegemony in Italy triumphantly assured. Philip the Bold had nothing to do with the first of these projects, for at the time of his brother Louis of Anjou's attempt in 1382–4 to conquer Naples and install Clement VII in Rome, he was busy in Flanders and France. A second, and much more ambitious, scheme, in which he was deeply concerned, was planned in 1390–1. A French army of 15,000 lances, each consisting of a knight, a squire (*piliardus*) and a page, all mounted, and led by King Charles VI in person, was to invade Italy with the help of Giangaleazzo Visconti. It was on this occasion that Philip the Bold paid his only visit to Italy, for in March 1391, accompanied by Louis of Orleans, he went to Milan to draw up with Giangaleazzo the terms of the treaty on which the enterprise was to be based. For various reasons this projected French invasion of Italy suffered the same fate as that of England five years before; nor was a third scheme, which involved the creation for the ambitious duke of Orleans of a central Italian kingdom to be called Adria, brought any nearer to fruition, in spite of a series of negotiations in 1393. In the event, French expansion in the peninsula was limited to the Angevin foothold in Naples, which was maintained after his father's death by Louis II of Anjou; to the transference to Louis of Orleans, in 1387 as part of his dowry, of the town and dependencies of Asti; and to the acquisition by Charles VI in 1396 of the sovereignty over the republic of Genoa. This last, had it not been for the intervention of Philip the Bold, might easily have fallen into the hands of Louis of Orleans. In fact, from 1395 on, the Italian ambitions of Louis, which were based on a close alliance with his father-in-law Giangaleazzo, were opposed and restrained at the French court by Philip the Bold and Queen Isabel.

If French policy in Italy before 1396 was characterized by a lack of realism and an excess of ambition, after this date it degenerated into an incoherence which was mainly due to the rivalry of Philip and Louis. This, in the last three or four years of Philip's life, when Louis was able to challenge him more effectively, became apparent in all

---

[1] For the above, see Leroux, *Nouvelles recherches*, 1–50; for what follows, Jarry, *BEC* liii (1892), 213–53 and 505–70 and *Origines de la domination française*; Mirot, *Politique française en Italie*; de Boüard, *Origines des guerres d'Italie*; and Peyronnet, *MA* lv (1949), 301–42.

branches of French diplomacy: in her relations with Italy, Germany, England and the Church. France indeed, particularly after 1400, demonstrated her internal weakness by displaying two rival foreign policies: that of Philip the Bold, in favour of peace with England, withdrawal from the obedience of Avignon, alliance with Rupert of Wittelsbach and Florence; and that of Louis, diametrically opposed to it: war with England, loyalty to Avignon, alliances with Wenzel against Rupert and with Milan against Florence.

From this sketch of Philip the Bold's control and use of French diplomacy we must turn now to look briefly at his position inside France between 1392 and 1404. The quarrel between him and Louis of Orleans has exercised the pens of numerous historians;[1] and there is no need to treat it in detail here. From about 1395 signs of friction became apparent: over the affairs of Italy; over the Great Schism; over certain tolls which Louis had imposed in his territories to the prejudice of Flemish commerce.[2] These differences were exacerbated by the mutual jealousies and animosities of the two duchesses, but it was not until the last few years of Philip's life that Louis was able to challenge him seriously, and even then Philip was able, by means of superior statesmanship, resources and prestige, to crush every attempt of his nephew to gain control of the government. In December 1401 the quarrel was about to flare up into open violence. Both dukes mustered troops in the capital, and the citizens of Paris were able to admire, among Philip's contingents, the warlike state of the bishop-elect of Liége, John of Bavaria—'non speciem presulis sed Hectoris aut Achillis representans', as a chronicler puts it—with his seven knights and forty-five squires.[3] France was saved from the horrors of civil war by the successful mediation of the dukes of Berry and Bourbon and the queen: on 14 January 1402 Philip and Louis promised to put an end to their hostile preparations and to be good friends, and on the following day they dined together at the same table. After this there was no further resort to arms, but Louis made several vain attempts to acquire a share of political power. On 18 April 1402, profiting by the absence of Philip and the temporary sanity of his brother the king, he put himself in charge of extraordinary taxation— *aides pour la guerre*—in the whole of the northern half of France, but

---

[1] Especially, Jarry, *Orléans*, Mirot, *CABSS* xii (1937), 48–9 and d'Avout, *Armagnacs et Bourguignons*.
[2] Van Nieuwenhuysen, *Recette générale*, 61–2.
[3] Zantfliet, *Chronicon*, cols. 359–60 and ACO B1526, f. 305.

in June he was forced to share this post with Philip, and early in July to relinquish it. In 1403 Philip succeeded in excluding his rival from any but a very subordinate share in the regency which would be necessary in the event of the king's death, and further improved his potential control over the succession by marrying his grandchildren into the royal family. Louis's attempts, after 1400, to shoulder his way into the government of France and, if possible, to gain control of it, were thus thwarted successfully by Philip, though he maintained power only at the cost of internal disorder and a growing incoherence in external affairs.

The internal condition of France was at this time rapidly deteriorating, and the struggle for power between Philip and Louis was by no means the most damaging of the many evils that now beset her.[1] While the life of the court became ever more elaborate and expensive, the royal administration was allowed to decline both in efficiency and probity, and its officers devoted themselves by fraudulence and embezzlement to their own enrichment. The chancellor, Arnaud de Corbie, tripled his already large annual salary of 2,000 *livres*, and lesser men followed suit. The generosity or insanity of Charles VI also permitted the state to be plundered from within by the princes of the blood, who became constant recipients of gifts and pensions from the royal treasury. Thus Louis, duke of Bourbon, received 12,000 francs per annum from 1382; John of Berry was enjoying a pension of 18,000 francs per annum in 1383 and 36,000 after 1400; and Louis of Orleans was at one time receiving nearly 100,000 francs per annum.[2] All three were also frequently permitted to collect part or all of the royal taxes or *aides* in their lands for their own personal use. Philip the Bold by far surpassed his relatives in the art of plundering, or diverting to his own use, the financial resources of France: he drew a regular annual pension; he enjoyed almost the whole of the proceeds of royal *aides* in his own territories; and, between 1382 and 1403, he caused a shower of royal gifts to descend on himself, which reached the enormous total of one and a third million *livres*.

This division or dissipation of the resources of the state among the royal princes was by no means limited to its finances, for they arrogated to themselves the judicial rights of the crown; purchased or

---

[1] See, in general, Coville, *Les Cabochiens*, 1–70, d'Avout, *Armagnacs et Bourguignons*, 13–31 and 56–73, and Perroy, *Hundred Years War*, 219–27.
[2] *Choix de pièces inédites*, i. no. 25 (see the text, there is a misprint in the heading); Lacour, *Jean de Berry*, 237; Pocquet, *MSHDB* vii (1940–1), 127 n. 1.

annexed territories belonging to the royal domain; found sinecures for their creatures in the royal administration and made use of royal troops for their own aggrandizement. Nor was Philip the Bold alone in his use of French resources for the construction of a state for himself and his descendants; indeed, France at this time seemed to be on the brink of disintegration. Royal control had been virtually excluded by John of Berry from Berry and Poitou and by John of Montfort from Brittany. Louis of Orleans, having obtained the duchy of Orleans at the expense of the royal domain (as Philip had the duchy of Burgundy) and added to it the counties of Blois, Angoulême, Périgord and other lands in France, had extended his territorial activities beyond her frontiers by the acquisition of Luxembourg and a powerful group of vassals in its neighbourhood extending northwards to include the duke of Guelders, and south to Lorraine. With fewer resources and less skill, but with equal or greater ambition, he was evidently trying to emulate his uncle Philip in creating for himself a more or less independent state, partly within and partly outside France.

Philip the Bold was pre-eminent among those who busied themselves with the dismantling of the French state, not only in the degree of real power which he obtained but also in the use to which the resources thus made available to him were put and in the scope of his political vision. His employment of French resources, both military and financial, to secure and pacify his Flemish inheritance between 1379 and 1385, has already been described, and in the pages which follow the numerous other ways in which Philip was able to make use of his control of France in the interests of his own lands will become abundantly clear. Indeed the formation of the Burgundian state would have been quite impossible without the political support and material resources of France; and these were assured by his skill and perseverance in maintaining his position there.

CHAPTER FOUR

The Crusade of Nicopolis

The crusade against Islam was still a living force in Western Europe in the fourteenth century.[1] It was carefully nurtured by a group of eccentric visionaries; it was kept in the forefront of European diplomacy by the popes, for whom it was, along with Anglo-French peace, an altruistic and non-controversial aim of some propagandist value; and it was implemented from time to time on a moderately large scale and with usually disastrous results, by the princes and chivalry of Christendom, and of France in particular. Although by now nearly devoid of political significance, the crusade was of considerable importance to secular rulers, for it was one of the few undertakings which brought them prestige and renown whether it succeeded or not. Thus the expedition to Hungary in 1396, known as the crusade of Nicopolis (modern Nikopol), though it ended in disastrous failure, played a considerable part in the emergence of Burgundy as a European power, for it was essentially a Burgundian enterprise, launched and financed by Philip the Bold and led by his eldest son, John of Nevers, who succeeded him in 1404 as Duke John the Fearless.

The fourteenth century was perhaps the Golden Age of the 'armchair crusader': of enthusiastic writers on the crusade who devised elaborate but purely theoretical and literary schemes for the successful reconquest of the Holy Land.[2] In the opening years of the century Pierre Dubois had suggested that crusaders should be put into uniform and accompanied by bands. In his *Liber de Fine* Ramon Lull entered a plea for a crusade against the Moorish kingdom of Granada, but this was rejected by the crusading propagandist Burcard, who

[1] For this chapter I have drawn widely on Delaville le Roulx, *France en Orient*, and, to a lesser extent, on Atiya, *Nicopolis*.
[2] For what follows, see Jorga, *Philippe de Mézières*, and Atiya, *Crusade in the later Middle Ages*, and references given there.

outlined a grandiose scheme for a European crusade aimed directly at Syria, though it was to be preceded by the conquest and annexation of Serbia and Byzantium. The Venetian, Marino Sanudo, had introduced economic warfare into crusading theory: he suggested a blockade of Egypt to smooth the way for the military conquest which should follow it. The Frenchman, Philippe de Mézières, spent years canvassing for a proposed new crusading Order of chivalry, to be called the Order of the Passion, and actually persuaded a number of leading nobles in the principal Western European countries to enlist in its ranks. As a matter of fact, almost every fourteenth-century crusading leader founded an Order of chivalry with a specific crusading purpose: Peter I of Cyprus, the Order of the Sword; Amadeus of Savoy, the *Chevaliers de l'Annonciade*; and Louis of Bourbon, the Order of the *Escu d'Or*.

The crusade, in the fourteenth century, was not nearly so impressive in fact as it was in theory. The earliest expedition seized the island of Rhodes in 1306-8 from the Christian Greeks of the Byzantine Empire. Another, in 1344, successfully conquered Smyrna from the Turks. In 1365 Alexandria itself, the second city of Mameluk Egypt, was captured but abandoned a few days later after hideous scenes of loot and carnage. This futile act of aggression had most unfortunate repercussions in the West: it severely damaged the commerce of Venice; it interfered considerably with the luxury trade with the East, and inflated the prices of silk, spices and other Eastern products; it provoked a wave of persecution against the Christians of the Near East, and was the indirect cause of a retaliatory raid on Cyprus in 1426 which was accompanied with frightful devastation. In the year after this sack of Alexandria a new crusade was led eastwards by the count of Savoy, Amadeus VI. Gallipoli was captured from the Turks, but after this the expedition was diverted against Bulgaria, and ended without significant result, except the acceleration of the collapse of that Christian kingdom. Even more disastrous and ineffectual was Louis of Bourbon's expedition to Tunis in 1390, but both he and Amadeus returned from their crusading adventures as popular heroes. Besides these Mediterranean enterprises, an almost annual crusade was organized during the fourteenth century by the knights of the Teutonic Order in Prussia, which was aimed in particular at the heathen Lithuanians, but which did not cease with their conversion to Christianity in 1386. These annual campaigns were so popular that they were explicitly mentioned by King Charles V of France in 1376, when he found it necessary to prohibit French knights and squires from leaving the country without his express permission.[1]

Philip the Bold seems always to have been keenly interested in crusading activities, and it is said that he took the Cross in 1363 with his father King John the Good.[2] Burgundian knights and squires took part in Amadeus of Savoy's crusade of 1366, and several persons intimately connected with Philip, for instance Guy and Guillaume de la Trémoille, Philippe d'Artois, count of Eu, Philippe de Jaucourt, and Philippe de Bar, were prominent on Louis of Bourbon's crusade, the two last, at any rate, receiving sums of money from Philip to help with their expenses.[3] One of these, Philippe d'Artois, took a small force out to Hungary in 1393 to help King Sigismund against the Turks, and all of them, except Philippe de Jaucourt, accompanied John of Nevers there in 1396. In these years, too, Burgundian knights swelled the ranks of the crusaders to Prussia, and their duke maintained close contacts with the Grand Master of the Teutonic Order. A chamberlain and familiar of Philip, Bertaut de Chartres, was sent to Prussia in 1380 to effect the release of some of the duke's subjects who had been imprisoned there; and some years later, apparently in 1388, Philip earned the gratitude of the Grand Master of the Teutonic Order by arranging a treaty of alliance between it and France, by means of which it was formally taken under the protection of the French crown.[4] Almost every year he paid out sums of money to help his knights defray their expenses on the 'voiage de Prusse'. In 1391, for instance, Louis de Poissy, Pierre de la Trémoille, Jehan de Sempy and Jehan de Hangest accompanied Jehan Boucicaut, and all of these, as well as others, were afterwards recompensed by Philip.[5] Although it would probably be inaccurate to state that these expeditions were actually sent by Philip,[6] he certainly encouraged and frequently subsidized them, and we do know that in 1394 he sent a company of crossbowmen, mostly Genoese, together with a gift of

---

[1] *Mandements de Charles V*, no. 1263.

[2] Jorga, *Philippe de Mézières*, 166 n. 5. For what follows, see the lists in Atiya, *Crusade in the later Middle Ages*, 519–28.

[3] ACO B1487, fos. 91 and 92.

[4] ACO B11932, ducal letter of 19 Feb. 1380/1, and *Cod. dipl. prussicus*, iv. no. 61.

[5] ACO B1487, f. 85a–b and B1495, fos. 41b–43b.

[6] Pot, *R. Pot*, 33, claims that Palamède Pot spent a year in Prussia by order of Philip, but in fact the entry in the accounts of the receipt-general whence his statement is derived only says that the *payment* to Pot was made by Philip's command (ACO B1479, f. 153).

wine, to the Grand Master, for the Grand Master's letter thanking him has survived.[1]

For some years before 1396 Philip the Bold had been toying with the idea of a crusade. In 1391 he sent Guy de la Trémoille to Venice and Hungary on important matters which he had 'très à cœur': surely in connection with a projected crusade?[2] By 1394 a definite scheme had emerged in the form of a joint crusade to be led by the dukes of Burgundy, Lancaster and Orleans, but at this time no decision had been made about its goal, for in July 1394 we find Philip writing to William of Namur stating that he planned to lead a crusade in the following year, with the dukes of Lancaster and Orleans, either to Hungary or Prussia.[3] When this letter was written Renier Pot was visiting the king of Hungary as ambassador of Philip and Louis of Orleans, and Philip's chamberlain, Pierre de la Trémoille, was enquiring, on his master's behalf, from the Grand Master of the Teutonic Order about the crusading prospects in Prussia.[4] Before the end of the year, however, the decision to go to Hungary had been made, and in January 1395 Philip the Bold's marshal, Guillaume de la Trémoille, was in Venice at the head of an embassy representing the three dukes. He waited there at least until 4 February, hoping to meet a Hungarian embassy which was on its way to France, and then left for Hungary.[5] Early in March King Sigismund's ambassadors arrived in Venice, and, after obtaining a promise of Venetian participation in the projected crusade, they journeyed on to enlist support in France. At Lyons, on 8 May, they were met and welcomed by Philip and Louis, but these princes were then engaged on a joint visit to Benedict XIII at Avignon, and it was not until early August that the Hungarian ambassadors were able to meet them in Paris for serious discussions. They had not, however, wasted their time in the meanwhile, but had employed it on a visit to Bordeaux to see the third leader of the crusade, John of Gaunt, duke of Lancaster. As late as May 1395 Philip still intended to lead the crusade in person,[6] and it

---

[1] *Cod. dipl. prussicus*, v. no. 57. See too Wigand of Marburg, *Chronik*, 654–6.

[2] Pot, *R. Pot*, 33.

[3] Letter printed by Cartellieri, *P. der Kühne*, 145–6; for its date, cf. ADN B1280/18296 with B18824, f. 201.

[4] Pot, *R. Pot*, 38 and ACO B1503, f. 82b; *Cod. dipl. prussicus*, v. no. 57 and ACO B1503, f. 86.

[5] *Mon. spect. hist. Slavorum merid.*, iv. 338–9 (wrongly attributed by Atiya, *Nicopolis*, 36, to 21 January 1394, instead of 1395) and *Cal. State Papers, Venice*, i. nos. 115 and 117.

[6] Cartellieri, *P. der Kühne*, 148–9.

must therefore have been in the second half of 1395 that its whole character was altered by his decision to send his eldest son, John of Nevers, in his place, and by the withdrawal of its other two prosspective leaders, the dukes of Lancaster and Orleans.[1] It then became, and remained, a specifically Burgundian enterprise.

Perhaps the most important of all the necessary preparations for a crusade was finance. Philip the Bold did not in fact have to meet the whole cost of the Nicopolis expedition, because the French nobles who accompanied John of Nevers, but did not form part of his retinue, went at their own expense with their own followings. Still, his expenses were bound to be on a very large scale, and in the summer of 1394 he began the complicated business of levying special taxes or *aides* for his projected crusade. A start was made with Flanders, which, impoverished by the troubles of 1379–85, was likely to prove unco-operative and difficult. Since he himself was occupied at this time in Brittany, Philip entrusted the negotiations to his wife Margaret, helped by John of Nevers. She was instructed, on 12 July 1394, to demand 100,000 nobles,[2] and was permitted to lower this to 90,000 nobles in case of opposition.[3] In fact, after some prolonged and hard-fought bargaining, the Flemish succeeded in lowering their contribution to 65,000 nobles. By October 1394 further contributions from this area had been fixed: Antwerp and Malines were to provide 4,000 nobles; Lille, Douai and Orchies, 10,000 francs; and Artois, 20,000 francs. On 19 August a councillor of Philip, Pierre de la Tanerie, *maître* of the *chambre des comptes* at Lille, was commissioned to receive the Flemish *aide*,[4] and the task of levying these moneys began that autumn.

At the end of the year a budget for the year 1395 was drawn up by Philip's financial advisers in order to ascertain what was available,

---

[1] The latest evidence of co-operation seems to be the dispatch by Louis and Philip of joint letters to Sigismund in the autumn of 1395, *IAPCA*, i. 142.
[2] The noble was originally an English gold coin introduced by Edward III in 1344 and eventually having its weight stabilized at 7·78 grams. In Flemish records the word usually refers to the imitation of this introduced by Philip the Bold in 1388, having a value slightly inferior to its English counterpart.
[3] ADN B18824/23870 and B1280/18296. For the next sentence, see the correspondence between Margaret and Philip, 17 July–12 October 1394, ADN B18822, fos. 153–181b, partly printed and analysed in *Documents pour servir à l'histoire de la Maison de Bourgogne en Brabant et en Limbourg*, nos. 17–30.
[4] *IAGRCC*, iii. 97–8.

or could be made available, for his crusade.[1] In this remarkable document, which throws much light on the Burgundian finances, and will concern us again later, the equivalent in francs is given for the sums voted in Flemish nobles, and the grand total of special taxes granted or to be requested for the crusade is reckoned at 220,000 francs, of which Flanders (including the clergy and Lille, Douai and Orchies), Malines, Antwerp and Artois had already voted some 170,000 francs; the duchy and county of Burgundy were to contribute 30,000; and the counties of Rethel, Nevers and Charolais between them 20,000. Other sources of income are then detailed, the probable ordinary expenses for the year assessed, and the figure of 400,000 francs calculated as available to Philip 'pour son voiage' is finally increased to 520,000 by the addition of a further *aide* from Artois of 20,000 francs, a loan of 50,000 from Giangaleazzo Visconti of Milan, and a gift of the same amount from the king of France. However, the whole of this sum, which exceeded the normal annual revenue of all Philip's territories, was certainly not received by him, and it is equally certain that the whole of what was raised was by no means set apart for the crusade.[2] The process of levying money for it continued throughout 1395, and even on the eve of its departure in 1396 loans were still being raised from the Flemish towns. Moreover, in spite of the careful financial preparations, and in spite of the 3,000 nobles and 24,685 francs paid over to John of Nevers on his departure, and more than 26,000 francs sent on after him, he still found it necessary to borrow 10,800 ducats at Vienna.[3]

Other important matters besides finance had to be settled before the crusade could start. Bulls were procured from Pope Benedict XIII permitting John to appoint his own confessor and to communicate with the infidel, and conferring plenary absolution on him in the case of his death on the expedition. Equipment of all kinds was purchased without any regard to cost, for the crusade was fitted out as if it were destined for one of those colourful parades through the streets

---

[1] Printed, Delaville le Roulx, *France en Orient*, ii. no. 5. The analysis in Atiya, *Nicopolis*, 139, is inaccurate and the headings misleading. See below, pp. 228–9.
[2] Van Nieuwenhuysen, *Recette générale*, 100, and Prevenier, *RBPH* xxxviii (1960), 358 n. 2. For Philip's annual revenue, see below, pp. 227–30.
[3] Van Nieuwenhuysen, *Recette générale*, 146–7. The ducat was a Venetian gold coin weighing 3·5 grams, having the same fineness and weight as the gold florin. Although its intrinsic value was slightly inferior to that of the franc, the two are often treated as equivalent in the accounts (see below, p. 77).

of Paris which normally accompanied the chivalrous festivities of the age, and Philip spared no pains to ensure that his son's retinue should surpass those of his followers in the splendour of its accoutrements. Twenty-four cartloads of green satin tents and pavilions were provided or made for it, and more than two hundred persons were issued with John's livery. Four huge banners, painted by one of the foremost artists in France, Colart de Laon, displayed the figure of the Virgin Mary in gold surrounded by escutcheons and fleurs-de-lis, while others bore the count's name and device. Hundreds of smaller pennons were provided to decorate the tents, and twelve trumpeters were lavishly equipped in heraldic costume to stand before John's own tent. Everything was embroidered, emblazoned and burnished with gold and silver. A complete range of kitchen equipment was specially made for the expedition, as well as forty dozen bowls and thirty dozen pewter plates.[1]

These preparations must have been nearing completion when, on 28 March 1396, a council was held by Philip the Bold in Paris to decide on the final arrangements and draw up a list of personnel to accompany John of Nevers. Fortunately a document recording the results of this deliberation has survived.[2] It opens with a list of twenty-two knights who are ordered by Philip the Bold to go 'au voiage de honguerie' with John of Nevers. The number of knights and squires to be brought by each of these twenty-two knights is laid down, and the total number of men-at-arms involved is eighty-four. Next follow the names of those who are to constitute John's household during the expedition. Of the 148 persons mentioned, some sixty or more are knights and squires, and there are twenty crossbowmen and ten archers. Thus John contributed about 150 men-at-arms of his personal company to the crusading army, a mounted contingent more than twice as large as what was probably the next largest single contingent, that of the marshal of France, Jehan Boucicaut, which is said to have numbered seventy. The members of John's contingent were ordered to report at Dijon by 20 April 1396, where they would receive four months' pay in advance. A supplementary document throws further light on the organization of the crusade. Five principal Burgundian knights of John's company were to act as his permanent council: Jehan de Vienne, admiral of France, Guy and Guillaume de la Trémoille, Philippe de Bar and Oudart de Chaseron. Further, should he so wish, John was to take counsel with five other

[1] David, *P. le Hardi, train somptuaire*, 37–8; Plancher, iii. 149 and *Documents concernant l'histoire de l'art*, 737–8.   [2] Printed, Atiya, *Nicopolis*, 144–8.

knights, not of his own company: Jacques de Bourbon, count of La Marche, Henri de Bar, Enguerrand de Coucy, Philippe d'Artois, count of Eu and constable of France, and the marshal, Jehan Boucicaut. This document ends with some elementary disciplinary regulations, and the curious, but, as we shall see, significant statement, that John of Nevers and his company ought to insist on being in the van of the battle: 'Item que monsieur le conte et sa compagnie a a requerir lavantgarde'. It is noteworthy that John's company was drawn from all the Burgundian territories. Flanders, for instance, contributed at least twenty-one knights and fifteen squires,[1] and, among the Flemish, were five bastard uncles of John of Nevers, illegitimate sons of Louis of Male: Louis le Haze and Louis le Frison, Jehan-sans-Terre, Victor and Renault.[2]

The leader of the crusade, John of Nevers, was twenty-four in the spring of 1396. As a boy of eleven he and his youthful companions had broken windows in the ducal castle at Rouvres, and at the age of sixteen or seventeen he took part in his first tournament.[3] He had acted as his father's lieutenant in the two Burgundies when he was still only fourteen.[4] Later, probably in 1389, he had been ordered by Philip to help the chancellor to investigate the complaints of the citizens of Malines against one of his officers, and he actively assisted his mother in 1394 when she was struggling to persuade the recalcitrant Flemish to grant the 100,000 nobles demanded by Philip for the crusade.[5] But in spite of these signs of maturity and of Philip's confidence in him, John was kept under the closest supervision and in complete dependence on his father. He had never been entrusted single-handed with any important business, nor had he ever been permitted to wield authority of his own. He remained, as he had grown up, entirely subservient to his father. Until the departure of the crusade he had never even possessed his own independent household organization, for, though he had a household, it was treated as an appendage of either his father's or mother's, whichever was convenient at the time, and was paid for out of their funds. He was often not even allowed to receive gifts made to him by the king and others. Thus when, on 6 April 1396, Charles VI granted him by royal letters

[1] Froissart, Kervyn, xv. 397–8.
[2] The three former were killed on the expedition. On Louis of Male's bastards, see, de Lichtervelde, *ASEB* lxxviii (1935), 48–58.
[3] *Inventaires mobiliers*, ii. nos. 839 and 2641.
[4] Plancher, iii. no. 82, and p. 76.
[5] *IAM*, iii. 4–6 and ADN B18822/23258; 23260; 23266 etc.

a parting gift of 10,000 francs, 2,000 francs were paid over by the royal receiver-general Michel du Sablon to Philip the Bold's *maître de la chambre aux deniers* for use in his own household, though the receipt was issued in John's name! Of the remaining 8,000 francs, 5,000 were paid to Philip's receiver-general of all finances in July, and only 3,000 were actually received by John of Nevers.[1] No moneys ever reached John from his own county of Nevers, the administration of which was entirely in his father's hands. Instead, he received an allowance, which was raised to two francs a day in 1389.[2] This was the prince chosen to lead the crusade against the Ottomans, and it is in the light of his situation and upbringing that one must interpret the document discussed above: nothing was left to John of Nevers himself. His council, and even the personnel of his household, were constituted by his father before he set out. Surrounded by some of the most experienced captains of war in the West, he should have been in capable hands. He was evidently not expected to contribute to the crusade anything in terms of practical leadership, but it was his presence, and his nominal leadership, as well as his father's authority, inspiration and finance, that stamped it with the character of a Burgundian enterprise.

Compared to the piratical or visionary character of so many of the crusades, that of Nicopolis stands out, in its broad conception, as eminently sound. Since the early years of the fourteenth century, a new power had emerged in Asia Minor, that of the Ottoman Turks. By the middle years of the century most of northern Anatolia was united under them, and they had already set foot on the European continent at Gallipoli. In the years after 1359, under their sultan Murad, they began the systematic conquest of the Balkans. Adrianople fell to them in 1361, and in 1365 Murad made it his capital. After the battle of Kosovo, Serbia was theirs, and Murad's successor, Bayazid, who promised to feed his horses at the altar of St. Peter's, completed the conquest of Bulgaria in the years after his accession in 1389, thus extending the Ottoman conquests to the Danube, the southern frontier of Hungary. Here was a new and terrible threat to Christendom, which for generations had enjoyed command of the European shores of the Mediterranean. Now, a large part of the Balkans was in

---

[1] ACO B1503^{bis}, f. 88b, B1508, f. 25b and B1511, f. 159b. The receiver-general was the official who presided over the financial office called the receipt-general. See below, pp. 146–8. In this chapter it is invariably the receiver-general or receipt-general of all finances which is referred to.

[2] Van Nieuwenhuysen, *Recette générale*, 120.

the hands of the infidel, and the work of military conquest was being completed and consolidated by swarms of settlers. Of the three powers chiefly affected by the rapid and relentless expansion of the Ottomans, Byzantium, reduced by them to the status of a city-state, was mutilated by internal dissension; Venice was unlikely to react violently, for her commercial interests dictated a policy of peaceful negotiation with the Turks; but Hungary, in the person of King Sigismund, was now ruled by a statesman who seems to have had a clear vision of the danger. He certainly played a large part in the genesis of the Nicopolis crusade. For him its aim was evidently the modest but sensible one of protecting his kingdom by inflicting a crushing military defeat on Bayazid, but some at least of the Western leaders entertained lofty though fantastic ambitions of reconquering the Balkans; even of crossing the narrows and crushing the Ottomans once and for all in their own homeland; and Froissart includes the recovery of Jerusalem among the expedition's aims![1] Be this as it may, the idea of meeting the Ottoman threat by concentrating the military resources of Christendom for a decisive stand on the Danube, and perhaps an offensive to the south of it, was an excellent one.

The Burgundian character of the Nicopolis expedition was carefully stressed by Philip the Bold in the arrangements for its departure. On 5 April 1396 he accompanied his son to the French royal abbey of St. Denis outside Paris for devotional purposes, and on the following day John bade farewell at Paris to the king. But the expedition was to depart, not from the capital of France, but from Dijon, the capital of the duchy of Burgundy. Here, on and after 13 April, a number of nobles, including the count of Savoy, and all the members of John's family, gathered at the ducal court. Here, too, the constable, Philippe d'Artois, Jacques de Bourbon, Henri de Bar and Enguerrand de Coucy assembled,[2] doubtless with their own followings, and it seems likely that most of the other French knights, besides John's company, did the same. On the eve of the departure Philip and his wife Margaret and John of Nevers attended a solemn mass in the abbey church of St. Bénigne, and the banners of France and Burgundy were carried in procession round the town.[3]

In the afternoon of 30 April John, with his own company and household, left Dijon for the final rendezvous at Montbéliard. Thence the crusaders marched to Regensburg, where they were able to embark on a flotilla of boats and sail down the Danube past Vienna,

---

[1] Kervyn, xv. 220.   [2] ACO B1503^{b18}, fos. 97–100b.
[3] Bazin, *MSE* (n.s.) xxx (1902), 120.

where John's brother-in-law Duke Leopold IV of Austria welcomed him towards the end of June, to Buda, the capital of Hungary. By the time they left Buda, in company with King Sigismund of Hungary, the Franco-Burgundian crusaders had been joined by contingents from Germany, England and elsewhere, as well as by the Hungarian army and two French knights who had travelled out via Venice: Enguerrand de Coucy and Henri de Bar. It seems to have been at a council of war held in Buda that the crusading leaders came to a fatal and strategically erroneous decision. Sigismund, who was expecting Bayazid to invade Hungary at any moment, counselled a defensive concentration on his southern frontier north of the Danube, but he was over-ruled by the Franco-Burgundian leaders, who preferred an immediate offensive into the Ottoman-held territories south of the river which, until recently, had formed part of the Christian kingdom of Bulgaria. The Danube was crossed at the Iron Gate by Orsova, and, after the reduction of the Ottoman garrisons of Vidin and Rahova (modern Oryakhovitsa) and the virtual destruction of the latter, the crusaders laid siege to the important fortified town of Nicopolis. Since they had brought no siege-engines with them, they had to resign themselves, after failing to carry the city by assault, to reducing it by blockade. The atmosphere in the besieging army seems to have been dominated by an element of jovial hilarity and insouciance quite out of keeping with its situation, which might at any moment have become exceedingly dangerous. In fact, Bayazid, nicknamed the Thunderbolt, was deftly encompassing its destruction. Abandoning his projected siege of Byzantium, he hurried north-west to concentrate his forces at Philippopolis (modern Plovdiv), 110 miles south of Nicopolis, and, advancing thence directly on Nicopolis, he encamped on 24 September some four miles from the city. Not until that very day were the crusaders convinced of his approach, a fact which becomes intelligible when we realize that they did not trouble themselves with reconnaissance and that Jehan Boucicaut, one of the most renowned soldiers of the age, had ordered that anyone found guilty of spreading alarm and despondency by announcing the approach of the enemy, was to have both his ears cut off!

It is quite fruitless to attempt to assess the numbers engaged in the battle which took place outside Nicopolis on 25 September 1396: probably none of the commanders on either side knew his own numerical strength at all accurately. The Christian army was federal in character, for the Hungarian and Franco-Burgundian contingents were quite separate entities without any unified command, and by their side fought a third army, of Wallachians, under their prince Mircea, a vassal of Sigismund. To their strategical error the crusaders now added a serious tactical one. Sigismund, who was familiar with the Ottoman practice of throwing out a screen of irregular light-armed troops in front of their main army, and who doubted the loyalty of Mircea and his Wallachians, planned to place these troops in the van, together with his own Hungarians, and to reserve the Franco-Burgundian heavy cavalry for a decisive blow at Bayazid's main force. But the crusaders would have none of this, insisted, with foolhardy enthusiasm and without any appreciation of tactics, on themselves occupying the van, and rode out to meet the enemy with chivalrous impetuosity and in considerable disorder, without further consulting Sigismund, who was left in some doubt as to their intentions and dispositions for battle. The battle of Nicopolis thus opened with a fierce cavalry charge of Franco-Burgundian and perhaps other Western crusaders, numbering probably less than one thousand men-at-arms.[1] In the face of this, the Ottoman cavalry screen dispersed to either flank, and then fell back to the rear, revealing a forest of pointed stakes, behind which a considerable proportion of their infantry, including archers, was massed. This obstacle was surmounted, though not without considerable losses from the Turkish archers, and the attack was then pressed home against the enemy infantry, which was overcome after a fierce struggle. Prudence and exhaustion now brought the forward movement to a halt, while the crusaders, many of whom had dismounted, rallied to their leaders. But, instead of waiting for the Hungarians to come up to their support, they resolved to attack the squadrons of Turkish cavalry which now confronted them. Once more, they were wholly successful, but, once more, counsels of prudence were brushed aside, and the exhausted crusaders struggled uphill in pursuit of the Turkish fugitives, spurred on by the mistaken belief that the whole Ottoman army had been put to flight. Bayazid, with his hitherto uncommitted reserves, was in fact waiting concealed beyond the hill, and, observing the blind temerity of his assailants, he directed the whole of these reserves against them. A few crusaders managed to flee, but the rest were surrounded and either cut down where they stood or taken prisoner, while Sigismund, who had been abandoned by his auxiliaries on either wing, was driven off the field by Bayazid's Serbian allies with heavy losses and considerable danger to his person. Although his losses probably exceeded those of the Christians, Bayazid had won a decisive victory, not so much by

[1] Froissart, Kervyn, xv. 315, was told they numbered less than 700.

his own military skill, though his initial dispositions and subsequent handling of his troops were tactically beyond reproach, as because of the extraordinary presumption and rashness of the Franco-Burgundian crusaders. Once more the fatal military weakness of Western chivalry was demonstrated. As on the fields of the Cephisus and of Courtrai, to name but two examples, the brilliant *élan* and tense excitement of the attack, inspired by the most exaggerated sentiments of renown, of military superiority and, worst of all, of honour, had led the knights and squires of the French-speaking world to ugly catastrophe.

Although Sigismund contrived to make good his escape down the Danube with a handful of followers, almost the whole of the Franco-Burgundian army was either killed or captured. Bayazid himself supervised the dispatch of a number of his prisoners on the day after the battle, but at least three hundred, including John of Nevers and those of his companions who had survived the battle, were spared. Philip the Bold's marshal, Guillaume de la Trémoille, Jehan de Vienne, the admiral of France, Louis le Haze, bastard of Flanders, Oudart de Chaseron, Philippe de Bar, Bertaut de Chartres and other leading members of the Burgundian nobility and intimates of Philip, had been left dead on the field, and several of those spared by Bayazid died before they could return home. Some idea of the tragic loss involved is given by a letter from the *gens des comptes* of Dijon to the chancellor of Burgundy, Jehan Canard, in answer to queries from the chancellor and Philip himself concerning the offices vacated by those killed at Nicopolis. This letter was written on 16 March 1397, at a time when accurate news of the fate of individual crusaders was still not available, and the *gens des comptes* had to content themselves with sending a list of sixteen persons, including two bailiffs, two castellans, and six captains of ducal castles, who were known to have gone to Hungary, and who were all salaried officers of the duke. In the event, twelve of these sixteen never returned.[1] Nothing was known in France of the disaster until rumours began to circulate early in December. At first the tragic tidings found no credence, and at Paris the first survivors who ventured to relate their terrible experiences were thrown into the provost's prison as rumour-mongers. But real anxiety was caused by the return, and the reports, of two of the constable's servants, and on 7 December and the following days a stream of messengers were hurriedly sent from the French court,

---

[1] Cf. Froissart, Kervyn, xv. 423–4 with Atiya, *Crusade in the later Middle Ages*, 523–8.

where Philip then was, to Italy and the East as well as to Austria, in search of more definite information.[1] Finally, on Christmas Eve, Jacques de Heilly arrived at Paris with letters from John of Nevers and instructions from Bayazid to request the initiation of negotiations with a view to the ransom of his prisoners. Philip's first messenger, his chamberlain Guillaume de l'Aigle, reached Turkey in January with Venetian help, and, after presenting some elaborately worked pieces of harness to Bayazid on Philip's behalf, was allowed to see the prisoners before returning to Paris, which he probably reached in April 1397.

Meanwhile, a solemn embassy to Bayazid, which included the governor of the county of Burgundy and the sovereign-bailiff of Flanders, Jehan de Vergy and Gilbert de Leuwerghem, and one of Philip's secretaries, Robert Dangeul, set out on 20 January. With it Philip sent a selection of the most sumptuous and splendid gifts that the West could offer an Eastern potentate: ten superb chargers, complete with their harness and led by seventeen grooms in white and scarlet livery, hounds, gyrfalcons, the very finest examples of cloth and tapestry, a dozen pairs of gloves, and some choice pieces of plate.[2] This unusual embassy was entirely successful, and on 24 June 1397 a convention was drawn up at Mikhalitch (modern Karacabey) fixing the ransom for all the prisoners of note at 200,000 ducats, to be paid by Philip the Bold. Twenty-eight thousand ducats were paid over on the spot in cash by John of Nevers, who had borrowed them from the nephew of the king of Cyprus, Jehan de Lusignan, and two Genoese merchants of Pera; and Bayazid accepted promises for the rest from a group of merchants and princes of the Genoese Aegean colonies, among them Francesco Gattilusio, the ruler of Mitylene, who pledged himself for 110,000 ducats. The prisoners had to guarantee to repay these sums before they left Venice on the homeward journey, and once this guarantee was ratified by Philip the Bold's ambassadors, both parties were free to return home.

After nine months in captivity at Gallipoli and Bursa, John of Nevers and his companions travelled home in a leisurely fashion. They stayed at Mitylene for more than a month in July and August, and stopped again with the Hospitallers at Rhodes, before finally reaching Venice in October. There, or at Treviso or in the neighbourhood, their homeward journey was necessarily interrupted for several months while they found means to discharge their financial

[1] *Commerce et expéditions militaires de la France et Venise*, no. 19 and ACO B1511, fos. 63b–64.   [2] David, *P. le Hardi, train somptuaire*, 38–40.

obligations. Those who had effected their release in the previous summer by pledging the payment of the ransom or paying the first instalment of it in cash, had now to be repaid or at least satisfied with new sureties, and some at least of the numerous debts which had been incurred since then had to be paid off. Administrative measures to deal with this situation were promptly taken by Philip the Bold. On 26 September 1397 one of his most experienced financial officers, Oudart Douay, a *maître* of the Dijon *chambre des comptes*, was commissioned to keep a special account of the moneys to be set apart for the ransom and return of John of Nevers,[1] and throughout the winter he was kept busy at Treviso under the supervision of a special committee appointed by Philip to control and expedite all matters concerning the ransom, and later authorized to raise loans for it as necessary.[2] Behind the complex operations of transferring funds to Oudart Douay, of satisfying creditors, and of raising new loans, was the genius and energy of Philip the Bold's councillor Dino Rapondi, a merchant banker, native of Lucca, but established in business at Paris and Bruges.[3] A member of the committee mentioned above, Dino had been employed by Philip, along with the chancellor, in organizing the levy of the special *aide* for the ransom recently voted by the Flemish. On 15 November, however, he was sent to join John of Nevers at Treviso, and here he, too, spent the entire winter. It was Dino who actually transferred the funds (*c.* 150,000 francs) which made up the greater part of Oudart Douay's receipt from the Burgundian receipt-general to Italy. The rest of Oudart's receipt, some 50,000 francs, came from a new series of loans which were raised at Venice in January 1398 and repaid by the receiver-general in the winter of 1398–9.[4] Only about a quarter of Oudart's funds can be readily identified as devoted to the ransom itself, and this money was used to repay to the Hospitallers of Rhodes and two Genoese Aegean merchants a sum of 52,000 ducats which they had between them paid to Bayazid, probably in August. The rest was used to repay a number of debts, totalling nearly 100,000 ducats, which John and his companions had incurred with Genoese merchants, either while they were still in

[1] Partly printed and analysed by Delaville le Roulx, *France en Orient*, ii. no. 23 and Pocquet, *AB* ix (1937), 296–302.
[2] BN Coll. de Bourg. 53, f. 190.
[3] See especially, Mirot, *BEC* lxxxix (1928), 299–389, and below, pp. 220–1.
[4] Cf. Delaville le Roulx, *France en Orient*, ii. 88 with ACO B1514, fos. 286b–291b. The receiver-general's account for 1398 is missing, but probably recorded the repayments not in that for 1399. This is the receiver-general of all finances; see above p. 67 n. 1.

Turkey or on the way home; to recompense the creditors with lump sums of about twenty-five per cent of the value of their loans, which looks rather like concealed interest; to defray the daily expenses of John's household between 22 November 1397 and 21 May 1398, which, including his return journey from Treviso to Ghent, totalled 9,684 francs; and for other miscellaneous purposes.

While he was at Treviso, Dino Rapondi transacted for Philip another financial operation of some importance.[1] King Sigismund of Hungary had generously promised to contribute half of John's ransom money, but found himself quite unable to raise the necessary 100,000 ducats. Dino Rapondi therefore paid it for him, apparently to John of Nevers, and received in exchange from Sigismund an annual rent of 7,000 ducats which the republic of Venice had been paying him. Venice, however, refused to accept the transference of this rent, and ceased to pay it, while Dino was presumably re-imbursed, and his claims to the rent taken over, by the duke. The affair led to prolonged negotiations between the dukes of Burgundy and Venice, and was not finally closed until 1424, when Philip the Good, the third Valois duke, agreed to abandon his claims to the rent of 7,000 ducats.

In the spring of 1397, before the arrangements for John's release had been made, Philip the Bold had begun to seek the extra funds which this was bound to require. His new appeal came very soon after the taxation of 1394 and 1395 for the preparation and launching of the crusade, and both in Flanders and Burgundy he was forced by popular opposition to lower his demands.[2] In April the Flemish were required to vote 150,000 nobles, but they were unwilling to do this, and it was only after protracted negotiations that they agreed to a sum of 100,000 nobles, to be levied over a period of two years.[3] The Estates of the duchy of Burgundy were asked to vote 80,000 francs, which was double their usual *aide*, but in August Philip was compelled to accept their offer of 50,000.[4] The county of Nevers contributed 10,000 francs; Charolais, 5,000; Artois, probably 20,000; Lille, Douai and Orchies, probably 12,000; the Champagne territories,

---

[1] The history and significance of this operation remain obscure. Besides Delaville le Roulx and Atiya, see, on it, Mirot, *BEC* lxxxix (1928), 361, and Silberschmidt, *Orientalische Problem*, 153–4 and 169–70.
[2] Delaville le Roulx (*France en Orient*, i. 325) mistakenly supposes that these *aides* were agreed to and raised without any *débat*. Atiya, *Nicopolis*, Appendix IX, 155–6, 'Money raised by the duke of Burgundy', is unreliable and contains several errors.   [3] *Handelingen*, nos. 375–84.
[4] BN Coll. de Bourg. 53, fos. 78 and 155b.

2,000; and the city of Besançon, 3,000. The county of Burgundy may have escaped, since it had voted 12,000 francs as recently as July 1396,[1] and there is some doubt about the contribution of the county of Rethel. In any case the total amounted to well over 300,000 francs, and, after this had been collected, further taxes 'for the rest of John of Nevers' ransom', were levied in 1400: 12,000 francs from the duchy of Burgundy; 2,000 from the county of Charolais; and 2,000 from the *terres de Champagne*.[2] The Flemish, however, firmly refused to vote the 30,000 nobles required from them for this purpose in 1400.[3]

While the internal resources of the Burgundian state were being exploited to the full, Philip the Bold did his best to make use of his power and status among the European princes to persuade or compel them or their territories to come to his aid. There was, of course, no difficulty with France, where his position in the government allowed him a large measure of control over the royal finances. In October 1397 he persuaded Charles VI to give him, or simply helped himself to, 84,000 francs, which was stated to be a contribution towards the ransom, and we may surmise that the further 40,000 francs made over to Philip from various royal *aides* on 20 and 21 November was obtained for the same purpose, or on the same pretext.[4] Elsewhere, Philip was unsuccessful. The good offices of the count of Savoy and Albert of Bavaria, regent of Hainault-Holland, were enlisted, but, though the former was the brother-in-law and the latter the father-in-law, of John of Nevers, neither contributed any money.[5] Even the Estates of Brabant were approached, but they also refused to help, although they expressed their sorrow and regret at the disaster which had overtaken the ducal house of Burgundy.[6]

Although the product of the *aides* voted in Flanders and elsewhere began to flow into the ducal treasury in the autumn of 1397, not enough was immediately available for the extrication of John of Nevers and his companions from Treviso in the following winter. The crisis came early in 1398, and special measures had to be resorted to. In February 10,000 francs were raised on some jewellery which Philip borrowed from his brother John of Berry, and at the same time Philip pawned some of his own plate for 20,000 francs.[7] In February

---

[1] Plancher, iii. no. 180.
[2] BN Coll. de Bourg. 53, fos. 206, 208 and 213.
[3] *Handelingen*, nos. 483–7 and ACO B1526, f. 81b.
[4] Pocquet, *MSHDB* vii (1940–1), 105.
[5] Bazin, *MSE* (n.s.) xxx (1902), 132.
[6] Froissart, Kervyn, xvi. 265–8.
[7] ACO B1514, fos. 290b–291 and Plancher, iii. no. 185.

and March, too, his officials were busy raising loans from the towns of Artois and elsewhere by means of the sale of rents, and well over 15,000 francs was realized in this way.[1]

After an enforced delay at Venice and Treviso of at least three months, the leading survivors of Nicopolis finally started for home on 23 January 1398. A month later, on 22 February, John of Nevers made his formal entry into Dijon. An extraordinary outburst of enthusiasm greeted him and his companions. Everywhere in the Burgundian dominions he was welcomed like a conquering hero with gifts, festivities and popular acclaim. As he traversed the duchy of Burgundy and, after a visit to the French court in Paris on 10 March, Artois and Flanders, enthusiastic municipal delegations met him outside the towns. He was preceded into Lille on 19 March by three minstrels and a trumpeter. After joining his father at Ghent on 22 March, they both indulged in a veritable triumphal progress through the chief towns of Flanders and Brabant, visiting Brussels, Malines, Antwerp, Sluis, Bruges, Ypres, Courtrai, Oudenaarde and Tournai. Thus ended the disaster of Nicopolis, in a blaze of glory which somehow conjured up triumph out of defeat and tragedy. The fame and prestige of the house of Burgundy had been successfully promoted, and it was now linked for ever with the proud and almost magic tradition of the crusades.

The financial repercussions of John of Nevers' expedition to Hungary were felt long after the enthusiastic scenes which marked his return. Unfortunately, the loss of one of the annual accounts of Philip the Bold's receipt-general of all finances, that for 1398, has made it impossible for the historian to trace these repercussions in detail. That matters dragged on for a long time is clear from the fact that fresh *aides* for the ransom were being levied in 1400, at a time when the ambassador of the Genoese rulers of Mitylene and Enos (modern Enez) was demanding from Philip the settlement of outstanding debts of over 100,000 ducats, which were still being repaid late in 1401.[2] In the previous year another outstanding debt, of 15,000 ducats, had been repaid to one of the leading Hospitallers, Dominique d'Allemagne, but at least one debt, incurred in 1397 or 1398, was not liquidated till 1403.[3] If we assume that Philip did eventually discharge all his debts—and there is no evidence to the contrary—we may attempt to ascertain what was the total cost of the ran-

[1] Van Nieuwenhuysen, *Recette générale*, 178.
[2] ACO B1526, fos. 93–4.
[3] ACO B1519, fos. 279 a–b and B1532, fos. 117b–118.

som and return of John of Nevers and his companions. The ransom itself was 200,000 ducats. Now, although a ducat was treated as equivalent to a franc or *livre* of Tours for purposes of *receipt*, the receiver-general normally debited 105 francs to his account for every 100 ducats *paid out*. The payment of the ransom therefore actually cost Philip 210,000 francs.[1] The two embassies to the East, those of Guillaume de l'Aigle and Jehan de Vergy, including the gifts sent to Bayazid, cost Philip some 10,000 francs, and he distributed at least 64,000 francs in gifts to the released prisoners after their return.[2] To these sums must be added Oudart Douay's expenses other than on the ransom itself, probably about 150,000 ducats but perhaps less; and 3,600 francs in recompenses or interest to creditors plus 9,000 francs for expenses in transferring funds, sums which were debited to the receiver-general's account for 1399. These sums total 446,600 francs, but the actual total paid out by Philip must have been considerably larger than this, especially as the receiver-general's account for 1398 is missing. We cannot surely be far out in assessing the total at half a million francs.

It has already been noted that the first series of *aides* raised by Philip for John's ransom yielded over 300,000 francs. Those levied in 1400 produced a further 16,000, and, when we add to their combined total the 124,000 obtained by Philip from Charles VI in autumn 1397, the grand total of 440,000 francs approaches the half-million required. Since all these moneys were specially raised for this occasion, it seems unlikely that the Burgundian financial resources were severely strained. While the normal, ordinary receipts and expenses continued at the accustomed level, special, extra moneys were raised to deal with this special situation. This conclusion is borne out by an examination of the accounts of the receipt-general and by the very moderate economy measures of the years after Nicopolis. True, on 18 May 1399, Philip ordered certain annual pensions to be reduced for one year by a total of 7,000 francs, and a number, perhaps the majority, of ducal officials suffered temporary reductions in their salaries by way of forced loans or otherwise, but this sort of economy occurred at other times in Philip's reign, and was probably practised to obtain or

---

[1] ACO B1514, fos. 54b, 286b–287, 296b etc. It may have cost more than 210,000 francs, for Dino Rapondi was, on one occasion at least, allowed 110 francs for each 100 ducats he paid out on behalf of the duke, B1514, f. 291. The details that follow are from the accounts of the receipt-general of all finances, ACO B1511 and 1514.

[2] List in Atiya, *Nicopolis*, 143. See also Mirot, *BEC* lxxxix (1928), 362.

conserve ready cash, rather than to meet a long-term need.[1] On the whole, the history of the Nicopolis tragedy amply demonstrates the remarkable extent of the financial resources already available to the first Valois duke of Burgundy.

[1] Plancher, iii. 153 and no. 192; BN Coll. de Bourg. 53, fos. 63 and 193; see below, pp. 235–6.

CHAPTER FIVE

The European Scene

In the Nicopolis crusade Burgundy, perhaps for the first time, acted as a major European power. Her ruler, Philip the Bold, embarked independently on a military enterprise of the first magnitude which was based on the fullest use of the combined resources of all his territories. But, besides this single significant enterprise, a whole series of smaller events, of interlocking policies, of skilful adaptations to circumstances and exploitations of opportunities, helped to establish Philip not just as count of Flanders or duke of Burgundy, or even regent of France, but as ruler of a new political entity— Burgundy. Under his able guidance this new entity evolved, internally, towards some sort of unity, and externally, as a European power. It is the purpose of the present chapter to examine this second development and to depict Philip the Bold acting in Europe, rather than inside his own dominions, as an independent ruler, in his own interests and for the benefit of his own house.

In the last two decades of the fourteenth century the European political context was favourable for the emergence of a new power, and by far the most propitious area for this was along the boundary between the kingdom of France and the Holy Roman Empire, which, roughly speaking, between Antwerp and Lyons, followed the course of the rivers Scheldt, Meuse and Saône. Philip the Bold's territories, though they straddled the border in the north and south, lay for the most part in France. After 1384 they extended from the North Sea southwards almost to Lyons. Artois in the north, Rethel between Rheims and the Meuse, and the duchy of Burgundy with Nevers, were entirely French. Flanders only just extended into imperial territory, but the county of Burgundy lay wholly within it.

Philip the Bold's position, as it were in the no-man's-land between France and Germany, was favoured by certain circumstances and developments. In the first place, the Empire was weak, for political authority, which had never taken on a very marked monarchic or centralized aspect there, was now widely fragmented among the princes, towns and petty rulers; and the independence of the Electoral Princes had been written into the imperial constitution by the Golden Bull of 1356. The emperor Charles IV (1346–78) was in many ways a notable statesman, but his energies and authority were concentrated in his hereditary Bohemian kingdom, and he had no control over events on the western boundaries of his Empire. In 1377, when he visited the Low Countries, his brother Wenzel of Luxembourg, duke of Brabant, was the only one of the three principal rulers who deigned to meet him. In 1378 he was succeeded by his ineffective son Wenzel of Bohemia, under whom imperial authority disintegrated still further, and Germany was soon plunged into civil war and chaos. If, on the one side, Philip was confronted with a powerless Empire, which incidentally had no army to buttress its diplomacy, on the other stood France, still, in spite of the reverses and crises of the 1350s, by far the most powerful continental state in the West. But France, as we have seen, was in Philip's pocket. He had nothing to fear from Germany and everything to gain from France.

While circumstances in France and Germany worked very much in Philip's favour, in the Low Countries he was able to exploit a situation which had been consciously engineered by his father-in-law Louis of Male, a hard, unscrupulous ruler whose brilliantly opportunist foreign policy and largely peaceful reign should not be lost sight of behind the tragedy of its closing years. His principal achievement was the substitution of Flanders for Brabant as the Low Countries' most powerful state. In 1356 his armies marched into that duchy and, over-running almost the whole of it, compelled Wenzel of Luxembourg and his wife Joan to sign the humiliating treaty of Ath, which transferred two of their most flourishing cities, Malines and Antwerp, to Flanders; recognized Louis of Male's rights to the succession of Brabant; and permitted him to use the title duke of Brabant, a right of which he availed himself in his official documents. The decline of Brabant under Wenzel and Joan was accentuated by their defeat at Baesweiler in 1371 at the hands of the dukes of Guelders and Jülich and the capture of Wenzel on the field of battle, as well as by internal developments, which involved the transference of a considerable degree of power from the ruler to the people, meeting in the Estates and acting in the Council of Cortenberg. Hainault-Holland, Louis of Male's other neighbour, had passed into the hands of William of Bavaria, of the house of Wittelsbach, in 1354–6, but in

1357-8 he went mad, and Louis was able to act as arbitrator between his two brothers, each of whom claimed the regency. With his help, Albert of Bavaria obtained it, and remained henceforth for the most part his staunch ally. Thus the local situation in the Low Countries, like the general situation in Western Europe, was highly propitious when Philip the Bold appeared on the scene in 1384-5 as the first ruler of a new Burgundian state.

Philip the Bold nurtured and extended his influence in Europe in all sorts of ways, but there were four principal activities, carried out in the interests of himself and his house, which had important repercussions on the European scene: the arrangement of a system of marriage alliances, the acquisition of territories, the maintenance of diplomatic relations with other European rulers, and the disposal of his lands among his children. These must be examined in turn.

Marriage Alliances

Between 1371 and 1391 Margaret of Male bore Philip at least eleven children, of whom seven survived the perils of childhood and adolescence. Here was ample material for matrimonial politics: three boys and four girls. The eldest son, John, who later acquired the sobriquet Fearless, was born on 28 May 1371, became count of Nevers in 1384, and succeeded his parents in their principal territories in 1404-5. Anthony, born in 1384, was promised Rethel in 1393, and Philip, born in 1389, followed John as count of Nevers in 1405. Both Anthony and Philip were killed in 1415 on the field of Agincourt. The girls were Margaret, born in 1374, Catherine (1378), Bonne, born in 1379 but who died unmarried in 1398, and Mary (1386).[1] It was the custom of rulers at this time to marry their children for purely political or financial motives—King John the Good of France sold a daughter to the despot of Milan to raise cash for his ransom—and without any regard for their age or inclinations. Child marriages were common: Charles of Orleans, married at the age of eleven, found himself three years later a widower with a daughter on his hands; and in 1396 the son of the duke of Brittany, then aged six, married a five-year-old daughter of Charles VI. With betrothals perfectly permissible at an even earlier age, a child, from the very

[1] I have tried to establish these and the many other dates mentioned in this chapter as accurately as possible, but I have not thought it necessary to justify, in the notes, every instance where my date differs from that given by some other modern writers.

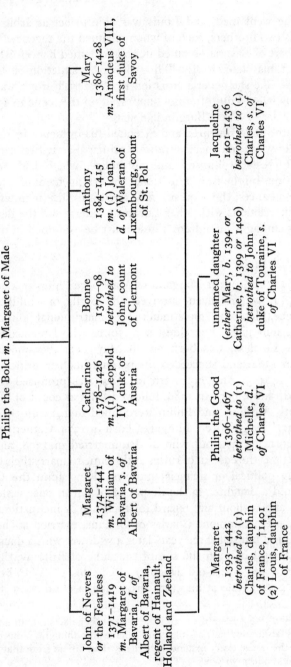

Marriages and betrothals of Philip's children and grandchildren during his lifetime (1342–1404).

moment of birth, was useful political material, to be actively exploited.

The first matrimonial alliance planned by Philip the Bold for his children was with the house of Habsburg.[1] When the initial exchange of embassies took place, in 1377, there were two Habsburg princes, the brothers Albert and Leopold, both the third of the name, who described themselves as duke of Austria, though in fact they had divided the ancestral territories between them, Albert taking Austria, and Leopold the rest. This arrangement made Leopold a neighbour of Philip the Bold, for he held a group of territories and seigneurial rights centred on Ensisheim in Upper Alsace, which gave him the titles of count of Ferrette (Pfirt) and landgrave of Upper Alsace, and made him effective master of this area, which lay on the northeastern boundary of the county of Burgundy. There is every reason to suppose that Philip appreciated the advantages of an alliance with the Habsburgs and that he envisaged the possibility of detaching the county of Ferrette, which was the most westerly piece of the extensive Habsburg territories, and adding it to his own dominions. On the other hand, the initiative seems to have come from Leopold, for the earliest evidence of Austro-Burgundian negotiations at this time is of a meeting between his emissaries and Philip at Dijon, at the end of April 1377.[2] Guy de Pontailler, marshal of Burgundy, was in charge of the negotiations on the Burgundian side, and these continued throughout the rest of the year. Early in April 1378 Philip again received Leopold's ambassadors at Dijon, and presented them with some plate he had bought for this purpose from members of his household. Finally, in July, the ambassadors of both sides met at Remiremont and drew up a marriage treaty between Leopold's son and namesake and Margaret of Burgundy, then aged four, which was afterwards ratified by the two dukes. Margaret and Leopold were to be married within a year of their both attaining the age of ten; Philip was to give his daughter a dowry of 100,000 francs to be paid in annual instalments of 20,000 francs, and Duke Leopold was to settle on her and her heirs 15,000 francs' worth of annual rent in the county of Ferrette and Upper Alsace, and a further 10,000 for her life

[1] For what follows, see Plancher, iii. 52–3, 100–4, 126 and nos. 62, 86, 89, 113–15, 121, 150, 160, 161, 166 and 167; Leroux, *Nouvelles recherches*, 92–3; Stouff, *Catherine de Bourg.*, 38–44 and David, *P. le Hardi, train somptuaire*, 45–9. I have not seen Hartl, *Österreichisch-burgundische Heirat*.

[2] *Inventaires mobiliers*, i. no. 3158. Philip was still at Vincennes on 20 April (ibid., p. 581 n. 1). For the next two sentences, see Dumay, *MSBGH* xxiii (1907), 39–40 and *Inventaires mobiliers*, ii. nos. 236, 273 and 316.

only. Effectively, Leopold had promised to hand over the county of Ferrette to his son and Margaret, but this would only be transferred to the house of Burgundy in the unlikely event of their being without issue. Philip had secured an ally and provided handsomely for his eldest daughter, and he could look forward, during her lifetime at any rate, to an extension of Burgundian influence in Alsace and to the termination or at least diminution of the incessant disputes and raids on the borders of this area and the county of Burgundy. The alliance was now to be cemented by one of those elaborate and colourful personal meetings of rulers which invariably accompanied, and apparently did not hinder, the humdrum diplomacy of the age. This took place on the borders of the counties of Burgundy and Ferrette in January 1379. Both dukes arrived with large followings, which indulged in the usual jousts and festivities at Philip's expense. He had treated this expedition almost like a military operation, summoning the Burgundian nobility to attend in person, and ordering the clergy to furnish the transport they were bound to provide in case of war, and he took with him his tapestries, and a quantity of silver plate to distribute to the Austrians.[1]

In matrimonial alliances, as in other matters, there were priorities, and when, in 1384, he was confronted with compelling reasons for marrying one of his daughters without delay into the Low Countries branch of another German family, the Wittelsbachs, Philip the Bold found it necessary to send an embassy to Austria in January 1385 to ask Duke Leopold to accept his second daughter, Catherine, now aged six, instead of Margaret, as the future wife of his son Leopold. This request was accepted without demur, and without the demand of any important changes in the marriage treaty, except the stipulation that Catherine and Leopold were to be married by 29 September 1385, and that she should be handed over to her husband immediately after the ceremony. The wedding was deferred, however, and a new situation arose when Duke Leopold was defeated and killed by the Swiss at the battle of Sempach on 9 July 1386. After some delay, another treaty was made, on 6 September 1387, this time between Philip the Bold and Duke Leopold's brother Albert, and later in the month six deputies on either side were appointed to supervise the transference to Catherine of the rents assigned to her in the county of Ferrette and the neighbourhood. The wedding was celebrated at Dijon between 14 and 17 September and followed by a further agreement between Philip and Albert over the details of Catherine's

---

[1] *Itinéraires*, 508 and *Inventaires mobiliers*, ii. no. 345.

dowry. At this time she was still only nine years old, and the stipulation in the marriage treaty that she was to leave the Burgundian court directly after the wedding was tacitly ignored by her parents. The young duchess of Austria remained at home with her mother, and it was only in May 1392, nearly five years later, that the marriage was finally consummated at Dijon.[1] But even then Philip and his wife refused to let Catherine leave, and a whole succession of delays and excuses intervened before the impatient Leopold was at last, on 18 September 1393, permitted to fetch his fifteen-year-old wife from Margaret of Male's favourite castle of Germolles and take her off to his own territories. At the last she was handsomely provided for by her parents. Her trousseau, which had been assembled for the most part at Arras and transported thence to Dijon in two carts decorated with her escutcheons, each drawn by five horses, included plate, jewellery, tapestries, a fur coverlet, clothes, wine, fruit, two silver basins, a hat of cloth-of-gold decorated with twenty rubies, twenty sapphires and ninety pearls, and much else besides. Catherine also received parting gifts from members of her family: her seven-year-old sister Mary, for instance, gave her a gold chess set.

The history of this protracted affair by no means ended in September 1393, for, after the prompt payment in 1385 of the first instalment of his daughter's dowry, Philip paid no more, and further negotiations were required before, in 1403, Leopold finally transferred the county of Ferrette to his wife, and, on 6 February 1404, ordered his officers there to do homage to her. Philip had still not paid the second instalment of Catherine's dowry when he died on 27 April 1404, and the story thus drags on into the reign of his successor John the Fearless, and indeed beyond it. Philip the Bold, however, had secured his foothold in Alsace and his Habsburg ally at the least possible cost to himself. If he had behaved badly both towards his daughter and her husband, he had done well for Burgundy.

A year after Catherine another daughter, Bonne, had been born to Philip and Margaret, and on 6 June 1382 a marriage treaty was drawn up between Philip and the duke of Bourbon, by the terms of which Bonne was to marry the latter's eldest son John, count of Clermont, and this was renewed in almost identical terms on 21 April 1386. Two years later, early in 1388, there was talk of marrying her to Louis II of Anjou, king of Sicily, but this ceased when it was discovered that she was already promised to the duke of Bourbon's son. The betrothal took place in July 1394, but the marriage was deferred,

[1] *Itinéraires*, 543.

probably because of Bonne's poor health, and forestalled by her death in 1398.[1]

It seems that, soon after his succession to the county of Flanders at the beginning of 1384, Philip the Bold began to think seriously of continuing and consolidating Louis of Male's policy of alliance with Albert of Bavaria, regent of Hainault-Holland.[2] Both he and Albert had children of marriageable age, and in January 1385 Philip released his eldest daughter Margaret from her engagement to Leopold in order to leave her free to marry William of Bavaria, Albert's son. He had been urged to do this by his wife's aunt, Joan of Brabant, who was an enthusiastic supporter of such an alliance, not least because of her fear that the marriage, then being projected, of William and the duke of Lancaster's daughter Philippa, would strengthen the influence of England in the Low Countries and thus increase the power of her sworn enemy the duke of Guelders, who was at this very moment contemplating an alliance with England and a war of aggression against Brabant. After a continual exchange of ambassadors in the second half of 1384, a conference was held at Cambrai in January 1385 between the rulers of the three leading powers of the Low Countries, Philip the Bold, count of Flanders, Joan, duchess of Brabant, and Albert, regent of Hainault-Holland, which marked Philip's début in the complex but important foreign policy of this area. At this conference his plans were nearly upset, and then modified, by the demand of Albert's wife that, if her son was to marry a Burgundian princess, then one of her daughters should marry a Burgundian prince. There is a clear hint, in Froissart,[3] that Philip regarded each of his children as a separate diplomatic or political instrument and intensely disliked the idea of using two stones to kill one bird. Albert's wife's attitude, that if she had to part with a son in this way, she ought to seize the opportunity to marry off a daughter as well, is equally understandable. In the event, and in spite of Philip's earlier plan of marrying John of Nevers into the French royal family, a double Burgundian-Wittelsbach alliance was agreed to at Cambrai. John of Nevers was to marry Margaret of Bavaria, and Margaret of Burgundy was to wed William of Bavaria.

[1] See Plancher, iii. 71, 86–7 and nos. 74 and 94; le Fèvre, *Journal*, i. 509–10 and David, *P. le Hardi, train somptuaire*, 51.

[2] For what follows, see the documents in Plancher, iii. nos. 78, 87, 88, 90, 91, 92, 93 and 95 and *Cartulaire de Hainaut*, ii. nos. 625, 627, 629, 630 and 632–5. For recent accounts see Laurent and Quicke, *Origines de l'État bourguignon*, 118–30 and David, *Misc. Roggen*, 57–76.

[3] Kervyn, x. 310; SHF, xi. 189–90.

Philip the Bold, of course, could have had no inkling that this alliance would eventually lead, in the next century, to the incorporation of Hainault-Holland into the Burgundian state. He was, however, establishing potential claims on these territories, and at the same time cementing an alliance with a powerful and influential neighbour. The value of Albert's friendship was demonstrated at once, for Brabant was explicitly mentioned as part of John of Nevers' inheritance in his marriage treaty with Margaret of Bavaria, a fact which implied Albert's support of the Burgundian succession to that duchy. Later in this same year, too, he sent troops to Philip's aid against the rebels of Ghent. The financial side of this double marriage alliance was heavily weighted in Philip's favour, for, while Albert promised to give his daughter a dowry of 200,000 francs, Philip only had to provide his with 100,000. In effect, therefore, Philip was able to marry off his daughter without a dowry, while Albert had to provide 100,000 francs for his, half of which he promised to give to John of Nevers 'pour en faire sa volonté'—to do what he liked with.

Although all the essentials for the double wedding had been settled in January at the conference of Cambrai, much remained to be done. The date, after one postponement, was fixed for 12 April, and Philip was soon busy borrowing jewellery from his brother of Berry, transporting tapestries from Arras and Hesdin, and moving some fifty jousting horses from Paris to Cambrai in preparation for the tournament which was to be held after the weddings. Because of the consanguinity of the future couples, dispensations had to be procured, and since at this time there were two rival popes, the precaution was taken of obtaining dispensations from both, though Urban VI's did not arrive until some time after the wedding. Meanwhile, Philip had borrowed twelve horses from the duke of Brittany and made use of his controlling position in France to borrow some hats and circlets from Charles VI, not to mention the crown jewels or a large part of them, in order to add lustre to the appearance of his wife and children, and he even persuaded the king to come to Cambrai in person for the ceremonies. These, and the festivities which accompanied them, formed one of the most brilliant spectacles of the age, celebrated by poets and chroniclers alike.[1] Philip alone had supplied a thousand jousting lances for the tournament.[2] His livery was red and green, and the quality of the cloth was carefully graded according to the standing of the wearers. Thus Philip himself, John

[1] Doutrepont, *Littérature française*, 369–70.

[2] *IADNB*, iv. 3 and, for the next sentence, *Inventaires mobiliers*, ii. no. 1213.

of Nevers, and twenty prominent knights wore velvet *en graine*; fifty-four other knights were issued with velvet *sans graine*; and 247 squires, servants, minstrels, falconers and other officers and menials of the court wore liveries of satin. The ladies and their attendants were dressed in cloth-of-gold. When Charles VI arrived outside Cambrai on 11 April 1385 he was greeted by Philip and Margaret, Albert and his wife, Joan of Brabant, and the nobility of north-eastern France and the Low Countries. The marriage contracts were sealed after dinner that day, and no significant changes were made to the agreements drawn up in January. William, Albert's son, was to be given territories in Hainault which included the county of Ostrevant, was made Albert's heir, and renounced any claim to the succession of the duke and duchess of Burgundy which he might have through his wife. The weddings were celebrated on 12 April in Cambrai cathedral, and were followed by a sumptuous banquet in the bishop's palace and a tournament in the market-place in which the king of France himself participated, together with knights and heralds from France, the Low Countries, Spain, Scotland and Germany. The prize was a jewelled clasp, which was removed from the bosom of the duchess of Burgundy and presented to a young knight from Hainault. The expenses of this magnificent entertainment must have been considerable. The livery which Philip issued to his court and retinue cost 34,000 *livres*, and the gifts which he distributed after the wedding came to nearly 78,000. The money, however, was certainly well spent, for the celebrations at Cambrai served as yet another useful and striking demonstration of the power and prestige of Philip the Bold.

In the summer of 1385 Philip could well have congratulated himself on having married, or arranged the marriage of, all his surviving children except the one-year-old Anthony. When, in August 1386, another girl, Mary, was born, her future husband was selected and her marriage treaty signed within three months of her birth. A chronicler relates how the news of this event reached Philip at a time when the ambassadors of the count of Savoy's mother were with him, endeavouring to find means to end a series of disputes between the subjects of Savoy and Burgundy along the frontier between the county of Burgundy and the *pays de Vaud*. The new-born child was at once put to political use and promised in marriage to the three-year-old son of the count of Savoy. If there is any truth in this story, it clearly shows that one of the principal motives which drew Philip into an Austrian alliance in 1377–8 was at work again in 1386: the protection and security of his most exposed and turbulent territory, the county of Burgundy. What we do know is that, in the autumn of 1386, Philip the Bold and the count of Savoy, Amadeus VII, were both in Flanders with the king of France and many others, intent on crossing the Channel and invading England, and that the marriage treaty of their children Mary and Amadeus was drawn up at Sluis, the planned embarkation port, on 11 November. Philip promised for Mary the same handsome dowry he had promised, but not paid, his other two daughters, 100,000 francs, and agreed to hand her over to her future parents-in-law, to be brought up at their court, as soon as she was seven. But, as with Catherine, so with Mary, he evidently had no intention of keeping his word. True, Mary was married on 30 October 1393 within a month or two of her seventh birthday, but she did not leave the Burgundian court for another ten years. Three days after her wedding Philip had become part-regent, with his brother John of Berry, of Savoy, and during the following years he intervened in its affairs and controlled the movements of his future son-in-law Amadeus VIII, so that there was nothing to prevent him indefinitely postponing Mary's departure, apart from his own promise. Eventually, however, on 29 October 1403, Amadeus was allowed to collect his wife from Tournus and take her off to Savoy. Like Leopold of Austria, he had had to wait a long time, but, like him, he was at least partly compensated for this delay by the magnificence of his wife's trousseau, for Mary took with her a gold crown encrusted with jewels, gold and silver plate, a complete set of equipment for her private chapel, coverlets, tapestries, saddles, horses, carts, chests and all the elaborate paraphernalia of the itinerant courts of the time.[1]

Anthony, the only other child of Philip who was married in his father's lifetime, was born in August 1384, and was promised in marriage to Joan, daughter of Waleran of Luxembourg, count of St. Pol and Ligny, on 19 February 1393.[2] Waleran was one of the most powerful of Philip's vassals in Artois. He had rendered important services to his lord, accompanying him, for instance, on the campaign against Guelders in 1388, and was to render more in the future. That

[1] For the above, see Dupin, *Chronique*, cols. 499–501, Plancher, iii. 97–8, 198 and nos. 107, 216, 217, and David, *P. le Hardi, train somptuaire*, 49–50 and 132–5. David claims that this Mary was born in August 1380 (49), but there were in fact two Marys; the first, who is referred to as alive in 1382 (ibid., 188), must have died soon afterwards.
[2] For what follows, see Plancher, iii. 131–2, 183–4, and nos. 156–9, and Schoos, *Burgund und Orleans*, 98–107.

Philip valued his friendship and support is shown by the fact that he received one of the highest annual pensions of all his allies and retainers, 8,000 francs.[1] He had invaded the duchy of Luxembourg on his own account soon after Duke Wenzel's death in 1383, probably with the immediate aim of recovering debts rather than of actually conquering the duchy. He did, however, have a claim to its succession which was reinforced in a practical way in 1384 when his brother, Pierre de Luxembourg, afterwards canonized, became bishop of Metz; and, in the autumn of 1392, he attacked Luxembourg again, penetrating to the walls of the capital. Although there was no mention of it in the treaty Philip now signed with him, the duchy certainly entered into Philip's calculations, for this alliance brought one of those most concerned with its affairs, and a possible pretender to its ducal throne, much more firmly under his influence; it was, indeed, one of the earliest moves of the house of Burgundy towards the annexation of Luxembourg. By the treaty of February 1393, the count of St. Pol was to give the castellany of Lille, which he held as a fief from Philip the Bold, to his daughter and her descendants, as well as some other territories, and Philip and Margaret agreed to transfer the county of Rethel, which lay next door to Luxembourg, to Anthony. The wedding, which in this case was delayed for ten years, took place, with the usual pomp and ceremony, at Arras on 25 April 1402. In fact, Waleran never made good his claims to Luxembourg, but Anthony succeeded, after Joan's death in 1407, in staking a better claim for himself by taking, as second wife, the actual heiress of Luxembourg, Elizabeth of Görlitz.

Philip the Bold did not rest content with the control and political exploitation of the matrimonial arrangements of his own children, but turned his attention, at the end of his life, to his grandchildren, whose parents were apparently quite willing to put their offspring at his disposal for this purpose. Apart from a scheme in 1399–1400 of marrying Catherine, then the youngest daughter of John of Nevers, to Peter, son of King Martin of Sicily, which was cut short by that prince's death,[2] his plan for them was evidently a kind of mass alliance with the

---

[1] Plancher, iii. 178.
[2] Vielliard and Mirot, *BEC* ciii (1942), 136–7. I am much indebted to Mr. Peter Rycraft, of Merton College, Oxford, for kindly supplying me with transcripts of two documents in the Archives of the Crown of Aragon at Barcelona (R2243, f. 57b and R2352, f. 44), which show that it was Philip who planned this alliance and started the negotiations for it; that the daughter of John of Nevers in question was Catherine; and that she was born before

French royal house. All the children of Charles VI and Isabel, including, most importantly, their eldest son the dauphin, prospective king of France, were to be provided with Burgundian consorts. With his own children, Philip had cemented a ring of alliances on his eastern borders and staked some territorial claims there; with his grand-children, he was determined to secure his western frontiers and the continued co-operation of a friendly or possibly subservient France.

On 9 July 1394, seven months after the birth of his first grandchild, Margaret of Nevers, Philip signed the contract of her marriage to the then dauphin, Charles of France.[1] They were betrothed in January 1396 and Margaret was henceforth known as 'madame la dauphine'. In spite of Charles's death early in 1401 Philip, with the active support of Queen Isabel, and brushing aside the efforts of Louis of Orleans to marry his daughter to the new dauphin Louis, succeeded in May 1403 in reforming and consolidating the Franco-Burgundian alliance in a remarkable manner. No fewer than four separate marri-ages were now envisaged, between the children of Charles VI and the grandchildren of Philip the Bold. Margaret of Nevers was to marry the dauphin Louis; the only legitimate son of John of Nevers, who succeeded him in 1419 as Philip the Good, was promised Michelle of France; another (unnamed) daughter of John of Nevers was to marry John, duke of Touraine; and another Charles of France, aged three months, was to wed the daughter of William and Margaret of Ostrevant, Jacqueline of Bavaria, born in 1401. These marriages were all agreed to in May 1403, at Paris.[2] Thus did Philip the Bold prepare

---

May 1400 (cf. David, *P. le Hardi, train somptuaire*, 55 and n. 4, who suggests winter 1400–1).

[1] BR 7381, fos. 27–8. For the next sentence, see David, *P. le Hardi, train somptuaire*, 135 and Thibault, *Isabeau*, 379 n. 2.

[2] See the documents concerning the first three in Plancher, iii. nos. 212–15. See also Thibault, *Isabeau*, 379–81. David, *P. le Hardi, train somptuaire*, 140, produces incontrovertible evidence for the fourth, but on p. 141 (though not on pp. 188–9) unaccountably suggests that there were only three. The text of the undated and incomplete document printed by Hulshof, *Oorkonden*, no. 39, from two seventeenth-century transcripts, in which Charles VI agrees to the marriage of Charles of France and *Jeanne* (sic) of Bavaria, is corrupt in several places and, since much of it is verbally identical with the 1403 docu-ments printed by Plancher and there is no other reference to this *Jeanne* of Bavaria, one can only assume that *Jeanne* is an error for *Jaquette* or *Jaqueline* and that the document in question dates from 1403 and relates to the fourth marriage mentioned above. When the chronicler Zantfliet, *Chronicon*, col. 359, records the dauphin Charles's death in January 1401 and adds that he had been married to Jacqueline of Bavaria ('qui jam in conjugium sumserat

the way, by means of a veritable web of marriage alliances, for the continued close association of France and Burgundy. In the event, in spite of his efforts, a dauphin grew up, and eventually became king, without a Burgundian wife, for Louis died in 1415, Jacqueline married John of Touraine instead of Charles, and it was this Charles who succeeded to the throne of France as Charles VII. Although, because of this, the marriage alliance with France lost some of its force after Philip's death, his handling of matrimonial politics in general was masterly, if unscrupulous. While he had no compunction about breaking the terms of a treaty or failing to pay a promised dowry, he invariably succeeded in exacting his share of the bargain. If his methods were unprincipled, his aims were impeccable, for, in selecting consorts for his children and grandchildren, he seems to have had three objects in view: the strengthening of his position in the Low Countries; the protection of the unruly frontiers of the county of Burgundy; and the maintenance of a close connection with France. In all three Philip was in the main successful, and all of them helped to enhance the status of Burgundy as a European power.

Expansion

Apart from the lands he acquired through marriage, Philip the Bold was involved in the addition or attempted addition to the Burgundian state of three important territories: the county of Charolais; the towns and castellanies of Lille, Douai and Orchies; and the associated duchies of Brabant and Limbourg. The first was acquired by Philip; the second was retained in spite of his promise to return it to France; and the third was obtained by him for his son Anthony. Philip's transactions over all three areas had one thing in common: they were carried out in a quite unscrupulous manner with blatant dishonesty and with a complete disregard for the interests of others, whether they were the kingdom of France, his generous and ageing aunt Joan of Brabant, or even his own children. He appears, in the history of these acquisitions, as a stern, ambitious and unprincipled statesman, who permitted nothing to interfere with his plans of territorial aggrandizement and consolidation. There are few other aspects of his political career which throw so much light on his

---

Jacobam'), he is certainly confusing him with the Charles of France born two years later, for Jacqueline was not born until 1401, and the Charles of France who died in January 1401 was, as we have seen, betrothed at the time of his death to Margaret of Nevers, and had been since 1396.

motives and outlook, and none which emphasizes so clearly his aspirations as the ruler, or even the creator, of a single, independent political entity, Burgundy, whose interests came before all others.

Apart from his equivocal behaviour afterwards, Philip's acquisition of the county of Charolais was a straightforward example of the purchase by a feudal ruler of a fief which had hitherto, though forming part of his territories, been held by a vassal doing homage for it to him.[1] This county, centred on the town of Charolles, lay in the extreme south of the duchy of Burgundy. Philip bought it on 11 May 1390 for 60,000 francs from John III, count of Armagnac, who was acting on behalf of his brother Bernard, count of Charolais, and his officers took possession of it on 30 June, the day the purchase money was paid over. In order to raise this, Philip found it necessary to make use of a sum of 50,000 francs, which was half Margaret of Bavaria's dowry. This, according to the terms of her marriage treaty, had been set aside, in the treasury of Cambrai cathedral, by her father Albert of Bavaria, for the purchase of lands for her and her heirs. Albert allowed Philip to use this fund for the purchase of Charolais, but Philip had to guarantee, on 13 May, to invest Margaret and her heirs with 50,000 francs' worth of land in the county, that is to say, roughly five-sixths of it, before 1 October following. Philip, however, disregarded this solemn promise and kept the county of Charolais in his own hands. Henceforth it formed part of his domain as duke of Burgundy and was exploited and administered directly by him. The only concession he made to good faith was to permit Philip, son and heir of Margaret of Bavaria and John of Nevers, who was born in 1396, to use the title count of Charolais, and the unfortunate Margaret had to wait until 1420 before this Philip, having succeeded her husband as Philip the Good, allowed her to enjoy the revenues of the county for the rest of her lifetime. In this matter Philip the Bold had evidently acted solely in the interest of the territorial unity of his possessions, regardless alike of the claims of his daughter-in-law and of conscience.

We have already seen how, at the time of Philip's marriage in 1369, the towns of Lille, Douai and Orchies, with their dependencies, were ceded by King Charles V of France, Philip's brother, to Louis of Male, count of Flanders.[2] On this occasion the historian was

---

[1] For what follows, see Plancher, iii. 117–19, 540–1 and nos. 132, 140–5, 147–9; van Nieuwenhuysen, *Recette générale*, 132. Charolais had been alienated from the ducal domain in the thirteenth century.

[2] See above, pp. 5–6.

presented with the unedifying spectacle of Philip the Bold secretly swearing two quite contradictory oaths: to his brother, Charles, that he would return these towns to France as soon as he succeeded to the county of Flanders; and to Louis, his father-in-law, that he would never allow them to be parted from Flanders. Philip's subsequent behaviour over this transaction throws a clear light on his character and on his political relationship to France. These three towns formed, with their dependencies, a compact Walloon-speaking area south of the river Lys, which was often referred to as *Flandre gallicante*, in contrast to *Flandre flamigante* to the north of that river. Long subject to French influences and sympathies, though from the earliest times forming part of the county of Flanders, it had been ceded to France by Count Robert of Flanders in 1312. It was one of the many key frontier areas which had succumbed to French expansion, and Charles V would have been acting in a way diametrically opposed to the true interests of France if he had returned it permanently to Flanders. No doubt he trusted in the good faith of his brother Philip, and he evidently had no reason to suppose that Philip would not act in the interests of France. In 1386, two years after Philip's succession to Flanders, Charles VI and his council approached him with a view to the honouring of his engagements. The debates which followed were prolonged and bitter. The good bishop of Chartres, Jehan le Fèvre, who had important business at Paris on 15 December 1386, was told that he was wasting his time

> quar entre nossegneurs faisoit tourble, pendant lequel on ne entendroit point à nous; et je sceus à part que ce estoit pour les trois chasteleries Lile, Douay et Orchies que le roy veult que le duc de Bourgongne li rende et le duc ne le veult mie.[1]

The same trouble recurred on 7 January, but eventually matters were settled in a curious document sealed on 16 January 1387 which sets out in detail the arguments used on either side.[2] Philip produced numerous excuses for keeping Lille, Douai and Orchies in his hands: he admitted that he had, some time before his marriage, given his assent to certain letters promising to return them on Louis of Male's death, but claimed that this was only to obey his brother and in the expectation that he would not be kept to his promise in the subsequent agreements. He claimed, too, that Charles V had no intention of making use of these letters, and that they were in any case invalid, since at that time Philip had no right to make any disposition con-

---

[1] Le Fèvre, *Journal*, i. 329. [2] Plancher, iii. no. 100.

cerning these territories. In spite of the palpable weakness of Philip's position and the hypocrisy of many of his statements, the decision was made in his favour, though possession of Lille, Douai and Orchies was only guaranteed to him and his immediate successor as count of Flanders.

The influence which he wielded at this time in the French government, and the brutal way he made use of it in his own interests, is equally apparent in a closely connected incident. It will be recalled that Charles V's cession of *Flandre gallicante* to Louis of Male in 1369 had not been by itself a sufficient inducement to that hard bargainer to part with his daughter in marriage to Philip the Bold. He had had to be bribed as well, and to the tune of 200,000 francs, a sum which Charles V and Philip had shared between them, each paying half. Now, in January 1387, Philip, with a quite remarkable lack of scruple and probably partly as a *quid pro quo* for his not being granted Lille, Douai and Orchies in perpetuity, persuaded the king to repay his share of this sum, as if it were owed to him by the French crown, and, by royal letters of 10 January, Charles VI duly ordered him to be paid 100,000 francs out of the *aides* in France.[1] Thus everything that could conceivably have been extracted from France as a result of the Franco-Flemish wedding of 1369 was successfully, if brutally, obtained by Philip the Bold, acting, not as a French prince, but as the ambitious ruler of a new state.

The third major complex of territories with the acquisition of which Philip was concerned was formed by the combined duchies of Brabant and Limbourg and certain detached territories east of Limbourg.[2] His attempts in this direction derived directly from the claims to the succession of Brabant established by his father-in-law through his wife Margaret of Brabant and recognized in the treaty of Ath. These could only materialize in the event of the death without issue of the duke and duchess of Brabant, Wenzel and Joan, and it so happened that Philip the Bold's accession to Flanders occurred a month after Wenzel's death in December 1383, when this possibility became a certainty. He at once took up Louis of Male's rights, and a large part of his diplomacy in the Low Countries between 1384 and his death twenty years later was devoted to their implementation. To this end he pursued a consistent policy based on the use of French resources and on the exploitation of the widowed Joan's weaknesses,

[1] BN Coll. de Bourg. 53, f. 41.
[2] What follows, to p. 100, is based on Laurent and Quicke, *Origines*, and *Geschiedenis van Vlaanderen*, iii. 21–54.

financial, administrative and political, as well as of her affection for himself and his wife.

The succession to Brabant actually claimed Philip's attention before he took possession of the county of Flanders: future possibilities of territorial expansion were evidently to be explored and consolidated before present acquisitions were so much as visited. On 4 March 1384 he sent an embassy to Brabant which included one of his most trusted secretaries, Gilles le Foulon, and an experienced councillor, Olivier de Jussy, and he himself was at the capital, Brussels, in the second half of the month, accompanied by his wife Margaret and an escort of eighty-nine knights and squires.[1] Joan agreed in principle to the Burgundian succession to her territories and permitted Philip's Flemish functionaries to examine, in the archives of Brabant, those documents which supported his claim to the duchy. A more practical kind of support was obtained by the distribution of gifts and the issue of fief-rents or pensions in return for homage to some seventeen of Joan's leading nobles and officials, some of whom were also made chamberlains or councillors of Philip. Many of those who received fief-rents from him at this time had accepted them formerly from Louis of Male, but a curious development of this policy now appears for the first time, for a number of Philip's new liege-men were granted additional pensions, on his authority, by the king of France. Thus he made use of his control of the French government to augment the pensions of his new protégés. While this work of political seduction was in progress, the finances and financial administration of Brabant were submitted to a searching scrutiny, with a view to their reform, by Philip's receiver-general, Amiot Arnaut. These contacts with the government of Brabant soon bore fruit, first in a monetary convention between Flanders and Brabant which regulated the production of a joint coinage in the two territories and laid the basis for a monetary offensive against Brabant which Philip initiated soon afterwards, and, in the following year, in the inclusion of Brabant and Limbourg in John of Nevers' inheritance, as defined by his marriage treaty of 11 April. Soon after this, political and military events gave Philip a further opportunity to extend and strengthen his hold on Brabant.

[1] Plancher (iii. 74) and Laurent and Quicke (*Origines*, 79 n. 4) considerably exaggerate the size of this escort, which was assembled at Tournai on 13 March, by adding to it troops summoned to Lille a month later for Philip's Flemish visit. Cf. their statements with la Chauvelays, *MAD* (3) vi (1880), 101–4, and see ACO B1461, fos. 168–71.

Politically, Joan's situation at this time was by no means enviable, for throughout the last thirty years of the fourteenth century Brabant was threatened by a powerful and aggressive neighbour on her eastern frontier: the duchy of Guelders. Between 1372 and 1402 this was ruled by the warlike William of Jülich, who in 1393 inherited the duchy of Jülich from his father, and so combined both duchies under his rule. Warfare was Duke William's principal interest and occupation, and when this was not available on his own frontiers, he was prepared to travel to Prussia or Africa to find and enjoy it. Politically, he was anti-French, and seems to have conceived himself as the bastion of the Germanic Low Countries against Franco-Burgundian influences and infiltration. He was allied with King Wenzel of Germany, who had inherited the claims of his uncle and namesake to Brabant and tried without success to get them accepted in 1384. He was in close diplomatic contact with England, and, soon after Duke Wenzel of Brabant's death, he had laid claim to the castles and dependent territories of Millen, Gangelt and Waldfeucht, east of Limbourg, which were in the possession of Brabant but formed enclaves inside the boundaries of the duchy of Jülich. On 14 September 1386, after a local military success against Brabant, he openly declared war on Joan. Philip promptly sent two knights, Guillaume de la Trémoille and Oudart de Chaseron, to establish liaison with Joan's forces, but the services of the two hundred menat-arms which he sent across Flanders in October on the eve of the projected invasion of England from Sluis were not in the event required, William and Joan having signed a truce in the meantime. The negotiations which followed made it clear that the former had no intention of abandoning his aggressive intentions. Though required by Albert of Bavaria's arbitration of 23 October to relinquish the disputed town of Grave, he fortified it instead, and at the very moment when he purported to be negotiating a peace with Joan and Philip at 's Hertogenbosch in June 1387, his ambassadors were returning from England with an Anglo-Guelders offensive alliance, according to the terms of which, in return for an annual pension from Richard II of £1000, William promised to declare war on both France and Burgundy. In the face of this threat Joan, in February 1387, had found it necessary to ensure Philip's continued military support by ceding to him most of her sovereign rights over the towns and dependencies of Limbourg, Rolduc, Wassenberg and Sprimont, on the right bank of the Meuse. She had in fact previously mortgaged her rights over these territories to members of the local nobility, but

Philip had little or no difficulty in redeeming these mortgages, and from May 1387 enjoyed control of a nucleus of territory in the area of Limbourg.

The persistent military enthusiasm of William of Jülich soon presented Philip the Bold with better and more dramatic opportunities for intervention in Brabant-Limbourg for, on 12 July 1387, according to the terms of his treaty with England, William sent formal challenges to both Philip and Charles VI. That sent to Charles began with the insulting words 'Karole qui vos dicitis regem Francie', and in both, Richard II was pointedly described as 'king of England and France'.[1] By October Philip had a Burgundian force under Guillaume de la Trémoille some two hundred strong, with a similar number of local knights, acting against Guelders in the Limbourg area; and, after December, when Joan and William signed another truce, he forced Joan to pay for these troops—though they were protecting his own recently acquired territories—by threatening their withdrawal. This was an astute move, as well as an economy, for it increased Joan's financial difficulties still further, and finance was her principal weakness, which Philip was to exploit to the full. In 1388, in spite of some delays and even opposition, he was able to persuade the French government to allow Charles VI to lead an army against the impertinent duke of Guelders, who was by then once again busily occupied conducting military operations against Brabant.

The French campaign to Guelders in the autumn of 1388 was in many ways a remarkable affair. This elaborate and costly expedition, ostensibly mounted to rescue Brabant from the clutches of a bellicose rascal who had affronted the military honour of France, was deflected by Philip the Bold along the lengthy and difficult Ardennes route through Luxembourg, in order to save his coveted Brabant from the expense and even horror of the passage of a French army. On the other hand, King Wenzel, the duke of Luxembourg, readily gave Charles VI permission to march through his duchy to invade the territories of his vassal and ally. Pope Urban VI had a more considered view of his political interests and, interpreting William's aggressive behaviour towards Brabant and France as an attack on his French rival Clement VII, furnished him and his supporters with crusading indulgences.[2] From the French point of view, the whole episode was farcical in its results. No battle was fought, for William of Jülich had enough military science not to be tempted

[1] *Choix de pièces inédites*, i. no. 39 and Cartellieri, *P. der Kühne*, 128–9.
[2] Remy, *Grandes indulgences pontificales*, 204–6.

to leave the ramparts of Roermond for a dubious pitched battle in the open, though he encouraged his irregulars to harass and cut off the French stragglers or attack them in their tents at night.[1] The only advantage to France in the treaty of Körrenzig, which, after keeping Charles VI waiting for nearly three weeks, William of Jülich eventually signed on 12 October, was the absurd clause requiring him to give the king of France a full year's notice before his next declaration of war! But if the campaign was a failure for France, it was entirely successful for Burgundy, for it had the effect of assuaging William's desire for military adventures against Brabant, and secured the frontiers of that duchy for a decade. This success was achieved, too, at very little cost, for Philip the Bold helped himself to 200,000 francs from the French treasury in compensation for his expenses 'dans l'armée que le roi a fait faire ès parties d'Allemagne' and elsewhere in the service of the French crown,[2] and, as if this were not enough, sent an embassy to Joan soon after his return from Guelders to settle accounts with her. She was quite incapable of paying him the 15,000 *vieux écus* he demanded for his services, but persuaded him to write off at any rate the greater part of this debt by further territorial and other concessions, and, in the summer and autumn of 1389, she ceded to him the *seigneuries* of Fauquemont, Millen, Gangelt and Waldfeucht, thus rounding off his possessions on the right bank of the Meuse. Again, these had to be redeemed from the mortgagees to whom Joan had pawned them, but this was accomplished by Philip without much difficulty and indeed with some financial assistance from her. At the same time, largely as a result of Philip's monetary offensive against Brabant, which was based on the devaluation of his own currency in direct infringement of the common standard set up by the 1384 convention, and enforced by his quite illegal closure of the Louvain mint when it struck similarly debased coins, Joan ceded the Brabant coinage rights to Philip, though retaining half the profits. This unscrupulous dismemberment of Joan's authority over Brabant was consummated on 28 September 1390, when the duchy was secretly transferred to Philip and Margaret and their heirs, Joan keeping the usufruct for life.

Unfortunately for Philip the Bold, neither the succession to Brabant nor its ownership were in the gift of Joan alone. Although the rights of the weak and frequently intoxicated Wenzel could be

---

[1] *Hist. Gelriae*, 94. For the next sentence, see *Gedenkwaardigheden*, iii. no. 132.
[2] Pocquet, *MSHDB* vii (1940–1), 101 and Plancher, iii. 106.

and were disregarded, the people of Brabant, recently organized in the three Estates of clergy, nobles and representatives of the towns, had to be consulted, and they refused to countenance the annexation of their country by another power. Their opposition forced Philip to abandon the plan he had adumbrated in his will in 1386, of incorporating Brabant after his death with his other dominions, and instead, in 1393, he set Brabant-Limbourg aside as the eventual inheritance of his second son Anthony, though still without the consent of the Estates. Meanwhile he missed no opportunity of tightening his stranglehold on these territories. In 1394 a scheme was considered, and then dropped, for making John of Nevers vicar or governor-general of Brabant-Limbourg,[1] but in summer 1396 some real progress was made: Anthony was recognized as heir by Joan, Philip and Charles VI, and Joan made over all her remaining rights in the duchy of Limbourg to Philip, as well as those in the scattered territories to the east. Henceforth, the duchy of Limbourg was his, and in September 1396 he received the homage of his new vassals there. The last mortgages in this area were redeemed in 1397, by which time he had succeeded in attaching to his interest most of the rather turbulent local nobles, many of whom became his fief-rentiers, though they were quite prepared to declare war on him, as a group of them had done in 1394, to ensure the prompt payment of their rents.

In 1397–9 Philip once again had to come to the rescue of Brabant against her aggressive eastern neighbour. An excuse for war was offered to William at the end of June 1397 by a quarrel in 's Hertogenbosch in which one of his officers was involved. In August, collecting allies in the shape of the archbishop of Cologne and three neighbouring bishops, he invaded Brabant. The chronicler relates that on this occasion Joan was bold enough to send him a herald who, holding a naked sword in his hand, challenged him to fight a pitched battle with her either where he stood, within three days, or, if he chose to withdraw to his own territory, after five days.[2] In September she actually delivered a successful counter-blow across the Meuse, and, early in 1398, signed a treaty with Liége, while Philip authorized a force of eighty men-at-arms and forty archers to serve with her for

[1] *Documents pour servir à l'histoire de la Maison de Bourgogne en Brabant et en Limbourg*, nos. 31–4.

[2] De Dynter, iii. 130–1. For this and what follows to p. 102 below, ibid., 131–57; *Brabantsche Yeesten*, ii. 334–97 and nos. 159–61 and 167–71; and van Berchen, *Geldersche kroniek*, 41–4. See, too, *Geschiedenis van Vlaanderen*, iii. 54–9.

three months.[1] In March, taking advantage of Brabant's critical situation on the eve of war, he tried, at a meeting in Brussels, to persuade the Estates to accept his son Anthony as heir in return for his help in the war against Guelders. Waleran of Luxembourg, count of St. Pol, whose father had died a hero's death fighting for Brabant at Baesweiler in 1371, who himself had rendered important services to Brabant, and whose daughter Joan was to marry Anthony, was entrusted with the task of expounding to the assembled Estates the arguments in favour of this.[2] However, in spite of the subsequent personal intervention of Philip, they firmly refused to make any decision about Joan of Brabant's successor, and, shortly afterwards, refused also Philip's request for an *aide* for the ransoming of John of Nevers. This double setback did not deter Philip from continuing his military support of Brabant, and on 19 April he joined the alliance between Brabant and Liége, promising to keep three hundred troops in the field as long as they did the same.[3] His contingent, under Waleran of Luxembourg, played an important part in the successful campaign which followed, when the allied armies penetrated as far as Roermond, Aachen and Jülich.

Philip's persistence was finally rewarded during his next visit to Brussels, when, on 29 September 1403, the Estates of Brabant at last accepted Anthony as Joan's heir, but, to obtain this favourable decision, he had to promise to restore to Brabant Limbourg and Antwerp, which had been stripped from her, the former by Philip himself in 1396 and the latter by Louis of Male in 1357. It was thus only after many years of negotiation, and as a result of important concessions, that he persuaded the Estates to accept the Burgundian succession. Even then, Philip had to be content with an arrangement which entailed the complete abandonment of his earlier plans for the annexation of Brabant-Limbourg or its incorporation with his other territories after his death, though it did at least ensure that it would remain, under Anthony and his successors, closely attached to Burgundy. In the spring of 1404 Philip set out once more for Brussels, this time to receive the government of Brabant, which the now aged Joan had decided to relinquish to him. What he would have done with it we do not know, for his death intervened on 27 April, in the Stag Inn at Hal, and on 7 May Joan resigned in favour of his widow Margaret, who appointed Anthony her lieutenant and

---

[1] La Chauvelays, *MAD* (3) vi (1880), 111–12.
[2] Draft instructions printed by Kervyn, Froissart, xiii. 342–5.
[3] *Régestes de Liége*, iii. no. 594.

governor on 19 May. In December 1406, after the death of both Margaret of Male and Joan of Brabant, Anthony finally became duke of Brabant.

There were two other additions or prospective additions to Philip the Bold's territories which are important enough to mention here. On 16 March 1382 Charles VI ceded to him a group of castellanies in Champagne: Beaufort, Nogent l'Artaud, Lassicourt and Soulaines, with their dependencies. Though small, these lands were a most welcome addition to those Philip acquired in this area by inheritance two years later: Jaucourt, Isle-Aumont, Chaource and Villemaur. Together, the *terres de Champagne* formed a complex of lands and rights based on castles or fortified towns and lying, apart from Nogent l'Artaud on the Marne, in the neighbourhood of Troyes. The other territories, which were conditionally given to Philip by his brother Duke John of Berry on 28 January 1388, were the county of Étampes and the lands of Gien and Dourdan, which, by a very profitable deal, John had acquired from the widow of his brother Louis of Anjou in exchange for his rights over the Italian principality of Taranto. Of these territories, the most valuable to Philip would have been Gien on the Loire, which would have formed an extension of the county of Nevers towards Orleans and Paris. In the event, however, the gift never materialized, and was revoked by John of Berry after the murder of Louis of Orleans in 1407.[1]

Philip the Bold often had to be content with the acquisition of financial, judicial or political rights over neighbouring territories, rather than the lands themselves. By far the most important of these were the rights he obtained in 1401 and 1402 over the duchy of Luxembourg. Long before this, Philip had made his first moves in the development of Burgundian influence in this important frontier region, for, in 1388, taking advantage of his passage through Luxembourg with the French army, he had acquired two vassals from among the local nobility by persuading them to do homage in return for annual pensions.[2] Soon after this he took another step in the same direction. In 1391 he and Duke Robert of Bar signed a mutual defence and security treaty with Jost of Moravia, to whom King Wenzel had mortgaged Luxembourg on 24 February 1388.[3] This treaty, in which Jost of Moravia is described as duke of Luxembourg,

---

[1] For this paragraph, see Pocquet, *MSHDB* vi (1939), 118–19; Lacour, *Jean de Berry*, 293; and Plancher, iii. 64, 111–12 and nos. 71, 110 and 111.
[2] Laurent and Quicke, *Origines*, 225 n. 3; Pocquet, *MSHDB* viii (1942), 145.
[3] *Choix de documents luxembourgeois*, nos. 2 and 3.

not only made provision for the mutual defence of the three neighbouring territories of Bar, Luxembourg and Rethel, but also included
detailed agreements for the suppression of criminals and disturbers
of the peace and, in an effort perhaps to implement the high-sounding
aim expressed in the preamble—'vraye et perfaite union et amour
entre nous et noz subgés de noz pais'—set up a council of six persons,
two appointed by each signatory, with appellate jurisdiction and some
administrative powers over all three territories.[1] Since Jost never
visited Luxembourg during his fourteen-year reign,[2] and Robert of
Bar, whose territories were in any case relatively small, was a vassal
of Philip for some lands he possessed in Flanders, it is probable that
Philip was the preponderant partner in this alliance. This treaty was
followed, in 1393, by another move towards Luxembourg, already
mentioned: the drawing up of a marriage treaty between Anthony of
Burgundy and Joan of St. Pol. Joan's father, Waleran, who had
invaded and pillaged a large part of Luxembourg in 1392, repeated
this aggression in 1395,[3] but after this both he and Jost of Moravia
accepted the arbitration of the dukes of Berry, Burgundy and
Orleans, which was finally pronounced on 5 March 1399.[4] Henceforth, at any rate, Philip's policy was based on a close understanding
with Jost, and bore fruit on 8 March 1401 when Jost placed Luxembourg under his protection and entrusted its administration to him.[5]
This arrangement was in some respects only a logical extension of
those made in the 1391 treaty, for we find Philip on 31 August 1401
ordering the governor of Rethel and his officers to lend their assistance
to their colleagues in Luxembourg, a thing they had been instructed
to do under the terms of the treaty, and when a garrison was installed
in Luxembourg by Philip in December 1401 'pour la garde et
deffense dudit duchie de Lucembourg en laide du marquis de
Moravie', half of it was raised in Rethel, and the governor of Rethel
reviewed the troops before they departed.[6] This state of affairs was,
however, radically altered in the following year when, on 18 August,
Jost sold his mortgage on Luxembourg to Philip's rival, Louis of
Orleans, for 100,000 gold ducats and an annual rent of 10,000 ducats.

[1] *Trésor des chartes de Rethel*, ii. no. 742.
[2] Schötter, *Geschichte des Luxemburger Landes*, 115.
[3] Ibid., and see Ulveling, *Invasions dans le Luxembourg* and *Urkunden und
Quellenbuch der altluxemburgischen Territorien*, ix. no. 647.
[4] Jarry, *Orléans*, 195.
[5] *Table chronologique . . . de Luxembourg*, no. 370.
[6] Cartellieri, *P. der Kühne*, 153–4; ACO B1526, f. 304; and see also B370
(quittance of 8 March 1401/2).

Within a few weeks Louis took possession of the duchy and Philip's influence there was extinguished.[1]

The explanation of Jost's *volte-face* lies in the situation in Germany at this time. After his cousin Wenzel's deposition from the German throne on 20 August 1400, Jost had tried, in the spring and summer of 1401, to supplant him on the throne of Bohemia. He had transferred the administration of Luxembourg to Philip at the very moment when he was gathering forces to attack Wenzel. Early in 1402, however, the situation was changed by the intervention of Wenzel's brother Sigismund, king of Hungary, who, in February and March 1402, gained control of Wenzel's person and of his kingdom of Bohemia. Sigismund was consistently opposed during the rest of the year by Jost, and it is probable that Jost's sale of Luxembourg to Louis of Orleans represented part of his effort to come to Wenzel's aid, for Louis was a powerful and enthusiastic partisan of Wenzel, whereas Philip the Bold had been lukewarm or even openly hostile towards him, and, throughout 1401, had been in friendly contact with his rival Rupert of Wittelsbach,[2] who had been elected king of the Romans in his place by a majority of the Electors on 21 August 1400. It seems unlikely that the opportunity to acquire Luxembourg was ever open to Philip, for Jost must have realized that it would be against his own interests and those of his house of Luxembourg to sell it to a partisan of their Wittelsbach rivals, though it might be politic to place it for a time in Philip's hands. Jost, in the summer of 1402, needed money and allies in support of Wenzel, and these he could acquire through Wenzel's ally Louis of Orleans, but not from Philip the Bold. Philip seems to have accepted this rebuff as inevitable, though he kept in touch with Jost after the sale by sending him an embassy in September 1402.[3]

A number of towns and bishoprics in the neighbourhood of

[1] *IAGRCL*, iv. nos. 1420 and 1421; *Documents luxembourgeois*, nos. 84, 88, 91, 92 etc.; and Jarry, *Orléans*, 274–5.

[2] *Deutsche Reichstagsakten*, iv. nos. 294, 298 and v. nos. 154–6, and ACO B1526, f. 76b.

[3] ACO B1532, f. 103a–b. For German and Bohemian affairs I have used Bachmann, *Böhmens*, ii. 120–41. Schoos, *Burgund und Orleans*, 141–2, adds nothing to Cartellieri, *P. der Kühne*, 100–1, and the sources already cited, and his picture of an angry and disappointed Philip, suddenly deprived of Luxembourg when he thought it was falling into his lap, or prevented only by lack of funds from buying the mortgage from Jost (p. 149), does not carry conviction. Leroux, *Nouvelles recherches*, 98, followed by others, supposes that Luxembourg was transferred to Philip in March 1401 in an attempt to gain his support for Wenzel.

Philip's territories were subjected to more or less successful attempts by him to maintain or acquire varying degrees of control over them. He was most successful in the city of Besançon, an enclave in the county of Burgundy in which jurisdiction was shared between the Emperor, the archbishop and the family of Chalon. In 1386, against the opposition of the two last, Philip persuaded the citizens to place themselves and their city under his protection, and even to make him an annual payment of 500 francs in return for this service, which included the stationing of a ducal official near the city at Châtillon-le-Duc. He seems to have made better use of this so-called *garde* of the city than those of his predecessors who had enjoyed it, for, in 1397, Besançon voted 3,000 francs towards the payment of John of Nevers' ransom; in the following year Philip's arbitration was accepted in a quarrel between the archbishop and the city; and in 1400, when he quelled a dispute which had arisen over the jurisdiction and behaviour of his officers in Besançon by blockading the city, he was able to exact from it a fine of 10,000 francs. He was also successful in extending his influence over the archbishopric. In 1391 he contrived to end in his own favour an old and vexatious quarrel between the dukes of Burgundy and the archbishops of Besançon over their respective coinage rights at Auxonne, and this success was followed, on 16 November 1393, by his attendance in person at the official entry into the city of a new archbishop, Gerart d'Athies, whose appointment was due to him, and who was in fact a councillor of his.[1]

Besançon, because it was an enclave in his territories, was particularly subject to Philip's intervention. Elsewhere his activities were frequently limited to influencing ecclesiastical appointments in his favour, as at Verdun, where, in 1378, he managed to place a candidate of his own, Liébauld de Cousance, on the episcopal throne.[2] At Cambrai he was more successful in other respects. The counts of Flanders had in the past acquired the right to an annual tax in the Cambrésis called the *gavène*, and after he inherited this in 1384 with the county of Flanders, Philip the Bold showed himself a zealous protector of the church of Cambrai. He seized every opportunity offered him of judging disputes there or referring them to his council at Lille, and he obtained from Clement VII the gift of a benefice in the cathedral. In 1388, when the see was vacant, attempts were made

---

[1] *Songe Véritable*, 308; *Itinéraires*, 234. For Philip and Besançon, see especially Gollut, *Mémoires*, cols. 855–6, 860–1, 894 and 906–7; Clerc, *Franche-Comté*, ii. 208–12, 269–71 etc.; and Piquard, *PTSEC* (1929), 193–200.
[2] Roussel, *Verdun*, i. 343.

to place it under the protection of Wenzel and the Empire, but, as a result of an appeal to him by the chapter, Philip occupied the episcopal castles and submitted the imperial partisans to the judgement of his council, which imposed heavy fines on them. On 22 July 1388 he formally took the bishop of Cambrai and his see under his protection, charging for this service a mass and 100 silver marks annually. This rapid extension of his influence was not, however, maintained, for a decade later he failed to obtain the promotion of his candidate, Louis de la Trémoille, bishop of Tournai, to the see of Cambrai. He managed to persuade the chapter to postulate him, but they admitted to Pope Benedict XIII that they had only done this for fear of displeasing Philip, and Benedict, affirming that he would rather have a tooth torn out of his mouth than confirm Louis de la Trémoille's postulation, appointed Pierre d'Ailly, adding that if he were prevailed upon to refuse, he would appoint a countryman of his, that is to say a Spaniard. Philip, who had already caused one candidate to withdraw, now wrote to Pierre d'Ailly asking him to decline, but d'Ailly remained firm, and had the temerity, in a reply which he drafted but may not actually have sent, to remind Philip of the day of judgement in terms readily intelligible to an administrator and ruler: 'quant il faudra compter en la grant chambre des comptes'.[1] Such was Philip's influence over the chapter that not a canon was to be seen in the cathedral when Pierre d'Ailly arrived there in June 1397 for his formal inauguration as bishop, and the High Mass which he celebrated without them was disturbed by the interruptions of ducal partisans. In the end the affair was patched up, and Philip had to accept the unwanted bishop. In spite of this setback, however, he had done something to prepare the way for the subsequent annexation of Cambrai and the Cambrésis by his successors.

There was one other city on the borders of his territories over which Philip tried to extend his influence. This was Tournai, which was particularly important to him because it was the seat of a bishop whose diocese included part of his county of Flanders. The town, together with the Tournaisis, was actually French. In 1388 a bishop of Philip's own choice, Louis de la Trémoille, had been elected, and was personally installed by him on 21 April 1392;[2] but he was able to

[1] De Saint Aubin, *BEC* cxiii (1955), 125–6, and see 114. For this paragraph I have also used Dupont, *Cambrai*, ii. 23–33, Dubrulle, *Cambrai*, 299–304, and Salembier, *d'Ailly*, 117–23.

[2] *Itinéraires*, 227. For the next sentence, see *Extraits analytiques des registres de Tournai*, i. 52.

make very little progress with the city. In November 1402, for instance, he asked it for an *aide* of 4,000 francs, but was firmly rebuffed.

The way in which a town like Tournai might be tempted into the Burgundian orbit is well illustrated by a decision of the council of Flanders copied out on 4 October 1402 by the secretary and archivist Thierry Gherbode.[1] In the course of a dispute with the abbey of Eename near Oudenaarde, which happened to be in imperial territory, the magistrates of Tournai had appealed to the *Parlement* of Paris and obtained thence letters in their favour which they asked the council at Lille to enforce on their behalf. The council refused to do this, on the grounds that, though it was prepared to uphold the authority of the Paris *Parlement* in French Flanders, it could not do so in imperial territory, and suggested instead that the magistrates might like to submit the whole case to them, when justice would be done and effectively enforced. It is doubtful if this specious offer was accepted, for this would have entailed the recognition by Tournai of the jurisdiction of the council of Flanders, but the fact that it was made at all indicates the constant pressure which the advantages of comital jurisdiction enabled Philip's council to exert on neighbouring territories.

Diplomacy

It is reasonable to suppose that, when Philip the Bold planned and carried out the aggrandizement of his house and lands by means of marriage alliances and the acquisition of territories and rights, he was acting as an independent ruler in the interests of Burgundy as a whole; but, in the complex field of what we should now call foreign policy, other interests were often prominent. His relations with some of his neighbours, for instance those with the counts of Savoy, have already been discussed because they seem to be merely those of a loyal French prince. On the other hand, relations like those with the Hanse, which were purely commercial and Flemish in significance, must find their place in an account of Philip's activities as count of Flanders. There remain numerous contacts with other rulers which do not fall readily into either of these categories, and which certainly helped to enhance his status as a European ruler. In the years after 1396 especially, he frequently entertained at his table foreign ambassadors, particularly those of England and Germany, but also, on occasion, those of the Spanish kingdoms and Venice. Neighbouring rulers, some of whom, like the count of Namur and the duke of Bar, were

[1] AGR Trésor de Flandre (1), 1629.

his vassals for part of their territories, visited him at Paris or Conflans, among them the duke of Lorraine and the bishop-elect of Liége. The value of these contacts was demonstrated in December 1401, when Philip, on the brink of open civil war with Louis of Orleans, assembled his forces at Paris; for the count of Namur, the bishop-elect of Liége, and Ferry, brother of the duke of Lorraine, all brought contingents to swell the ranks of his army.[1]

Much light is thrown on Philip's diplomatic contacts by an examination of the detailed expenses entered under the heading 'Ambassaderies, voiages et grosses messageries' in the annual accounts of his receiver-general of all finances, though these neither include all expenses of this kind, nor do they always disclose the purpose of the various embassies. As a sample, we may set out the foreign embassies recorded in one of these accounts, that for 1 February 1400–31 January 1401.[2]

Name of ambassador	Destination	Purpose of embassy	Date of order to pay ambassadors
Jehan de Villeroy	England	New Year's gifts to Richard II and the duchess of Gloucester.	23 March 1398/1399
Guillaume de Vienne Gerart de Bourbon Robert Dangeul Rogier de Coulongne	Wenzel, king of the Romans	'certaines choses secretes'	30 May 1399
(squire with letters)	Henry III, king of Castile	?	3 Dec. 1399
Guillaume de l'Aigle	The Morea	To collect the head of St. George which had been given to Philip.	21 Jan. 1399/1400
Jehan Blondeau Amiot Arnaut	Lombardy, Venice and elsewhere	'certaines grosses besongnes'	10 Feb. 1399/1400
Rogier de Coulongne	The Diet of Frankfurt	Concerning the Schism and the government of the Empire.	22 May 1400
Rogier de Coulongne with two ambassadors from Denmark	The duchess of Bar	?	29 Oct. 1400

[1] ACO B1526, fos. 304b–307b.   [2] ACO B1519, fos. 69–86.

Philip's contacts with Italy were frequent and varied. Some, like those which led to the commercial treaty with Genoa in 1395, were of mainly Flemish significance;[1] others were connected with the county of Savoy, where Philip acted as regent after 1393.[2] Some, however, are of more general interest. In November 1402, for instance, after the death of Giangaleazzo Visconti of Milan, three Burgundian ambassadors arrived in Florence with an offer to arbitrate a peace in North Italy.[3] Although this was shrugged off by the wily Florentines, it is a good example of Philip's interest in European affairs and of his efforts to exert an influence of his own on them. With Venice, too, he was in frequent contact, between 1379 and 1396 chiefly over damages done to his subject Hugues de Vienne, who was inadvertently attacked by a Venetian fleet near Rhodes when returning from the Holy Land in September 1379, and over a scuffle between Venetians and Burgundians in Beirout some ten years later.[4] After 1396, as we have seen, the crusade of Nicopolis led to prolonged and none too amicable negotiations between Venice and Burgundy, and to contacts with the Genoese princes and merchants of the Aegean, with the king of Hungary, and with the Ottoman Turks. At the other end of the Mediterranean the influence of Burgundy was also felt. In 1381 Philip sent a chamberlain, Oudart de Chaseron, and a councillor, Olivier de Jussy, on a journey to Sardinia,[5] and he was in touch, particularly in 1398–1400 concerning the Great Schism, with King Martin I of Aragon, with whom he had an alliance or confraternity.[6]

The Inheritance

Over the years, by marriage, purchase, persuasion or gift, Philip the Bold had acquired a princely inheritance, the territorial basis of a European power. Theoretically, he had carved three apanages out of his lands, for John and Anthony had been granted respectively the counties of Nevers and Rethel, and the county of Charolais had been promised to Margaret of Bavaria and her heirs. But, as we have seen in the case of the last mentioned, these apanages were perfectly fictitious. The county of Nevers, with the associated barony of Donzy,

[1] See below, p. 180.
[2] See, e.g., ACO B1526, f. 87b; Jorga, *Thomas III*, 138; and Gabotto, *Ultimi principi d'Acaia*.
[3] *Commissioni di Rinaldo degli Albizzi*, i. 20.
[4] Perret, *Relations de la France avec Venise*, i. 58–66.
[5] ACO B11934, quittance of 20 July 1389.
[6] Alpartils, *Chronica*, 268–304. See, too, above p. 90.

had been transferred to John in 1384, but to the end of his life Philip administered it and received the revenues from it;[1] and Anthony, though he had been promised Rethel in 1393, was not formally given it until his marriage in 1402; and even after then there is not a scrap of evidence that he was allowed to share in its administration or revenues. Indeed Philip continued till his death to be described, at any rate in the county itself, as count of Rethel, and the only concession, in the documents printed in the *Trésor des chartes de Rethel*, to Anthony's possession of it, is a solitary reference to Philip in 1403 as 'ayans le gouvernement de mon tres redoubté seigneur Antoine, conte de Rethel.' [2]

Although he was strong enough to keep all these territories together under himself, Philip could never ensure such unity after his death, and we can trace in a series of documents the succession of plans he devised for the partition of his lands among his three sons. These plans were made with the utmost care, and drawn up in minute detail in an effort to provide for every eventuality.[3] In 1385 and 1386, before Philip was born, the problem was relatively simple, and in John of Nevers' marriage treaty and the will which Philip made in September 1386 on the eve of his projected invasion of England, John was to have the two Burgundies and Brabant-Limbourg and, at any rate in the will, Flanders as well, while Anthony was to be content with the scattered and less important territories of Artois, Rethel and Nevers. Some years later, in 1391, Margaret published a remarkable document in which she made Philip her heir in all her lands, and explicitly stated that she did this because of the excellent way he had ruled them, and because of the youth and inexperience of her eldest son John of Nevers. Yet at this time John was twenty years old! In 1393, when a new partition scheme was elaborated, he was still the principal heir, with the two Burgundies, Flanders, and, eventually, Artois and probably Rethel. Anthony was to begin with the two last, but resign them when he became duke of Brabant-Limbourg on Joan's death. Philip, born in 1389, had now to be taken into

[1] The receipts from Nevers continue to appear in the accounts of Philip's receiver-general of all finances, and not in those of John's *chambre aux deniers* analysed by Mirot, *ABSHF* (1938), 133–6. For the administration, see e.g. the references to officers appointed by Philip in *IACOB*, ii. 108, 276 etc. and Mirot, *MSAN* xxxviii (1936), 127.

[2] *Trésor des chartes de Rethel*, ii. no. 807. The receipts of Rethel appear in the accounts of Philip's receiver-general of all finances for 1402 and 1403: ACO B1532 and 1538.

[3] Printed, Plancher, iii. nos. 90, 105, 151, 156 and 201.

account, and he was to be allotted Nevers-Donzy by John when John succeeded his father as duke of Burgundy. This arrangement was in principle preserved in the final partition act of 1401, except that Rethel was now added to Philip's lands. In all these schemes, incidentally, it was naturally assumed that Margaret would continue to rule until her death in her own lands of Flanders, Artois, Rethel and the county of Burgundy.

Although the detailed provisions of these different schemes make a complicated history, their broad lines reveal a masterly appreciation of future possibilities on the part of their author. What Philip clearly aimed at, after his death, was the maximum unity consistent with the satisfaction of his three sons. Furthermore, in every scheme from 1386 onwards Flanders and the two Burgundies were kept together, which shows that he intended them to form the permanent nucleus of the Burgundian state. At first he evidently hoped that Brabant would form part of this nucleus, but local particularism there forced him to separate it from Flanders, and it then formed a convenient inheritance for Anthony. The youngest son, Philip, was left with bits and pieces, two of which, Rethel and the Champagne lands, were relatively small and isolated. Apart from Brabant-Limbourg, then, which Philip had in any case failed to annex, and a necessary but modest competence for his youngest son, the Burgundian state was to be handed over intact by him to his principal heir, John of Nevers. He had transformed it into a European power, and he disposed of it in such a way as to ensure, as far as possible, that it would remain one.

In the record of the speech made on Philip's behalf to the Estates of Brabant in Brussels in March 1398,[1] there is a passage which throws valuable light on his views about the position of Burgundy in Europe. The Estates were told that Philip the Bold and his children, since they were already in possession of Flanders, and since Philip's son (*sic*) William of Ostrevant was likely to become count of Hainault-Holland, would be better placed to govern and defend Brabant than any other ruler. Then follows this significant statement: 's'il estoit mestier ils [i.e. Philip and his sons] auroient la puissance de France et d'Angleterre'. Here, Burgundy is evidently conceived both as an entity apart from France and as a European power. Philip may not have thought consistently along these lines—he never got out of the habit of beginning his documents with the words 'Philippe, filz de roy de France'—but the existence of statements of this kind, together

[1] Kervyn, Froissart, xiii. 342–5.

with the actions and policies outlined in this chapter, surely compel
the historian to accept him as the conscious ruler of a viable political
entity, Burgundy, even though this might seem to be a mere adjunct
of France.

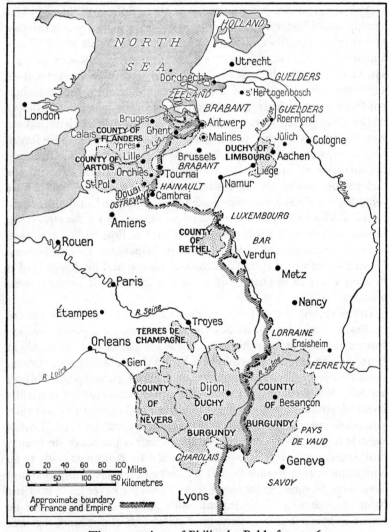

2. The possessions of Philip the Bold after 1396

CHAPTER SIX

The Burgundian State

In the twenty years between 1363 and 1384 Philip the Bold had acquired power in France and influence outside it, but he possessed only the duchy of Burgundy. Like Berry and Brittany, this was in itself an embryonic state, with its own institutions and resources,[1] but, like them, it was only one among several large and powerful fiefs of the French crown. In 1384, when he succeeded to the five counties of Burgundy, Nevers, Rethel, Artois and Flanders, Philip's situation was radically changed, and, in the last twenty years of his life, he was ruler of what can only be described as a powerful, independent and more or less unified state. Its power and independence have been discussed in their European setting in the preceding chapter. Here, we shall be concerned with the internal structure of the state, its administration, institutions and actual working, and some light will be thrown on the degree of unity which it attained.

Although Philip the Bold's possessions consisted of a number of discrete feudal territories, these were by no means entirely distinct political units when they became his, for a certain amount of fusion between them had already taken place. The counties of Burgundy and Artois had been united under a single ruler since 1330. At first, in 1330–61, this ruler was the duke of Burgundy; later, 1361–82, it was Margaret of Artois, whose dominions included also part of the county of Nevers; and, finally, for two years before Philip's accession, these two counties had been in the possession of the count of Flanders, who had also ruled the county of Rethel and part of Nevers for some sixty years. Soon after he acquired these territories in 1384, Philip the Bold, abandoning these rather haphazard dynastic groupings, set about reorganizing them for administrative purposes into two broad geographical divisions: in the south, the duchy of Burgundy with the counties of Nevers and Burgundy on either side of it; and, in the

---

[1] See Perroy, *BIHR* xx (1943–5), 181–5.

north, Flanders and Artois, which were contiguous, and Rethel. Each group of territories was equipped with its own institutions and administration, and these must be separately discussed before the central government of the Burgundian state is examined.

The Two Burgundies

'The two Burgundies' is a convenient phrase to designate Philip the Bold's southern group of territories, which included also the *terres de Champagne*, frequently regarded as a dependency of the duchy; the county of Nevers with the more or less dependent barony of Donzy; and, between the duchy and county, the *vice-comté* of Auxonne and the *terres d'Outre-Saône*.

In each of Philip the Bold's individual territories, with the exception of the two most important, Flanders and the duchy of Burgundy, a single officer, the governor, normally represented his authority and stood at the head of the local administration. It is true that when Philip was absent from his own territories, his wife Margaret often acted as his personal representative, and described herself as 'ayant le gouvernement' for him. She did this frequently in the 1370s and 1380s in the duchy of Burgundy and, after 1384, in all his lands; but her position, as a sort of vice-regent, did not affect the structure of the state. On the other hand, the governors were a vital part of it. In the duchy, this office existed only during the first two decades of Philip the Bold's reign. At first the governor's powers there were military and temporary, for he was appointed only during the duke's absence.[1] The commission of Eudes de Grancey in December 1369 seems, however, to have been on a permanent basis, as was that of the marshal of Burgundy, Guy de Pontailler, appointed governor of the duchy in 1381; and the attributions of both of these extended beyond the military sphere. Guy de Pontailler, however, is referred to as governor of Burgundy only in documents of 1381-4, apart from a single reference in 1387, and, though he may theoretically have remained governor until his death in 1392, it is likely that the office fell into abeyance during his tenure of it, for we hear no more of a governor of the duchy during the rest of Philip's reign.

The absence, after about 1385, of a governor of the duchy was evidently due to the presence at Dijon of the ducal council, which

[1] ACO B380, appointment of J. de Montaigu, 9 January 1365/6; Plancher, iii. no. 8; *Itinéraires*, 458, 472, 481 and 486. For what follows, see Plancher, iii. nos. 41 and 68, and Dumay, *MSBGH* xxiii (1907), 160–222. On the governor of Burgundy in general, see Richard, *MSHDB* xix (1957), 101–12.

removed the need for such an officer. But in the outlying and newly
acquired counties of Nevers and Burgundy he could not be dispensed with, and remained the chief executive officer throughout
Philip's reign, holding office continuously over a period of years.
Thus Philippe de Jaucourt, governor of Nevers between 1384 and
1391, was succeeded on 26 January 1391 by Guillaume de Champ-
lemis, who remained in office until July 1403;[1] while Jehan de
Vergy was governor or 'guardian' of the county of Burgundy between
1386 and 1404, and the surviving records reveal him acting on
numerous occasions as the principal agent of Philip's authority there,
in a military, administrative and diplomatic capacity.[2]

Partly because of the impetus given to it by King John the Good of
France when he acted as regent of the duchy in the years after 1350,
the council at Dijon was already, in the first years of Philip's reign
as duke, the real head and centre of the administration.[3] It kept him
informed by letter of what was going on; it directed the levying of a
subsidy in the autumn of 1363 and took measures to suppress the
opposition to it; and in August 1364 it ordered the raising of a local
tax to pay for the redemption of a castle from a company of pillagers
who had seized it.[4] By this time it already possessed a nucleus of
members who attended more or less regularly at its sessions, to some
of whom the task of auditing accounts and looking after the ducal
domains was particularly entrusted. Thus Guy Rabby, *clerc des
comptes* in 1354 and 1366, was in the latter year described as 'estably
sur l'audition des comptes';[5] André Pasté, Jehan de Baubigny and
Dymenche de Vitel were *maîtres des comptes* in 1371-4;[6] and these
gens des comptes formed a distinct enough section of the council to
give their corporate advice to the duke on his finances.[7] The council

[1] Mirot, *MSAN* xxxviii (1936), 136. For P. de Jaucourt, see, e.g., below
p. 157.
[2] ACO B380, ducal letter of 5 July 1386; *IACOB*, ii. 338; Plancher, iii.
pp. 137-8, 147-8, 189, and nos. 172 and 180; and below, p. 166.
[3] For what follows I have drawn largely on Lameere, *Grand conseil*, especially pp. v-xi; Pocquet, *MSHDB* iv (1937), 5-77; *Ordonnances du duché*
and *Ords. franc-comtoises*; Blondeau, *MSED* (n.s.) iv (1924), 90-106 and
(n.s.) v (1925), 79-103; Registre des Parlements de Beaune; Andt, *Chambre
des comptes*, i; Riandey, *Organisation financière*; Faussemagne, *Apanage
ducal*; and *Hist. des institutions françaises*, i. 209-47.
[4] *Itinéraires*, 460; Vernier, *MAD* (4) viii (1901-2), no. 7, pp. 308-9; and
Plancher, iii. no. 19.
[5] *Ordonnances du duché*, p. cix; ACO B1423, f. 25; and *Itinéraires*, 471.
[6] Plancher, iii. no. 46; BN nouv. acq. f. 3589, no. 23; and Aubrée, *Mémoires*,
ii. 79-80.   [7] Plancher, iii. no. 51.

was concerned with the administration of justice as well as finance, indeed it regularly acted as a court, both of first instance and appeal, and from at any rate 1372 onwards one or more councillors, called *maîtres des requêtes*, were charged with preparing cases for it and receiving petitions to the duke. The judicial sessions of the council, usually held on Sundays after mass, were recorded in a register called, in 1367, the 'papier ou sont escript toutes memoires, toutes presentacions de gens, qui ont este adjournez tant pardevant les gens du conseil comme des comptes' and, later, the 'registre des causes et appointemens amenez en la chambre des comptes' or the 'livre des journees sur le fait de la justice'.[1] The second of these titles is explained by the fact that at this time and throughout Philip the Bold's reign the sessions, since there was no separate council chamber at Dijon, were usually held in a room which, because the accounts were audited and stored in it, was called the *chambre des comptes*.[2] The first illustrates the absence of any thoroughgoing distinction between the two groups of councillors, which becomes even more apparent when the pages of this register of its judicial proceedings are turned over, for the *gens des comptes* are present at the great majority of meetings recorded in it on exactly the same footing as the other councillors, and on occasion they even meet by themselves to dispatch judicial business. We are evidently dealing with a single institution, whose regular membership consists of six or eight councillors, three or four of whom are financial experts sitting separately from time to time to audit accounts, but by no means forming an entirely distinct institution like the *chambre des comptes* at Paris.

After the acquisition of his wife's inheritance in 1384 and the pacification of Flanders at the end of 1385, Philip and his advisers turned to a thorough reorganization of government and institutions. An important *ordonnance* of 11 July 1386 concerned the *chambre des comptes* at Dijon and has even been regarded as marking its foundation.[3] This *ordonnance* was the direct result of an investigation by two *gens des comptes* from the Paris *chambre*, Jehan Creté and Oudart de Trigny, who were commissioned and paid by Philip to 'veoir, visiter

[1] The first two are the contemporary titles of ACO B11402 and B94. The third is a reference in ACO B15, f. 31b.
[2] This *chambre* had originally been in the precincts of the ducal palace, but was moved in *c.* 1367 by Philip the Bold, and installed in some neighbouring buildings, which had originally formed the *hôtels de Rouvres* and *de Neuilly*. See Picard, *MCACO* xvii (1913–21), pp. xcv–xcvii. It is called the *chambre des comptes* at least as early as 1369, see ACO B11402, f. 5b.
[3] Printed, Riandey, *Organisation financière*, no. 6.

et reformer, se mestier est, le fait et estat de la dite chambre des comptes de mondit seigneur a Dijon'[1]—yet another example of the way in which Philip used his position in France to further his own interests. The *ordonnance* which followed extended the competence of the *chambre des comptes* to the counties of Burgundy and Nevers and the *terres de Champagne*; organized the *maîtres* into two alternating pairs, one to deal with the accounts of the duchy and the *terres de Champagne*, and the other those of the two counties; permitted them when in difficulty or doubt to call in other ducal councillors to help; defined their duties in the administration of the finances and the ducal domain; ordered them to keep a *livre des mémoriaux* in which to record ducal orders and their own decisions concerning these two matters, as well as the oaths of bailiffs and others on taking office; and laid down other detailed regulations for their duties and conduct.

This *ordonnance* neither created a new institution nor even separated the *chambre des comptes* from the rest of the council. This is proved by the *registre des causes*, for, right up to the end of Philip the Bold's reign, the judgements recorded there are still made, more often than not, 'par messieurs du conseil et des comptes'.[2] Even more illuminating in this respect is the *livre des mémoriaux* which the *gens des comptes* were instructed to keep by the 1386 *ordonnance*, and which still fortunately survives at Dijon.[3] In spite of the fact that it is called the 'livre des memoires de la chambre des comptes a Dijon', this book is a record of business transacted at ordinary meetings of the council, normally held in the *chambre des comptes* every week or ten days. Throughout the years 1386–1404 those taking part in these meetings and decisions include councillors, who invariably head the list of those present, as well as *gens des comptes*, even when the matters discussed concern the finances or domain. The formula varies. Often we are simply told that some matter was discussed and agreed in the *chambre des comptes* by ——, and a list of names of six or more councillors and two or three *maîtres des comptes* follows, but often the list of names is preceded by some such formula as: 'par messieurs du conseil et des comptes ou estoient. . .' Thus, after the 1386 *ordonnance*, as before, the *gens des comptes* and the councillors continued to act together in almost all matters save the audit of accounts, and this remained true even after Philip the Bold's *ordonnance* of 1402, which instructed the *gens des comptes* to cease concerning themselves with

[1] ACO B1465, f. 40b.   [2] ACO B94.
[3] ACO B15.

the judicial business of the council.[1] This *ordonnance* was not enforced, and was in fact directly contradictory to one of two years before which had conferred the title of councillor on the *maîtres des comptes* specifically so that they could handle 'requestes' when their colleagues were absent.

The *ordonnance* of 1386 not only reorganized the internal arrangements of the Dijon *chambre des comptes*, it also extended its jurisdiction to the whole of Philip the Bold's southern group of territories, thus conferring on their financial administration an important degree of centralization. Although the *ordonnance* is silent about the council, its competence must have been similarly extended at this time, for we frequently find it dealing with the affairs of the counties of Nevers and Burgundy. When the chancellor was present, he presided, and, in his absence, it was to him that the council particularly looked for advice and guidance, though it often received orders direct from the duke. Its duties were so multifarious as to defy brief description. In general, it was the permanent representative of Philip the Bold's authority in the two Burgundies. It was one of the higher courts of justice; it controlled the financial organization and the civil service; it concerned itself with the domains, with general security, with the levying of taxes, with juridical questions, with the appointment of minor officials, with the coinage, with accounts. As Philip's reign proceeded, he came to rely on it more and more. At first, in the 1370s, he himself spent half of each year in the duchy, and, when he was absent, his wife Margaret was usually there to act on his behalf. In the 1380s, however, his visits were shortened to an annual two or three months, and, from 1396 on, the Dijon council had to work without any personal contact with the ruler or his lieutenants, for Philip never again visited the duchy; his duchess settled at Arras and seldom if ever left Artois after 1398; and there is no trace, after 1396, of the chancellor visiting Dijon and presiding over the council there, as he had done for a few days in 1387, 1389, 1391, 1395 and 1396.[2] It was perhaps this growing separation of the council from the duke and chancellor which led to the only change in its organization between 1386 and 1404: the institution in September 1400 of a president.[3]

Although the administration of Philip the Bold's southern group

[1] Andt, *Chambre des comptes*, i. 206 and n. 2, and 211. For what follows, see Plancher, iii. no. 197.
[2] His visits are recorded in ACO B15.
[3] ACO B15, f. 53b and *Ordonnances du duché*, pp. clxiii–clxiv.

of territories was centralized in the council at Dijon, this was by no means true of its muniments, for the duchy and county of Burgundy, the county of Nevers, and even the barony of Donzy, each continued to possess its separate *trésor des chartes* or archive repository. The *trésor* of the duchy had been moved from the castle of Talant to the ducal palace at Dijon in 1365 by Guy Rabby, a ducal councillor who was already *garde des chartes* before Philip became duke. Other trusted Dijon councillors followed him in this office: Jehan Potier in 1382 and Jehan Couiller, dean of the ducal chapel, ten years later. In the county of Burgundy, where the archives were kept in the castle of Poligny, Philip also took over the services of an existing *garde des chartes*, Perrenin de Plaigne, who was succeeded in 1397 by Aubry Bouchart. In the county of Nevers the bailiff, Jehan Blandin, is described as 'garde des chartes du comté de Nivernais'; in the barony of Donzy, this office was discharged in the last years of the century by a castellan who looked after the muniments in the castle of Druy. It is difficult to establish what degree of centralization of these various record offices was effected by Philip the Bold, but, from 1384 onwards, it seems that the regional repositories ceased to grow, the new documents from all the southern territories being stored in the *trésor* at Dijon. Steps were taken, too, to make the content of the regional offices more available to the administration at Dijon: in 1397, for instance, the *trésor* at Poligny was reorganized and inventoried by two ducal commissaries, one of whom was a clerk of the Dijon *chambre des comptes*. Besides these different *trésors*, the *chambre des comptes* was itself an important and central archive repository, since all the accounts and related documents from the southern group of territories were stored there.[1]

The absence of specialization which is so typical a feature of medieval government, and which is so apparent in the Dijon council, did not hinder the evolution of specifically judicial institutions, and in Burgundy a hierarchy of courts had evolved by the middle of the fourteenth century and lay open to the reforming schemes of Philip the Bold. At the base of this hierarchy were the numerous petty tribunals of mayors, provosts and castellans, and the manorial and other seigneurial courts, representing respectively municipal, ducal and feudal justice. From these courts appeals went to the bailiffs' assizes, which were held about once a month at different places in

---

[1] For the above, see *IACOB*, ii. 276 and 403; *IADB*, i. 9; *Inventaires mobiliers*, i. no. 432; Duhem, *BAB* (1936), 145–63; and Richard, *BEC* cv (1944), 123–51.

each bailiwick. The bailiff judged both civil and criminal cases at first instance and on appeal. Side by side with his assize three more or less specialized courts existed: those of the *gruyer*, the officer concerned with the administration of the *eaux et forêts*; the *maître* of the Chalon fairs; and the chancery of the duchy. The chancery exercised a *jurisdiction gracieuse* over private contracts and other acts which were sealed by it and over disputes arising from them, and its court, called the *chancellerie aux contrats*, sat in six local seats in the duchy, in each of which there was a lieutenant of the chancellor. This chancery tribunal had originally been presided over by the chancellor himself, but, in 1368 and from 1387 onwards, we find in his place and acting for him a 'gouverneur de la chancellerie et lieutenant de monsieur le chancelier ou duchie de Bourgogne', as he was called in 1391.[1] In the duchy, appeals from the bailiffs' assizes and the courts of *gruyer*, *maître* of the Chalon fairs and chancery lay with a special appeal court sitting at Beaune about six times a year, called the *auditoire des causes d'appeaux*. This court also heard appeals from the Dijon council, which, as a court, itself exercised wide though ill-defined appellate and first-instance jurisdiction, and, from it, appeals went to the supreme court of the duchy, the *Parlement* of Beaune. In the county there was no special court of appeal, and appeals from the bailiffs' assizes there went directly to the county's own *Parlement* at Dôle. The twin *Parlements* of Beaune and Dôle were similar in most respects, and sat irregularly, though, after 1388, almost annually. The only important difference between them was that appeals from Beaune went to the Paris *Parlement*, since the duchy was part of France, while at Dôle the *Parlement* was sovereign. A third *Parlement* met from time to time at St. Laurent-lès-Chalon to administer sovereign justice to the inhabitants of the vice-county of Auxonne and the *terres d'Outre-Saône*.

Although Philip the Bold did not radically alter this rather unwieldy system of courts, he did introduce a number of reforms in the direction of efficiency and centralization. Thus the Beaune *Parlement*'s procedure was improved, its sessions made more frequent, various abuses removed, and an effort made to detach it from the Paris *Parlement*. To accomplish this last, Philip tried, though with little success, to dissuade litigants from exercising their right of appeal to Paris. He did, however, succeed in achieving its complete detachment from Paris as regards personnel, for, while the president of Philip's first few Beaune *Parlements* was a royal officer sent from the Paris

[1] Aubrée, *Mémoires*, ii. 8 and ACO B15, f. 27.

Parlement, the last of these French presidents held office in 1393, and, thereafter, the president was always a ducal officer or councillor. In 1400 another important innovation was effected when Antoine Chuffaing became the first permanent president of the Beaune *Parlement*, for, before then, the president had been appointed *ad hoc* for each session. At the same time Chuffaing was also made president of the Dijon council, of the Dôle *Parlement*, and of the *auditoire*. Thus a considerable measure of centralization and uniformity was achieved between these bodies, which was increased by the fact that they now had a treasurer and *greffier* in common, as well as identical personnel, for the courts were mainly staffed by the same hard-working legal experts who met regularly in the council at Dijon. The appointment of Chuffaing to the presidency of the Dôle *Parlement* alongside that of the higher courts of the duchy was one of the last in a series of attempts of Philip the Bold to bring the judicial administration of the county into line with that of the duchy. The most important of these was the *ordonnance* of the Dôle *Parlement* of 20 May 1386, which was confirmed by the Duke on 11 July—the very same day as the promulgation of the *ordonnance* concerning the *chambre des comptes* at Dijon. The objects of this Dôle *ordonnance*, to remove abuses, improve procedure and the system of appeals, and to introduce a measure of order and efficiency, were, however, only partly attained.

The financial administration of Philip's southern group of territories formed part of the central administration of finances, but certain elements of it were essentially local or regional. It was partly centralized at Dijon, where the *chambre des comptes* checked and audited the accounts and, with the council, supervised the activities of the financial and domanial officials of all the southern territories, as well as exercising jurisdiction over them. The *chambre des comptes* was not an office of receipt, nor was it responsible for ordering or authorizing the multitude of individual payments made by the ducal officers, for this task of controlling expenditure in detail was entrusted to the ducal treasurer. Most of the minor local officials, provosts, castellans, *grènetiers* and the like, collected and spent moneys and made up accounts of these receipts and expenses which they brought to the *chambre* for annual audit. In each bailiwick a more senior accounting officer, called, in the duchy, the receiver of the bailiwick, who centralized the surplus revenues of the minor officials, did the same. In the two Burgundies, these balival receipts were to some extent centralized by the receiver-general of the duchy and county of Burgundy, to whom their surplus cash was normally transferred.

This officer, in his turn, paid over some of his moneys direct to the central receiver-general of all finances and expended most of the rest on his behalf. Side by side with the receiver-general of the duchy and county were the receivers or receivers-general of Nevers, of Donzy,[1] and of the *terres de Champagne*, for these also paid their surpluses to the receiver-general of all finances or spent them on his behalf, thus escaping from the jurisdiction of the receiver-general of the duchy and county.

The financial organization very briefly outlined here as it existed after 1386 must on no account be imagined as a tightly organized or centralized hierarchy. In the first place, an important group of receipts, those from *aides* voted by the Estates of the duchy and other territories, were usually collected and accounted for by special receivers responsible directly to the receiver-general of all finances. Secondly, in spite of their name, the receivers and receivers-general expended money as well as collecting and receiving it, and, besides the routine local expenses of repairing buildings, holding courts, sending messages and so on, others quite unconnected with them were assigned to their receipts by the duke or his central financial officers. In 1381 the castellan of Beaune had to bear the cost of Philip the Bold's New Year's gift to his wife, which amounted to 1,000 *livres*, and, in December 1386, the cost of some prescriptions made up for the ducal doctors by a Paris chemist was assigned to the receipt-general of the duchy and county.[2] Thus, while the receipts of the financial officers in the two Burgundies were of local origin, their expenses often had nothing to do with their own areas, being incurred directly on behalf of the central government.[3]

After the annexation of Charolais to the domain in 1390, the duchy of Burgundy was divided into six bailiwicks: Dijon, Autun, Auxois, La Montagne or Châtillon, Chalon and Charolais.[4] The county of Burgundy consisted of two, Amont and Aval, and the county of Nevers and the barony of Donzy each formed a single one. The institution of receivers in each bailiwick in 1366 had divested the bailiff of his financial duties, and he had become primarily a judicial

[1] From 1391 on the receiver-general of Nevers was also receiver-general of Donzy, but he made up two separate accounts, so that the two receipts-general were not merged; Mirot, *MSAN* xxxviii (1936), 128 and 141.

[2] *IACOB*, i. 366 and *Inventaires mobiliers*, ii. 210 n. 2. See also below, p. 147.

[3] For the *grèneterie*, which was rapidly losing importance at this time, see Richard, *MSHDB* x (1944–5), 117–45.

[4] On the bailiffs of the duchy, see, besides the works already referred to, Bouault, *RB* xxiii (1913), 76–84 and *AB* ii (1930), 7–22.

and police officer, but he was still kept busy in all sorts of ways as the representative of the ducal authority in his bailiwick. He had to publish the ducal *ordonnances* and carry out the instructions of the government; he had to summon the men-at-arms of his bailiwick in case of war; and his presence might at any time be required at the Dijon council. He possessed a large staff of officials to help him, including one or more lieutenants, who could hold his assizes for him if necessary; a handful of councillors; and a *procureur* whose par-

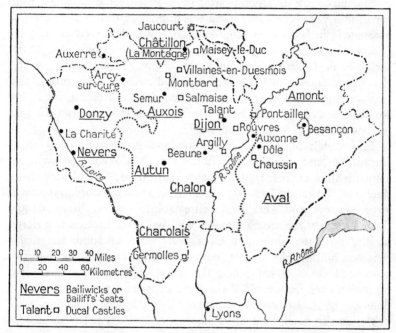

3. Sketch-map of the two Burgundies and Nevers

ticular task was to defend the interests of the duke in all legal matters. He was assisted, too, by numerous sergeants: in 1370 the bailiff of Dijon was allowed forty of these auxiliaries, and the smallest number in any one bailiwick was twenty-three in that of La Montagne.

Below the rank of bailiff were a number of officers primarily concerned with the administration of the ducal demesne lands: the provosts and the castellans. The latter presided over units of the domain centred on a ducal castle, the captain of the castle being often a quite distinct and purely military officer. While most of the castellans were salaried accounting officers, many of the provosts held their *prévôtés* in farm and made what they could out of them. Certain non-territorial elements of the domain were looked after by special officers or administrations. Thus the ducal wine supplies were controlled by a *visiteur et gouverneur des vins et des celliers du duché*; the *eaux et forêts* had their own administration called the *gruerie*, with its master-foresters and other officials; and the ducal castles and buildings also had their specialized services *des œuvres de maçonnerie* and *charpenterie*. For the purposes of the last two administrations the duchy and county, at any rate after 1398, were treated as a single unit, for in that year Jehan Bourgeois was appointed *maître des œuvres de maçonnerie* in both, and Hugues Douay was described as 'maistre charpentier du duc de Bourgogne en ses duché et comté de Bourgogne et de Charolais'.[1] Another important administrative service, that of the ducal artillery, which included cannon, ammunitions and siege-engines of all kinds, was likewise partly centralized, for Pierre Roy was described, when he took office in 1398, as *artilleur* of Philip 'en ses duche et conte de Bourgogne'.[2]

This sketch of the administration and institutions of the two Burgundies and associated territories would be incomplete without some mention of their representative institutions. The Estates of the duchy of Burgundy had met together on numerous occasions from 1352 onwards, and were thus well established when Philip became duke. Of the three orders which composed these Estates, the clergy usually sent two representatives from each of some ten major religious houses; the nobles, who received individual summonses, numbered about twenty; and the third order normally sent two representatives from each of the eight or more largest towns in the duchy. The Estates could be convened only by the duke and, after 1386, usually assembled at Dijon before one or more councillors appointed for this purpose by him. Occasionally Philip himself addressed the Estates, or deputed his son, wife or chancellor to do so.[3] Their function was at this time limited to the voting of taxes, but they had some influence over the appointment of the officers commissioned to levy them. These officers, called the *élus* and appointed *ad hoc* for each tax or *aide*, were in theory elected by the assembled

---

[1] Canat, *BM* lxiii (1898), 447; see, in general on Philip the Bold's *maîtres des œuvres*, ibid., 245–72, 341–57 and 439–73. For Jehan Bourgeois, see Monget, *Chartreuse*, i. 290. After 1395 the two administrations were placed under a single officer, see below, p. 158.

[2] ACO B15, f. 49b and Garnier, *Artillerie*, 211.

[3] See, e.g., Plancher, iii. no. 75 and p. 88; ACO B15 fos. 10a–b and 24.

Estates, one by each order, and then empowered to proceed by the duke. In fact Philip was able in most cases to obtain his own nominees, and the majority of the *élus* were his officers or councillors. Thus, in 1391, the three *élus* were the mayor of Dijon for the commons, the bailiff of Dijon for the nobles, and a leading Dijon councillor and dean of the ducal chapel, Jehan Couiller, for the clergy; and the two last were again *élus* in 1393.[1]

Little is known of the representative institutions in Philip the Bold's other southern territories. In the county of Burgundy he seems sometimes to have persuaded the two Estates of clergy and commons in each of the two bailiwicks to vote separate *aides*, but, on occasion, following a precedent of 1358, he certainly summoned the three Estates of the whole county.[2] The county of Nevers had its own Estates which, in 1387 and probably at other times, were convened by the governor of Nevers and consisted of two orders only, nobles and clergy. Taxes were apparently voted by them to Philip in 1386, 1387, 1392, 1394 or 1395, 1397 and 1403, and perhaps in other years.[3] Finally, *aides* in the county of Charolais, in spite of its annexation to the duchy in 1390, continued to be voted separately and, after 1393 at any rate, by its own Estates.[4]

This brief examination of the administration of Philip the Bold's southern group of lands shows that in some respects that of the duchy acted as a sort of nucleus round which the rest of the administration was formed, while in others it was a model. This was due to the fact that the duchy had already been Philip the Bold's for twenty years before he acquired the other territories, while its institutions and administration, introduced or reorganized on the lines of those of France by John the Good in the years after 1350, were far in advance of them. The council and *comptes* at Dijon, before which all the ducal officials in the area had to take their oaths of office and which exercised jurisdictional powers over them all, was the only completely centralized institution, but its wide, indeed almost universal, powers and multifarious activities made these territories a single administrative unit. True, the financial organization was decentralized, since there were four separate receivers-general, but all of them, as well as

[1] Plancher, iii. 121 and 132. For the Estates of the duchy, see Billioud, *États de Bourgogne*.
[2] For the county, see especially Plancher, iii. 121, 133, 147–8 etc.; Prost, *PTSEC* (1905), 115–22; van Nieuwenhuysen, *Recette générale*, 67. Clerc, *États généraux*, i. 53–61, is unreliable.
[3] *IACOB*, ii. 147, 275; BN Coll. de Bourg., 54, f. 54; and see above, pp. 64 and 74.   [4] Laroche, *MSHDB* vi (1939), 145–94.

the other financial officers, submitted their accounts to the *chambre des comptes* at Dijon. Again, while the duchy and county had quite separate judicial systems, the judges and members of many of the courts came under the jurisdiction of the Dijon councillors, who themselves formed the membership of the higher courts of both duchy and county. Even over the decentralized representative institutions a measure of unity was imposed by these councillors, for it was they who organized the meetings of the Estates and were mainly responsible for the collection of the subsidies they voted.

The Low Countries

Like 'the two Burgundies', the phrase 'the Low Countries' is more convenient than accurate, for Philip the Bold's dominions in this area actually comprised Artois, Rethel and the towns and dependencies of Lille, Douai and Orchies, *'Flandre gallicante'*, all of which are now in France, as well as the rest of Flanders, *'Flandre flamigante'*, with Antwerp, Malines, and, after 1390, Limbourg, and they excluded the whole of the rest of the Low Countries. Although Philip acquired them at the beginning of 1384, no effective government could be organized in these territories until after the submission of Ghent at the end of 1385, so that the administration and institutions described here were only introduced or perfected in 1386.

Philip the Bold's use of governors as the chief executive agents in his different territories followed exactly the same pattern in the Low Countries as in the two Burgundies. They were only employed on a permanent basis in peripheral areas where an extra reinforcement of the ruler's authority was desirable, and in Flanders, as in the duchy of Burgundy, they ceased to be appointed during Philip's reign. In 1384, Guy de Pontailler and Jehan de Ghistelles shared the governorship of Flanders, and in 1385 Jehan de Ghistelles is described as governor or captain and governor, but between 30 August 1387 and the summer of 1389, the office was held by Philip's nephew, William of Namur, who enjoyed very wide powers and whose competence extended to Malines and Antwerp as well as Flanders. He attended meetings of the *audience* and the ducal council at Lille, presided occasionally over assemblies of the Four Members of Flanders and dealt with their complaints, undertook commercial negotiations with the Hanse, and so on. On the other hand, he was only appointed in the absence of Philip, Margaret or John of Nevers, so that he was, in fact, a temporary vice-regent rather than a permanent official.[1] In

[1] *IADNB*, i (1863), 191–2, i (2), 318, and iv. 3; ADN B1681, fos. 29a–b;

July 1389 Jehan de Ghistelles reappears as governor of Flanders, but this can only have been a temporary measure, for on 14 July 1392 we find him appointed captain-general of Flanders, a post which he was still holding in 1393.[1] Although he continued an active and leading member of Philip the Bold's Flemish administration during the rest of the reign, there is no trace, after 1393, of his acting again as governor or captain-general, and we may assume that the former office was allowed to lapse.

In Flanders, the governor was a novelty, first introduced by Philip the Bold. In Artois, surprisingly, there is no sign of a governor in Philip's reign. On the other hand a French governor of Lille, Douai and Orchies had existed before this area was ceded to Flanders in 1369, and the office was preserved by Louis of Male and Philip the Bold. In French hands this was a key frontier territory, and the governor's authority was supreme, but under Philip the Bold his real importance must have declined, for between 1390 and 1400 the governorship was held in plurality by Pierre de le Zippe, whose duties as president of the council of Flanders probably permitted him to discharge only the formal functions of the governorship of Lille, such as presiding over the feudal court of justice there.[2] In the outlying territories of Limbourg and Rethel the governor was a permanent officer in effective charge of the local administration. In the latter, where Louis of Male had had a governor, we find Henri de Vouziers suppressing bands of pillagers from Germany in 1391, keeping Philip informed of the course of a dispute with Liége in 1395, and concerning himself, in 1401–2, at Philip's request, with the affairs of Luxembourg.[3] In Limbourg, Philip installed Scheifart de Mérode as governor in 1390, but he resigned in 1394 and was replaced by Jehan d'Immersele. Here, too, the governor was invested with wide powers and was the principal representative of the duke: in June 1395, for instance, Jehan d'Immersele was negotiating a treaty of alliance on Philip's behalf with the duke of Guelders.[4]

The counterpart, in the Low Countries, of Philip the Bold's

Buntinx, *Audientie*, table II; *Handelingen*, nos. 54, 74, Appendix no. 1, etc. For the Four Members, see p. 138 below.

[1] *IADNB*, i (1), 218; ADN B1597, f. 47; *IADNB* i (1863), 234.

[2] His commission is printed in *Textes historiques sur Lille et le Nord de la France*, i. no. 28.

[3] *IADNB*, i (1863), 213, and iv. 12; *Régestes de Liége*, iii. nos. 578–83; and Cartellieri, *P. der Kühne*, 153–4.

[4] Ernst, *Limbourg*, v. 166–7 and 167 n. 1; *Documents pour servir à l'histoire de la Maison de Bourgogne en Brabant et en Limbourg*, no. 35.

council at Dijon was the council of Flanders at Lille.[1] Like the Dijon
council, it stood at the head of the administration in its area and was
closely associated with a *chambre des comptes*. During Louis of Male's
reign a group of councillors had begun to function as a sort of standing
committee of the council, at first at Ghent, and after 1379, when
Louis was driven out of Ghent and Bruges, at Lille. Here was an
embryo *chambre du conseil*: the first beginnings of a permanent council consisting of a small number of specialized, salaried councillors
meeting regularly in a fixed place, on the lines of the council which
Philip the Bold had found working at Dijon when he became duke of
Burgundy in 1363, and in contrast to the earlier, amorphous, ambu-
latory council of the counts of Flanders, though this continued to
exist side by side with it. A similar phenomenon is evident in the
development of the Flemish *chambre des comptes*. Already, some years
before 1382, the accounts of Louis of Male's bailiffs were being
audited by temporary committees of councillors including at least one
maître des comptes. At first, the audit of accounts was carried out in
different Flemish towns, or even outside the county at Hesdin, but
after 1382 this was invariably done at Lille, in a special room in the
château or *Palais de la salle* which was called the *chambre des comptes*
and in which the audited accounts and related documents were
stored.[2] Thus, when Philip the Bold inherited Flanders in 1384 the
structure of government, with its emergent *chambre du conseil et des
comptes*, was already approaching that of the duchy of Burgundy, and
the latter could be used as a model to put the finishing touches to the
former.

As early as October 1384 Philip the Bold had set on foot the restoration of the room in the *Palais de la salle* at Lille called the *chambre des comptes*[3] and, while this work was still in progress, on 6 July
1385, he appointed a commission, exactly on the lines of those of
Louis of Male, to audit the accounts of the financial officers of Flanders and Artois and at the same time to undertake the organization of
a permanent institution having its headquarters in this room and
taking its name from it. The personnel of this commission is of
exceptional interest, for it consisted of two leading Flemish council-

[1] The chief modern authorities for what follows in the the rest of this section
are Monier, *Institutions centrales* and *Institutions financières*; Buntinx,
Audientie; idem, *APAE* i (1950), 57–76; Nowé, *Baillis comtaux*; Foucart,
Gouvernance; de Lichtervelde, *Grand commis; Hist. des institutions françaises*,
ii. 343–426; and Leclercq, *PTSEC* (1958), 87–92.
[2] *J. Froissart's cronyke*, ii. and ADN B4563/11433.
[3] ADN B4563/11433.

lors of Louis of Male, Colard de la Clite and Henri d'Espierre; a *maître des comptes* of Louis of Male, Jehan le Brune; a councillor of Margaret of Artois and *maître des comptes* at Arras, Jehan Blarie; a *maître* of the *chambre* at Dijon, Regnaut Gombaut; and a *maître* of the Paris *chambre des comptes*, Jehan Creté. These experts, drawn from all quarters and from four different auditing organizations, were hard at work by August 1385.[1] In September, the chancellor himself was occupied at Lille with the intricacies of administrative reform, and, somewhat later in the year, a detailed memorandum on the state of the administration in Flanders and Artois was submitted to him for Philip to act on. Unfortunately the authors of this report are unknown. After discussing numerous difficulties which would have to be cleared up—such as whether or not to continue the annual payments to Louis of Male's pensioners, the problem of the arrears of rent caused by the recent troubles, and the question of the replacement of unsatisfactory bailiffs and other officers—they continue:

> . . . il semble quil soit de necessite a monseigneur dauoir conseil ordonne a Lisle et resident audit lieu continuelement pour le gouvernement des pais de Flandres, de Malines, Enwers, la terre de Blaton et des contes d'Artois et de Rethelois.

They point out the difficulty of centralizing the control of finances at Dijon and suggest that it would be better to have a 'chambre de comptes et de conseil' at Lille with a personnel of at least seven: three councillors 'pour le fait de justice', two to audit accounts, a *greffier* and a clerk. They then submit short lists of possible candidates for these and other posts.[2]

The outcome of all this searching activity was the important *ordonnance* of 15 February 1386, with its accompanying instructions.[3] While the *ordonnance* of July 1386 regulating the central administration of the two Burgundies dealt only with the *chambre des comptes* there, the Flemish *ordonnance* was concerned with both the council and the *gens des comptes*, though the resulting institution was very similar to its Burgundian counterpart. At Lille there were to be two resident councillors 'sur le fait de justice' who were empowered to add other Flemish councillors to their number, and to whom control of

---

[1] ADN B18822, fos. 67, 70, 71 and 72: letters to the *gens des comptes* at Lille from various officials, 2–21 August 1385. For this commission, see van Nieuwenhuysen, *Recette générale*, 14.

[2] ADN B881/11574.

[3] Printed in *Textes historiques sur Lille et le Nord de la France*, i. no. 39 (*RN* xvi (1930) 108–12).

the entire administration of Flanders, Malines and Antwerp, as well as the maintenance of law and order, was explicitly entrusted. They could receive complaints against comital officials, suspend them from their offices, and summon malefactors of all sorts before them, and they were to employ their spare moments in examining the archives of the count, 'pour estre mielx instruiz de ses faiz ou temps avenir'. They were instructed to keep Philip fully informed of everything of note that happened, and, with the help of 'les autres gens ordonnez sur les comptes', to supervise the domanial administration In all difficult matters the *maîtres des comptes* were to assemble with their colleagues, and each group was enjoined to keep a register of its acts and decisions. Pierre de le Zippe, one of the two councillors 'sur le fait de justice', was appointed president.

This *ordonnance* was by no means definitive, and a number of changes were introduced in the succeeding years. Thus a further set of detailed instructions was issued for the *chambre des comptes* regulating the audit of accounts and related matters,[1] and the powers of the president were carefully defined: he was to preside at all meetings; he could punish a colleague who was late by withholding his wages for the day; and the other councillors were not to read, write, chat or amuse themselves in any other way while he was talking. The numbers laid down in 1386 were not kept to, for the size of both *conseil* and *comptes* gradually increased. By 1400 there were five instead of two councillors 'sur le fait de justice', and in 1401 a second president was appointed; the solitary clerk of the *chambre des comptes* was soon joined by a colleague; and the number of *maîtres des comptes* had increased by 1395 from three to four.[2]

In functions and competence the Lille council was exactly like that at Dijon. The area of its competence, perhaps intentionally, was not fully defined in the 1386 *ordonnance*, but a glance at its archives shows that it exercised just the same powers in Artois and Limbourg as it did in Flanders, and the accounts of the receivers and bailiffs of all Philip's northern territories, including Rethel,[3] were audited in the *chambre des comptes*. Internally, too, the resemblance between the two councils was very close. At Lille, as at Dijon, the council and the

---

[1] *IAGRCC*, i. 74–80 (no. 3) and, for what follows, ADN B881/14581.
[2] ADN B1597, f. 56; B4079, fos. 35a–b; B1598, fos. 28, 75a–b, 88b; B4082, f. 36b; B4080, f. 40; B4081, fos. 46b–47; B1599, f. 103b etc. The original three *maîtres des comptes* were Jehan de Pacy, Thomas de le Beke and Henri Lippin (*Textes historiques sur Lille, RN* xvi (1930), 109 n. 1).
[3] ADN B1845/11690.

chambre des comptes formed in most respects a single institution, and, in the early years, the councillors 'sur le fait de justice' even joined with the *maîtres des comptes* in the audit of accounts, though this practice was stopped in 1389.[1] When they met together, Pierre de le Zippe acted as joint president, they shared one or more messengers (*chevaucheurs*), and their joint clerk, Pierre Joris, was succeeded in 1401 by a *greffier* of the *chambre du conseil et des comptes*.[2] On the other hand, the Lille council and *comptes* evidently achieved a greater degree of separation and specialization than their counterparts at Dijon, for we find the *chambre des comptes* acting on its own, not only, after 1389, in the auditing of accounts, but also in all sorts of domanial, financial and administrative matters.

Much of the original correspondence of the Lille *chambre des comptes* has survived: the duchess writes asking about her rents; the chancellor wants to know how certain newly appointed officials are getting on and why the sovereign-bailiff of Flanders did not submit his accounts for audit along with those of the bailiffs; Philip the Bold writes from Arras asking why an *ordonnance* which the *chambre des comptes* was ordered to publish in all the bailiwicks had not yet come to the notice of the bailiff of Arras; and bailiffs write excusing themselves from coming to the *chambre* with their accounts on the appointed day. All these flimsy paper letters were carefully stored away in the *chambre des comptes* after the date of their arrival there had been noted on the back. From this we can ascertain that letters from Ghent, Bruges, Sluis or elsewhere in Flanders, as well as from Arras, were often delivered at Lille within twenty-four hours of their dispatch, while three days, or often much longer, was required from Paris.[3]

What this correspondence reveals, functioning under the control of the chancellor and ultimately of the duke, is an active and efficient institution, centrally placed at Lille to administer the domains and finances of the ruler and supervise his officers and servants in his northern group of territories. This *chambre des comptes* has its own correspondence and archives and frequently acts entirely on its own, but it is closely linked to the council, which, in its turn, is

---

[1] ADN B4074, f. 62 and *J. Froissart's cronyke*, ii. 458; *IADNB*, i (2), 74. In 1394, however, Jehan de Nieles, one of the councillors 'sur le fait de justice', was ordered to help out in the *chambre des comptes* (*IADNB*, i (2), 74).
[2] ADN B1598, f. 103b and B1599, f. 65b.
[3] This correspondence is ADN B17599–17605 (1386–99) and AGR Acquits de Lille 977 (1400–1).

primarily concerned with law and order in general, with politics, with the relationship of the Flemish towns to the comital administration, and, most important of all, with justice.

The organization of the governmental archives in the Low Countries was very similar to that in the two Burgundies. As at Dijon, so at Lille, the *chambre des comptes* was itself an important central archive repository, since the accounts of all the financial officers in the northern territories, the documents relating to them, and the *chambre*'s correspondence, were stored in it. The other Flemish muniments were divided, when Philip acquired these territories, between the *trésors des chartes* of Ruppelmonde and Lille, while the muniments of Artois were kept at Arras and looked after by a 'garde des comptes, lettres et escriptes' of Artois.[1] Rethel also had its own *trésor des chartes*. Two significant measures of centralization were applied by Philip the Bold to this archive administration. After 1385 most of the new documents relating to his northern territories which did not automatically go to the *chambre des comptes* at Lille were placed in the *trésor* there, so that the other offices, though still existing, ceased to expand much, and the current muniments were readily available at Lille either in the *trésor des chartes* or in the *chambre des comptes*. Then, in 1399, Philip appointed his secretary Thierry Gherbode, who had already inventoried the Flemish archives at Ruppelmonde and those of Brabant and Limbourg at Nivelles, *garde des chartes* of all his northern territories.[2] His first task, after his appointment, seems to have been an inventory of the archives of the *chambre des comptes*, for he was working on this in 1400 and 1401.

At the end of the fourteenth century the judicial institutions of Flanders were quite unlike those of the duchy of Burgundy, and there was no centralized hierarchy of courts under the control of the ruler. His weakness in this respect is well illustrated by the powerful municipal jurisdictions, which were quite outside his control, as well as by the judicial status of the bailiffs who, unlike those of Burgundy, were not judges, but only convened and presided over their courts. Nor was there any regular mechanism of appeal to their tribunals from the seigneurial, ecclesiastical and municipal courts. In Artois, on the other hand, the bailiffs acted as judges in the French style;

---

[1] ADN B881/11754; B18822/23387. For Rethel, see *Trésor des chartes de Rethel*, i. pp. xix–xx.

[2] For this paragraph, see van Nieuwenhuysen, *Recette générale*, 18–19 and Richard, *BEC* cv (1944), 156–9; for the next sentence, *Documents concernant l'histoire de l'art*, 793.

their assizes were reformed by Philip in an important *ordonnance* of 1386.[1]

In Flanders, the absence of an organized central court of justice had been made good in Louis of Male's reign by the emergence or creation of the *audience* (*audientie*). This was a special, periodic, judicial session of the comital council, which, by 1386, was an old-established and quite popular institution. Its proceedings were normally held in Flemish and it met at intervals of two months or so in the principal Flemish towns. It was preserved unchanged by Philip the Bold, and served as a kind of cloak to conceal his new central court of justice, the *chambre du conseil* at Lille, from popular suspicion. These two courts existed side by side throughout his reign, with identical personnel, functions and jurisdiction and, in the early years, even sharing the same register in which to record their proceedings.[2] They formed a sort of duplicate supreme court which normally sat in the *chambre du conseil* at Lille, but at intervals metamorphosed itself into the *audience* and met in some other Flemish town. The main difference between the two divisions of this court lay in the fact that the *audience* was merely a court, while the *chambre du conseil*, as we have seen, had other and more important functions. The judicial attributions of the council, whether it sat in the *audience* or the *chambre*, were identical. It judged at first instance crimes like treason or disobedience of comital decrees, as well as complaints against bailiffs and other officials, jurisdiction over which was in any case reserved to the count. Much more important, it gradually evolved an appellate or quasi-appellate jurisdiction by acting as arbitrator in disputes between local jurisdictions, especially between the smaller municipal and seigneurial courts, and by hearing complaints against the judgements of lesser courts. It had cognizance, too, over the count's officers and servants, who could have recourse to it for protection and also be effectively disciplined by it when necessary.

The judicial registers of the *chambre du conseil* have survived complete from 12 March 1386 throughout the rest of Philip the Bold's reign,[3] and in them the business transacted at each session is meticulously recorded month by month, sometimes with the relevant documents copied in, and, especially towards the end of the reign, with the names of the councillors present at each session. Apart from

[1] *IAPCA*, i. 141 and 144.
[2] RAG, Raad van Vlaanderen, J3.
[3] RAG, Raad van Vlaanderen, J3–8. The minutes of the *audience* from the first of these registers are printed by Buntinx, *Audientie*, 289–416.

the first, which includes also the minutes of the *audience*, these registers are very like their counterpart, the *registre des causes* of the Dijon council, a similarity which no doubt reflects Philip's attempts to introduce as much uniformity as possible into the administrations of his two groups of lands.

There were two other judicial institutions in Philip the Bold's northern territories which cannot be passed by in silence: the feudal courts of justice, and the *procureur général*. The former, which consisted of a number of regional courts of fief-holders, the *salle de Lille*, the *salle de Ypres*, the *château de Douai* and so on, with a more or less central court at Lille called the *chambre légale* which was reconstituted by Philip the Bold, were rapidly ceasing to be of any real importance.[1] Traces of a *procureur général* are found from 1390 onwards, but it is only in January 1396 that the office emerges from obscurity with the appointment of Jacques de la Tanerie, whose commission still survives.[2] His jurisdiction comprised Antwerp and Malines as well as Flanders, and his duties were to inform himself of all crimes which concerned Philip the Bold and to arraign their perpetrators on his behalf before the *chambre du conseil et des comptes* at Lille, or the *audience*, and in general to defend and safeguard his judicial rights. He was, in fact, a sort of public prosecutor or attorney-general, and his office was closely modelled on that of the Paris *procureur général*, which had already been copied at Lille, as well as in Artois, where a certain Tassart le Jone was Philip's *procureur général* between 1384 and 1398.[3]

The financial organization which Philip the Bold set up in the Low Countries in 1386 was, like most of the rest of the administration, similar to that of the two Burgundies. In Flanders, however, it was complicated by the presence of a separate organization for the collection of and accounting for a large proportion of the domanial resources which remained outside the competence of the *chambre des comptes*. These revenues, many of them in kind, were levied by special receivers and paid by them directly to the receipt-general of Flanders, while their accounts were audited, not by the *chambre des comptes*, but by a special institution which, after 1385, was likewise fixed at Lille, called the *chambre des rennenghes* or *hauts-renneurs*. The two organi-

---

[1] For the *salle de Lille*, see Monier, *Lois, enquêtes, et jugements des pairs du castel de Lille*.   [2] ADN B1598, f. 26; see too Buntinx, *Audientie*, 139 n. 2. [3] *IAPCA*, ii. 126; *IADNB*, iv. 10, 28, 31; and, especially, ADN B932/18700, which gives details of his activities and expenses between 30 June 1389 and 2 February 1390.

zations of *rennenghes* and *comptes* were not, however, entirely separate, for both were under the supervision of a special official, called the *contrôleur des comptes des offices de Flandre*, who worked in close co-operation with the *chambre des comptes* and to whom the task of examining the accounts and checking the payments of both the bailiffs and the *rennenghes* was entrusted.[1]

Apart from the *rennenghes*, which were confined to Flanders, a full measure of centralization in the northern territories was achieved by the Lille *chambre des comptes* in the audit of accounts and in the control of the accounting officers. On the other hand, the collection of moneys remained, as in the two Burgundies, more or less decentralized. True, in 1382 Artois had lost its separate receipt-general,[2] and henceforth a large proportion of its revenues were centralized in the receipt-general of Flanders, Artois, Malines and Antwerp, or paid out on its behalf, but a separate receiver of Rethel, paying his moneys, like the receiver-general of Flanders, directly to or on behalf of the receiver-general of all finances, continued to exist, and, in 1390, another receipt-general, that of Limbourg and Philip's lands beyond the Meuse, was created. Moreover, as in the two Burgundies, so in the northern territories, special receivers or receivers-general were usually appointed to collect the *aides*. Lower down the ranks of the financial organization there was one important difference between Flanders and Burgundy, for in Flanders the bailiffs themselves kept accounts and collected moneys which they either spent or handed over to a receiver-general, though, since most of the domanial revenues escaped them, they handled relatively small sums. Two important changes in their accounts were introduced by Philip the Bold: from 1385 they are invariably in French instead of Flemish, and most of them are entered in registers instead of unwieldy rolls.[3] These bailiffs' accounts were made up and presented for audit to the *chambre des comptes* at Lille, usually by the bailiff in person, at fixed dates three times a year. In Artois, although the bailiffs had originally been accounting officers, by Philip's reign most, if not all, of their financial duties had been taken over by a receiver in each bailiwick. At Antwerp and Malines an officer called an *écoutète* collected and accounted for the comital revenues.

---

[1] ADN B1599, f. 100 b; and B4079, f. 33b, where he is called 'controller of the bailiffs and *rennenghes* of Flanders'. For the *rennenghes*, see Thomas, *BCHDN* xxxiii (1930), 168–70.

[2] *IAPCA*, ii. 233 and van Nieuwenhuysen, *Recette générale*, 6.

[3] See J. Froissart's *cronyke*, ii. and *IAGRCR*.

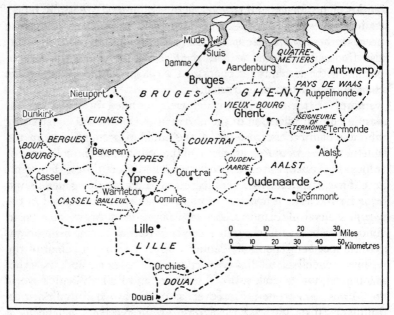

4. Map of Flanders showing the castellanies at the end of the fourteenth century. After Nowé. The bailiff of Ghent exercised ill-defined powers over the bailiffs of Vieux-Bourg, Pays de Waes and the Quatre-Métiers

The general administration of Philip's northern territories was in the hands of the bailiffs. In Flanders the area ruled by the bailiff was called a castellany, and there were sixteen of these at the end of the fourteenth century. Artois was divided into a dozen bailiwicks, and there was a solitary bailiff for the county of Rethel. Apart from their specifically judicial and financial functions, the bailiffs were responsible for the maintenance of law and order and the publication and enforcement of comital *ordonnances*, and they were kept busy, in Flanders, executing the commands of the sovereign-bailiff, an officer instituted by Louis of Male in 1372 to supervise them, who, in Philip the Bold's reign, was the chief executive and judicial officer in that county. The bailiffs were also at the beck and call of the council at Lille, the chancellor, and the count himself, and their activities were by no means confined to their own castellanies. In 1399, Jehan de Latre, bailiff of Ypres, sent in a detailed claim to the *chambre des comptes* for expenses incurred on journeys outside his castellany, including visits on the sovereign-bailiff's orders to the castellanies of Lille and Cassel to arrest malefactors; and another to that of Bailleul;

but his claim for expenses in visiting Comines and Warneton on the council's orders to publish a monetary *ordonnance* was disallowed because these places were inside his castellany.[1] The bailiffs were also frequently charged with military duties, and not the least important of their many functions was to keep Philip the Bold, the chancellor and the Lille council fully informed of everything that went on. This was particularly important in the powerful and often hostile city of Ghent, and the accounts of Danckart d'Ogierlande,[2] who was bailiff there from 1389 to 1411, show that he was indefatigable in this respect. On 21 September 1390 he sent a messenger to inform Philip and the chancellor of the hostility of the citizens to the recent monetary reforms; in 1392 he had to report a riot; and early in 1394 he was able to forewarn Philip that a deputation from the dissatisfied city was on its way to him to request his presence there. Evidently nothing of importance could happen in Ghent without the government being notified at once.

There were numerous other comital officials in Flanders besides the bailiffs, two of which, because of their special importance, ought to be mentioned here: the *écoutète* of Antwerp and the maritime bailiff of Sluis. The *écoutète* was normally a minor official, but in Antwerp he took the place of a bailiff. Indeed, when the bailiff of Courtrai was appointed *écoutète* of Antwerp in 1395, this was regarded as promotion.[3] The maritime bailiff of Sluis, called the *bailli de leaue* or *bailliu van den watre*, was in most respects a typical bailiff, but his jurisdiction, instead of extending over a castellany, covered the estuary leading up to Bruges, called the Zwin, the harbour and port of Sluis, and crimes committed at sea. With six sergeants to help him, he patrolled the waters of the Zwin, made sure that goods were unloaded at the Damme and Bruges staples and not elsewhere, and enforced the port regulations. Despite his name, his headquarters were in fact at Mude, opposite Sluis on the other side of the mouth of the Zwin.[4] A host of minor officials in each castellany acted as auxiliaries of the bailiffs or sometimes independently of them—*sousbaillis*, many of whom had acquired the title of bailiff; sergeants; *écoutètes*, and the like. Many of them were urban officials, and some, like the *écoutète* of Bruges, had important judicial attributions.

In a brief summary such as this, many aspects of the administration,

[1] AGR Acquits de Lille, 187–9.
[2] AGR CC, 14106–14108. See, too, Cartellieri, *P. der Kühne*, 141–2.
[3] De Lichtervelde, *Grand commis*, 24.
[4] I have not been able to see Mauricette, *Le bailliage de l'Eau de l'Écluse*.

for instance coinage and sea-defences, to name but two, must be passed over in silence, but something must be said of the representative institutions in Philip's northern territories. Only in Artois was there a regime of Estates comparable to that of the duchy of Burgundy. Here, the three orders had met almost annually since 1361 and had acquired the right to vote an *aide* which had become fixed at 14,000 francs. Normally granted annually, this was levied by the king of France and shared by him with the count. On at least three occasions, in 1389, 1394 and 1397, Philip the Bold convened the Estates of Artois and persuaded them to vote an extra *aide* to himself alone. These Estates enjoyed no control over the administration of the county, nor did they wield any political influence.[1]

In Flanders an original and most important representative institution had evolved spontaneously in the fourteenth century, and was extremely active in Philip the Bold's reign. This was formed by the so-called *vier leden* or Four Members of Flanders,[2] three of which, Bruges, Ypres and Ghent, were urban; while the fourth, the Franc of Bruges (*het Brugse Vrije*), was mainly rural, for it was in fact the castellany of Bruges and included all the country surrounding that town from Dixmude to Eekloo and Biervliet. Throughout Philip's reign the representatives of these Four Members held, on average, over thirty meetings (*parlementen*) each year. They addressed joint complaints to the count; they negotiated with him when he requested an *aide*, or jointly refused it; they even helped him to negotiate commercial treaties with England and the Hanse.[3] Very occasionally their meetings were attended by representatives of the other Flemish towns and the castellanies. Compared to the Four Members, the three Estates of Flanders, which first appear in Philip's reign, are of little significance, and only seven meetings can be traced: in September 1384, 1386, probably 1386–8, 1390, and three in 1401.[4] In every case

[1] Hirschauer, *États d'Artois*, i. In vol. ii, 11–12, the author records two separate *aides* voted to Philip in 1389 and 1390, though probably there was only one, and he places the 1397 *aide* in 1396.

[2] For what follows, see *Handelingen*. Two recent articles have revolutionized our knowledge of the Four Members in the fourteenth century: Prevenier, *ASEB* xcvi (1959), 5–63 and idem, *RN* xliii (1961), 5–14.

[3] See Chapter 8 below.

[4] For this and what follows, see Cartellieri, *P. der Kühne*, 138–41; de Lichtervelde, *Grand commis*, 81 and n. 218; and *Handelingen*, nos. 7, 106, 417–21, 531, 533, 537, 599 and 601. For the meeting at Lille in September 1384, see Leman, *RHE* xxv (1929), 249. The purpose of the 1386 meeting is unknown. For the meeting in 1386–8, see *IAGRCC*, v. 245. No indication is given of where or when this meeting took place, but it cannot readily be identified

they appear to have been summoned by the count, in 1386–8 to help organize an investigation into the domanial rents at Bruges; in 1384 and 1390 to hear Philip's views about the Schism; and in 1401 to try to solve a dispute between him and Ghent. In 1398 a meeting of the Estates which had been called by the Four Members was forbidden by Philip; in March 1403 there were meetings of two Estates only, clergy and commons. The relative unimportance of the Estates is not only demonstrated by the infrequency of their meetings, but also by the fact that the third Estate was as often as not only represented by the Four Members. Because of this, the Estates take on the character of mere afforced meetings of the Four Members.[1]

To what extent are we justified in considering Philip the Bold's northern territories as a single political and administrative unit? The answer is that the contiguous counties of Flanders and Artois, the isolated lands of Rethel and Limbourg, the detached cities of Malines and Antwerp, were all effectively ruled from the centre through the *chambre du conseil et des comptes* at Lille, the activities of which were closely supervised from Paris or Arras by the chancellor, who played a much more important part in the government of this area than of the two Burgundies. In justice, in finance, in every branch of administration, as well as in political and economic matters, the *conseil* and *comptes* at Lille were actively engaged throughout these territories: together they formed a genuine and powerful central institution which imparted a very real measure of centralization, and even unity, to them.

Central Government

In addition to its regional institutions at Dijon and Lille the Burgundian state under Philip the Bold was equipped with central institutions and officials, most of which formed part of the ducal court or household (*hôtel*). During the first half of the twenty-year period 1384–1404 this was at or near Paris for about half of each year, but between 1394 and 1404 it became virtually fixed there, apart from spells in Artois in 1396 (three months), 1399 (four months), and 1401 (five months), and occasional visits elsewhere. The chancellor, too,

---

with the 1386 meeting, for it was held in Philip's presence and apparently without the deputies of the smaller towns, whereas the 1386 meeting was held in Ghent on 18 February 1386 when Philip was near Mantes, and the additional deputies were present (*Itinéraires*, 185 and *Handelingen*, no. 7).
[1] It is unfortunate that I have not been able to make use of W. Prevenier's forthcoming book, *De Leden en de Staten van Vlaanderen (1384–1405)*, which is to be published by the Koninklijke Vlaamse Academie. See p. xiv above.

resided more or less permanently at Paris from 1385 onwards. While Paris was thus the real seat of Philip the Bold's government, the true centre of the state was the person of the duke himself. All major policy decisions, all important legislative *ordonnances*, nearly all appointments of officers and servants and all diplomatic missions emanated from him. Furthermore, there is abundant evidence of his frequent personal intervention in almost every conceivable matter which concerned him or his lands. In these multifarious activities he made especial use of the so-called 'aulic' council and the chancellor. The former, which in contemporary documents is called simply the *conseil* or, occasionally, the *grand conseil*, was quite unlike the highly institutionalized councils at Dijon and Lille. It was amorphous, met irregularly, had no fixed meeting-place, permanent personnel or even clerk, and it has left no records. It was made up of any officers, relatives, or friends of the duke who happened to be with him at the time. Most, but not all, of these had the title councillor. When the duke was in Flanders or Burgundy this 'aulic' council would on occasion be afforced by the Lille or Dijon councillors. Certain persons appear in it regularly: the chancellor, for instance, and familiars of Philip who were with him continuously over long periods, like Philippe de Bar and Oudart de Chaseron, both of them knights. Its function was advisory and legislative, and in both capacities it was entirely subordinate to the duke, none of whose authority was delegated to it.[1]

It was Philip the Bold who established the chancellor as the most important and powerful of all the central officials of the Burgundian state. When this came into existence, in 1384–7, there were three different chancellors. In Burgundy, the chancellor of the duchy presided over a group of chancery courts, while in Flanders the provost of the church of St. Donatian at Bruges was titular *chancelier de Flandre*, though he had long ago been stripped of the powers which were now concentrated in the hands of the *chancelier du comte*. Philip allowed the offices of chancellor of the duchy and chancellor of the count of Flanders to lapse. In place of the former, a governor of the chancery of the duchy was deputed to preside over the chancery there.[2] In place of the chancellor of the count of Flanders, Philip in 1385 appointed Jehan Canard *chancelier de monseigneur le duc*, and

[1] Lameere, *Grand conseil*, especially 3–7, and ADN B1597, f. 40b.
[2] See above, p. 120. The office of chancellor of the duchy of Burgundy probably lapsed in 1387, for the last occupant, Nicolas de Tholon, is last mentioned as chancellor in September of that year (Plancher, iii. no. 116),

he remained throughout the reign his right-hand man and the undisputed head of the administration and secretariat in all his territories. Living for the most part in his Paris *hôtel*, he controlled and directed the activities of the *chambres* at Lille and Dijon, and from time to time visited them in person. His letters enquiring about the behaviour of a new official and asking for information of every kind are a characteristic feature of the correspondence of the Lille *chambre des comptes*. He occupied himself with all aspects of government, whether financial, domanial, political or religious, and his advice and decision were constantly sought by the rest of the administration. He was the linch-pin of the state, and it is in his activities and powers that its unity is most apparent.[1]

In his court, Philip the Bold possessed an instrument for the dispatch of embassies, the execution of decisions, the publication of letters and the conveyance of instructions to all parts of his scattered territories. It is not perhaps going too far to say that one of the principal functions of the court was to provide this service and ensure a constant contact between the central authority and the rest of the state. Although almost any member of the ducal court might be used in this way, these agents of the central executive authority were usually drawn from among the councillors, secretaries, chamberlains, squires and *chevaucheurs* who were constantly in attendance on the duke. There is some evidence of specialization: the secretaries, more often than not, were used for the internal administration, squires and chamberlains for foreign embassies, while the *chevaucheurs* were mere messengers. Many of the secretaries were important men who were also councillors: senior officials who were intimately concerned with the highest affairs of state. Few of them seem to have been attached permanently to the court, but nearly all did spells of service there or with the chancellor, and even when residing in their own homes—

while in November 1387 a governor of the chancery of the duchy was instituted. The chancellor of the duchy was often called, in official documents, *chancelier de Bourgogne*, a title which has frequently been accorded to Jehan Canard, though not on the authority of the official sources, where he is invariably qualified as *chancelier de monseigneur le duc*. Evidently he was the direct successor of the chancellor of the count of Flanders, rather than of the chancellor of Burgundy.

[1] See the details of his journeys in the ducal service in the accounts of the receipt-general of all finances, ACO B1465 *et sqq.*, and see too his letters to the Lille *chambre* in ADN B17599–17605 and AGR Acquits de Lille 977. On the chancellor's powers in general, see Dumont, *APAE* xv (1958), 33–61, especially p. 48.

Thierry Gherbode at Lille, Gilles le Foulon at Sluis, Jehan Hue at Arras or Robert Dangeul at Paris—they were often sent off on missions by the duke. Councillors, too, were always available at court, and there were a number, like Jehan de Saulx and Dino Rapondi who lived in Paris, or Jehan Despoullettes at Arras, who were in any case usually near at hand. All the members and servants of the court were paid a daily allowance out of the household funds, and received extra payments when they were sent away from it on ducal business.[1]

So far only the unspecialized elements of the central government have been mentioned, for the duke and his council, the chancellor, and their executive agents in the court, were concerned with all aspects of government and administration. But there were also specialized services, dealing with justice and finance.

There was no supreme judicial tribunal in Philip the Bold's state. In theory, the supreme court was the duke in his council, but this jurisdiction had been delegated to and divided between the council and *audience* in Flanders and the council and *Parlement* in Burgundy, and appeals from the Lille council and the Beaune *Parlement*, since both were in France, went to the Paris *Parlement*. In France the *maîtres des requêtes de l'hôtel* formed a sort of subsidiary central court which dealt with all kinds of petitions and requests addressed to the king, but in Burgundy this jurisdiction, too, was decentralized, for the *maîtres des requêtes* seem to have been divided between Lille, Dijon and Paris. Thus Jehan de Nieles was a resident member of the Lille council; Pierre Paris and Michel de Laignes seem to have acted at Dijon in conjunction with the council there; while Jehan du Drac, Jacques du Val, Jehan de Saulx and probably Pierre Blanchet, lived in Paris, at any rate intermittently.[2]

There was another judicial service, which may be mentioned here for want of a more convenient place: the duke's legal representation

[1] This paragraph is based on an examination of the accounts of the receipt-general of all finances, ACO B1465 *et sqq.*

[2] Nieles was appointed to the Lille council in 1393 and was second president in 1401, ADN B1597, f. 56 and B1599, f. 103b. For Michel de Laignes in the Dijon council, see ACO B11402, fos. 28b, 34 etc., and see too, *Ordonnances du duché*, p. clxxxix and n. 5. For Pierre Paris, ACO B15, f. 15b etc., and see too, Pocquet, *MSHDB* viii (1942), 143–4 and *Ords. du duché*, pp. cxxviii, cxci, etc. For Jehan du Drac, see van Nieuwenhuysen, *Recette générale*, 15; ACO B1495, f. 47b; and *Testaments enregistrés au Parlement de Paris*, no. 38. For Jacques du Val, Pocquet, *MSHDB* viii (1942), 143 and ACO B1470, f. 41 etc. For Jehan de Saulx, ACO B1526, fos. 73a–b etc.; and for Pierre Blanchet, ACO B1479, fos. 30, 56b etc. and ACO B15, f. 37b.

at courts other than his own. In the Middle Ages the multitude of different and often rival jurisdictions—feudal, ecclesiastic, royal and communal—and the frequent absence of adequate definitions of their respective competences, led to the maintenance by kings, nobles, bishops and towns of proctors and advocates attached to the courts of other jurisdictions. There were two types of court near or in Philip the Bold's territories in which cases concerning him were likely to be heard, and which could be relied on to seize every opportunity to infringe his judicial rights: the spiritual courts of the bishops, and the assizes of neighbouring French royal bailiffs and provosts. In each of these his permanent legal representation seems to have consisted of a resident *avocat* with a *procureur* to help him. This was evidently the case at any rate in the episcopal courts of Thérouanne, Arras and Tournai, and in the royal courts of Mâcon, Sens, Villeneuve-le-roi (modern V.-sur-Yonne), Amiens, Péronne and Laon.[1] Much more important than these, however, was the ducal legal representation at Paris, and particularly at the *Parlement* of Paris, where it was known as the *conseil du Parlement de Paris*.[2] This council normally consisted of five or six *avocats* and one or two *procureurs*, and many of the former were or became famous, for they included a cardinal, two presidents of the Paris *Parlement*, a chancellor of France and Philip the Bold's chancellor, Jehan Canard. Its function was to look after the duke's interests in the Paris *Parlement*, follow cases which concerned him, act as his agent there and, in particular, to defend his judicial privileges. One of the most zealously guarded of these was his right, as a peer of France, to have cases concerning him judged directly in the Paris *Parlement*, thus by-passing all the lower crown jurisdictions, including those of the French bailiffs; and this privilege goes some way in explaining the large number of cases with which Philip's council at the *Parlement* was kept busy.[3] Another

---

[1] Thérouanne: *IADNB*, i (1863), 220; Arras: *IAPCA*, i. 140 and *IADNB*, i (1863), 234; Tournai: ADN B4073, f. 53 and *IADNB*, iv. 39; Mâcon: *Inventaires mobiliers*, i. 501 n. 6; Amiens: *IAPCA*, ii. 125, 128; *IADNB*, i (1863), 233 and iv. 2; Péronne: *IAPCA*, ii. 129; Laon: *IADNB*, iv. 33, 37. See too, Pocquet, *MSHDB*, viii (1942), 140.

[2] *Ordonnances du duché*, p. ccx n. 4. For what follows, see Aubrée, *Mémoires*, ii. 74–5; *Registre des Parlements de Beaune*, pp. lxi–lxv, and Pocquet, *MSHDB* viii (1942), 140–3.

[3] See, e.g. *IAPCA*, i. 141, where Charles VI orders the royal bailiff of Amiens to transfer for this reason the cases concerning Philip the Bold in Artois to the Paris *Parlement*, and ADN B932/18700, where Philip's *procureur général* in Artois is busy extricating cases from the neighbouring royal

source of trouble for it were the frequent appeals direct to Paris from the duke's own lower jurisdictions in Burgundy, for these were illegal appeals *omisso medio*, and had to be referred back by the Paris council to the Beaune *Parlement*, which was the only court in the duchy whence appeals lay direct to Paris. A number of perfectly legitimate appeals remained to be heard at Paris and to occupy the ducal council there. In the duchy, Philip's disputes with Dijon went to the Paris *Parlement* on appeal;[1] in Flanders, disputes with Ypres, with the abbey of St. Peter at Ghent, and with Yolande of Flanders, countess of Bar, were taken there on appeal against the judgement of the council at Lille;[2] and disputes between Philip and French neighbours like the bishop of Tournai also on occasion went to Paris.[3]

There were other legal officers maintained by Philip the Bold in Paris to safeguard his rights there. A *procureur* was attached to the royal chancery, and another to the *Châtelet*. Furthermore, certain ducal secretaries were deputed by Philip to 'poursuir ses besongnes devers le roy, ses chambres de parlement, des comptes, son chancelier et ailleurs a Paris ou mestier sera'. In 1386 Jacques du Val fulfilled this function; ten years later two of these secretaries were established at Paris, Jehan Hue and Pierre de Courlon.[4]

The central financial administration of the Burgundian state, which consisted of the *chambre aux deniers*, the receiver-general of all finances, and the treasurer, was closely interrelated with the two regional organizations already described; indeed, in many respects, the whole administration formed a single entity. The *chambre aux deniers* was the accounting office of the ducal court or household, but it was also a central institution of the state, for it drew its funds from all parts of the ducal territories as well as directly from the receiver-general of all finances, and it spent them centrally on the ducal person and court, of which it formed part.[5] At first, from 1363 onwards, the responsibility for accounting for the daily expenses of the court was probably entrusted to the household stewards or *maîtres d'hôtel*, while

courts so that they can be heard at Paris. See too, Plancher, iii. 129–30 and nos. 162 and 163.   [1] AD B138, f. 34b, and see below, p. 162.
[2] *Geschiedenis van Vlaanderen*, iii. 242; Fredericq, *Rôle politique*, 174–5; *Chartes et documents de l'abbaye de Saint-Pierre à Gand*, ii. nos. 1490, 1493 and 1497; and *IADNB*, i (1863), 199 etc. For appeals from Flanders in general, see van Caeneghem, *AFAHB* xxxvi (1956), 191–2 and idem, *Études offertes à Pierre Petot*, 61–8.   [3] E.g. ADN B1599, fos. 94b–95.
[4] Pocquet, *MSHDB*, viii (1942), 143, and ACO B1508, f. 35.
[5] See especially, though with reservations, *Itinéraires*, pp. vi–xi and xx–xxvii, and Canat, *Marguerite de Flandre*, especially p. 10.

the treasurer, or some member of the household staff, an almoner or chaplain, made up the annual account of these expenses. In 1371 a clerk, Regnaut Gombaut, was specially charged with this task, and his annual accounts for 1371–7 still survive at Dijon,[1] but the title *maître de la chambre aux deniers* only appears with Nicolas le Convert, who succeeded him on 3 June 1377 and is called 'maistre des garnisons et de la chambre aux deniers.'[2] From 1381 there was an unbroken succession of *maîtres de la chambre aux deniers* whose function it was to make up these annual accounts of the household. The *chambre aux deniers* included among its personnel, besides the *maître de la chambre* and the *maîtres d'hôtel*, two or more *clercs des offices de l'hôtel*, and a *contrôleur de la dépense de l'hôtel*.[3] The *chambre* met every day to record and verify the court's expenses. These were divided into two sections: the wages or daily allowances of all the members of the household with their horses and attendants (*gaiges*), and the purchases made by the different household offices: *paneterie, échansonnerie, cuisine, écurie* and so on (*vivres*). They were entered in a long column on one side of narrow strips of parchment called *escroes*, several bundles of which are still to be found in the departmental archives at Dijon. The number used for each day, as well as their size, increased as the reign drew on. In 1378 two or three *escroes* about fifteen inches long by seven inches wide were sufficient, but by 1386 five or six were required each day, and they had increased in size to about nine inches by twenty-four. The daily expenses of the different household offices were entered on the *escroes* by the *clercs des offices* and they and the *gaiges* were verified and totalled by the *maîtres d'hôtel*. These totals were then copied by the *contrôleur* from the *escroes* into a book called the 'contrerolle de la depense de l'ostel'. It was from this book that the *maître de la chambre aux deniers* made up his annual account, which included also full details of the moneys paid into the *chambre* by the various ducal receivers, as well as some miscellaneous items of expense. It was he who was responsible for receiving and distributing the funds allotted to the *chambre*, and his account, as well as the 'contrerolle', had to be submitted for audit to the *chambre des comptes* at Dijon.[4]

[1] ACO B1436/bis, ter, 7, 13, 17 and 23.
[2] His commission, ACO B1451, fos. 13a–b.
[3] There was at least one *clerc des offices* as early as 1364, and there were two in 1365 (*Inventaires mobiliers*, i. 114 n. 5 and 542 n. 2). For the *contrôleur*, who first appears in 1363, see *Itinéraires*, pp. xxv–xxvii.
[4] The chief surviving *escroes* are ACO B320/2 (December 1371); B320/4

The importance of the *chambre aux deniers* was limited. In the first place, the duchess, from 1384 onwards, and John of Nevers from 1398, had their own quite separate *chambres*, and the expenses of their households were only borne by Philip's *chambre* when they were with him.[1] Secondly, a large proportion of household and court expenses, especially the purchases of equipment of all kinds, horses, vehicles, tapestries, clothing, jewellery and so on, escaped the *chambre* altogether and were paid for chiefly by the receiver-general of all finances, except between 1386 and 1392, when a special accounting officer, the *argentier*, was charged with purchases of jewellery, plate, tapestry and clothing.

While the *chambre aux deniers* was primarily concerned with expenditure, the receiver-general of all finances, like his junior colleagues the regional and local receivers, was occupied more or less equally with the collection and disbursement of funds.[2] Although he was placed at the apex of the hierarchy of ducal receivers, there was no centralization, in his office, of receipts and expenditure. Indeed the transport of specie was as far as possible avoided by a system of assignments (*assignations*), though this was less used in Flanders than elsewhere. This system entailed the assignment of a given expense to the receipt of some convenient receiver. When an assignment was made by the receiver-general of all finances on to, say, the receipt of Rethel, the receiver-general recorded the sum involved among his receipts, while the receiver of Rethel actually paid it out and accounted for it among his expenses. A large proportion of the 'receipts' of the receiver-general of all finances were in fact assignments of this kind: the money never was received by him, but was simply paid out on his behalf by some other receiver. The same is true of the accounts

---

(August–October 1378); B321/bis (January 1385); B321/3 (January–February 1386); B321/4 and 5, B322/2 and B326/2 (May 1396). The surviving 'contrerolles' are ACO B323 (1388–9); BD MS. Baudot 1106 (1389–90); ACO B326 (1396) and B329 (1399). For the accounts of the *maître de la chambre*, see *Itinéraires*, pp. xxv–xxix.

[1] There seems to be no mention of Margaret's *chambre aux deniers* before the appointment of Jehan de Vrechy as *maître* in December 1384 (ACO B1463, f. 26). For John's *chambre*, see Mirot, *ABSHF* (1938), 88. He had been given his own *chambre* for the Nicopolis crusade (van Nieuwenhuysen, *Recette générale*, 120), but this was only temporary. For the *argentier*, see e.g., *Inventaires mobiliers*, ii. no. 1388.

[2] For what follows, see van Nieuwenhuysen, *Recette générale* and Pocquet, *MSHDB* iv (1937), 5–77. I have also made use of the remarkably complete series of accounts surviving at Lille and Dijon.

of the receiver-general of the duchy and county of Burgundy and of those of many other receivers. Alongside these assignments there was a system of direct cash payments, for the receiver-general of all finances, as well as his junior colleagues, needed sums of ready money to meet the numerous expenses which were not assigned to another receiver. In both systems the regional divisions of the financial administration were respected. Thus, while the receiver-general of all finances could make assignments on and receive moneys from any receipt, the receiver-general of the duchy and county neither received funds from, nor made assignments on, the receivers of Nevers, Donzy and the Champagne lands, for these were outside his jurisdiction. Similarly, the receiver-general of Flanders and Artois never received funds from Rethel and Limbourg, the receivers of which paid moneys into and received assignments from the receipt-general of all finances. Again, the local receivers of the duchy bailiwicks could not have payments assigned to their receipts by the regional receivers of Nevers, Donzy and Champagne, but only by their own regional receiver, the receiver-general of the duchy and county of Burgundy, or by the receiver-general of all finances.

The decentralization of receipts and expenses, which was achieved as a matter of necessity and facilitated by the system of assignments, meant that, in spite of his title, the receiver-general of all finances actually received only a small proportion of the ducal revenues. True, the numerous assignments he made to other receivers were recorded in his accounts as receipts, but these other receivers were constantly making payments of their own which escaped him altogether. Moreover, though he was responsible for most of it, the receiver-general of all finances shared the cost of court, administration, diplomacy and other central expenses with many of the regional and local receivers. Thus, he supplied funds to the *maître de la chambre aux deniers*, paid for salaries of councillors, gifts made by the duke and purchases of all kinds for the duke and his court, but so also did the receivers-general of Burgundy and Flanders. The duchess's annual allowance or pension of 6,000 francs was in 1390 paid to her by five different officials:[1]

treasurer of Dôle	2,000
receiver of bailiwick of Chalon	1,000
castellan of Chaussin	500
castellan of Verdun-sur-le-Doubs	500
receiver of Rethel	2,000

[1] ACO B1474, paper note formerly attached to f. 22b.

In spite of this decentralization, the receiver-general of all finances, because he alone had universal powers of making assignments and receiving funds, and because he bore the brunt of the central expenses of the state, was an authentic and indeed vitally important member of its central administration.

The history of the office of receiver-general of all finances may be briefly told. After an early experimental period, Amiot Arnaut was appointed receiver-general of finances in 1372 and held office until 1386. He included in his receipt moneys from the duchy of Burgundy and those which came from France in the form of royal gifts, and, between 1384 and 1386, revenues from all Philip's newly acquired territories, and made assignments on these sources of revenue. In these years there was no separate receipt for the duchy, though Amiot Arnaut has been regarded as only a glorified receiver-general of the duchy,[1] in spite of the fact that his receipts were never limited to it, and that he was never called by this title. In 1386-7, however, a receipt-general of the duchy and county was set up, and the task of the receiver-general thus considerably eased. From 1387 onwards no further changes were made in the receipt-general of all finances, except for the temporary fusion, between 1391 and 1397, of the offices of receiver-general and treasurer in one person.

The whole of Philip the Bold's financial administration was controlled by a single central official, the treasurer, or *trésorier et gouverneur des finances*. This title had at first been held by the receiver-general, but in 1372 the treasurer became a separate officer of co-ordination and control. In 1384-6 and 1400-4 the experiment was tried of dividing the office into two, with one treasurer for the northern territories and another for the southern. The treasurer did not keep an account, nor did he receive and disburse funds. His principal occupation was the countersigning and dispatch of ducal orders or *mandements* for specific payments and assignments, and the authorization of countless others on the duke's instructions. He kept a watchful eye on the receiver-general of all finances, whose payments and assignments had to be authorized by him, supervised the financial administration, and was responsible for the duke's finances as a whole. Although he thus imparted a considerable measure of centralization to the financial organization, he had no jurisdiction over the *chambres des comptes*, the functions of which were of course quite different from his own. There was in fact no need for an official placed over the two *chambres* to co-ordinate their work, for the Dijon *chambre* was the

---

[1] E.g. van Nieuwenhuysen, *Recette générale*, 1.

senior of the two, and it audited the central accounts of the receiver-general of all finances, the *argentier* and the *maître de la chambre aux deniers*. The verification of these accounts entailed a continual exchange of correspondence and extracts of accounts between the two *chambres*, which well illustrates the subordinate status of the Lille *chambre*.[1]

Conclusion

In spite of its many close links with France, its judicial dependence on the French crown through the Paris *Parlement* and the fact that much of it was juridically part of France, the Burgundian state under Philip the Bold formed a distinct political and administrative entity. It was ruled by the duke himself, acting with the advice of his council and the help of his household, treasurer, and, most important of all, his chancellor. It did not consist of an amorphous scattering of separate administrations, for in the two Burgundies, as in the Low Countries, the central *chambres du conseil et des comptes* exercised the ruler's authority over a whole group of territories and over every aspect of their administration. Each of these units was firmly under the control of the centre, and in both the administration was organized on the same lines. Parts of this structure had evolved separately in Flanders and Burgundy before Philip acquired them, but its centralization and co-ordination was due to him and required a radical governmental and administrative reorganization which was carried out in the years 1385-7. It was then that the *chambres du conseil et des comptes* were set up or reorganized at Lille and Dijon, and an all-powerful *chancelier de monseigneur le duc* was instituted; not to mention the reorganization of the financial administration and the reform of the judicial system in the counties of Burgundy and Artois. Because of this work, Burgundy became a state instead of remaining a haphazard dynastic grouping of territories. But Philip the Bold's state was by no means original: it was copied from France. Just as he employed French resources and French administrative personnel, so Philip unashamedly modelled his administrative institutions on those of France. The transformation of the chancellor into a veritable prime minister, the institution of the treasurer, the employment in Flanders of a *procureur général*, and indeed almost all his innovations, were imported from France, and the detailed working of the financial

---

[1] E.g. ACO B1463/bis and ter: bundles of extracts of accounts sent by Lille to Dijon and vice versa; a questionnaire from Dijon to Lille, etc., 1386-96.

administration, the courts of justice and the rest, was invariably modelled on French practice. This fact does not, however, affect the principal conclusion to be drawn from an examination of Burgundian administration and institutions under Philip the Bold: that Burgundy, by medieval standards at any rate, was, from 1384–7 onwards, a real political and administrative entity. Burgundy was a state.

CHAPTER SEVEN

The Two Burgundies under Philip the Bold

The two Burgundies differed from each other in almost everything but name, language and approximate area. In the county, which was part of the Holy Roman Empire, a turbulent feudal nobility pursued its private quarrels and enjoyed its traditional judicial immunities regardless of the count's authority. On the other hand, long before Philip acquired the duchy, its Capetian dukes had established their power on the firm basis of an extensive domain and an efficient administration; they had enjoyed for centuries an undisputed succession and the protection of the French crown; and they had given the duchy both political stability and prosperity. While the county was a peripheral frontier region of little importance, the duchy, which yielded more than five times as much revenue, provided Philip with an administration, with developed institutions, and with a trained secretariat. Moreover, he had already ruled it for twenty years before he acquired the county.

Philip the Bold was a French prince who had no connection with Burgundy before 1363. Between then and his marriage in 1369 he spent about four months in each year there, but in the 1370s this increased to an average of six months. In 1380, when Charles VI succeeded to the French throne, Philip became much more deeply involved in French affairs and, after this, especially after the acquisition of his other territories in 1384, his visits to Burgundy became fewer and shorter, though they were still annual or nearly so until his last brief stay there in the spring of 1396 to see John of Nevers off on his crusade. Philip's wife Margaret, although she was Flemish, very soon settled down to reside in Burgundy. Indeed, throughout the 1370s she was there more or less permanently, whether at Rouvres, Talant, Jaucourt, Montbard or Dijon, and she often acted as her husband's lieutenant when he was away. In the 1380s she began to accompany him more frequently on his visits to France and the Low Countries, and, in spite of the purchase and reconstruction for her of the castle of Germolles, spent less time in Burgundy. Even in the early 1390s, however, she was still there for prolonged periods, for instance from March 1393 to June 1394, but there seems to be no evidence that she visited Burgundy after 1397, and, in the last years of the reign, she resided at Arras in Artois. The county of Burgundy was seldom visited by either Margaret or her husband.

When Philip the Bold became duke of Burgundy in 1363 the duchy, like much of the rest of France, was in a critical condition, owing principally to the chaos caused by the English campaigns before and in 1360 and to the activities of the bands of unemployed soldiers known as companies. Since the death of Eudes IV in 1349 there had been no ducal authority worth the name, and, apart from the brief reign of the youthful Philip of Rouvres, the duchy had been administered by the crown of France. In 1360 an enormous financial burden had been imposed on it when it was held to ransom first by Edward III and then by the demobilized soldiery which had united to form the so-called Grand Company. After Philip of Rouvres' death in 1361 its succession was disputed by Charles the Bad, king of Navarre, and in these years it suffered too from the hostile incursions of the nobility of the county, whose sympathies lay with England rather than with France, as well as from visitations of the plague, especially in 1361.

Philip's appointment on 27 June 1363 at the age of twenty-two as royal lieutenant-general in the duchy, which was followed in June 1364 by his public institution as duke, came thus at a dangerous moment in its history, and the danger was increased by his personal indifference to it at this time. It is true that he reached Dijon within two weeks of his appointment as royal lieutenant, and summoned troops to meet there at the end of July, but early in August he returned to Paris, leaving the duchy in the hands of a governor. Although in September he was back again, and remained in the duchy throughout the following winter, he did not visit it at all between April and November 1364, and in 1365 he was absent from July to the end of the year, in spite of reiterated appeals from the council at Dijon. He was evidently enjoying the life of the royal court, and, while the duchy was being threatened and even pillaged by companies of disbanded mercenaries, and neither the marshal nor the ducal troops had been paid, he calmly ordered twelve pairs of pointed shoes (*souliers à la poulaine*) to be sent to him from Dijon, and asked the hard-pressed *gens des comptes* there to send him funds to pay his debts at tennis and support the other pleasures of court life.[1] Philip the Bold, in fact, played a surprisingly small part in the crises and eventual recovery of the duchy in the early years of his reign there.

Two military problems faced the administration of the duchy in and after 1363: the war with the county and the ravages of the companies. The former was soon disposed of, for it was officially terminated within a year, and even its unofficial aftermath was over before the end of 1365.[2] Although this war was partly only a continuation of earlier hostilities against the duchy by the Comtois nobles, it was exacerbated by a dispute over the possession of the lordship of Chaussin, and by the Emperor Charles IV's investment of Philip the Bold with the county early in 1362, for this was a direct challenge to its ruler, Margaret of Artois, who had succeeded to it with the support of the inhabitants after Philip of Rouvres' death in 1361. It was the threat from the county that had forced Philip to summon troops in July 1363, but other events intervened, and it was not till December, after he had taken into his employment two of the leaders of the companies, Seguin de Badefol and Arnaud de Cervole the Archpriest, that Philip was able to organize a counter-attack. This achieved the recapture of one or two castles, but had to be abandoned when other companies threatened the duchy. It was followed by an abortive attempt of Philip in February 1364 to make peace with Margaret of Artois, and by further sporadic hostilities which his captains, Arnaud de Cervole and Jehan de Montaigu the governor of the duchy, failed to press to a conclusion, chiefly because of the activity of the companies in the duchy. Philip's army was in large part a temporary coalescence of some of these companies, whose leaders were apt to desert him at any moment, especially if their wages were not promptly paid. One of these captains who had not been paid for his services, Arnaud de Talebardon, was remunerated in an unusual manner. In February 1364 Philip the Bold made over some ducal prisoners to him on the understanding that he would accept their ransom-money in lieu of wages for his troops. Some of these men had the good fortune, later that year, to fall in with the clerk of a ducal receiver travelling to Dijon with funds for the administration. He was forcibly relieved of 141 gold francs which Arnaud de Talebardon retained as the second instalment of the money owed him by the duke. He even had the

---

[1] Petit, *P. le Hardi*, 172–3.
[2] For what follows, see Vernier, *RCB* i (1904), 1–23 and 183–203; Chérest, *Archiprêtre*, 142, 151–4, 225–302; and Petit, *P. le Hardi*.

effrontery to write out a receipt in due form for this sum, which Philip, in spite of its evident irregularity, later ordered the *gens des comptes* at Dijon to accept.[1]

While some of the Comtois nobles, notably Jehan de Neufchâtel, the count of Montbéliard Henri de Montfaucon, and Hugues de Chalon, actively prosecuted the war through the summer of 1364, the two rulers, Philip and Margaret of Artois, encouraged by King Charles V, recommenced peace negotiations, and a preliminary treaty was signed on 25 July, which was followed in September by the grudging acceptance of truces with Philip by the disaffected Comtois nobles. But the peace between the governments of the duchy and county did not deter these nobles from renewing hostilities in the following spring. In March Jehan de Neufchâtel seized the town of Pontailler, only to fall into the hands of Guy and Guillaume de la Trémoille, who sold him to the duke for 8,000 *livres*. This redoubtable enemy of the duchy, who was a pensioner of Edward III, was thrown in irons into the dungeon of Semur, and remained there until August 1369. After his capture, others took up arms to avenge him, and, in the summer of 1365, Chaussin was seized and the lands dependent on it so ravaged that they were still a desert ten years later. During 1365, however, intermittent hostilities gave way to further negotiations, and by the end of the year all parties had at last agreed to make peace. From December 1365 Philip's relations with the county and its unruly nobility seem to have been friendly, and on 3 January 1371 he entertained Henri de Montfaucon's son Estienne Hugues de Chalon, and several other Comtois nobles to dinner at Auxonne.[2] He certainly had no difficulty in remaining on friendly terms with the Countess Margaret, whose granddaughter he had married in 1369. In that year Philip signed a treaty of alliance with her, the count of Savoy and Hugues de Chalon, and in 1375 the rulers of the two Burgundies amicably settled certain matters of dispute between them.[3]

The companies were a much more serious threat to Philip's newly acquired duchy than the activities of a handful of hostile Comtois nobles.[4] The armies which had been used by either side in the Anglo-French fighting which preceded the peace of Brétigny in 1360 con-

---

[1] La Chauvelays, *MAD* (3) vi (1880), 42 and Chérest, *Archiprêtre*, no. 18.
[2] *Itinéraires*, 63.   [3] Above, p. 13, and Plancher, iii. no. 52.
[4] For what follows, see Finot, *Recherches*; Chérest, *Archiprêtre*; Vernier, *MAD* (4) viii (1901-2), 219-320; *Itinéraires*, especially pp. 455 ff; and Petit, *P. le Hardi.*

sisted entirely of mercenaries, but there were two distinct types of these: the feudal contingents which served according to fixed rules based on the old feudal duty of military service, and which were led and mustered by loyal vassals of the lord or ruler; and the arbitrarily recruited bands of soldiers maintained by the captain (or *condottiere* as he was called in Italy) whose private army they formed, and who rented out his and their services just as he pleased. These independent bands of military adventurers, known as companies, were already active on their own account before the peace of Brétigny, but after it many more of them, no longer finding employment in the Anglo-French struggle, moved off on their own to exploit the alternative sources of income presented to them by the possibility of pillage, ransom and the sale of safe-conducts. Burgundy suffered as much as almost any other region of France or Italy from their attentions, which began there as early as 1355, reached a peak in 1360–2, and continued throughout the first few years of Philip the Bold's reign.

These attentions took various forms. A group of companies might traverse the duchy from north to south, cutting a broad swathe of devastation as it passed; an isolated band might destroy some villages and remove their livestock after killing or mutilating the inhabitants; and from time to time a castle or fortified town would be seized and either held to ransom or used as a base for pillaging excursions into the surrounding countryside. When one company was bought off, another would take its place. The history of the companies in Burgundy is thus a piecemeal, disconnected one of sieges, raids and pursuits. They operated sometimes independently and sometimes on behalf of King Charles the Bad of Navarre. Their leaders and rank and file came from all parts of France as well as from elsewhere in Western Europe, including England.

In October 1363 one of these companies, moving by night and hiding by day in the woods, surprised La Charité-sur-Loire near the western frontier of the county of Nevers. Early in November Philip ejected a band of brigands from Arcy-sur-Cure in the north-west corner of the duchy, but, as soon as he had left, they returned and threw the ducal coat of arms he had erected there into the river Cure. The possessors of La Charité soon became a menace: in February 1364 they were threatening Châtillon-sur-Seine and Auxerre, both in the extreme north of the duchy. In the summer, a mercenary captain actually penetrated the *basse-cour* (bailey) of the ducal castle at Argilly near Beaune, and made himself and his men at home there for some days. At this time operations against the companies were hampered by lack of funds to ransom the fortresses they had captured: the marshal of Burgundy, Guy de Pontailler, had to pledge himself for a sum lent for this purpose by Arnaud de Cervole, and actually became Arnaud's prisoner for a time when the ducal administration failed to find the money to repay him. In the autumn, however, some real, though temporary, progress was made: between July and November 1364 the provost of Dijon hanged 120 malefactors; in September Philip at last forced the group of companies holding La Charité to surrender; and in October one of the most redoubtable captains, Guiot de Pin, was executed at Chalon after he had been purchased by the ducal council for 200 *livres*.

This state of affairs continued during the succeeding years, and the course of events need not be described in detail. Meanwhile, a succession of schemes to find employment for the companies elsewhere, if possible some distance away, failed to alleviate the situation. In the spring of 1365, at a time when a project to seize Philip's person became known to the ducal administration, an attempt was made to dispatch all the companies on a crusade against the Ottoman Turks, but the few who set out on this dubious enterprise got no further than the Rhine, whence they were driven back into France by a hostile population stung into action by their pillaging activities. Later in the year Bertrand du Guesclin, the famous constable of France, managed to lead some of the companies off on his expedition to Spain to place the French candidate on the throne of Castile, but his passage through the duchy of Burgundy, with his army of companies, which Philip did his best to prohibit,[1] was little different in its effect from the passage of a hostile army. In any case many had refused to accompany him and, of those who did, a number returned in 1367, after his defeat at Navaretta, to continue their depredations in the duchy and elsewhere. In the spring of 1366 another opportunity presented itself: the Green Count, Amadeus VI of Savoy, was about to set out on a crusade against the Ottoman stronghold of Gallipoli. Arnaud de Cervole, one of the most renowned captains of his time, who had rendered important assistance to Philip the Bold since 1363, agreed to assemble the companies at large in the duchy of Burgundy and lead them on this expedition, but he was assassinated in the midst of these commendable efforts, and, in spite of the free transport down the Saône which Philip the Bold arranged for them, a considerable number still remained in the duchy. Yet another attempt to remove the companies was made in the autumn of 1367 when King Charles V

---

[1] *Inventaires mobiliers*, i. no. 511.

hired the services of John of Armagnac, count of Charolais, Philip's leading Burgundian vassal, to lead them out of the duchy, but this too was a failure.[1] In 1368, however, a concerted military effort against them was largely successful, and, in any case, after that year the reopening of hostilities between France and England helped to diminish their numbers and divert their activities from the duchy.

If the companies were no longer, after 1368, an unremitting evil for the inhabitants and administration of the duchy of Burgundy, their incursions and escapades punctuated its history during the next twenty years, though with decreasing frequency. In the 1370s we hear of them annually. In 1382–3 some men-at-arms in the Mâconnais were preparing to enter the duchy; in 1383 a company of Bretons threatened it; and in 1385 a messenger was sent by the bailiff of Chalon to warn Philip that the count of Armagnac 'li entendoit faire guerre en son pays de Bourgogne'.[2] Within a few months of its acquisition by Philip early in 1384, the county of Nevers was invaded by a group of companies, and the governor, Philippe de Jaucourt, had to introduce garrisons into the towns and castles

> pour résister et aler à l'encontre de Teste Noyre et de pluseurs ennemys du royaume, et aussi à l'encontre de Jehan Labbé et autres cappitaines de gens d'armes de rotes et de compaignie, lesquelles gens d'armes voloient passer et séjourner en la comté de Nevers . . .

and, in January 1387, he had to assemble troops to dislodge a number of irregulars, said to be in the service of the count of Armagnac, from the neighbourhood of Donzy.[3] Even as late as 1391 we hear of some 'grosses compaignies' near Avignon which menaced the south of the duchy, and there was another alarm in 1402–3 caused by some men-at-arms near Vienne.[4]

The activities of the companies in 1363–9 constituted a serious and immediate threat to the security of the duchy which was met by calling out its feudal contingents to pursue the malefactors, or besiege the fortresses they had seized; by strengthening the garrisons; by taking measures to ensure the rapid withdrawal of movable goods and livestock from the countryside into the castles and walled towns in case of emergency; and by persuading or bribing the companies to move elsewhere. All these essentially short-term measures were tried

---

[1] La Chauvelays, *MAD* (3) vi (1880), 57–63.
[2] *IACOB*, i. 425 and ii. 260.
[3] Mirot, *MSAN* xxxviii (1936), 148 n. 1.
[4] *IACOB*, i. 426 and 428.

with varying degrees of success, and, when the menace of the companies was eventually relaxed, the duke and his administration turned to the long-term problems of security and defence. Above all, they embarked on a large-scale building programme entailing the reconstruction and repair of the principal ducal castles and residences. This work was partly financed from the profits of justice, all of which, according to ducal *ordonnances* of 1384, 1391 and 1396, were to be applied to it, as well as, after 1396, from the profits of the ducal salt monopoly in the duchy.[1] It was carried out by two allied administrations *des œuvres de maçonnerie* and *charpenterie*, each of which was in the charge of at least one *maître*, and both of which, after 1395, were under the control of a single officer, Oudart Douay, who was appointed by Philip the Bold 'sur le fait des ouvraiges et reparacions des chasteaulx, forteresses et maisons de monditseigneur'.[2] This building programme was inspired by Philip's personal interest. Like his brother Charles V, he was an enthusiastic builder. His visits to works in progress both in the duchy and elsewhere are mentioned on numerous occasions in the accounts because of his habit of tipping the workmen, and he often intervened personally in a particular project. Thus in 1383 when the *château* of Argilly was under repair he had a new chimney-piece in the hall specially copied from a very fine one he had noticed in his brother's superb and newly built *château* at Creil.[3]

There is little evidence, in the 1360s, of major works of reconstruction to the ducal *châteaux* in the two Burgundies.[4] The times were probably too uncertain and the necessary funds not forthcoming. Instead, we read of work on the armaments of Argilly, including repairs to cross-bows; of a new lantern for the use of the watch at Rouvres and new cords for a siege-engine there. This sort of work continued in the 1370s: the cannon received attention at Chaussin; at Argilly four painted bronze banners were set up, and the craftsmen responsible for them painted and decorated several of the rooms; at Montbard, Jaucourt and elsewhere glaziers were at work on the windows; at Rouvres gardens were laid out with a maze and Philip's room and the *pourtal de l'entrée* were painted; and at Montbard the

[1] BN Coll. de Bourg. 53, fos. 26 and 106; ACO B15, f. 44 and BN Coll. de Bourg. 72, f. 319.   [2] See above, p. 124 and n. 1; ACO B15, f. 39b.
[3] Petit, *P. le Hardi*, 22–6.
[4] For this paragraph, see *Inventaires mobiliers*, i. 202 n. 5, 287 n. 5, and nos. 213–17, 1113, 1380, 1384, 1888, 1889, 2116, 2118, and 2426; ibid., ii. 270–5 and nos. 388–90 and 1123; *IACOB*, ii. 55, 77, 191–3, 291, 355 and 428–9.

stone window-seats in the *chambre rouge*, which were too cold for the duchess, were replaced with wooden ones. But much more substantial works, major schemes of restoration or rebuilding, new towers and the like, got under way from about 1370 onwards. The works at Maisey-le-Duc were in progress from 1372 and a new tower is mentioned there in 1384. New towers were also constructed at Pontailler, Villaines-en-Duesmois and Chaussin in the late 1370s and 1380s. At Salmaise and Jaucourt important works were undertaken in the 1380s and 1390s, and the castle of Germolles was completely rebuilt by the duchess.[1] In 1402–3 Jehan Bourgeois, *maître des œuvres de maçonnerie*, inspected the works at Saulx-le-Duc, Villaines-en-Duesmois, Maisey-le-Duc and elsewhere.

Besides the ducal *châteaux*, the capital of the duchy, Dijon, benefited from the ducal building programme. Its streets were ordered to be paved by a ducal *ordonnance* of 1375, and the mayor was authorized to levy a special tax on the citizens to help finance this work. But, in spite of a contribution from the duke, funds seem to have been inadequate, and the work was not finished until 1396.[2] In the same way the walls and fortifications of the town were restored between 1359 and 1390 or later, chiefly at the expense of the citizens,[3] and in spite of the reluctance which they showed in 1386 to continue this expense: they claimed that the fortifications were already perfectly adequate, and that if further work really was necessary, then the clergy and nobles ought to pay for it. Philip the Bold's generosity towards Dijon seems to have always been somewhat limited. In 1382, for instance, he saved the municipal clock of Courtrai in Flanders from the flames to which the town was consigned after the battle of Roosebeke, and presented it to Dijon, but the cost of reassembling it, together with the famous Jacquemart, and placing it on one of the towers of the church of Notre-Dame, where part of it still remains, had to be met by public subscription.[4]

Work on the ducal palace at Dijon was begun as soon as Philip took over the duchy. He added a new tower to it, and also a wall to enclose the *enceinte* of the palace on the east side, which, owing to the disrespectful custom of the inhabitants of obeying the call of nature

[1] For Germolles, see Picard, *MSE* (n.s.) xl (1912), 147–218.
[2] *Inventaires mobiliers*, i. no. 2310 and p. 436 n. 2; ACO B15, f. 33b and Plancher, iii. no. 126.
[3] *IACD*, iii. L, 34–5 and 92–7. For the next sentence, see Plancher, iii. no. 103.
[4] Fredericq, *BARBL* (1909), 379–90. The figure of a man wielding a hammer, which strikes the hour, was only later called 'Jacquemart'.

there, was painted red and decorated with a row of large white crosses. The accounts do not tell us whether or not this religious symbolism had the desired effect. In 1387 work was in progress on the chapel of the ducal palace, later called the Sainte-Chapelle, and, the following year, a bathhouse was being fitted out in an adjoining house. It is curious to learn that the storks which tried to nest on the chimneys of the ducal palace were driven off. In 1386 a man was paid to remove their nests, and later, iron grilles were fixed on the chimneys to make it impossible for them to build there.[1]

On the whole, Philip the Bold's reign in the duchy was marked by a general acceptance of his policies and even his taxes, a picture which contrasts to some extent with that obtaining in the county of Burgundy. The scanty surviving direct evidence about his popularity in the duchy comes from the accounts of the castellans and other local judicial officers who from time to time punished some unfortunate individual, usually by way of a fine, for saying rude things about his duke. Thus one person was fined for maintaining that the prior of Moûtier-en-Bresse 'valait mieux que le duc de Bourgogne', and another for stating that if a certain person, whom he named, were as well dressed as the duke, 'il seroit aussy beaux comme Monseigneur, et qu'il [the duke] estoit trop noirs et laiz homs'. Others were fined for likening the duke to 'un chien foireux', or for criticizing a solemn procession in aid of the removal of the companies by suggesting that the ducal troops were just as bad. No general conclusion can of course be drawn from this sort of thing, nor from the frequent minor clashes of members of the populace with the local officers of the ducal administration. A minstrel, provoked by a ducal sergeant, had wounded the latter with his *cornemuse* 'bagpipes'; another sergeant had his beard pulled in a tavern by an inhabitant of Villiers-les-Hauts who afterwards claimed that he did this 'non mie par maul, mas pour oster dessus sadite barbe une miote de pain qui y estoit'.[2]

Much more indicative of the general feeling towards Philip the Bold's administration is the attitude to the *aides* or extraordinary taxes which were voted by the three Estates. Here we find, in general, a ready acquiescence interrupted by occasional opposition. Sometimes, as with Philip's first subsidy voted in 1363, or his attempt to levy an *aide* in the county of Charolais in 1383 before it became his own, this

---

[1] For this paragraph, see *Inventaires mobiliers*, i. nos. 429–32; Petit, *Entrée*, 45–50; and Picard, *MCACO* xvii (1913–21), pp. cccxcvii–cccc.

[2] For these and similar incidents, see *IACOB*, i. 423; *Inventaires mobiliers*, i. nos. 1621, 600, 968, 526 and 425; and Petit, *P. le Hardi*, 428–33.

opposition was directed against the actual levying of money;[1] at other times the Estates themselves opposed the duke's demands, or exacted concessions from him in return for their vote. In 1382 they granted the *aide*, but only on condition that no other *aides* were levied during the year, and that food purveyed in the duchy for the ducal household would be paid for and ducal creditors in the duchy satisfied, out of the proceeds; and Philip also had to promise to make provision for the expulsion of Jews and Lombards.[2] In 1391 they were able in part to dictate how the 30,000 francs they voted were to be spent: the duke was to have 10,000 'pour en faire son plaisir' and the other 20,000 were to be used exclusively to pay his debts in the duchy.[3] There is at least one clear case of the successful lowering by the Estates of the required subsidy: in August 1397 Philip asked them for 80,000 francs to help finance the payment of his son's ransom, but had to be content with only 50,000.[4] In general, however, the inhabitants of the duchy duly accepted his repeated financial demands, and one can only assume that the burden thus imposed on them was not oppressively heavy.

It was often the case in fourteenth-century Europe that opposition to established governments was confined to or originated in the towns, the more important of which had everywhere acquired varying degrees of civic autonomy, and a fierce and possessive enthusiasm for their often monopolistic or restrictive privileges. In agricultural Burgundy there were few towns of importance, though some half-dozen, the chief of which were Dijon, Beaune, Montbard and Semur, had acquired *communes*, that is to say, had been granted municipal constitutions, and certain privileges that went with them. Of these, Dijon alone, with its 10,000 or so inhabitants[5] and its enhanced status as capital, was capable of presenting problems of a political sort to the ducal administration, and even these frequently had the character of private, juridical disputes between the town and its ruler.[6]

Although on 26 November 1364, when he made his formal entry into Dijon, Philip had solemnly sworn to respect its privileges, it was

---

[1] Vernier, *MAD* (4) viii (1901–2), 308–9 (no. 7) and Pocquet, *RHDFE* (4) xviii (1939), 393–5. See too, Petit, *P. le Hardi*, 373–6, 380, etc.
[2] Plancher, iii. no. 75.
[3] Plancher, iii. no. 133, and Petit, *P. le Hardi*, 396.
[4] BN Coll. de Bourg. 53, fos. 78 and 155b.
[5] Humbert, *PTSEC* (1958), 51.
[6] For what follows, I have used Plancher, iii. nos. 35, 103, 124 and 125; *Recueil de pièces servant à l'histoire de Bourgogne*, pp. 367–82 and 395–7; *Chartes de communes*, i. nos. 61–9.

not long before complaints on either side flared up into an open quarrel. In March 1366 a jurisdictional dispute caused the duke to abrogate the municipality and take its jurisdiction temporarily into his own hands, and in the following year we hear of open opposition to the ducal captain of Dijon, Olivier de Jussy.[1] Ten years later something approaching a revolt occurred as a result of a quarrel over the election of the mayor. When Philip tried to seize the goods and persons of some citizens who had on this occasion actually taken up arms against his administration, he found the mayor and aldermen united behind them, and a military demonstration with 'foreign' troops from the county of Burgundy was necessary in November 1377 to subdue the town.[2] After this, a succession of lesser quarrels occurred throughout the rest of Philip the Bold's reign, many of which were only settled with the help of the Paris *Parlement*. A lengthy decree of that body of 14 July 1386 confirmed a detailed agreement between the duke and the town which redefined a number of important principles. Municipal statutes were only valid if approved by the duke; the municipality had no power to exempt people from ducal taxes without his leave; and public works—roads, bridges and fortifications—in the town were admitted to be a matter for the duke to decide about, even though the town paid for them.

All this, however, was in vain. A new dispute arose in 1387 and was referred to the Paris *Parlement*.[3] In 1389 Dijon was at fault in attempting to impose its taxes on the ducal *gens des comptes*, who were traditionally exempt from these dues. In 1395 it was the duke's turn to give offence: his bailiff at Dijon had most improperly imprisoned some inhabitants of Dijon in the castle of Talant, outside the town. Soon after this, in 1396, the municipality was again taken over by the duke, and the town was governed for nearly a year by Guillaume Chenilly, the ducal receiver in the bailiwick of Dijon. Some years later, in 1402, Philip was able to persuade the aldermen to elect a mayor of his choice, Lambert de Saulx, but the juridical bickering still continued: in 1403–4 there was trouble over the burning of a necromancer and his books by the bailiff of Dijon, and the provost gave offence in the matter of wine measures. It may be noted, in passing, that the complete series of minutes of the town council or meetings of the mayor and aldermen of Dijon, for the years 1383–1404, are still to be found among the communal muniments there, preserved in quarto-size paper volumes called the *papier du secret*

[1] Plancher, iii. 25.   [2] Petit, *P. le Hardi*, 324–6.
[3] AD L341, f. 90. For what follows, see AD B138, 139, 144 and 145.

which constitute a mine of information about the relationship of the town with the ducal administration and many other matters.[1]

The defence of juridical privileges by private vested interests was not confined to Dijon, for the bishops of the duchy, whose seats were at Langres, Autun, Auxerre and Chalon, were equally tenacious in the maintenance of their rights. Indeed, the early history of Philip the Bold's relations with the Church in the duchy consists largely of an interminable series of complicated judicial disputes which were often referred to the Paris *Parlement* or to Avignon. Some of them had been taken over by Philip along with the duchy in 1363. Documents concerning these disputes still clutter the departmental archives at Dijon. In 1371–2 the bishop of Autun had tortured a ducal sergeant so that he could no longer walk; in 1397–8 pennons were put up by the duke at St. Jean-de-Verdun to denote his judicial rights there, but the bishop of Chalon's privileges were thereby infringed, and he appealed to the Paris *Parlement*; in 1370 the officers of the bishop of Langres retaliated against a ducal infringement of his judicial privileges by putting the town of Châtillon under an interdict, and the bishop followed this up by excommunicating the captain of the castle and the bailiff of La Montagne.[2]

More interesting than these disputes is the way Philip the Bold tried to avoid them by persuading the chapters to elect or the pope to appoint bishops of his own choice. This was the method he had tried with the mayoralty of Dijon in 1402. When applied to the bishops, it met with some success. Both Philip and the Duchess Margaret sent embassies to Avignon in May 1374 with a view to obtaining the appointment to the see of Chalon, then vacant, of Philip's chamberlain and councillor Pierre de la Trémoille. In the event they were too late, for the vacancy had already been filled. Next time, however, the duchess was more careful: she ordered the ducal bailiff at Chalon to inform her at once when the bishop died. This happened in 1386 and, in the following year, Philip succeeded in placing one of his own men, Olivier de Martreuil, who had been a member of the *Parlement* and *auditoire* of Beaune, on the episcopal throne of Chalon.[3] A year later,

---

[1] AD B130–46.

[2] *IACOB*, ii. 174–5, 406, and *Inventaires mobiliers*, i. no. 1127. For disputes, especially in the 1360s, between the bishop of Autun and the ducal bailiff, see de Charmasse, *MSE* (n.s.) xxvi (1898), 1–135 and Berthollet, *Évêché d'Autun*, 92–7. For disputes with the bishop of Chalon, see Bazin, *MSHAC* xiv (1914), 273–6.

[3] Aubrée, *Mémoires*, ii. 45 n.c.; *Inventaires mobiliers*, i. no. 2021 and p. 377 n. 1; and Gras, *MSHDB* xv (1953), 33–4.

in 1387, the chancellor of the duchy of Burgundy, Nicolas de
Tholon, was promoted to the see of Autun, and in 1401 he was
succeeded, as a result of Philip's intervention, by another ducal
councillor, though this last died almost at once.[1] The two bishops
who followed one another at Auxerre after 1382 were both prominent
in the royal service,[2] and Philip was either unable or did not attempt
to influence appointments there. At Langres, on the other hand,
Louis de Bar, who was elected bishop in 1395 and administered the
see until after Philip's death, was closely connected with him: two of
Louis' brothers, Philippe and Henri de Bar, died on the Nicopolis
expedition, the former having for long periods resided at the ducal
court, where Louis de Bar himself was entertained on occasion.[3]

Before we leave the duchy, one further fact must be mentioned.
The recurrent visitations of the plague in the years and even decades
after 1348, coupled with the ravages of the companies, had caused
considerable mortality. Indeed, it seems likely that in the first half of
Philip the Bold's reign as duke, if not throughout it, the population
declined rapidly. A complete quantitative assessment of this is
impossible, but the figures of the taxable hearths all tell the same tale:
Nuits-Saint-Georges had 242 *feux* in 1377 but only 111 in 1400, and,
in the bailiwick of Chalon, forty-five per cent of the hearths seem to
have disappeared between 1360 and 1382. There is other evidence,
too, which points to widespread mortality between 1398 and 1400.[4]

There was nothing sudden or revolutionary in Philip the Bold's
acquisition of the county of Burgundy early in 1384: the ground had
been prepared long before.[5] For more than a century France had been
expanding slowly eastwards as, bit by bit, imperial territory was
nibbled away and annexed to the French crown. The line which
divided the two Burgundies was of course part of the Franco-
imperial frontier, and thus the dukes, taking part in this movement,
had extended their eastern boundaries at the expense of the counts.
Nor had they confined their attentions to the frontier, for they had
acquired territories and rights of various kinds in the interior of the
county. Before the end of the thirteenth century they had made their
first attempt to unite the county with the duchy, and Eudes IV had
actually achieved this union, which persisted from 1330 to 1361.

---

[1] Plancher, iii. 110; Aubrée, *Mémoires*, ii. 16 n.e.; and ACO B1528, f. 45.
[2] Lebeuf, *Mémoires*, i. 483–506.
[3] Daguin, *MSHAL* iii (1880–1901), 139, and *Itinéraires*, 322.
[4] *IACOB*, v. 107–8; Gras, *AB* xv (1943), 289–92; and Garnier, *Recherche*.
[5] See Richard, *Ducs de Bourgogne*, 226–8.

In considering Philip the Bold's relations with his people, the county presents a very different picture from the duchy. There were no towns of significance save for Besançon, which was not in fact part of the county; administrative and judicial institutions were either non-existent or relatively primitive; and Philip himself scarcely ever visited it. Moreover, the history of the county is in any case poorly documented, and Philip the Bold's reign there has received little attention from modern scholars. Although this area, dominated by a turbulent feudality, was theoretically administered by the council at Dijon with the help of the ducal governor, in fact Philip's authority was imposed and with difficulty extended chiefly through the *Parlement* of Dôle, which had the great advantage of being relatively old-established and therefore generally accepted. This institution, which was summoned approximately every other year throughout Philip's reign, was presided over by his faithful Dijon councillors, afforced in the early years by some of Margaret of Artois' councillors and officials, and was directly under his control. As a supreme court, it was the equivalent in the county of the *Parlement* of Beaune in the duchy, but, since the *Parlement* of Dôle was not in France, no appeals lay from it to Paris.

Although the Dôle *Parlement* had met in 1384 and 1385, the first important meeting in Philip's reign took place in May 1386. It was marked by the promulgation of a general *ordonnance*, soon afterwards confirmed by the duke, the object of which was the reorganization of the judicial system and the reform of procedure to bring both more into line with the practice of the duchy.[1] This *ordonnance* aroused widespread discontent among the nobles, whose judicial rights it infringed, and at the next two *Parlements*, in 1387 and 1388, its most offensive clauses were either repealed or modified. Further surrenders followed: in 1390 a long list of complaints was sent to the duke by four leading nobles, and countered with vague or ambiguous promises and one or two minor concessions; and in 1393 Philip found it expedient to repeal certain privileges of *bourgeoisie* he had granted to various individuals, which had the effect of removing the recipient from the jurisdiction of his lord and placing him under the special protection of the duke. But, if Philip was compelled to give ground, or abandon earlier claims, in the field of judicial rights in general, these years saw the successful imposition of his authority over one of the

---

[1] For what follows, see especially, Gollut, *Mémoires*; Plancher, iii; Clerc, *Franche-comté*, ii; *Ordonnances franc-comtoises*; and Blondeau, *MSED* (n.s.) v (1925), 79–103.

more rebellious nobles of the county, Jehan de Chalon, prince of Orange and baron of Arlay. In April 1390 Jehan de Chalon was party to the assassination of a ducal sergeant who had made himself particularly odious to him. Summoned to answer for his misdeed before a special tribunal, he failed to appear, and, while the ducal governor of the county, Jehan de Vergy, assembled troops and seized two of his castles, he himself was formally banished. Worse was to follow, for, in 1391, he fell into the hands of the duke and was imprisoned, first at Lille and then at Vantoux in the duchy. When he was finally pardoned, two years after his arrest, he had to accept the annexation of some of his lands to the ducal domain and construct a chapel in the parish church where the unfortunate sergeant had met his death. He also had to endow a thrice-weekly mass for the sergeant's soul.

The affair of Jehan de Chalon was a triumph for ducal authority in the county, and in the ensuing years this was further consolidated, principally by means of the Dôle *Parlement*. In 1401 another incident, closely similar, again demonstrated Philip's power, though it also showed the difficulties of enforcing his decisions. One of the Comtois nobles, Humbert de Villars, claimed that Montréal and other lands of his were allodial, and that the count of Burgundy had no rights of suzerainty over them. When he was summoned before the Dôle *Parlement* early in 1401, Humbert de Villars was unable to discredit the ducal *procureur*'s evidence of his vassality, and he was condemned to a fine of 1,000 francs and the confiscation of Montréal and its dependencies. To this double indignity he refused to submit, and retired to fortify his castles against further ducal action. In the event, Montréal was only annexed to the ducal domain in October 1402, after the governor of the county had called out the feudal levies and assembled an army of six hundred lances and four thousand others with which to lay siege to the castle. On the whole, Philip the Bold seems to have earned the respect and obtained the co-operation if not obedience of the Comtois nobility. It is perhaps significant that they willingly went to the help of his governor against Humbert de Villars, and that among the besiegers of Montréal was Jehan de Chalon himself. Furthermore, in the winter of 1400–1, fifteen Comtois nobles, led by Jehan de Vergy, had formed an escort for Philip in distant Paris.[1]

In this sketch of Philip the Bold's reign in the two Burgundies much has necessarily been omitted. Nothing has been said of his

[1] Bazin, *MSE* (n.s.) xxx (1902), 145.

considerable additions to the ducal domain; no mention has been made of the administration of the salt-industry of Salins; the treatment of Jews and Lombards; ducal wine-production; and the history of the mint at Auxonne, all of which would find a place in a detailed history of Burgundy at this time. The two Burgundies, however, were only a part of Philip the Bold's state, and we must turn now, in the next chapter, to that other vitally important part of it, the county of Flanders.

CHAPTER EIGHT

Philip the Bold, Count of Flanders

A detailed description of Flanders under Philip the Bold would be
out of place in this account of the formation of the Burgundian state.
The few salient features of his rule with which we shall be concerned
have been chosen partly because of their significance for the history
of Burgundy as a whole, and partly for their value in illustrating
Philip's policies and difficulties in Flanders. What follows is therefore
selective rather than systematic, and it is because of this that little or
no mention has been made of the comital mints and coinage, the
regulation of industry, the relations of the count with his vassals, and
many other problems.

The situation which faced Philip when he took over Flanders early
in 1384 was much worse than that of the duchy of Burgundy in 1363.
In the latter the disturbances and devastation were the work principally of the detested companies, and the ducal authority was supported by the bulk of the populace; but in Flanders they were
the result of a prolonged civil war initiated by a revolt against the
count. The way in which, in 1384 and 1385, Philip re-established
internal peace and the comital authority has been described in
Chapter Two, and his reconstruction of the administration and
governmental institutions of Flanders in 1385-6 has occupied us in
Chapter Six. In spite of this excellent initial work, the aftermath of
revolt formed a persistent background during the whole of the rest
of Philip's reign. For more than a decade after the peace of Tournai
his government was engaged in the prosecution and punishment of
the rebels, and concerned with the often rather sinister activities of
those who, banished from Flanders, had sought refuge in England,
Zeeland or elsewhere.[1] In 1387, indeed, a large-scale conspiracy, in
which these *bannis* and their English friends, allied with dissident

[1] ADN B1598, fos. 66b, 70, 75b; and AGR CC 13675, f. 15b and 13678, f. 80.

elements in Ghent, were closely involved, was unearthed by the government; and as late as 1400 there was a plot to hand over Saaftinge castle to the *bannis*, this time acting in concert with the Zeelanders.[1] Much of the devastation occasioned by the revolt had still not been repaired when Philip died in 1404. Domanial rents, for instance, were still in arrears in 1389 and 1396, and some had to be lowered in 1402, and this state of affairs was explicitly blamed on 'the troubles'.[2] The town of Ruppelmonde had been 'du tout arse, gastee et destruite' and in 1388 was 'encore presque toute desolee'; Courtrai was described as 'presque toute arse, gastée et destruite'; Grammont and Aalst suffered the same fate, and no attempt was made to restore the former's fortifications until 1403.[3] Damme was still in ruins in 1398.[4] At Ypres the suburbs had been entirely destroyed and some canals had been rendered useless, and, although the town was re-fortified in 1388–96, economic decline and depopulation followed inevitably.[5] Much more evidence of the same sort could be cited to prove that the widespread damage caused by the revolt was but slowly repaired. The economy of Flanders had in fact suffered a setback which was never wholly made good, and which struck particularly at the wealth and industry of her great cities.

It was not only the economy of Flanders which had suffered from the six years of revolt and war between 1379 and 1385, for her security and the security of her rulers had been undermined by the decay and destruction of her defences. Everywhere town walls were in disrepair, and most of the comital castles had suffered more or less severe damage, or even, in some cases, demolition. It was in these circumstances that Philip the Bold inaugurated a programme of re-building and repair as soon as he acquired Flanders in 1384, and continued to lavish funds and care on it throughout his reign, just as he had done, and continued to do, in his duchy of Burgundy.

The financing of this reconstruction of Flemish castles was by no means undertaken by Philip alone. As with Burgundy, so with Flanders and Artois, a series of ducal *ordonnances* from 1386 on made over the profits of justice to this purpose.[6] The local inhabitants, too, were made to pay directly for the fortifications designed to protect as

---

[1] Cartellieri, *P. der Kühne*, 129–38 and de Lichtervelde, *Grand commis*, 61.
[2] ADN B1597, f. 44b; 1598, f. 52b; 1599, f. 92b. See too, *IADNB*, iv. 27.
[3] ADN B1681, f. 45b; *IAC*, i. no. 61; AGR Trésor de Flandre (1), 978.
[4] ADN B1598, fos. 90a–b.
[5] Vandenpeereboom, *Ypriana*, ii. 110, 113–15, and *IAY*, ii. 303–5.
[6] ADN B1597, f. 2; 1598, fos. 47b and 76; 1599, fos. 22, 86b–87, etc.

well as to overawe them: Bruges and the Franc of Bruges contributed 23,000 *livres* of Paris to the new castle of Male;[1] the town of Courtrai was charged with purchasing properties and clearing a site for the castle there, and paid 2,000 francs towards the expense of building it; and the castles of Sluis and Oudenaarde were partly financed out of local contributions or *aides*. The two last were also subsidized with funds from another source: the French crown. In March 1402, for instance, Charles VI ordered all the arrears owed to the Paris *chambre des comptes* by the royal receivers to be used to help defray the expenses of the Sluis fortifications. Philip appointed Jehan Despoullettes, lately his receiver-general of all finances, to extract what he could from this source, and, when it realized a mere 2,500 francs, he renounced it, and took instead the promise of two lump sums, amounting to 50,000 francs, on specified royal receipts.[2] The king also paid, at first directly and subsequently by way of a special annual grant to Philip, for the maintenance of the garrison of Sluis castle, which comprised, in 1397, the captain, thirty-nine other men-at-arms, forty crossbowmen, forty *compagnons de pié*, six porters, two chaplains and two cannoneers; as well as for the garrison at Oudenaarde.

The works at Sluis, on the southern side of the entrance to the Zwin, which were begun in 1384 and continued throughout Philip's reign, were by far the most ambitious and elaborate of all his building projects in Flanders.[3] Between 1389 and 1397 nearly 100,000 francs were paid out for this purpose by the receiver-general of all finances alone. The site, which, together with the town of Sluis, was in the possession of William of Namur, was acquired by Philip in 1386 in exchange for Béthune; a bargain very much to Philip's advantage, but which William, one of his leading vassals, was in no position to resist. Two quite separate buildings were involved, standing on either side of the harbour mouth and linked when necessary by a

---

[1] Van Nieuwenhuysen, *Recette générale*, 141–2. For Courtrai, see *IAC*, i. no. 56. For another local *aide* 'pour l'avancement des ouvrages des chasteaux et maisons de Flandres', see Prevenier, *RBPH* xxxviii (1960), 354.
[2] Pocquet, *MSHDB* vi (1939), 138. For royal funds for Oudenaarde, see AGR Nelis, *MS. Analyses des chartes. Trésor de Flandre* (2), *acte* of 25 May 1388, and ADN B1846/11746. For the next sentence, see Plancher, iii. no. 177.
[3] For the start of the works, see above, p. 33; for the finances, van Nieuwenhuysen, *Recette générale*, 143; and for the acquisition of the site, Plancher, iii. 86, *IADNB*, i (1863), 194–6 and i (2), 353. See too, on the *tour de Bourgogne*, *IAB*, iii. 277–81 and, on the castle, *Cron. de Tournay*, 315.

chain: the castle of Sluis and the *tour de Bourgogne*. The castle, originally constructed of wood, was rebuilt in the years after 1384 in stone. The works were visited in 1387 by the royal architect, Raymond du Temple, and, in 1389, by the duchess.[1] The *tour de Bourgogne*, which was an entirely new structure, was begun in 1394 amid considerable difficulties caused by the sea, which several times breached the dikes constructed round the site to enable the foundations to be laid down. Indeed, work on these dikes became so urgent at one time that it was carried on at night by means of torches and lanterns.[2] John of Nevers laid the first stone on 4 September 1394 at a time when the duchess was able to report to her husband that the castle 'est tresbel ouvrage'. The fact that the *tour de Bourgogne* was finished within two years is a tribute to the skill and perseverance of Dino Rapondi, Philip's councillor and financial expert, who was entrusted with the financing and probably also with the general direction of the works.[3]

Besides Sluis, three other castles were entirely rebuilt by Philip the Bold. That at Oudenaarde was begun in October 1385 and was probably finished within ten years or so, for the accounts of the years 1395–1403 show that by this time only very small sums were being spent on it.[4] Work on a new castle at Male on the outskirts of Bruges, to replace the old one which had been burnt down in 1382, was begun in April 1390 and completed in 1396.[5] At Courtrai the castle had also been destroyed in 1382 but, although in 1386 Philip had enlisted the help of the town in replacing it, actual construction on the new castle was not begun until June 1394. Not only have the complete series of accounts of this work survived, which show that rather more than 60,000 *livres* of Paris was spent on it between March 1394 and December 1399, but also the original contemporary plans, carefully drawn on an entire skin.

In the 1390s this building programme, which had at first been limited to Sluis and Oudenaarde, was extended to include the repair and partial reconstruction of castles all over Flanders and Artois. At

---

[1] *Inventaires mobiliers*, ii. no. 1826 and Moranvillé, *le Mercier*, 110 n. 1.

[2] *IADNB*, i (1863), 239. For the next sentence, see Cartellieri, *P. der Kühne*, 147.

[3] He submitted an account for expenses on the *tour de Bourgogne*, 1 Feb. 1394–1 Dec. 1395, ADN B17602 (list of accounts of various fortifications); see too, Mirot, *BEC* lxxxix (1928), 349–52, and *IAB*, iii. 280–1.

[4] AGR CC 26479–26480.

[5] Cafmeyer, *ASEB* lxxxiii (1940–6), 120–6. For what follows, see Lavalleye, *ASRAB* xxxv (1930), 158–68. The accounts of Courtrai castle are AGR CC 26604–26614.

Antwerp the castle moats, which had fallen into such a state of disrepair that houses had been built in them, were cleared out and restored in 1393–5 on Philip's instructions and at the town's expense; at Nieuport the fortified church of St. Laurence, which did duty as a castle, was restored in 1394–8; and at Lille and Douai castles major works were in progress in 1389–1400.[1] Moreover, castles at Beveren, Aardenburg, Warneton, Ruppelmonde and elsewhere in Flanders, as well as many of those in Artois, Rethel and Limbourg, were restored in these years.[2]

Besides undertaking this work on his Flemish castles, Philip encouraged the towns to repair or rebuild their own fortifications. At Bruges these had been almost entirely reconstructed at the town's expense in 1383–4; at Sluis the defensive works begun at Louis of Male's behest in 1382 were continued throughout Philip's reign; and at Ypres the walls, which had received a severe battering during the English siege of 1383, were rebuilt in 1388–96.[3] The town of Limbourg received some financial assistance from the duke in 1398 to help defray the costs of repairing its fortifications. Thus, while the restoration of the comital castles facilitated the military control of the county against the possibility of further rebellion, the walls of its cities were rebuilt to secure its defences against the external threats of neighbouring powers like England and Guelders.

Although in the decade between their marriage in 1369 and the revolt of Ghent in 1379, Philip and Margaret visited Ghent and other places in Flanders almost annually, these contacts were not maintained when Philip became count in 1384. He was present in Flanders in 1382, 1383 and 1385 in a purely military capacity, to campaign against the rebels, and in 1384 and January 1386 he made his *joyeuse entrée* into the principal Flemish towns. After these five consecutive annual visits, *Flandre flamigante* 'Flemish Flanders' was more or less ignored by its ruler, except for two grand tours, when he spent a few days in each of the chief towns, the first in the winter of 1389–90, and the second, with John of Nevers, in 1398. Apart from these, visits to Flanders by either Philip or Margaret were infrequent, usually short, and often only incidental to a trip to Brabant: they are

[1] *IAGRCC*, iv. 264–6; ADN B17602 (list of accounts of various works); *IADNB*, i (1863), 232–60 *passim* and iv. 16, 19, 23, 26, 33; *Documents concernant l'histoire de l'art*, 674–5.

[2] *IADNB*, i (1863), 233, etc.; iv. 33–4; and van Nieuwenhuysen, *Recette générale*, 139–40.

[3] *IAB*, iii. n. 668; van Dale, *Sluis*, 47–54 and 160–73; and Vandenpeereboom, *Ypriana*, ii. 110, 113–14. For Limbourg, see ADN B1598, f. 91b.

recorded in Petit's *Itinéraire* of Philip the Bold in 1392, 1394 and 1401. While the Flemish were thus deprived of the presence of their rulers, they were also governed from outside their boundaries, for the administrative capital of Lille was south of the Lys in the French-speaking area of *Flandre gallicante*. On the other hand, it would be wrong to conclude from this that contacts between the people of Flanders and their count or his council at Lille were slight and infrequent, for the contrary was in fact true: if he did not deign to visit them, they, organized in the *vier leden* 'Four Members', were constantly sending deputations to him and his council, and, apart from the programme of castle-building, there was hardly a single aspect of government with which they were not intimately concerned.

Philip the Bold's relationship with his people was quite different in Flanders from that in the duchy of Burgundy, chiefly because in Flanders the populace was concentrated in a number of urban centres which individually enjoyed a much greater degree of autonomy than Dijon or the other Burgundian *communes*. Moreover, the most powerful of these—Ghent, Bruges and Ypres—regularly combined their political influence with that of the Franc of Bruges in the usually harmonious co-operation of the *parlementen* or meetings of the *vier leden* of Flanders. These Four Members, having arrogated to themselves some of the public attributes of the state, made it difficult or even impossible for Philip to rule without their active co-operation, especially as they exhibited a remarkable solidarity in defence of their common interests. Over their meetings and their activities in common he had little or no control. True, at the end of August 1391, at a council meeting in Lille at which their representatives were present, they were forbidden to meet together in future without the permission of the count or, in his absence, of his Lille council; but this was a verbal order only and seems to have been revoked or disregarded, for the *parlementen* of the Four Members continued to be held after this as often as they had been before.[1]

Although Philip had no control over the doings of the *vier leden* acting as a group, he was much better placed to intervene in the affairs of the individual *leden*, and, to an even greater extent, in those towns, like Courtrai and Oudenaarde, which did not form part of this privileged group. Everywhere, even inside the walls of Ghent, his bailiffs kept a watchful eye on the political and other activities of the townspeople. His deputies or financial officers could nowhere be

[1] *Handelingen*, Appendix No. 3, p. 436, and de Sagher, *ASEB* lxii (1912), 231, 237.

denied the right to inspect and audit the municipal accounts, and a copy of the accounts of every town save Ghent had to be deposited in the *chambre des comptes* at Lille.[1] Nor could municipal taxes be levied without his consent. The smaller towns for the most part recognized the jurisdiction of his *audience* and council, and their municipalities, like that of Dijon, were subject to at any rate partial sequestration by him. The administration of Courtrai, for instance, was in Philip's hands for five years and, when it was handed back, in 1399, he retained considerable powers over it.[2]

More important than any of these measures of control was the influence enjoyed by the ruler over municipal elections. The constitutions of the Flemish towns varied considerably, but in most of them the administration was entrusted to one or more benches of magistrates who were elected annually, and this annual renewal of the *loi* or magistrature was carried out by a group of comital deputies specially appointed for this purpose. At Bruges the two benches, each of thirteen magistrates, were wholly nominated by the count and, in practice, the other municipal offices were also in his gift. In 1398 the citizens attempted to make some alterations in the list of names which Philip had sent to his *commis* for the renewal of the *loi*, and, after a protracted squabble, he permitted them in future to put forward candidates of their own in place of some of his nominees for the second bench, provided this was done on the day of the renewal.[3] Whilst thus at Bruges virtually the entire magistrature was appointed by the count, at Ghent he exercised much less influence. Here the annual municipal elections took place on 14 August. The two benches of magistrates, each, as at Bruges, numbering thirteen, were selected by an electoral college of eight burgesses of Ghent, four chosen by the outgoing magistrates and four by the count or his deputies.[4] In other towns the count's powers were much more extensive and, within reasonable limits, a significant degree of control could be and was exercised by him over the municipal magistratures of Flanders. Moreover, the fact that the municipal accounts had to be passed by the comital deputies at the same time as the magistrature was renewed made this control even more effective.

[1] Richebé, *ACFF* xxii (1895), 141–84; van Werveke, *Gentsche stadsfinanciën*, 63–8; van Nieuwenhuysen, *Recette générale*, 26.   [2] *IAC*, i. no. 74.
[3] *IAB*, iii. no. 865. AGR Trésor de Flandre (2): copies of a ducal letter of 24 Aug. 1398 with list of ducal nominees and a 'memoire de la response faite par ceux de Bruges'; letters of Philip's *commis* to him, of 2 Sept. 1398, and from the Lille council to the chancellor of 21 Sept. 1398.
[4] *Rekeningen der stad Gent*, 522.

The interest of the government in the Flemish municipal elections is amply documented and well illustrated in a memorandum sent to Philip and his chancellor in 1386 by the council at Lille.[1] The councillors point out that the day for the renewal of the *loi* of Ghent is approaching and advise the duke if possible to carry this out in person at Ghent, or, failing this, to be as near to Flanders as possible. They also ask him to appoint one or two councillors to make secret enquiries at Ghent among his supporters to discover the most suitable candidates for municipal office.

In spite of the influence and even control which Philip exercised over the individual *leden*, on occasions indeed because of it, a number of incidents occurred in all of them, most of which were demonstrations against the government, whether they took the form of popular disturbances or outright disputes with the duke or his administration. The riot at Bruges in the autumn of 1386, during which the duke of Berry was attacked and unhorsed, was probably provoked by the behaviour of the French army which Philip had assembled at Sluis for the invasion of England; but those of 1387 and 1391 seem to have been due to the weavers, and were probably aimed at the government of Bruges rather than that of Flanders.[2] In Ghent there were at least two disturbances in 1392, about which little certain is known except that they were directed against the comital government. Opposition to Philip the Bold's religious policy and defence of municipal privileges against the activities of the comital officers were the probable motives. One of these disturbances, which broke out on 15 March, began with an attack on supporters and friends of the count. The bailiff, hearing that more of the same was promised for the morrow, took to his heels that same night and fled; and the government was sufficiently disturbed to make preparations for raising troops.[3]

---

[1] ADN B517/11715. The year is fixed by the reference to a meeting of the Hanse towns at Lübeck on 13 July, see *Hans. Urkundenbuch*, iv. nos. 873 and 874.

[2] Kervyn, *Flandre*, iv. 63–4; *IAB*, iii. 102–3, 233; *Cartulaire de l'ancienne Estaple de Bruges*, i. 371–3.

[3] AGR CC 13678, f. 13a–b; 14106, account for 8 Jan. 1391/2–6 May 1392, f. 11 and account for 6 May–16 Sept. 1392, f. 11b; van Dixmude, *Merkwaerdige gebeurtenissen*, 21–2; *IADNB*, i (1863), 220. See too, Cartellieri, *P. der Kühne*, 145 (no. 9), de Lichtervelde, *Grand commis*, 11 n. 12 and van Asseldonk, *Schisma*, 92 with references given there (n. 354). I do not know on what evidence Fris (*Gand*, 106) places the religious disturbance at Ghent in January 1392.

Besides the occasional riots in which some of them were involved, each of the Four Members engaged in at least one more or less serious and prolonged dispute with Philip or his officials. Bruges, as we have seen, quarrelled with him in 1398–9 over the renewal of its magistrature. The Franc of Bruges quarrelled with the comital administration in 1393 over the arrest by the bailiff of Ypres of some subjects of the Franc accused of homicide. The magistrature of the Franc had attempted to exercise jurisdiction over the bailiff by fining him 50 *livres* and asking his colleague of Bruges to collect the money from him, and to exert pressure on the government by going on strike. The affair went to the Lille council in July 1393 and was finally settled by Philip himself in March 1394 in a judgement against the Franc, which was condemned to a fine of 6,000 nobles.[1] Another quarrel of a similar kind broke out in 1398, but ended in a victory for the Franc. At Ypres there was a dispute in 1395 over the summons of some of the burgesses to the Lille council, and, towards the end of the reign, the magistrature was in conflict with the bailiff over certain alleged infringements of its privileges. In autumn 1401 it had threatened to apply, and perhaps actually applied, to the king of France for a royal governor to replace or supervise the comital bailiff.[2]

The most serious of all these quarrels was that between Ghent and the sovereign-bailiff of Flanders, Jacques de Lichtervelde, who had executed a burgess of Ghent convicted of conspiracy and treason, in spite of the fact that only the magistrature had jurisdiction over its own burgesses. This dispute, which originated in June 1400 as a delicate conflict of privileges, was within a few months converted, by the brutal and unilateral action of Ghent in banishing the sovereign-bailiff for fifty years, into a political quarrel of the most serious proportions. It lasted two years, necessitated at least thirty-five meetings of the Four Members, the other three of which took up a moderate position and tried to mediate, involved the king of France, the *Parlement* of Paris and the three Estates of Flanders; and was finally settled by an elaborate compromise: the offending sovereign-bailiff was quietly packed off on an extended pilgrimage to Palestine and elsewhere subsidized by Philip the Bold, while the magistrates of Ghent agreed to erase his name from their register of banishments.

---

[1] AGR Trésor de Flandre (1), 671–3; de Lichtervelde, *Grand commis*, makes this two separate disputes, pp. 16–17, nn. 35–6. For the next sentence, see ibid., 48–52.

[2] *Handelingen*, nos. 315–26; van Dixmude, *Merkwaerdige gebeurtenisse*, 22; *IAY*, iii. 5 and ADN B1363/14931 bis.

Philip seems to have had the last word, however, for Jacques de Lichtervelde took up office again in the autumn of 1403 after his return from abroad.[1]

While opposition to Philip the Bold was expressed, in the individual *leden*, in popular disturbances and quarrels with his administration, a much more general and consistent opposition was carried on by the Four Members acting together in their *parlementen*. From time to time they openly resisted his policies and administration, and submitted grievances to him. They complained of the damage done by his rabbits to the coastal dunes; they intervened on numerous occasions in his monetary policy and sometimes directly opposed it; and they repeatedly requested him to visit or reside in Flanders.[2] These complaints came to a head in 1398–1400, when they were reinforced by a number of protests against the activities of the comital council at Lille, prominent among which were demands that Flemish should be made an optional language at its proceedings as it already was in the *audience*, and that the powers of the *procureur général* 'qui est officier nouvel et non necessaire' should be severely restricted or abolished.[3] On the whole, Philip remained firm: he made no attempt either to muzzle the Four Members or to redress their grievances.

In spite of their constant criticism of Philip the Bold's regime, the Four Members played an active and constructive part in the government of Flanders. In particular, it was they and not, as elsewhere, the Estates, who were responsible for voting extraordinary taxes on behalf of the whole country. Their powers in this respect did not include Artois, nor the towns and dependencies of Antwerp, Malines, Lille, Douai and Orchies, all of which voted separately. Nor did they cover a number of miscellaneous and more or less local subsidies of a specialized kind, like that granted by Bruges towards the fortifications at Sluis. Whereas, in the duchy of Burgundy, the Estates seldom opposed the ducal request for an *aide* of, usually, 40,000 francs, which was made approximately every other year between 1380 and 1397, in Flanders Philip's requests for *aides* were much less frequent and were almost invariably bitterly opposed. The only consolation which Flanders offered him in this respect was the much larger size of its

---

[1] De Lichtervelde (*Grand commis*, 61–93, 105, 107) describes the quarrel in detail. See now also, *Handelingen*, nos. 501–55.

[2] *Handelingen*, no. 425 and ADN B1598, f. 98a–b (rabbits); *Handelingen*, *Index van zaken*, 'Munt' and 'Residentie'.

[3] ADN B865/14582. See too de Lichtervelde, *Grand commis*, 53–4, and *Handelingen*, nos. 315–26, 397–408, 415 ff, etc.

aides, which averaged well over 100,000 francs each. This meant that its average *annual* contribution in extraordinary taxes was greater than that of Burgundy: a fact which is doubtless related to its superior wealth.[1]

The most conspicuous feature of the Flemish *aides* in Philip's reign was the extreme reluctance of the Four Members to vote them, and the dilatory manner in which the Flemish paid them. At first, probably because the demands were limited and reasonable, they made little difficulty in voting the required sums: thus in 1384 and 1386 a monthly *aide* was readily voted; and early in 1388 the first major *aide*, of 100,000 francs, was granted to subsidize the war against Guelders, which seems to have been popular in Flanders. The Flemish, however, found it much easier to vote these taxes than to pay them. Payment of the 1386 *aide* was refused outright by some towns, and we learn from a letter of the duchess that the 1388 *aide* had still not been fully paid in August 1394.[2] After 1388 all Philip's financial demands were resisted, and either diminished or successfully refused. In August 1391 he asked for 60,000 nobles, and the instructions issued to his deputies appointed to negotiate this with the Four Members indicate the elaborate care he took to put his request in an acceptable form.[3] They were to explain the difficulties of keeping peace and order with inadequate funds; point out the expenses which Philip had incurred in entertaining the king in Burgundy the year before and in visiting Milan in the spring of 1391; and draw attention to the fact that, since he had become count of Flanders, he had been voted only one *aide*, and had abstained from requesting one for the marriage of his eldest son in 1385. This care was not wholly lavished in vain, for the Four Members, though they refused to vote the required sum, granted 45,000 nobles a month later.[4] In 1394, when Philip was raising money for his projected crusade, he entrusted the task of extracting a contribution from the

---

[1] See the tables below, pp. 232–3. For what follows, see Gachard, *Rapport* . . . *Lille*, 66–7; *Handelingen, Index van zaken*, 'Bede'; van Nieuwenhuysen, *Recette générale*, 68–70, 106–9, 173; and Prevenier, *RBPH* xxxviii (1960), 330–65.   [2] ADN B517/11715 and B18822/23260.

[3] They are analysed in ADN D. Godefroy, *MS. Inventaire chronologique de la chambre des comptes de Lille*, xi. 467, and wrongly numbered B1274/11993. I have not been able to find the actual document. Godefroy's analysis gives sufficient material for dating these instructions from internal evidence. For the conference with the Four Members to which Philip's deputies were sent with them, see *Handelingen*, no. 182.

[4] ADN B1597, f. 36b.

Flemish to his Flemish wife Margaret, but, in spite of weeks of protracted negotiation, she had to be content with a mere 65,000 nobles,
instead of the 100,000 her husband had hoped for. The same thing
happened in 1397 when funds were needed to ransom John of Nevers:
Philip asked for 150,000 nobles, but was granted only 100,000, after
prolonged wrangling and not before he had promised, as a *quid pro
quo*, to relax his policy of sequestrating the property of those who had
taken part in the revolt of 1379–85.[1] This was the last occasion on
which the Flemish acceded to their ruler's demands for extra funds:
in 1400 and 1403, when asked for 30,000 and 120,000 nobles, they
refused to contribute anything.

The other aspect of government with which the Four Members
were concerned in a positive way was the regulation of commerce
and the negotiation of commercial treaties. The prosperity of Bruges,
in particular, depended very largely on the exploitation of foreign
trade, for it was at Bruges that the products of the Baltic were exchanged with those of the Mediterranean. Moreover, besides this
transit trade, Flanders itself was a major exporting and importing
country, since her cloth industry depended on the import of wool from
overseas, chiefly England, and the export in all directions of its
finished or partly finished products. This flourishing commerce was
mainly in the hands of foreigners, for the Flemish themselves
exhibited few seafaring inclinations at this time, except when the
dubious attraction of piracy tempted them to act against their own
best interests. The overriding importance of foreign merchants in the
economy of Flanders is illustrated by the many grants of privileges
issued to them by the rulers and, not least, by Philip the Bold. Some
of these grants were made at the request of the Four Members; in all
of them, Philip's motives are clearly expressed in some such formula
as 'desirans de tout nostre povoir augmenter le fait de la marchandise'.
The most prized privileges were, of course, the rights of free ingress
and egress and of free commerce. They were confirmed or granted
by Philip the Bold to, among others, the Portuguese, Castilian and
Aragonese merchants visiting Flanders, and to the merchants of
Scotland, Ireland, Berwick, Newcastle, Norwich and La Rochelle.[2]

---

[1] Above, pp. 63, 74, and ADN B1598, f. 66b.
[2] Laenen, *Archives à Vienne*, no. 171 (Portuguese); Finot, *ACFF* xxiv
(1898), 126–32 and 329–41 (Castilian, Aragonese, etc.); *IAB*, iii. nos. 663
and 688 (Portuguese); ADN B1597, f. 8 (Scottish); *IAB*, iii. no. 689 and
Cartulaire de l'ancienne Estaple de Bruges, i. no. 483 (Berwick); *IAB*, iii. no
690 (Ireland); ADN B1598, f. 71b (Newcastle); *Cartulaire de l'ancienne*

In the case of larger groups of merchants, or of commercial powers, the simple grant of privileges was replaced by a regular commercial treaty, such as that with Genoa of 1395, in which, among other things, Philip promised to give the Genoese merchants in Flanders eight months' notice of expulsion.[1] Of commercial powers, two were especially important for Flanders: the Hanse or Hanseatic League, and England. The bulk of the Baltic trade with Flanders was in the hands of the former; most of the Flemish wool imports on which her towns depended were in the hands of the latter. In Philip's reign Flemish relations with both these powers were disturbed and difficult, and necessitated prolonged negotiation, much of which was carried out jointly by himself and the Four Members, thus exemplifying the constructive part which the latter played, at any rate in commercial affairs.

The Hanseatic League was at its apogee in the last quarter of the fourteenth century. Its member towns were scattered, in North Germany and especially along the southern shores of the Baltic and the North Sea, between Cologne and Reval, and met irregularly in a Diet which conferred on the Hanse something of the character of a federal state. Timber, furs, wax, salt, amber and other products were exported by its merchants to London, Bruges and elsewhere, while cloth, manufactured articles and Mediterranean commodities were imported. In this commercial network Bruges was a key point, for it was here that the Hansards had fixed the staple for a large part of their trade with Western Europe and the Mediterranean. Their principal weapon for ensuring the security and privileges of their merchants in foreign parts was the embargo or commercial boycott, and they had used this to good effect against Flanders in 1358–60, when the Bruges staple was removed to Dordrecht in Holland. When Philip the Bold became count of Flanders in 1384 relations between the Hanse and Flanders were approaching a similar crisis, chiefly owing to Louis of Male's policy of confiscation and reprisal against them, which was intensified when he discovered their sympathies and contacts with the rebels of Ghent in 1382. But, although the Hansards had already opened negotiations with Albert of Bavaria, the ruler of Holland, with a view to the restoration of their staple to

---

Estaple de Bruges, i. no. 496 (Norwich); Finot, *ACFF* xxi (1893), 103 (La Rochelle).

[1] *Documenti ed estratti,* i. *Brabante, Fiandra e Borgogna,* no. 3 and *Cartulaire de l'ancienne Estaple de Bruges,* i. no. 469.

Dordrecht, they remained open to further talks with the Flemish, no doubt because of the many advantages of Bruges. In the summer of 1386, when the Flemish heard that the Hanse was to meet in July at Lübeck to consider withdrawing its staple from Bruges,[1] a combined embassy from Philip and the Four Members hastened to the meeting and was able to arrange a conference at Cologne for 11 November 1386. In the event this was put off, and a new series of negotiations followed in the summer of 1387 at Dordrecht and Antwerp, during which the problem of reparations to the Hanse for damage done to its merchants by the Flemish proved insoluble. In the following summer the staple was finally withdrawn from Bruges and a commercial boycott of Flanders proclaimed and imposed.

Soon after the withdrawal of the Hansards from Flanders Philip set about trying to coax them back: in October 1388 he wrote to ask the Grand Master of the Teutonic Order to help fix a conference somewhere near Flanders, and in December he wrote to the Wendish towns asking them to arrange a meeting to finish the negotiations which had been broken off after the Antwerp conference of 1387. Contacts were maintained, and, at a meeting in Lübeck in September 1389, attended by the deputies of the Four Members and Philip's ambassadors, the Hanse laid down its conditions for the return of the staple to Bruges: the Flemish were to make a formal apology for the damages they had caused, as well as financial reparation. Agreement in principle, however, was not reached until November 1391, and even then discussions continued in 1392, nearly breaking down at one point when the Hanse demanded the removal from Philip's draft grant of privileges of a clause invalidating them automatically in the event of a Flemish revolt against him. Philip however yielded and ordered his secretary to remove the offending clause, while at the same time making it quite clear to the Four Members that the Hanse privileges would be revoked if the Flemish took up arms against him. At last, in December 1392, the Hanse restored its staple to Bruges, and in January 1393 one hundred Flemish burgesses made a formal public apology to the Hansards assembled in the Carmelite convent in Bruges. Nor was this the end of the story, for the unfortunate Flemish had also to dispatch pilgrimages in all directions: sixteen persons to Rome, sixteen to the shrine of St. James at Compostella, and four to Jerusalem. These moral reparations were combined with financial ones, and it was not until 1394 that the Flemish towns

[1] ADN B517/11715; see above, p. 175, n. 1.

completed the payment of the 11,100 lb. of Flemish *gros* which the Hansards had exacted from them.[1]

If, at the beginning of his reign as count, Philip was faced by a hostile Hanse intent on reparations or the commercial boycott of Flanders, his relations with England were even less auspicious for the prosperity of his newly acquired subjects. During the revolt of Ghent England had sympathized with the rebels: in 1383 a combined force from England and Ghent had laid siege to Ypres, at that time loyal to the count, and, in 1385, Ghent had accepted an English captain. In 1386 Philip the Bold planned to carry the war across the Channel from the invasion port of Sluis, but at the last moment the attempt was deferred, and later cancelled. Its aftermath was unfortunate for the Flemish, for, in the spring of 1387, they suffered from the attentions of an English fleet which lay for some weeks off Sluis, and even sent pillaging expeditions ashore.

In spite of these hostilities, neither Philip nor the English were seriously intent on prosecuting the war, and the unofficial talks at Calais in the autumn of 1387 between the English authorities there and the deputies of the Four Members of Flanders, were taken up by both sides. Parallel Anglo-French and Anglo-Flemish negotiations, the former at Leulinghen or elsewhere, the latter usually at Calais, were set on foot and continued intermittently during the ensuing years. They did not, however, result in a peace, but only in truces, which at first had to be renewed annually: a commercial one between England and Flanders, and a general one between England and France. The former was apparently firmly consolidated by 1390; the latter only in 1396, when Richard II married Isabel of France and the famous twenty-eight-year Anglo-French truce was proclaimed. Thus, in the first decade of his reign, Philip had achieved a two-fold success through a policy of co-operation with the Four Members: the restoration of uninterrupted commerce both with the Hansards and the English—the two powers on which the prosperity of Flanders so largely depended.

Apart from an isolated incident in 1396, Anglo-Flemish commerce seems to have flourished peacefully between 1388 and 1400. Then, in

[1] For the above, works like Lindner, *Wenzel* (ii. 251–9); Daenell, *Blütezeit der Hanse* (i. 76–88); Cartellieri, *P. der Kühne*; Bahr, *Handel und Verkehr;* Friccius, *HG* lvii (1932), 59–77; and Beuken, *Hanze en Vlaanderen*, have been supplemented by the printed sources: *Dortmunder Urkundenbuch*, ii; *Urkunden zur Geschichte der Hanse* in Mone's *Anzeiger*, vi (1837), cols. 126–36, 271–82, 382–9; *IAB*, iii; *Hansisches Urkundenbuch*, iv, v; *Recesse der Hansetage*, iii, iv; *Handelingen* (see the *Index van zaken*, 'Hanze').

the last years of Philip's life, it was once more seriously endangered, this time through events beyond his control.

At the end of the fourteenth century there emerged two distinct threats to the maritime trade of north-west Europe: piracy and renewed Anglo-French hostility. The English were not the only people responsible for the former, for the Four Members, supported by Philip, had laid their complaints of the piratical activities of the Zeelanders before Albert of Bavaria's ambassadors as early as May 1398, and a long series of discussions and conferences on this problem occupied the next three years. The deterioration of Anglo-French relations was due to elements in France hostile to Henry IV, who had usurped the English throne from Richard II in 1399. Prolonged attempts were made on all sides to palliate or remove these two potential harbingers of war. Thus, in spite of the sack of Alderney, Plymouth and the Isle of Wight, by unofficial French expeditions in 1403, Anglo-French talks continued at Leulinghen in the same year as well as in 1404. Similarly, Anglo-Flemish talks continued in 1403 and 1404 in the face of the mounting activity of John Hawley of Dartmouth and other noted English pirates, which led to Flemish reprisals, and both the Anglo-French and the Anglo-Flemish negotiations continued long after Philip's death in April 1404.

Owing to the absence of any systematic and scholarly study of Anglo-French and Anglo-Flemish relations at this time,[1] it is impossible to follow them in detail, and difficult to ascertain the real motives and the degree of enthusiasm of the participants. This is especially true in the case of Philip the Bold, but those historians who have portrayed him as encouraging the bellicose adventures against England of his rival Louis of Orleans, his vassal the count of St. Pol, and others, against the interest of his peace-loving Flemish

---

[1] Most existing accounts of the latter are incomplete and misleading, especially Hingeston in *Royal letters of Henry IV*, pp. xlviii–lxi; Varenbergh, *Flandre et Angleterre*, 469–89; Owen, *England and Burgundy*, 15–20; and Söchting, *HV* xxiv (1927–9), 182–3. Better, but still incomplete, is de Coussemaker, *ACFF* xxvi (1901–2), 282–90. Kervyn, *Flandre*, iv; Wylie, *Henry IV*, i; Cartellieri, *P. der Kühne*; and Huguet, *Aspects de la Guerre de Cents Ans en Picardie maritime*, are useful. The principal printed sources and inventories are: *Codex Germaniae diplomaticus*, ii. cols. 2127–32; *Foedera*, iii, iv; *Proceedings of the Privy Council*, i; Gachard, *Rapport . . . Lille; Royal letters of Henry IV; IADNB*, i (1863) and i (1) and (2); *IAB*, iii; Varenbergh, *Flandre et Angleterre*, 540–6; *Documents pour servir à l'histoire des relations entre l'Angleterre et la Flandre;* Cartellieri, *P. der Kühne*, 123–4 and 154–8; *Söchting, HV* xxiv (1927–9), 193–8; *Actes concernant les rapports entre les Pays-Bas et la Grande Bretagne de 1293 à 1468*, no. 3; *Handelingen.*

subjects, are surely mistaken. The evidence available so far is conflicting, but most of it points to Philip as an opponent of the war party in France.[1] At no time did he refuse to send his deputies to the Anglo-Flemish discussions at Calais. Between July 1402 and August 1403 these discussions only concerned reparations for infringements of the Anglo-French truce of 1396, and they were undertaken by the Four Members alone, not because Philip was unwilling to join them, but because it was the Flemish who had suffered at the hands of English pirates and who therefore demanded restitution or reparation.[2] When, in the summer of 1403, as a result of the requests of the Four Members for the neutrality of Flanders in the event of open war between England and France, Philip obtained from Charles VI permission to negotiate a separate commercial truce for Flanders, he became an interested party and consequently sent a strong delegation to the Calais conference in April 1404. Further indirect evidence of his policy is afforded by his relations with the Four Members, for there is no sign of that determined opposition which was invariably aroused when he pursued a policy which they radically disliked. True, they several times asked him to promise Flemish neutrality in the Anglo-French war, and they refused his requests, in 1400 and 1403, to raise troops for the defence of Flanders against a possible English attack. But otherwise there is every indication that Philip and the Four Members were acting broadly in concert in this matter. It may, incidentally, be noted that it was they, not he, who caused a delay of some months by absenting themselves from the conference they had arranged at Calais for 10 November 1403, a fact which leads one to wonder how far the Four Members themselves really were endeavouring to expedite the interminable parleying which occupied so many years.

No discussion of Philip the Bold as count of Flanders would be complete without some mention of the Great Schism and the Church. The county of Flanders was unequally divided between three dioceses: those of Thérouanne, Tournai and Cambrai. These were all of them effectively French sees and lay in the French archdiocese of Rheims. When, in 1378, the Great Schism broke out, the bishops of these

---

[1] See above, pp. 51–2.
[2] See the excerpt from a letter of the English ambassadors at Calais, *Royal letters of Henry IV*, 181, where a clear distinction is drawn between negotiations for a commercial truce or treaty, in which Philip would have to join, and negotiations for compensation for damages, which was a private matter for the parties concerned.

three dioceses followed the example of France and gave their allegiance to the French pope, Clement VII, while the Flemish populace, together with its count Louis of Male, opted for Urban VI. When Philip the Bold acquired Flanders early in 1384, this internal schism between the Flemish and their bishops was exacerbated by a new one between them and their ruler, for Philip was at that time a convinced supporter of Clement.[1]

During Louis of Male's reign various unsuccessful attempts had been made by France to bring Flanders into the obedience of Clement VII. The towns which submitted to the victors of Roosebeke were compelled to declare allegiance to Clement, but this transaction was for them a meaningless formality. Embassies were sent to Louis, but were totally without effect. Philip must have been gratified by the public conversion, within a month or so of his accession to the county, of the chapter of St. Peter's, Lille, to the obedience of Clement, but he could have had no illusions about the general situation of Flanders. Many of the nobles were open supporters of Clement, Yolande of Bar in particular; the ducal secretariat as a whole was in favour of Clement; and the French pope had numerous supporters in the French-speaking areas which, of course, included Lille; but the bulk of the populace, together with the powerful *communes* of Ghent, Bruges and Ypres, was firmly Urbanist. Force was out of the question, and when he signed the peace of Tournai in December 1385, Philip specifically allowed the citizens of Ghent liberty of conscience to follow the pope of their choice. But if he was tolerant, Philip was by no means neutral: he had presided in person over an assembly of the three Estates of Flanders at Lille in September 1384 at which his government's sympathies for the French pope were made abundantly clear. In the following years, however, no further moves of this sort were made. Evidently the government fully appreciated the difficulties. On 2 December 1386 Jehan le Fèvre, bishop of Chartres, recorded in his journal a conversation with Jehan Canard, bishop of Arras and chancellor of Philip the Bold. To his enquiries concerning the possibility of putting an end to the schism in Flanders, the chancellor replied in the negative: the Flemish, he observed, were more obstinate than ever.[2]

New hopes were raised on the death of Urban VI in 1389, in spite

---

[1] For what follows, see especially, Valois, *France et le Grand Schisme*, ii. 224–71; Nelis, *RHE* xxviii (1932), 34–69; Leman, *RHE* xxv (1929), 239–259; de Moreau, *Église en Belgique*, iv. 15–20, 27–31; van Asseldonk, *Schisma*; and the references given in these works.   [2] Le Fèvre, *Journal*, i. 327.

of the fact that he was at once provided with a successor. Early in 1390 the three Estates of Flanders were summoned to Oudenaarde and harangued by the chancellor; the powers of the officials appointed in Flanders by Urban were officially declared to have lapsed; and an embassy from Clement arrived in the county. Philip now initiated a policy of more definite persuasion, and, in spite of the bitter feelings which were roused in the spring of 1390 by the arrest—without Philip's knowledge—of an Urbanist legate in Flanders, the Flemish began to weaken and to drift over piecemeal into the obedience of Clement. By the end of 1393 this process had gone so far that almost the whole of Flanders had abandoned Urban or at least accepted the jurisdiction of the bishops who recognized Clement. Ghent alone remained firm—and even there supporters of Clement began to appear from 1390 on. Philip's striking victory had not, however, been won entirely through his own efforts. The defection of Bruges, for instance, from the Urbanist obedience, was largely brought about by the intemperate and even violent behaviour of the Urbanist official there, and his superior, Jehan du Mont.

Philip the Bold was well aware of the value of being able to appoint to ecclesiastical benefices, and he made particular use of the powers conferred on him in this respect or exercisable by him as ruler, in the interests of the French pope. Clement VII empowered him to confer one benefice in each of the cathedral and collegiate churches of Flanders on one of his chaplains or chapel clerks, and permitted him also to appoint to 120 benefices both in and outside France.[1] Other benefices were conferred by the pope on individuals recommended to him by Philip. In Flanders a special interest was taken by the government in some of the more important appointments. Thus in 1394 John of Nevers persuaded the aged Urbanist abbot of St. Bavo's, Ghent, to resign, and the monks, no doubt under the influence of the government, elected a supporter of Clement as his successor. At the same time, John of Nevers, hearing that Guillaume Vernachten, the provost of St. Donatian's at Bruges, was gravely ill, wrote to his father proposing his tutor, Baudouin de la Nieppe, as his successor. Philip encouraged his wife to influence the chapter of St. Donatian's on Baudouin's behalf, but in fact his election had to be deferred, because of the provost's survival, until 1397.[2]

If any general conclusions can be drawn from this brief and necessarily incomplete sketch of Philip the Bold's reign in Flanders, they

[1] BN Coll. de Bourg. 53, f. 107.
[2] ADN B18822/23245 and 23294; *IAB*, iii. 400 n. 1; and *IAEG*, no. 657.

must surely be favourable to him. He found the county in the throes of a civil war directed against the authority of the count. Not only did he restore it to peace, but, with the help of an efficient administration, a loyal personnel, and, above all, the council at Lille, he placed the comital authority on a firmer footing than it had ever been before. All this was done without alienating the sympathies of a proud and sensitive populace, for, though Philip quarrelled with the Four Members on more than one occasion, he was statesman enough never to push these quarrels too far. Moreover, in several important matters, such as the negotiations with the Hanse and England, and those with Albert of Bavaria over the piratical Zeelanders, he and they co-operated together for their common advantage. In his reign Flanders enjoyed a period of peaceful recovery from the turmoil of 1379–85, during which even its religious dissensions were palliated or removed: Philip the Bold brought it firmly yet gently into the Burgundian state, and ruled it wisely.[1]

[1] It is unfortunate that I have been unable to use the first volume of Philip the Bold's *ordonnances* (1381–1393) concerning the Low Countries, which is shortly to be published by the Commission royale des anciennes Lois et Ordonnances, edited by J. Bartier and A. van Nieuwenhuysen.

CHAPTER NINE

The Burgundian Court and Philip the Bold's Patronage of the Arts

Although the Burgundian court was the creation of Philip the Bold, he was not, in this respect, an innovator: he simply followed the princely fashions of the time. Everywhere, in the fourteenth century, court life flourished and grew in extravagance and complexity while the rulers themselves, acquiescing in or consciously encouraging the lavish display of material wealth which this growth entailed, became patrons of the arts on a scale hitherto unknown. Their courts, as well as that of the popes at Avignon, became the leading centres of cultural and artistic life, and it was for them that many of the finest products of late-medieval architecture, sculpture, wood carving, painting, book illumination, jewellery, goldsmithery, tapestry and music were made. In all this, as well as in the grosser and more ephemeral elements of court life—banquets, tournaments, processions and the like—Philip the Bold saw to it that Burgundy was second to none.

Wherever he went, the duke was invariably attended by knights and squires, councillors and secretaries, and other administrative officers.[1] His and their material needs were catered for by the various services or offices of the court: the *paneterie*, *échansonnerie*, *cuisine* and *écurie*, each in the care of a *premier écuyer* helped respectively by *écuyers panetiers*, *écuyers échansons*, *écuyers tranchants* and *écuyers d'écurie*, and staffed with numerous pages, waiters and other servants and menials. There were two other services of a lower status but equal importance: the *fruiterie* and the *fourrière*. The *paneterie* was

---

[1] For what follows, see especially Plancher, iii. 575–7; Canat, *Marguerite de Flandre*; and *Hist. des institutions françaises*, ii. 213–14. For the whole of this chapter I am much indebted to David's two fine studies, *P. le Hardi, train somptuaire* and *P. le Hardi, protecteur des arts*.

primarily responsible for the provision of bread, though it also purveyed salt and mustard. The *échansonnerie* was concerned only with the provision of wine for the duke and his court. The kitchen, which was much larger than either of these departments, was responsible for preparing and serving the two daily meals, dinner at midday and supper in the evening. The *écurie* looked after the horses,[1] while the *fourrière*, if the court was on the move, had to find and prepare lodgings for the night, as well as being responsible for tapestries and furnishing of all kinds. Lastly, the *fruiterie* supplied not only fruit, but also spices, candles and torches. Besides these permanent and essential services, others were attached to the court more or less continuously, or only intermittently. Among the quasi-permanent services were those provided by the musical chapel under the *premier chapelain*,[2] which was quite distinct from the chapel at Hesdin and the Sainte-Chapelle at Dijon, the confessors and almoners, physicians and barbers, minstrels or musicians, fools, dwarfs, giants and others. The services which were intermittently attached to the court included the *vénerie* 'ducal hunt' and *fauconnerie*, each comprising a staff of twenty or thirty persons, as well as the menagerie, the pride of which was the leopard given to Philip by Giangaleazzo Visconti of Milan, and which contained also a porcupine and a bear.[3]

It is not easy to assess the actual size of Philip the Bold's court at any one time. For one thing, it varied enormously according to the importance of the occasion, the number of guests, and the presence or absence of the duchess and John of Nevers. For another, the titles of many of its officers were used for honorific purposes: Dino Rapondi, the Italian banker and financial adviser of Philip the Bold, was *maître d'hôtel*, but it is unlikely that he ever served at court; and the eighty-seven chamberlains listed by one historian as holding office in 1384–6[4] were many of them only titular. Moreover, most of the court offices were collegiate, the officers serving by rota, like the ducal secretaries. Thus, of the six or eight *maîtres d'hôtel*, only two served at any one time. The few surviving *escroes*—the slips of parchment on which the daily expenses of the court and the number of persons and horses present were recorded—alone give an exact

---

[1] See Picard, *MAD* (4) x (1905–6), 307–439.
[2] Technically separated from the *hôtel* by an *ordonnance* of 1397, *Hist. des institutions françaises*, ii. 214 n. 3.
[3] *Inventaires mobiliers*, i. no. 2436 and pp. 463 n. 7 and 466 n. 2. For the *vénerie* and *fauconnerie* in Burgundy, see Picard, *MSE* (n.s.) ix (1880), 297–418.   [4] Beaune, *RNHB* (n.s.) i (1865), 49–56.

idea of the size of the court. On 4 December 1371, when both Philip and the duchess were at Rouvres, they were accompanied by one hundred persons, including *valets*, and seventy-six horses;[1] but later, especially after the acquisition of Flanders in 1384, the court grew much larger. On 25 January 1385, at Cambrai, it numbered 248 persons and 232 horses, and at Ypres a year later (19 January 1386), the duke and duchess were accompanied by 353 persons and 405 horses. It is easy to imagine the disturbance caused in all but the largest towns by the arrival of this imposing cavalcade with its train of thirty or forty wagons, and difficult not to sympathize with the *maîtres d'hôtel*, on whose shoulders fell the intricate task of its day-to-day organization.

The Burgundian court was lavishly furnished with all the elaborate trappings of the princely and chivalrous life of the age, which were concentrated round the person of the duke. It was the custom among rulers to prepare from time to time inventories of the contents of their *trésors*, and these, by describing in detail the personal belongings of the ruler, throw a great deal of light on his material surroundings, and therefore on the life of his court. It must be borne in mind, however, that in the fourteenth century a large proportion of a ruler's liquid assets took the form of plate and jewellery, so that much of what is listed in the inventories was destined neither for the table nor for personal adornment, but for melting down and sale whenever ready cash was required, or, at best, for the pawn-shop. The contents of the *trésor* was also regularly drawn on for the extravagant gift-exchange between princes and nobles which took place on New Year's Day under the name of *étrennes*.

A comparison of the inventories of the four sons of King John II— Charles V, Louis of Anjou, John of Berry and Philip the Bold—all of which have been published,[2] reveals, as one would expect, that Charles V's *trésor* was far superior to the others. He possessed, for instance, twenty-seven gold crosses or crucifixes for use in chapel, and sixty-three complete sets of chapel furnishings; while Philip the Bold had only nine crosses, some of them silver-gilt, and nine complete *chapelles*. The king easily surpassed the others in gold plate, with over two hundred pieces; and in jewellery, which included

---

[1] ACO B320/2. For the next sentence see ACO B321/bis and 3. For the *escroes*, see above p, 145.

[2] By Labarte, Moranvillé, Guiffrey and Dehaisnes respectively. For the first three, see below, p. 250, under *Inventaire*; the last is in *Documents concernant l'histoire de l'art*, 825–54.

forty-seven crowns. John of Berry excelled in gem-stones, with his fourteen named rubies; curios, with an ostrich's egg, a porcupine's quill and an elephant's molar; and relics—he had fifteen fragments of the True Cross. Philip the Bold's inventory was made at Paris a few weeks after his death. It lists his holdings in jewelled and other crucifixes and crosses, gold and silver-gilt statuettes, mostly of saints and including a 'St. Charlemagne', reliquaries, altar-pieces, vestments, service-books, plate, tapestry, banners and standards, clothes, hunting horns, bows and arrows and so on. Of special note is a large silver-gilt cup 'de bien ancienne façon' which, according to the inventory, had belonged to Julius Caesar, though this had not deterred Philip the Bold from engraving his own arms on the cover! Of curios, he had a solitary, but unusually large, boar's tooth. The subjects of many of his tapestries are noted. Among pious representations, we find the Coronation of the Virgin, the Creed and the Prophets, and the lives of various saints; but there are many more with secular subjects ranging from recent history—the battle of Roosebeke and Bertrand du Guesclin—to antiquity, through Arthur and Charlemagne, and including Semiramis of Babylon, the *Romance of the Rose*, the story of Jason and the Golden Fleece, and the Twelve Peers of France. The ducal wardrobe was of regal splendour: among many other things, it contained thirty-six superb *houppelandes* of satin, velvet or cloth-of-gold, together with the skins of 9,408 ermines for lining eleven *houppelandes* and one mantle. Two of the finest *houppelandes* were of crimson velvet with sleeves covered in pearls and precious stones. The Duchess Margaret's inventory, made after her death in 1405,[1] reveals, above all, her passion for personal adornment: five magnificent jewelled gold crowns, thirty necklaces, mostly of gold with pearls or gems, some 150 gold clasps, many of them jewelled, belts of gold studded with pearls, chains, fastenings, garters, rings, purses adorned with pearls, rosaries of gold, amber, coral and crystal, not to mention her entire wardrobe enumerated in detail, and all sorts of miscellaneous articles like ivory boxes, forks, spoons, towels, mirrors and a portrait of herself.

Of all the items in the inventories of Philip and his wife, the books are perhaps the most interesting. The two lists, the first made at Paris in 1404, the second at Arras in 1405, describe a single collection which was shared by the duke and duchess and which was under the care of a certain Richard le Comte, who discharged the combined offices of ducal hairdresser and *garde des livres*. Taken together, these

[1] *Documents concernant l'histoire de l'art*, 855–920.

lists evidently describe the great majority of Philip and Margaret's books, which were probably already, in the duke's lifetime, divided between his normal place of residence, Paris, and the duchess's at Arras. A very few books may have been moved from Paris to Arras in 1404–5, and thus appear in both lists. A certain number, which we know Philip possessed, appear in neither. So far as is known, there was no actual library at this time, the books simply being kept in chests.

It was in the 1360s that two of Europe's earliest princely libraries were installed, in the Louvre at Paris by Charles V, and at Pavia by Galeazzo Visconti; and Charles V and his brothers were among the first princes to collect books on a large scale, though Louis of Anjou's efforts in this direction seem to have been limited to removing forty of the finest books from the library of the Louvre directly after Charles V's death in 1380. Fortunately the contents of these collections are known through the published inventories, so that it is possible to ascertain, by comparison, how Philip the Bold's collection stood in relation to those of his brothers Charles V and John of Berry and to that of the contemporary Italian ruler, Giangaleazzo Visconti, son of Galeazzo.[1]

If we exclude Bibles, service-books, books of hours and the like, very few of which figure in the Pavian inventory, although there were over two hundred in the Louvre, Charles V and Giangaleazzo each owned about a thousand books. But, though the two libraries were similar in size, they were quite different in character: while the king of France possessed numerous works of romance, the despot of Milan had very few. While in the Louvre more than three-quarters of the books were in the vernacular, at Pavia five out of six were in Latin. Many more classical authors were to be found at Pavia than at Paris. True, both libraries had the Latin Aristotle, but, of the writers of ancient Rome, Paris could only provide Ovid, Lucan, Livy, Seneca and one or two others, against Pavia's Cicero, Caesar, Horace, Juvenal, Lucan, Livy, Ovid, Terence, etc. Not surprisingly, Pavia possessed Dante's *Commedia* and many of the works of Boccaccio and

---

[1] Delisle, *Recherches sur la librairie de Charles V*, ii, lists the books of Charles and John of Berry; Peignot, in his *Catalogue des livres des ducs de Bourgogne*, prints the inventories of Philip and Margaret's books, as does Dehaisnes, *Documents concernant l'histoire de l'art*, 839–40, 851–2 and 879–81. Identifications and much additional information are in Doutrepont, *Inventaire de la 'librairie' de Philippe le Bon* and *Littérature*. Pellegrin, *Bibliothèque des Visconti*, prints the inventory of 1426 which, with a few exceptions, describes the collection as it was under Giangaleazzo before his death in 1402.

Petrarch, all of which Paris lacked. The scope of the Pavian library was in general much wider than that of the Louvre, especially in medieval Latin writers: it possessed works of English writers like Bede, Anselm and Ockham, the two latter completely absent at Paris; and it was quite strong in scholastic theology, which was weak at Paris. Some things the two libraries had in common: the basic texts of canon and civil law, though at Paris these were mostly in translation; strong holdings in natural science, medicine, astrology and magic; and a certain amount of history. Paris excelled in one field, that of French vernacular literature: Delisle, in his summary of the contents of Charles's library, notes twenty-four Carolingian and seventeen Arthurian romances, as well as sixteen inspired by antiquity, and there were many others. Not that these were entirely lacking at Pavia, for it possessed some ninety books in French, most of which probably came from Giangaleazzo's mother, Blanche of Savoy.

Neither John of Berry's nor Philip the Bold's collection could compare in size with those at Paris and Pavia. Even including service and devotional books, John of Berry could only muster some three hundred volumes, while Philip's collection hardly exceeded two hundred. Although similar in character to the library of his royal brother, John of Berry's was much richer in illuminated books, of which he possessed some of the finest ever produced, notably the famous *Très Riches Heures* of the so-called brothers Limbourg. His selection of books showed, too, some leanings towards humanism, for he had Virgil's *Bucolics*; two Terences, one illuminated, the other glossed; Petrarch's *De remediis utriusque fortunae*; and even 'un grant livre ancien escript en grec.'

Of the formation of Philip the Bold's library we know a good deal. Some books came to him from Philip VI's wife Blanche of Navarre, in particular the famous Psalter of St. Louis; others must have been acquired by him with the duchy of Burgundy in 1363; while yet others were contributed by his wife Margaret of Male. A certain number came by way of gift: for instance the *Légende dorée*, the Bible, the Missal in French and the book of Arthurian romance which were given to Philip or his wife by Charles VI;[1] and the superb Book of Hours from John of Berry in 1402-3. But many of the acquisitions recorded in the accounts as gifts were in fact probably purchases, for

[1] These seem to be the only books which came to the Burgundian library from the Louvre in Philip the Bold's time. Three of them were given to the duchess in October 1381.

the 'donor' received a payment which was at least equal in value to the book. Among these purchases concealed as gifts should be included an illuminated Livy from Dino Rapondi in 1398; the French translation of Boccaccio's *De claris mulieribus* from Giacomo Rapondi in 1403; and Charles de Poitiers' gift in 1400 of the *Roman du roy Mellyadus et de Gyron courtois*. There is plenty of evidence in the accounts of direct purchases of books by Philip the Bold: in 1383 he bought a *Croniques des roys de France*; in 1386, a *Catholicon*; in 1393 a Breviary; in 1398–1400 an illuminated Bible, a *Légende dorée*, and the French translation of Bartholomew the Englishman's *Liber de proprietatibus rerum*. Most of these purchases were made in Paris, where Giacomo Rapondi was particularly active in supplying books to Philip. It was from him that in 1403 Philip bought three illuminated copies of Hayton's *Fleur des histoires d'Orient*, one for John of Berry, one for Louis of Orleans, and one for himself.

In the general character of its contents, Philip the Bold's library was very like that of the Louvre, though it was only one-sixth its size. His ignorance of Latin[1] no doubt explains the complete absence, apart from service-books and some devotional works, of that language in his library. Classical antiquity was very poorly represented by a handful of French romances inspired by it—the *Roman de Marques*, *Cassidore*, an *Istoire de Troyes* and possibly an *Ector de Troyes*, and two copies of the *Vœux du Paon*—and by French translations of Livy and Aristotle. The largest single group of books was devotional and religious: about half the eighty or so books listed in the 1404 inventory were from Philip's chapel and oratory. Besides his fine series of Bibles, Hours, Missals, Psalters and the like, Philip possessed a *Vie des saints*, the *Légende dorée*, lives of SS. Gregory and Bernard, St. Gregory's *Dialogues*, and devotional works in the vernacular like the *Échelle du ciel*, the *Charité* and *Miserere* of the recluse of Molliens, a *Complainte de Notre-Dame et autres choses*, etc. He was also well supplied with the secular literature of medieval France: among *chansons de geste*, he had *Aiol*, *Ogier de Danemarche*, *Elie de Saint-Gilles*, *Aymeri de Narbonne* and *Bueve de Hanstone*. He possessed a number of *romans d'aventures*, including *Robert le Diable*, *Cléomadès* and the *Histoire du châtelain de Coucy et de la dame de Fayel*. Besides some half-dozen Arthurian romances, he could boast three works of Chrétien de Troyes: *Lancelot*, *Cligès* and *Yvain*; and he possessed two collections of *fabliaux*, as well as an *Ysopet* and a *Roman de Renart*. There were two copies of the *Romance of the Rose*, while

[1] Langlois, *Notices*, 214.

lyric poetry was represented by a *Livre de Machaut*, two copies of the *Livre de cent ballades*, and two *Livres d'amour*. With the literature of the crusades and of travel in the East, Philip was quite well provided: he possessed *Li estoire d'Outremer et dou roi Salehadin*, Hayton's *Fleur des histoires de l'Orient*, two copies of Villehardouin, a Mandeville and two books called *Godefroid de Bouillon*, one of which was Gautier of Arras's *Eracles*. History was scantily represented by two *Chroniques de France* and two or three *Chroniques de Flandres*. Finally, there was a good selection of didactic works, ranging from such favourites as the bestiary, the *Roman de Sidrach*, the French translation of Bartholomew the Englishman's *De proprietatibus rerum*, and a *Jeu des échecs*, to Bonet's *Arbre des batailles*, two copies of Gace de la Buigne's *Deduiz de la chasse* and an illustrated French translation of Frederick II's *De arte venandi cum avibus*.[1]

Such, very briefly, was the collection which Philip the Bold created and which passed unscathed through John the Fearless to Philip the Good. Though much smaller than Charles V's library and less rich in illuminated books than John of Berry's, it still ranked among the foremost collections of the time, in size, beauty and range of contents. It was already one of the principal ornaments of the Burgundian court.

If we dwell on Philip the Bold's books, it is because they have a greater intrinsic interest for us than other aspects of the material surroundings of the court, such as the elaborate and ephemeral festivities and pageants which were its constant occupation. These, though designed primarily for the delectation of the aristocracy, had the important if subsidiary function of enhancing the ruler's prestige in the eyes of his humbler subjects. They were organized by Philip the Bold to attend events of all kinds—the conclusion of diplomatic negotiations, a wedding, the reception of a distinguished visitor—or even without such a pretext, and were invariably the occasion for martial exercises in the form of tournaments; for the display of sartorial splendour on a fantastic scale; for feasting and drinking, and for musical and other entertainments. The Burgundian court also took part, with equal brilliance, in the festivities laid on by the king in connection with royal events at Paris or elsewhere.

Among the purely Burgundian fêtes which Philip organized, three were perhaps outstanding: the double wedding at Cambrai in 1385; the reception of Charles VI in Burgundy in 1390; and Anthony's wedding at Arras in 1402. Some account has already been given of the

[1] BN fr. 12400.

first of these.[1] The second had been planned in 1383, then deferred till 1385, and again deferred in 1387, and it was not until February 1390 that Charles VI was formally received by his uncle at Dijon. Philip spared no pains on this occasion. Preparations for the reception were begun at least a month beforehand. One hundred and ninety-three knights and squires were issued with the royal livery of vermilion and white velvet or satin in honour of the king, while their womenfolk were decked out, at the ducal expense, in robes of cloth-of-gold and Damascus silk. The streets of Dijon were cleaned and decorated. The extensive gardens of St. Stephen's abbey were requisitioned for the tournament, the trees felled and many of the walls removed, and four hundred shields were painted with the coats of arms of Philip, John of Nevers, William of Ostrevant and Guy de la Trémoille, to decorate their stands. Philip, with his son and others, went out to meet the king at Tournus, and the two courts, united in a single impressive *cortège*, made their entry into Dijon on Sunday, 13 February. A huge marquee had been erected for the reception in the courtyard behind the ducal palace and, while the municipality of Dijon presented the king with six oxen and one hundred sheep, Philip distributed quantities of costly gifts—jewelled clasps, gold goblets, diamond rings and other plate and jewellery—to those present, who included the king of France, the exiled king of Armenia, the counts of Savoy and Geneva, the constable of France, and many other French nobles, as well as the entire nobility of the two Burgundies. This reception was followed by a banquet in the ducal palace, for which, since it was Lent, choice fish, including salmon, was brought from Bâle, and by the tournament in the gardens of St. Stephen's, not to mention another held specially for the townspeople. The jousting continued for three days and, while it was still in progress, Philip showed the king over his new religious foundation on the outskirts of Dijon, the famous Charterhouse of Champmol. Finally, on 17–20 February, he escorted his royal guest as far as the boundaries of his lands. All the other festivities in which the Burgundian court participated followed a similar pattern: the jousts, the gift exchange, the sartorial pageantry, were repeated every time, and, even when he was travelling on quite ordinary business, Philip maintained his extravagant appearance and sumptuous train.[2]

[1] See above, p. 87–8. For what follows, see Plancher, iii. 116–17; Petit, *Entrée* and *Itinéraires*, 532–5; *Inventaires mobiliers*, ii. nos. 3396, 3397, 3450–7, etc.

[2] See especially, David, *P. le Hardi, train somptuaire* and, for the next para-

Apart from the serious business of state, and the many hours spent in the saddle, the everyday life of the court was taken up with amusements of many kinds, and with devotion. We read in the ducal accounts of the court musicians or minstrels, who frequently performed before the duke, and whose journeys to their annual gatherings in the Low Countries he subsidized; and of the court jesters or *fous*. For relaxation, the duke indulged in hunting and tennis, chess and dice. But religious exercises occupied much more of his time, whether they took the form of reading a book of hours with the help of a lantern and spectacles, or of an occasional pilgrimage to Mont-St.-Michel or elsewhere in France. Philip attended mass nearly every day, and often meditated alone in his oratory. He carried his rosary and a portable reliquary with him wherever he went. A constant stream of alms issued from him and his entourage, carefully graduated according to rank, so that, if Philip gave three francs, the duchess gave two, and John of Nevers, one. Candles, sometimes painted with the ducal arms, and occasionally of almost grotesque size, were often burnt before statues of the Virgin Mary: those offered to Notre-Dame of Soissons in 1374 weighed fifty pounds each. Once a year the statue of the Virgin in Tournai cathedral was adorned at the duke's expense with a robe and mantle of cloth-of-gold lined with miniver and embroidered with his and his wife's arms. The church of St. Anthony at Pont-de-Norges benefited annually from Philip's charity, which there took a bizarre form: the gift of a fat pig for each living member of his family. All this emphasizes the religious element in court life, which was just as essential a part of it as the jousts and feasting, and the jewels and finery.

The literary patronage of Philip and his contemporaries is extremely hard to assess. Many of the writers of the day had aristocratic and court connections other than literary; and some, Christine de Pisan in particular, addressed their works more or less promiscuously to the princes whose favours they sought. The Burgundian court was certainly not a centre of literary activity, but it was the scene of a certain amount of literary patronage, exercised by the duke himself. In character, this patronage was essentially conservative, for it was limited to writers in the medieval tradition of chivalry and the crusade, of courtly love and of didactic and allegorical works. There is no sign, at the Burgundian court, of the humanism which

graph, this and Vernier, *MSA* lxiii (1899), 29–63 and Picard, *MAD* (4) xii (1910–13), 1–116.

was infiltrating into France at this time, and which is apparent, though to a limited extent, in John of Berry, Louis of Orleans, and Louis of Bourbon.

Of the writers who dedicated works to Philip or wrote at his request the best known is Christine de Pisan, whose father, a practising astrologer, had emigrated from Italy to the court of King Charles V, where, among others, the count of Savoy made use of his professional services to ascertain the most auspicious day for his son's wedding. Christine married one of the royal secretaries and subsequently wrote numerous works in French verse and prose, copies of which she presented to the queen, Louis of Orleans, John of Berry, and Philip the Bold. One manuscript of her *Epistre d'Othea*, written in 1401, has a dedication to Philip, and it seems certain that a copy of *Le chemin de long estude*, which was dedicated to Charles VI and the princes, was given to him by her.[1] For a New Year's gift in 1404 she presented him with another work, *La mutacion de fortune*, and this resulted, a few months before Philip's death, in his request to her to write what would amount to a quasi-official panegyric of his famous elder brother King Charles V. Thus Philip directly commissioned what proved to be one of Christine's most interesting works, the *Livre des fais et bonnes meurs du sage roy Charles V*, which, in spite of its idealized and sometimes obsequious character, is a valuable source of information for Charles's reign. Before it was finished, Philip was dead, and Christine, after deploring this event in a rather banal poem, completed the *Livre des fais* and used it on the following 1 January as a New Year's gift for John of Berry. There are many references to Philip in Christine's works, all of them flattering and sycophantic: 'l'excellent duc de Bourgoingne, Phelippe'; 'le tres venerable hault et poissant noble prince Philippe', etc., but similar phrases are used of all the other princes. If Philip was 'dulz, aimable, large comme un Alixandre,' Charles VI was 'plus large et plus liberal que oncques ne fu Alixandre'. But, to be fair to Christine, this fawning concealed the desperate enterprise of a woman who had been left, at the age of twenty-five, a penniless widow with three children: she wrote to live.[2]

Another writer patronized by Philip the Bold was Honoré Bonet or

[1] Written in 1403; there was a copy in his library in 1404, *Catalogue des livres des ducs de Bourgogne*, 49. Throughout what follows I have made use of Doutrepont, *Littérature*.

[2] For this paragraph, see de Pisan, *Œuvres poétiques*, and *Le livre des fais*; Pinet, *Christine de Pisan*, and Boldingh-Goemans, *Christine de Pizan*.

Bouvet, prior of Salon, a poor Benedictine priory in Provence, who was living in Paris at any rate between 1394 and 1404. Philip received from him a copy of his most famous work, the *Arbre des batailles*, which was dedicated to Charles VI in 1387. Three years later, an entry in the ducal accounts records the payment of 100 francs to Bonet for a 'livre de ystoires' he had 'given' Philip, as well as a mule and a greyhound,[1] and, some ten years later, Bonet wrote a special version of his treatise in praise of the *Romance of the Rose*, the *Apparicion maistre Jehan de Meun*, for Philip, apparently at the request of his chancellor, Jehan Canard.

Christine de Pisan and Honoré Bonet were among the best-known writers of the age, but both were outshone in literary merit by the poet Eustache Deschamps, disciple of Machaut and author of over a thousand ballades. Deschamps, like Christine, was by no means averse to currying favour at court by writing for or flattering the princes, but he was much less servile. After all he had the temerity, in his *Ordre de la Baboue*, to describe an imaginary drinking-club whose members all belonged to Philip the Bold's household; and, in the *Dit du gieu des dez*, he describes a drunken dicing-session at John of Berry's Paris *hôtel* in which Philip participated. Other poems present Philip in a more favourable light; in one he is even addressed as 'Bel Oncle'. The poet stayed, on one occasion at least, at the Burgundian court and, in 1393, Philip commissioned from him a French translation of his *Complainte de l'Église*, a polemical work on the Schism, Philip's interest in which is perhaps also shown in the gift to him, by the Dominican Martin Porée, of a treatise 'faisant mencion de la Restitution d'obéissance au pape', and in the dedication to him of two tracts on the same subject by a certain 'G'.[2]

[1] ACO B1479, f. 146, and, for what follows, Coville, *Vie intellectuelle*, 310–312. On Bonet, see the *Somnium*, ed. Valois, *ABSHF* (1890), 193–228; *L'Apparicion maistre Jehan de Meun et le Somnium; The Tree of Battles*; Langlois, *Notices*, 211–17.

[2] *Catalogue des livres des ducs de Bourgogne*, 50 and Valois, *France et le Grand Schisme*, iii. 78 n. 4 and 265 n. 7. For Deschamps, see *Œuvres complètes* and Höpffner, *Eustache Deschamps*. Philip seems to have commissioned one other translation from Latin into French, for Prost (*Inventaires mobiliers*, ii. no. 797) records a payment on 5 August 1383 to the regent-master of the 'Augustins' in Paris, who had translated for Philip from Latin into French a 'livre des Armoilles [*sic*] qu'un Cordelier . . . disoit avoir vu en plusieurs parties du monde . . . '. This must be a *livre des merveilles*, but it seems unlikely that it was either the *Mirabilia* of Jordan of Séverac, written in the 1330s (see Beazley, *Dawn*, iii. 215–35), for he was a Dominican; or the *Merveilles* of Odoric of Pordenone, for two authors of French translations

Philip the Bold was concerned in two notable additions to the literature of falconry and the chase. Gace de la Buigne had begun his *Deduiz de la chasse* for Philip's instruction in England in 1359; it was completed at Philip's request in the 1370s. Some time later the count of Foix, Gaston Phoebus, dedicated his *Livre de la chasse* to Philip and, in the *envoi* addressed to him, acknowledges that he is 'meistre de nous tous qui sommes de mestier de vénerie'.[1] The connection of several other writers with Philip the Bold seems to have been tenuous. Two of these, Froissart and Philippe de Mézières, were well known. The former, though he apparently had no direct contact with Philip, celebrated in verse the double wedding at Cambrai in 1385, as did a very inferior Brabantine poet, Jehan de Malines.[2] Froissart moreover, particularly towards the close of his chronicle, exhibits pronounced Burgundian sympathies and an unqualified admiration for Philip the Bold. The crusading propagandist Philippe de Mézières likewise had little direct contact with Philip, but the disaster of Nicopolis prompted him to address to the duke his *Epistre lamentable et consolatoire*.[3] The *Chronique rimée des troubles de Flandre*, a poem on the revolt of Ghent in 1379 and the succeeding years, may have been a direct product of Philip the Bold's literary patronage, for the author lavishes praise on Louis of Male, and refers to Philip in flattering terms. Philip's relationship with Jehan Creton, author of a metrical description of the last years and death of Richard II of England, remains obscure. We possess a letter of Creton's to Philip written in 1402, exhorting him to avenge Richard's death, and there is an entry in the ducal accounts recording Philip's purchase in 1402 from a Jehan Creton of a book 'faisant mencion de la prinse de feu le roy Richart'.[4]

---

of Odoric's work, sometimes known under this title, are already known, and neither of them was an Austin friar (Bossuat, *Manuel*, 537). The passage cited by Prost states that the Franciscan traveller had been with John, duke of Gironne, son of King Peter IV of Aragon and a nephew of Philip the Bold. The translator may possibly have been Jehan Corbechon, a well-known translator who was *maître en théologie* at Paris and an Austin friar; see Delisle, *Recherches*, i. 91–2.

[1] See Gace, *Le roman des deduis*; for Gaston Phoebus, see Paris, *MSS. françois*, v. 217–21.

[2] See Pinchart, *BBB* xii (1856), 28–37.

[3] Jorga, *Philippe de Mézières*, 499–504.

[4] Creton's poem is printed in *Archaeologia*, xx (1824), 1–423; the letter, ed. Dillon, ibid., xxviii (1840), 91–4. The entry in the accounts, ACO B1532, f. 168, is inaccurately transcribed by Peignot, in his *Catalogue des livres des*

Much more significant than the sporadic favours which Philip granted to writers like Christine de Pisan and Honoré Bonet was his consistent patronage of the youthful Jehan Gerson, who without it would probably never have become one of the most profound and influential theologians of the age. The origins of this patronage no doubt lay in the fact that Gerson was a subject of Philip's, having been born in a village near Rethel from which he took his name, but it was probably reinforced by Gerson's early fame as a preacher at Paris. As soon as he had completed his studies there, in 1393, Philip made him his almoner with an annual pension or salary of 200 francs, and, later in the same year, he secured for him the deanery of St. Donatian's at Bruges. In spite of this, Gerson continued to reside in the main at Paris, where he succeded Pierre d'Ailly as chancellor of Notre-Dame in 1395. As chancellor, Gerson was an influential figure in the capital and its university, but Philip's continued patronage of him does not seem to have been due solely to a desire to make use of him. From 1394 onwards, he opposed Philip's policy of the withdrawal of the obedience of France from Pope Benedict XIII, yet Philip retained him as almoner and, in 1400, when he thought of resigning his chancellorship and retiring to Bruges, the duke dissuaded him. The importance of this disinterested ducal support was later attested by Gerson himself, who described Philip as 'he to whom after God all my works are due'.[1]

One other aspect of Philip's literary patronage remains to be mentioned: in 1401 he was jointly responsible with Louis, duke of Bourbon, for the foundation of a *cour d'amour* or *cour amoureuse* in France. This was an aristocratic society whose object was to honour the female sex and cultivate lyric poetry. The foundation charter, which purported to be issued by the *prince d'amour*, laid down the constitution and rules of the court. Consisting, in the main, of three *grand conservateurs* of whom Philip was one, eleven *conservateurs*, twenty-four ministers, and various other officers, it was to meet from time to time to hear and pronounce judgement on poems submitted by its

---

ducs de Bourgogne, 32. The payment to Creton is actually described as a gift 'pour et en recompensacion dun livre . . .'. It is very probable that this Creton is the author of the poem. Another, or possibly the same, Jehan Creton, figures in the same and other accounts as Philip's *valet de chambre* (e.g. ACO B1532, f. 208b).

[1] Morrall, *Gerson and the Great Schism*, 6. See too Vansteenberghe, *RHE* xxxi (1935), 5–52. Gerson was still Philip's almoner in 1401, ACO B1526, f. 65.

several hundred members. It held a formal dinner annually on St. Valentine's Day, and the first of these dinners took place on 14 February 1401. Unfortunately, the history of this whimsical academy remains obscure and, if the registers, into which, according to the foundation charter, its productions were to be copied, ever existed, they have not survived.[1]

In spite of the favours he extended to many of the writers of his time, Philip the Bold's fame as a Maecenas has always depended on his artistic patronage; and rightly. This patronage was centred on his religious foundation at Dijon, the Charterhouse of Champmol, but was by no means limited to it, for the castle at Sluis, the duchess's *château* at Germolles, and the ducal palace at Dijon, as well as many other buildings, occupied the labours of Philip the Bold's sculptors, painters and craftsmen.

The Charterhouse of Champmol, a large and beautiful convent for twenty-four, instead of the customary twelve, Carthusian monks, of which scarcely a trace now remains, was conceived by Philip as a gigantic sepulchral monument for himself and his heirs.[2] As early as 1377 building materials were being assembled from local quarries, and work on an access road to the site had begun, but it was not till 1383 that the foundation stones were laid. From then on the work proceeded apace and, by 1388, when the church was consecrated, the construction of both it and the conventual buildings was probably completed, at a cost of over 75,000 francs. The project was under the care of a committee of Dijon councillors and others, among whom Dreue Felize, André Pasté and Amiot Arnaut were prominent. Amiot Arnaut looked after the finances and kept the accounts of the Charterhouse works between 1383 and 1412. The architect was Drouet de Dammartin of Paris who, at the same time, designed the ducal castle at Sluis. He had previously worked on Charles V's palace of the

---

[1] Potvin, *BARB* (3) xii (1886), 191–220; Piaget, *Romania*, xx (1891), 417–54; and ibid., xxxi (1902), 597–603.

[2] For what follows I have made special use of David's three works, *P. le Hardi, train somptuaire; P. le Hardi, protecteur des arts;* and *Claus Sluter.* Apart from the two former, the only other general study of Philip the Bold's patronage of the arts is that by Dehaisnes, *Histoire de l'art,* 485–525. Among the many works on Sluter and the Charterhouse, most of which are referred to by David in his *Claus Sluter,* I have found the following of special value: Monget, *Chartreuse de Dijon,* i; Drouot, *RBAHA* ii (1932), 11–39 and *AB* xiv (1942), 7–24; Troescher, *Claus Sluter;* Rolland, *RBAHA* v (1935), 335–44; Liebreich, *Claus Sluter;* Roggen, *GBK* i (1934), 173–213, ibid., iii (1936), 31–85 and ibid., xi (1945–8), 7–40.

Louvre with another royal architect, Raymond du Temple, and the latter probably lent his aid to his colleague both at Sluis and at the Charterhouse; certainly he visited both places with Drouet while the works were still in progress.

While Philip found his architects in France, nearly all his sculptors and artists were brought to Dijon from the Low Countries, though some of them found employment at Paris for a time, as it were on the way. Long before work on the Charterhouse had begun, in 1372, Philip had retained Jehan de Marville as *valet de chambre* and official *imagier* or sculptor, and settled him at Dijon, where he opened an atelier. It was this Flemish sculptor who was responsible for beginning work on the duke's tomb and on the famous portal of the Charterhouse church, with its five life-size figures of the Virgin Mary, Philip the Bold and his wife, and SS. John the Baptist and Catherine. Meanwhile, Philip evidently lost few opportunities of attracting the artists and craftsmen of the Low Countries to Dijon. In the midst of the negotiations at Tournai in December 1385 he found time to sign on one of the local sculptors, Claus de Haine, who agreed to work for some months in the following year on his tomb at Dijon; and, on his visit to Ghent after the peace, he engaged a certain Colart Joseph as *canonnier*. This Joseph left his workshop in Dinant to reside at Dijon for some years in the ducal service, and it was he who cast the metal pieces for the Charterhouse: the convent bell, chandeliers, the bronze eagle for the lectern, and an elaborate arrangement of columns supporting angels to surround the high altar. When Jehan de Marville died in 1389 his successor was ready to hand in Dijon, for the incomparable Claus Sluter of Haarlem in Holland had been working in Marville's atelier since 1385, having moved there from Brussels with several colleagues. On 23 July 1389 he was engaged as ducal *imagier* and *valet de chambre* on the same terms as Marville, and, between then and his death in 1405, Sluter carved the five portal figures which his predecessor had planned or designed; made some further progress on Philip's tomb; and completed the so-called *puits de Moïse*, which is generally recognized as one of the sculptural masterpieces of all time. Of this monumental Crucifixion only the pedestal, with its six full-size figures of prophets, remains *in situ*, and it is hard to imagine the work as it was left by Sluter, standing in the centre of the main cloister of the Charterhouse, which was one hundred yards square. The tip of the cross towered some twenty-five feet above ground level; below it St. John, the Virgin Mary, and Mary Magdalene stood on the hexagonal pedestal, which, carved with the prophets in high relief, rose out of a pool of water eleven feet deep. The whole structure was coloured and gilded, and within a few years of its completion a wooden roof was erected over it to protect it from the weather.

While Sluter, aided by his brilliant nephew and successor, Claus de Werve, was at work on the sculptures for the Charterhouse, he was also engaged by Philip on the decoration of his wife's *château* at Germolles, which was built in the 1380s under the supervision, and perhaps according to the designs, of Drouet de Dammartin.[1] It was in connection with the décor at Germolles that Sluter and the ducal artist Jehan de Beaumetz were sent by Philip in 1393 to inspect John of Berry's recently finished and elaborately decorated *château* at Mehun-sur-Yèvre. This was the finest of contemporary princely residences; everyone had heard of its artistic splendours, and, in the previous year, the mason and carpenter at work in Philip's Artois *château* of Hesdin had been sent there on a similar errand. At Germolles, in the years after 1393, Sluter carved a figure of the Virgin Mary for the portal, as well as one of those sculptured pieces of rustic inspiration known as *bergeries*. This one, carved in deep relief, depicted Philip and Margaret seated beneath an elm amidst a flock of sheep. The same motif was repeated within the *château*: in 1388, 180 sheep had been painted on the walls of the *chambre aux brebis*, reflecting, perhaps, Margaret's interest in rural life, for Germolles was really more of a farm than a castle.

Like the sculptors Marville and Sluter, Philip the Bold's principal painters enjoyed official status at court: they too were ranked among the *valets de chambre*.[2] In painting, as in sculpture, Philip employed the finest masters available: prominent among them were Jehan de Beaumetz and Jehan Malouel, who succeeded one another at Dijon, and Melchior Broederlam, who worked mainly in Flanders. All three were natives of the Low Countries: Beaumetz probably from Artois, Malouel from Guelders, and Broederlam from Ypres in Flanders. The first two had worked for a time in Paris before Philip brought them to Dijon; the last, apart from three years in Philip's service at Hesdin, lived and worked at Ypres and, before 1384, had been in the service of Louis of Male.

---

[1] For Germolles, see Picard, *MSE* (n.s.) xl (1912), 147–218.
[2] For what follows, I have used Kleinclausz, *RAAM* xx (1906), 161–76 and 253–68; Dimier, *GBA* (6) xvi (1936) (2), 205–32; Sterling, *Peinture française*; *primitifs*; the works of David cited above, p. 202, n. 2; and Panofsky, *Early Netherlandish Painting*.

Philip the Bold's artists were employed on all sorts of tasks, from decorating pennons and ensigns, to painting furniture, jousting equipment and retables. Jehan de Beaumetz was at work for several years in the 1380s decorating the chapel of the *château* at Argilly before he turned his attention to the vaulting of the Charterhouse church. In the 1390s he executed a series of pictures for the monks' cells there, and also painted altarpieces for some of the chapels, though this work was interrupted, in 1391–2, when he was charged with the decoration of four hundred ducal ensigns. Malouel, who succeeded him in 1397, continued the work of painting altarpieces for the chapels and, at the end of Philip's life, was busy colouring Sluter's *puits de Moïse*. It was Melchior Broederlam, the master of them all, who was required to paint the shutters of the two altar-pieces for the Charterhouse which still survive at Dijon, though one has lost its shutters. The construction of these altarpieces, and the carving of their central retables, had been specially commissioned by Philip from Jacques de Baërze, of Termonde in Flanders, and, when he had completed his work, the shutters were sent to Ypres to be painted by Broederlam, before the final installation of the Champmol altarpieces at Dijon. These exquisite masterpieces, together with Sluter's now dismembered sculptures, are the main surviving monuments to Philip's artistic tastes and patronage, and must be reckoned among the most remarkable works of art of the later Middle Ages.

Apart from the shutters of the Charterhouse altarpieces, Broeder-lam's artistic talents were employed, on Philip's behalf, chiefly in the castle of Hesdin in Artois, which was another centre of ducal artistic patronage. This castle had not only been provided, at the end of the thirteenth century, by Count Robert of Artois, with a magnificent park and menagerie, but also with a variety of curious mechanical devices known as 'engiens d'esbattement', which were installed for the amusement of the count's family and guests. There were statues which surprised the unwary visitor with words, or squirted jets of water at him as he walked past them; there was a trap-door in the floor which plunged him into a sack of feathers below; and in one room artificial rain, and even snow and thunder, could be produced. The castle was even fitted out with 'conduis pour mouiller les dames par dessous'. In Philip's time the mechanism of this elaborate horse-play was cared for by the resident ducal artist, described in the accounts as 'peintre du chastel de Hesdin et maistre des engiens d'esbattements', but the duke also employed Broederlam to supervise the restoration and repair of the *engiens*, to paint the gallery in which many of them were situated, and to carry out other miscellaneous interior decoration.[1]

While Philip's patronage of the greatest sculptors and panel-painters of the age has long been recognized and justly celebrated, his part in the history of book illumination has perhaps received less approbation than it deserves. True, he seems to have entered this field only towards the end of his life, and to have purchased, rather than commissioned, most of his finest books. But it was he who first employed the so-called Limbourg brothers, who later executed for the duke of Berry the famous *Très Riches Heures* now at Chantilly. It seems that Pol, Jehan (or Hennequin) and Herman Manuel were in fact nephews of Philip's artist Jehan Malouel, and, like him, came from Limbricht in Guelders, not from the duchy of Limbourg.[2] In 1400–1, when Jehan and Herman were goldsmith's apprentices in Paris, Philip gave them financial assistance on their journey to Guelders to avoid the plague. In 1402 the brothers were back again in Paris, and the duke now took Pol and Jehan into his service, installed them in the *hôtel* of his Paris physician Jehan Durant, and commissioned them to execute for him as well and as quickly as possible a 'très belle et notable' Bible. The contract stipulated that they were to engage in no other work until this book was finished. They were still at it a year later, but then they pass out of recorded history for a time, to reappear in 1411, along with their brother Herman, in the service of John of Berry. Thus the credit for discovering these remarkable artists, and of launching them on a successful career in France, must go to Philip the Bold.

Although there is ample evidence that Philip the Bold took great pleasure in paintings, illuminated books, and other works of art, his artistic patronage undoubtedly contained an element of ostentatious pride. Nor was it in the least original or enlightened. He was simply doing what his elder brother Charles V had done before him, and what almost all the princes of the age aspired to do, at least in some measure. When he brought the finest available artists from the Low Countries to work in Dijon, he was not making special and enlightened

---

[1] For this paragraph, see, in addition to the works already cited, Charageat, *BSHAF* (1950), 94–106, and Hommel, *Grand héritage*, 128.

[2] For a contrary view, see Dimier, *BSHAF* (1929), 46–9. Manuel is probably a corruption of Malouel, itself the French transcription of *maelweel* 'Paint-well'. On this paragraph, see especially, Durrieu, *Le Manuscrit*, ii (1895), 82–7, 98–103, 114–22, 162–8, 178–81; Hulin, *BSHAG* xvi (1908), 183–8; and Dimier, *GBA* (6) xvi (1936) (2), 205–32.

use of his position as ruler of Flanders as well as Burgundy, but emulating Charles V, who had done just this at Paris in the 1370s. Even his personal interest must not be exaggerated; after all, he never even saw the magnificent Crucifixion which Sluter carved in the Charterhouse cloister, for, at the time of his last visit to Dijon in 1396, work on this had scarcely begun. Nevertheless it may justly be claimed that Philip the Bold, not content with his administrative, diplomatic and political work, which brought the Burgundian state into being, equipped it with a brilliant court and with aesthetic trappings which, though common to the age, were second to none. In this, as in so many other respects, his successors had only to follow his footsteps.

CHAPTER TEN

The Burgundian Civil Service

The personnel who administered the Burgundian state did not form a civil service in the modern sense of the term, but, for want of a better one, the phrase may legitimately be used in this context, provided it is borne in mind that what is meant is the medieval equivalent of a modern civil service, not the thing itself. Although we shall be concerned here with the men themselves rather than with the functions and interrelationship of their offices—a subject already touched on in connection with the administration of the Burgundian state—some attempt must be made to assess the size of the Burgundian civil service and describe its broad structure.[1]

It is important to distinguish the members of the ducal civil service from the large category of persons who were the duke's servants, rather than his officials. Thus the innumerable sergeants, porters of ducal *châteaux*, and the like are excluded from consideration here, as well as the bulk of the court personnel: pages, valets, *écuyers* and the rest. Nor need we notice the many officials who devoted only a fraction of their time to the duke's affairs, such as his *avocats* and *procureurs* at the Paris *Parlement* and neighbouring 'foreign' courts.[2] It is doubtful, too, if some of the officials he shared with other jurisdictions, and classes of persons like the balival councillors in Burgundy or the local people commissioned to look after individual building projects, qualify for membership of the civil service. The most direct evidence about its size, excluding these categories, is afforded by an *ordonnance* of 1422, which shows that in the duchy of Burgundy alone it numbered about one hundred.[3] This figure is

---

[1] Much of the information in this chapter is derived from the accounts, but the following printed books have been particularly useful: Aubrée, *Mémoires*, ii; Gailliard, *Bruges et le Franc*; d'Arbaumont, *Armorial*, and Prost, *Inventaires mobiliers*.

[2] Above, pp. 142–4.   [3] Bartier, *Légistes*, 41–3.

probably valid also for Philip the Bold's reign, and it enables us to hazard the guess that the total in his time for the two Burgundies and related territories could scarcely have been less than 150. In the northern territories we are even more dependent on guesswork, but a known minimum of about fifty for Flanders alone gives us an approximate minimum total for the whole area, including Rethel and Artois, of one hundred. To this minimum combined total of at least 250 civil servants from the two groups of territories must be added the personnel of the central administration: a chancellor with a dozen or more secretaries; the central financial officers; and some, at any rate, of the so-called 'aulic' councillors: at least twenty-five persons in all. Philip the Bold's civil service was perhaps about three hundred strong.

This civil service had a pronounced geographical structure, for it consisted of a number of more or less separate local administrations, with little or no movement between them. Broadly speaking, Flanders was administered by Flemish officials; Burgundy by Burgundians; and so on; while the central administration was recruited for the most part from France, with a sprinkling of Burgundians. Although no section of the civil service was truly specialized in function, it contained several rather different groups of persons. The councillors, especially those at Lille and Dijon, were lawyers, usually with university degrees in both canon and civil law; the bailiffs, essentially unspecialized though with important judicial attributions, were drawn from the lesser nobility; while the secretaries and financial officers were more often than not of *bourgeois* extraction. These three groups, which consisted of what one might call fully professional civil servants, had almost entirely dispossessed the knightly amateurs of a much earlier age, although these still preserved a foothold in the administration of the late medieval state. In Burgundy, the higher nobility in the ducal service advised the duke in his 'aulic' council; administered and waged war; and undertook important diplomatic negotiations. Because of their functions as councillors and diplomats this class of persons cannot be excluded in the present context, though they themselves would certainly not have appreciated the application to them of the term civil servant.

The only section of Philip the Bold's civil service that had to be entirely recruited by him was the central administration, for elsewhere he was able to take over, more or less intact, an already numerous personnel. Thus in 1363 he acquired with the duchy of Burgundy, a receiver-general, Dymenche de Vitel; several councillors and *maîtres des comptes*, including Guy Rabby, Richard Bonost and Jehan de Baubigny, all of whom continued in his service at Dijon for over a decade; as well as knights like Thomas de Voudenay and Guillaume du Pailly, who served him as councillors just as they had served his predecessors, and bailiffs like Guillaume de Clugny, who was also a councillor.[1] In 1384 the local administrative personnel of Flanders, Artois, Rethel, Burgundy and Nevers were taken over by Philip with the counties themselves. Naturally, there were a number of replacements, for instance among the bailiffs of Flanders, but, by and large, the officials who had served Margaret of Artois and her son Louis of Male continued to serve Philip in the same capacity. Besides the local officials in Artois and the county of Burgundy, Philip acquired from Margaret of Artois a secretary, Robert Thoroude, and at least three councillors: Guy Ponche, Ancel de Salins and Jehan Blarie. Ancel de Salins had been Margaret's chancellor; Jehan Blarie, a canon of Beauvais, had been her *auditeur des comptes*; and both were employed by Louis of Male between her death in 1382 and his in 1384. It is probable, too, that Philip's receiver-general of all finances in 1397–1401, Jehan Despoullettes, had been in Margaret's service as a *clerc des comptes*.[2] In Flanders, it seems that as long as ten years after Philip's acquisition of the county, former civil servants of Louis of Male still formed a majority among the leading councillors and officials. This is certainly true of the councillors and others who received salaries of 150 francs or more from the Flemish receipt-general in 1394.[3] The first five councillors

---

[1] Vitel, Rabby and de Baubigny had been introduced into Burgundy from the royal civil service, Pocquet, *MSHDB* iv (1937), 15–17. For Vitel, see *Inventaires mobiliers*, i. 50 n.6. For Rabby, Bonost, de Baubigny and de Clugny in the Dijon council/*comptes*, see ACO B11402, *passim*. For Bonost, see *Registre des Parlements de Beaune*, 345, and Bartier, *Légistes*, 301; de Baubigny: Billioud, *États*, 191; de Voudenay and du Pailly: *Inventaires mobiliers*, i. 244 n.1 and 344 n. 4; de Clugny: *Registre des Parls. de Beaune*, 335–6.

[2] Thoroude: *Inventaires mobiliers*, ii. 623 n. 4; Ponche: *IAPCA*, ii. 128 and *IADNB*, iv. 10; de Salins: *Registre des Parlements de Beaune*, 331, Clerc, *Franche-Comté*, ii. 236, *IAPCA*, ii. 109, ACO B1461 f. 32b, B401 fos. 39b–40b, etc.; Blarie: *IAPCA*, ii. 121, van Nieuwenhuysen, *Recette générale*, 14, ACO B1461, f. 42b. It seems very likely that the Jehannin de Pouillettes of *IAPCA*, ii. 115, a *clerc des comptes* at Arras in 1380, is the later receiver-general, Jehan Despoullettes, who lived at Arras when not sent on ducal service, ACO B1514, f. 79b.

[3] ADN B4079, fos. 33a–b and 35. For their service under Louis, see Froissart, Kervyn, x. 539; van Nieuwenhuysen, *Recette générale*, 14 and 164–6; Nowé, *Baillis comtaux*, 375, and *IAB*, iii. 246 n. 1.

in this list, Pierre de le Zippe, Jehan van der Aa, Colard de la Clite, Guillaume Vernachten and Henri d'Espierre, had all been councillors of Louis of Male. Of the remaining five, Guillaume Slyp had certainly, and Jehan de Visch probably, been in Louis' service; while nothing certain is known of the earlier careers of Jehan de Poucques, Jehan de Nieles and Thiercelet de la Barre. Four *maîtres des comptes* and one financial officer also figure in this list, and, of these five, two, Pierre de la Tanerie and Jacques de Streyhem, had been in the service of Louis of Male. In sum, of the fifteen Flemish councillors and others receiving salaries of 150 francs or more from the Flemish receipt-general in 1394, eight or nine had been in Louis of Male's service. Many other officials of Louis of Male were employed by his successor. Henri Lippin, Louis' receiver-general, was retained in that position for a time by Philip before being made a *maître des comptes*; Jehan de Ghistelles, councillor of Louis of Male, became governor of Flanders under Philip; Louis' governor of Rethel, Josse de Halewin, kept his post under Philip until 1387; and Gerard de Rasseghem was taken over from Louis of Male and appointed governor of Lille in 1386.[1]

In spite of this wholesale appropriation of existing personnel, a certain amount of new recruitment was necessary, or became so as the years went by. In Burgundy, where this was almost exclusively local, many of the councillors and *gens de finance* introduced by Philip were of *bourgeois* extraction and came from or lived at Dijon, Autun, Chalon and other towns. Four at least of his receivers-general of Burgundy fall into this category: Jehan d'Auxonne was the son of a Dijon *bourgeois*; Guillaume Bataille lived at Autun; Oudart Douay was mayor of Dijon in 1401-2; and Joceran Frepier came from Chalon.[2] André Pasté, one of Philip's Dijon *maîtres des comptes*, was probably a brother of Louis Pasté of Dijon and certainly lived there, and, of the legists he enrolled in the Dijon council, Mathe de Bezon lived at Chalon, and Dreue Felize and Jehan de Verranges at Dijon.[3]

---

[1] Lippin: van Nieuwenhuysen, *Recette générale*, 164; de Ghistelles: Limburg-Stirum, *Cour des comtes de Flandre*, 148-51 and above, pp. 126-7; de Halewin: *Trésor des chartes de Rethel*, ii. nos. 632, 670, 728, etc.; de Rasseghem: Buntinx, *Audientie*, 85-8.

[2] See respectively *Inventaires mobiliers*, ii. 427 n. 4; ibid., 315 n. 3. and ACO B2299, f. 1; *Invs. mobs.*, i. 595 n. 6; ACO B1494, f. 1.

[3] See respectively *Inventaires mobiliers*, i. 583 n. 4 (where Prost suggests that A. Pasté may originally have moved from Paris to Burgundy with J. Blanchet) and Debrie, *AB* ix (1937), 304; ACO B364/2, quittance of 26 May 1389; *Registre des Parlements de Beaune*, 333-4; and ACO B1465, f. 36.

In Flanders, the receivers-general were all recruited locally, and the three engaged by Philip himself, rather than inherited from his father-in-law, were probably all citizens of Bruges: Pierre Adorne, Francois de le Hofstede *dit* le Cupre, and Jehan le Chien or den Hond.[1] Moreover, the sovereign-bailiffs, the *procureur général*, the *contrôleur des comptes* and the majority of the other officials recruited by Philip were Flemings. But he introduced a number of Frenchmen into the *chambre du conseil et des comptes* at Lille: of the councillors, Thiercelet de la Barre was probably French, and Jehan de Nieles came from Artois; and, of the *maîtres*, Thomas de le Beke and Jehan de Pacy were imported from Paris and were almost certainly French.[2]

The fact that French was the official governmental language in Flanders meant that there was bound to be a preponderance of French-speaking personnel in the administration, but, apart from the minority of Frenchmen at Lille, these seem to have been recruited from *Flandre gallicante* rather than from outside the county, and there were many among them who, like Colard de la Clite, Henri d'Espierre and Pierre de la Tanerie, had already been in the service of Louis of Male. The shortage of Flemish-speaking councillors was a source of concern to the government: in 1394 the Duchess Margaret was complaining that she could not permit Jehan de Poucques away from her because 'je nai autre maistre dostel qui saiche le langange', and, in 1402, when the ducal secretary Daniel Alarts was appointed a Lille councillor, it was explicitly stated in his commission that this was because there were few councillors there who, like him, knew Flemish.[3]

In recruitment and promotion the civil services of Flanders and Burgundy were quite separate entities. While there are notable examples of Philip engaging artists and craftsmen in the Low Countries for service in Burgundy—the sculptor Jehan de Marville and the *canonnier* Colart Joseph, for instance[4]—there is no evidence of any such movement among his administrative personnel. In the other direction, we do occasionally hear of Burgundian civil servants and

---

[1] See respectively Gailliard, *Bruges et le Franc*, iii. 104 and van Nieuwenhuysen, *Recette générale*, 166; *IAB*, iii. 116, 117, etc. and van Nieuwenhuysen, *Rec. gén.*, 167; *Handelingen*, no. 124.

[2] Van Nieuwenhuysen, *Recette générale*, 17. Before he became a Lille councillor in 1393, Jehan de Nieles had been a councillor in the bailiwick of St. Omer (*IADNB*, i (1863), 234), and was also an *élu* for the *aides* in Artois (ADN B1597, f. 56). For the presence of Frenchmen in Philip's Lille *chambre*, see Leclercq, *PTSEC* (1958), 89.

[3] ADN B18822/23280 and ADN B1599, f. 84a-b.   [4] Above, p. 203.

THE BURGUNDIAN CIVIL SERVICE 213

others being employed in Flanders, but only temporarily. Thus the marshal of Burgundy, Guy de Pontailler, served in Flanders and even became governor there for a short time, and Regnaut Gombaut, *maître des comptes* at Dijon, worked at Lille between 20 June and 5 November 1385, and again for fifteen days in 1388.[1] But these are isolated instances.

The central administration was much more amorphous than either of the regional ones, and recruitment for it was more varied. Its personnel was Franco-Burgundian, with the French element predominating among the secretaries, and the Burgundian in the knightly entourage of the duke, which supplied the 'aulic' councillors and diplomatic agents. Among the treasurers and receivers-general of all finances a rough balance was maintained: Robert d'Amance and Nicolas de Fontenay were probably both from Troyes or its neighbourhood; Josset de Halle, though living in Dijon, was originally from Brabant; Pierre de Montbertaut and Jehan Despoullettes were probably from Artois; Amiot Arnaut was from Montbard in the duchy, Pierre Varopel from Beaune, Joceran Frepier from Chalon, and Jehan Chousat was from Poligny in the county of Burgundy.[2] Only one of these, the last, worked his way up, so to speak, through the Burgundian civil service: all the others were appointed to high office directly Philip took them into his employment. This is not true, however, of two of his chancellors, Philibert Paillart and Nicolas de Tholon, both Burgundians, who served as councillors, and the former also as bailiff, before their promotion.[3] They, like Robert d'Amance among the financial officers, were in office before the acquisition of Flanders, and therefore before the emergence of a genuine central administration. There was in fact only one truly 'central' chancellor, Jehan Canard, a Frenchman promoted from Philip's council at the Paris *Parlement* to be head of the entire ducal civil service.[4]

---

[1] Above, pp. 128–9 and van Nieuwenhuysen, *Recette générale*, 14 and 29.
[2] Pocquet, *MSHDB* iv (1937), 30–1, *Inventaires mobiliers*, i. 249 n. 3 and ACO B1479, f. 145 (d'Amance); Pocquet, ibid., 37 and van Nieuwenhuysen, *Recette générale*, 48 (de Fontenay); *Invs. mobs.*, i. 53 n. 5 and Pocquet, ibid., 42 (de Halle); van Nieuwenhuysen, *Rec. gén.*, 46 and ACO B1514, f. 79a–b (de Montbertaut; the second reference shows that he was paid when away from his Arras *hôtel* on ducal service); above, p. 210, n. 2 (Despoullettes); Billioud, *États*, 191 (Arnaut); *Invs. mobs.*, ii. 260, n. 2 and Monget, *Chartreuse*, i. 26 (Varopel); ACO B1494, f. 1 (Frepier); van Nieuwenhuysen, *Rec. gén.*, 46 (Chousat).
[3] *Inventaires mobiliers*, i. 61 n. 8 and *Registre des Parlements de Beaune*, 340.
[4] Giard, *PTSEC* (1902), 23–8 and Pocquet, *MSHDB* viii (1942), 141.

The other group of professional civil servants in the central administration were the secretaries. Three of these were Flemish and carried
out most of their secretarial duties in Flanders, except when sent on
special missions by the duke. They were Daniel Alarts, Gilles le
Foulon or de Volre, *bourgeois* of Sluis, and Thierry Gherbode of
Ypres.[1] One, Jehan Hue of Avallon, was certainly, and another,
Jehan Potier, was almost certainly, Burgundian, but most of the others
seem to have been French, among them several who either came from
Paris or resided there more or less permanently.[2]

The Franco-Burgundian character of Philip the Bold's central
administration is very apparent in the nobles of his entourage, who
served him as 'aulic' councillors and diplomatic agents, for there was
scarcely a Fleming among them. The majority were Burgundian,
with a sprinkling of French knights: prominent among them were
Guy and Guillaume de la Trémoille, Oudart de Chaseron, Guillaume
de Vienne, Olivier de Jussy, Ancel de Salins, and Bertaut and Philippe
de Chartres.

This brief survey of the structure and recruitment of the Burgundian civil service has shown that a career in it never led from
Burgundy to Flanders or vice versa, and only occasionally was a
member of one of the regional administrations transferred to the
centre. Indeed there seem to be only two clear examples of this:
Jehan Chousat, a native of Poligny in the county of Burgundy, was
promoted in 1401 from treasurer of Dôle to receiver-general of all
finances; and Joceran Frepier became treasurer and governor of
finances in 1400 after serving as receiver-general of Burgundy.[3] At
first sight the career of Maciot Estibourt might be taken as an example of this, for he became *maître* of Philip's *chambre aux deniers* in

---

[1] See respectively ADN B1598, fos. 11b, 17a–b, 48, 120b and 1599, f. 43;
IAB, iii. 358, ADN B1599, f. 17, *Inventaires mobiliers*, ii. 179 n. 1 and ACO
B1519, f. 80b (Gilles le Foulon paid when absent from his Sluis *hôtel*); de
Coussemaker, *ACFF* xxvi (1901–2), 175–385.

[2] For Hue, see *Inventaires mobiliers*, ii. 111 n. 1; and for Potier, see ibid., no.
2779; *IACOB*, ii. 116; *IAPCA*, ii. 125; ACO B11402, f. 47b, etc. The
secretaries who were certainly or almost certainly French included Jehan
Blanchet, Pierre de Courlon, Robert Dangeul, Laurence Lamy, Jacques du
Val and Jehan Vie. Jehan Blanchet, originally from Sens, had a *hôtel* at
Dijon (Coville, *Col*, 15 n. 6 and ACO B15, f. 2); Pierre de Courlon was
required by Philip to live in Paris (ACO B1508, f. 97); and Jacques du Val
received a pension while he lived in Paris on Philip's behalf (ACO B1465,
f. 36).

[3] Van Nieuwenhuysen, *Recette générale*, 46 and 47, and Durrieu, *Le Manuscrit*, ii (1895), 82.

1380 after serving as a castellan in the duchy in 1377–8, but in fact his career had begun in the central administration, and it was from it that he moved into that of the duchy and not vice versa. *Clerc des offices* of the ducal household in 1365, he had been charged in 1369 with accounting for all the household expenses, a position functionally identical to that of the later *maître de la chambre aux deniers*, which he held in 1380–2. Between 1382 and 1391 he was receiver of the bailiwick of La Montagne in the duchy, but he reappears in the central administration in 1392–9 as *maître* of the Duchess Margaret's *chambre aux deniers*. Finally, in 1401, he was provided for with the post of *grènetier du grenier à sel* at Dijon.[1] His career was not untypical, ... Pierre du Celier and Amiot Arnaut joined the regional ad- ... of Burgundy after taking office at the centre. Pierre du ... *gruyer* of Burgundy in 1389 after serving for two years ...r-general of all finances, a post which he took up again in ...combining it with that of treasurer; and during these two ... was also castellan of Saulx-le-Duc. He ended his career in ...al service as receiver of Hesdin in Artois.[2] Amiot Arnaut, ...rving as receiver-general of all finances in 1372–86, became a ...*des comptes* at Dijon. He had been entrusted with the accounts ... construction of the Charterhouse of Champmol in 1383, a ...which occupied him for the remainder of Philip the Bold's ...n, and which he delegated to his brother Philippe when he was ...sent from Dijon on ducal business, which he frequently was, for ...e was employed, among many other things, as a diplomatic agent. He too held more than one office at a time, for he was receiver of the Dijon bailiwick between 1374 and 1384, and castellan of Saulx-le-Duc and Salives from 1399 to 1403.[3] It was most unusual for a ducal financial officer to hold high office for as long as he had, but in Arnaut's case it must be remembered that the central financial administration scarcely existed before 1384. More typical of careers in it are those of Pierre Varopel and Jehan Despoullettes. Appointed receiver-general of all finances in 1397, Jehan Despoullettes does not seem to have been employed again in the central administration after his retirement from this post in 1401, except briefly, in connection with some royal funds, in 1402.[4] His four-year term as receiver-general of all finances was rather longer than average: Pierre Varopel,

---

[1] *Inventaires mobiliers*, i. 542 n. 2; *Itinéraires*, p. ix, and ACO B1460, f. 17b.
[2] *Inventaires mobiliers*, ii. 440 n. 4, and van Nieuwenhuysen, *Rec. gén.*, 47.
[3] *Inventaires mobiliers*, i. 387 n. 4; Monget, *Chartreuse*, i. 23, 291, etc.
[4] See above, p. 170.

after two and a half years as *maître de la chambre aux deniers* and a spell of office as *maître des garnisons de l'hôtel*, became receiver-general of all finances on 1 June 1389, but vacated this office eighteen months later, after which we hear no more of him in the ducal service until his appointment as treasurer in March 1399, a post which death deprived him of a little over a year later.[1]

In marked contrast to the brevity of the careers in the central administration of Philip's *gens de finance*, which were also frequently interrupted by periods out of office, was the length of service there of his secretaries, who often retained office continuously for a decade or more, and even for life. Nor did they necessarily remain secretaries, for many were promoted in the ducal service. Daniel Alarts, w[ho] worked for some eight years with Louis of Male's *gens des c[omptes]* before he became a ducal secretary in 1384–5, was sent ba[ck as] *maître* to the Lille *chambre des comptes* after fifteen years' servi[ce as] secretary; and shortly afterwards, in July 1402, was promoted f[rom] being *maître des comptes* at Lille to councillor there.[2] Jacques [de] Val, after about ten years as secretary alone, was appointed *maî[tre] des requêtes* and councillor of the duke as well,[3] and Jehan Potier, [a] ducal secretary at least as early as 1374, appears in the ducal counci[l] at Dijon from 1379 on, and became also *garde des chartes* of the duchy before his death in 1392.[4] Several other ducal secretaries became councillors, including Robert Dangeul and Jehan Hue.

The ladder of promotion was much more pronounced in the regional administrations than in the centre. Both in Burgundy and Flanders it was customary for a financial officer to work his way up, as it were, through the ranks, and some of the councillors at Lille and Dijon had done the same. Thus Guillaume Slyp and Guillaume de Clugny served as bailiffs before they became councillors at Lille and Dijon respectively.[5] Although the *maîtres des comptes* were some-

---

[1] ACO B1460, f. 17b and B1462, f. 37; van Nieuwenhuysen, *Recette générale*, 114 and ACO B1463 bis, f. 2b; Pocquet, *MSHDB* iv (1937), 49.

[2] Besides the references cited above, p. 214, n. 1, see *Textes historiques sur Lille et le Nord de la France*, ii. no. 88 (*RN* xix (1933), 232–3) for Alarts signing as secretary in 1385.

[3] ACO B11402, f. 34 bis (sec. in 1374); B1461, fos. 42b–43 (still sec. in 1383–4); B1462, f. 94b (councillor and sec. in 1385–6); and B1465, f. 36 (sec. and *m. des requêtes* in 1386–7).

[4] BD Baudot MS. 954, f. 15; ACO B11402, f. 47b, etc.; ACO B15, f. 31b. For the next sentence, see *Inventaires mobiliers*, ii. 516 n. 5 and ACO B1526, f. 73.

[5] Nowé, *Baillis comtaux*, 375; ADN B4079, f. 35, etc. and *Registre des Parlements de Beaune*, 335–6.

times recruited from among the receivers, more often than not the aspiring *maître* served his apprenticeship as a clerk in the *chambre des comptes*. Thus at Lille, David Bousse and Dreue Suquet, both clerks, were promoted to *maître* in 1397, and in the *chambre des comptes* at Dijon, at least two of the *maîtres*, André Pasté and Nicolas le Vaillant, had been clerks there.[1] On the other hand Jehan Aubert, after at least four years as a clerk in the Dijon *chambre*, was promoted by Philip in June 1400 to be *maître* of Duchess Margaret's *chambre aux deniers*;[2] while Pierre Boiville, who served as *maître des comptes* at Dijon for the last ten years of his life, had previously been castellan of Villaines and receiver of the bailiwick of La Montagne.[3] Oudart Douay, too, one of Philip's most trusted financial officers, entered the Dijon *chambre* so to speak from outside, for he was appointed a *maître des comptes* there in 1389 after serving as castellan of Salmaise, *grènetier* of the duchy and receiver-general of the duchy and county. While a *maître*, he continued to hold important financial offices. He served another term as receiver-general of the duchy and county in 1390–1; kept account of the payment of the ransom of John of Nevers in 1397–8; and, from 1395 on, supervised the ducal rebuilding programme in the duchy of Burgundy. Moreover, apart from this distinguished career in the ducal service, he served a term of office in 1401–2 as mayor of Dijon.[4] In Flanders, one of the receivers-general recruited by Philip, Jehan le Chien, in office during 1402–4, had been a domanial receiver at Sluis, and had kept the accounts of the construction of Sluis castle in 1396–7. Bailiff of Aardenburg in 1398–1401, he was one of a commission of three appointed in the latter year to collect domanial arrears throughout Flanders.[5] While he had worked his way through the ranks before achieving high office, Pierre Adorne, receiver-general of Flanders in 1394–7, was introduced from outside, for, though he had been a leading member of the town government of Bruges, and treasurer there between 1390 and 1394, he had never previously been in the ducal service.[6]

Although it is often impossible to demonstrate the relationship of ducal officers with the same name, it is clear that nepotism was common in the ducal civil service. Many minor offices passed from father

[1] ADN B1598, f. 75 (Bousse and Suquet); *Inventaires mobiliers*, i. 583 n. 4 (Pasté) and ibid., ii. 428 n. 7 (le Vaillant).
[2] ACO B15, f. 42b and BN Coll. de Bourg. 54, f. 24.
[3] *Inventaires mobiliers*, i. 128 n. 3.
[4] *Inventaires mobiliers*, i. 595, n. 6; above, p. 73, and ACO B15, f. 39b.
[5] Van Nieuwenhuysen, *Recette générale*, 143, 167; *Handelingen*, index *s.v.* and ADN B1599, fos. 57 and 60.   [6] *IAB*, iii. 275.

to son, or from brother to brother. Thus Philip in 1399 permitted his secretary and maritime bailiff of Sluis, Gilles le Foulon, to make over certain duties and rights in the prisons near Sluis to his son Simonnet le Foulon; Pierre Alarts succeeded his brother, the ducal secretary Daniel Alarts, in a minor office at Sluis in 1395; and the bailiff of Arras, Pierre d'Esnes, was succeeded, on his death in 1397, by his brother Jehan d'Esnes.[1] In the southern territories, Guiot de Rup, who had been governor of the ducal wine cellars and *sommelier de l'échansonnerie*, was succeeded by his son when he retired in 1395; and the receiver of Beaufort, Jehan Leclerc, was succeeded in 1402 by his son Nicolas.

Philip the Bold had no qualms about finding employment for relatives of his civil servants. Denys de Pacy, illegitimate son of Jehan de Pacy, *maître des comptes* at Lille, was made a clerk in 1397 after four years' service in the *chambre* under his father, and was at the same time legitimized by the duke; and Jehan Slyp, brother of the bailiff of Bruges and ducal councillor Guillaume Slyp, held in succession between 1385 and 1409 the offices of bailiff of West Ypres, bailiff of Sluis, *écoutète* of Bruges, and maritime bailiff of Sluis.[2] The ducal secretary, Thierry Gherbode, was able to place his brother Jehan in the ducal service as *clerc des offices de l'hôtel*, and it seems likely that the bailiff of West Ypres and Sluis, Pierre Gherbode, was a relative of his. The father and son, Jehan and Pierre Blanchet, served Philip as secretary between 1363 and 1400, the latter becoming councillor and *maître des requêtes*; but perhaps the best example of two members of the same family in the ducal civil service is that of la Tanerie, from the lesser nobility of *Flandre gallicante*.[3] Two brothers, Pierre and Jacques, had distinguished careers in Philip the Bold's service in Flanders. Pierre was employed by Louis of Male in 1382 as clerk of the receiver of Antwerp, and fought at the battle of Roosebeke in that year. He was promoted by Philip to be receiver of the domain of Antwerp in 1387 and receiver-general of Flanders from 1388 to 1394, before settling down as a *maître* of the Lille *chambre des comptes*, in which office he remained, residing for the most part in his *hôtel* at Lille, till his death in November 1400. Numerous special

---

[1] ADN B1599, f. 17; ibid., 1598, f. 17; *IADNB*, iv. 26, 29. For the next sentence, see *Inventaires mobiliers*, i. 114 n. 7 and *IACOB*, i. 361–2.

[2] ADN B1598, fos. 64b, 75b; *IAB*, iii. 209 n. 1 and iv. 201 n.6. For what follows, see de Coussemaker, *ACFF* xxvi (1901–2), 175–385, and *Inventaires mobiliers*, i. 51 n. 6 and ii. 337 and n. 3.

[3] On the family, see Fremaux, *BSEC* xii (1908), 195–243.

tasks were allotted him: he kept account of the works at Nieuport castle in 1396–8 and of the funds raised for the Nicopolis crusade in 1394 and for John of Nevers' ransom in 1397; he acted as receiver of the domains of Biervliet and Harelbeke in 1394–1400; and, shortly before his death, he had been appointed Philip's treasurer and governor of finances for the northern group of territories.[1] His brother Jacques de la Tanerie must have been a man of parts, for his career was divided between the spheres of justice and finance. In 1384–6 he was acting at Lille as ducal *procureur* in the ecclesiastical court of Tournai. From this legal post he moved in 1388 to the financial one of receiver of Lille, and temporarily achieved high office in the central administration in 1395–6 as *maître de la chambre aux deniers* before returning to legal office in 1396 as Philip the Bold's first *procureur général* of Flanders.[2]

The tendency for several members of one family to be taken simultaneously into the ducal service is equally apparent in its non-professional element. Outstanding here is the case of the Burgundian noble family of la Trémoille. Three brothers, sons of Guy V and Radegonde Guenant, devoted themselves to Philip the Bold, Guy and Guillaume served him as chamberlain and councillor, and the latter succeeded Guy de Pontailler as marshal of Burgundy in 1392; both were killed on the Nicopolis crusade.[3] The third brother, Pierre, was also a chamberlain and councillor of Philip, and, like his brothers, was sent by the duke on numerous diplomatic missions: to Albert of Bavaria in 1393; to the Teutonic Knights in 1394; and to England in 1398. An attempt by Philip and his wife to place him on the episcopal throne of Chalon in 1374 failed, but another la Trémoille, Louis, became bishop of Tournai in 1388 as a result of Philip's influence, and thereafter ducal councillor.[4] Although the members of

---

[1] Van Nieuwenhuysen, *Recette générale*, 100 and 165–6; ADN B4080, f. 39b and B4082, f. 36b. For his *hôtel* at Lille see, e.g., ACO B1519, f. 70b and AGR Acquits de Lille 977, letter from the duchess to Jehan de Pacy, 8 Nov. 1400. A rather pathetic letter written at 3 p.m. on 5 Nov. 1400 survives among the correspondence of the *chambre des comptes* at Lille, in which Jacques announces his brother's death at 10 a.m. that day, AGR Acquits de Lille 977.

[2] Van Nieuwenhuysen, *Recette générale*, 166; ADN B4073, f. 53 and B4075, f. 60b. For his appointment as *procureur général*, see ADN B1598, f. 26.

[3] For Guillaume, see *Inventaires mobiliers*, i. 157 n. 6.

[4] For Pierre's diplomatic missions, see above, pp. 61–2; ACO B1500, f. 40; and B11926, certificate of expenses of Pierre de la Trémoille and Witart de Bours, chamberlains, on mission to England, dated 20 November 1398. For his attempted promotion to the see of Chalon, see above, p. 163, but note that Prost (*Inventaires mobiliers*, i. 376 n. 5) suggests that the candidate for the

this family were devoted servants and friends of Philip the Bold, it must not be imagined that there was anything exclusive about this devotion. The surviving accounts of Guy de la Trémoille show a remarkable spread of loyalty and obligations for, besides the 5,000 francs per annum he received from Philip, he accepted pensions at one time or another from the king of France, the duchess of Brabant, the count of Savoy, the despot of Milan, Giangaleazzo Visconti, and even the pope, and his income from these sources far exceeded that derived from his lands.[1]

One other example of a family in the ducal service cannot be omitted: indeed, no account of the ducal civil service would be complete without some mention of the famous merchants and bankers of Lucca, the Rapondi, who had settled at Paris and Bruges in the second half of the fourteenth century, for one of them, Dino Rapondi, played a major part in the formation of the Burgundian state, acting as Philip the Bold's chief financial adviser and agent, as well as banker, with the official titles of *maître d'hôtel* and councillor. One of the chief suppliers to the ducal and royal courts in the 1370s, Dino advanced his first loans to Philip at this time. The acquisition of Flanders in 1384 made him doubly useful to the duke, for he was admirably placed to supply Philip with cash in Paris or elsewhere, and recoup himself from the Flemish taxes and rents. In 1383 he had advanced a sum of 100,000 *écus*, which Louis of Male had imposed on Ypres and other towns after Roosebeke and made over to Philip, and at the same time he lent money to Philip on the strength of an *aide* from Antwerp. While directing the works at Sluis between 1391 and 1394, he was of particular value in raising the necessary funds; but it was in 1397–8 that he performed the most valuable and grandiose of all his services to Philip, in making possible the ransom of John of Nevers after the disaster at Nicopolis. Behind the political power of Philip the Bold was the wealth of Dino Rapondi.[2]

Dino Rapondi not only put his immense financial resources at the disposal of the duke, he also worked unceasingly in the ducal financial administration. In 1386 he visited Pavia to negotiate a loan for

---

see of Chalon may have been a different Pierre de la Trémoille. For Louis as a councillor, see, e.g., *IAB*, iii. 412 (1398).

[1] *Livre de comptes de Guy de la Trémoille.*

[2] For this and the next paragraph, see Mirot, *BEC* lxxxix (1928), 299–389; van Nieuwenhuysen, *Recette générale*, 40–1, 89–90, 144 and 149–51; above pp. 73–4 and p. 194; ACO B1500, fos. 44b–45 and B1526, f. 79; *Inventaires mobiliers*, i. 382 n. 6; and van Nieuwenhuysen, *RBPH* xxxv (1957), 59–61.

Philip from Giangaleazzo Visconti. In 1392 he was away from his Paris *hôtel* on ducal business from 28 March to 15 June, visiting Amiens, Bruges, Sluis and Lille; he undertook another journey to Lille from 20 August to 22 September; and a third to Lille, Bruges, and Ghent, on the instructions of the chancellor, between 7 October and 11 December. Flemish monetary and other affairs took him to Flanders again in 1393, between 8 January and 11 February, and 12 March and 23 July. He was still active in 1402, though by this time he could no longer ride, but had to travel in a carriage. The other members of the Rapondi family who were of value to Philip the Bold can hardly be said to have belonged to his civil service. Guillelmo, a brother of Dino, helped to finance his wedding in 1369; Giovanni, Dino's nephew, lent money to Philip and recouped himself from the ducal receivers, and Giacomo, another of Dino's brothers, supplied him with books.

The basic remuneration of Philip the Bold's civil servants was monetary: most of them received an annual pension or salary (*pension*) which acted as a kind of retaining fee, and were paid an additional daily wage when actually engaged on ducal business away from their homes or the court (*gaiges*). Thus the treasurer and governor of finances, in charge of the financial administration, received 1000 francs per annum after 1397, and was paid *gaiges* in addition at the rate of 3 francs per day.[1] The active, professional councillors for the most part received salaries of 300 francs, and 2 or 3 francs a day when travelling on ducal business; while the *maîtres des comptes* at Lille, the *procureur général* and *contrôleur des comptes* of Flanders, and the governor of the chancery in the duchy of Burgundy, were paid salaries of 200 or 250 francs.[2] The annual *pension*, augmented with daily *gaiges*, was by no means the only financial remuneration, for ducal gifts accounted for a large proportion of the earnings of many civil servants. Every year sums of money, often equivalent in amount to the annual salary of the recipient, were distributed throughout the civil service. The following table (figures in francs)[3], compiled from the accounts of the receipts-general of all finances and of Flanders, illustrates this.

---

[1] Van Nieuwenhuysen, *Recette générale*, 45.
[2] The salary of the Lille *maîtres* was raised in 1394-5 from 200 to 250 francs, cf. ADN B4079, f. 33b with B4080, f. 39b. For the governor of the Burgundian chancery, see Andt, *Chambre des comptes*, i. 70 n. 116.
[3] From ACO B1508, f. 85; ADN B4079, 4080, 4081 and 4082, fos. 33a–b, 39b, 78–83 and 36a–b respectively.

Name of officer	Rank or title	Annual pension	Amount received in ducal gifts in 1396
Jehan de Poucques	councillor and *maître d'hôtel*	300	900
Pierre Heyns	*contrôleur des comptes* of Flanders	200	200
Jehan de Pacy	*maître des comptes*	250	150
Pierre de la Tanerie	*maître des comptes*	250	200
Jehan de Nieles	councillor at Lille	500	300

These gifts to civil servants are a constant feature of the ducal accounts, and, in the case of the secretaries, seem to have been their chief form of remuneration. Some of them, Jehan Hue, for example, received annual *pensions*, but most of them apparently did not, and at least one, Jehan Vie, received no payments from the duke other than the occasional gift.[1] To judge from the accounts of the receipt-general of all finances, this source of remuneration provided the secretaries with an average annual income of about 50–100 francs. The distribution of the chancellor's sources of income is shown in the following table (figures in francs) compiled from the accounts of the receipt-general of all finances for the years 1392–6. As head of the ducal civil service, he was by far its most highly paid member, with an average annual income from the duke of over 4,500 francs.

ACO B no.	Period of account	Amount of 2000 f.p.a. pension actually paid	Total paid in gaiges	Total paid in gifts	Total income from duke
1495	7 June 1392–23 April 1393	1500	702	500	2702
1500	24 April 1393–31 July 1394	3000	988	1500	5488
1501	1 August 1394–1 Feb. 1395	1000	1720	1000	3720
1503	26 Jan.–31 Dec. 1395	1500	2530	750	4780
1508	1 Jan.–31 Oct. 1396	2000	1120	650	3770
TOTALS for whole period of four years and five months:		9000	7060	4400	20460

[1] ACO B1495, f. 22b and above, p. 144; ACO B1503, f. 97b.

Apart from their monetary income and minor perquisites like gifts of robes or wine, exemption from taxation and the like, the more outstanding among Philip the Bold's councillors and administrators could hope for recompense, during or after their service, in the form of ecclesiastical benefices or *anoblissement*. Jehan Potier, after serving Philip for at least twenty years as secretary, councillor, and *garde des chartes* at Dijon, was promoted in 1391 through his influence to the see of Arras, and, when he died before his installation could take place, the vacancy was filled by the ducal chancellor, Jehan Canard.[1] Another chancellor, Nicolas de Tholon, was provided with the bishopric of Autun when he resigned from the ducal service; another secretary and councillor, Robert Dangeul, became bishop of Nevers in 1401;[2] and many examples could be cited of Philip the Bold rewarding his civil servants with minor benefices, or even by obtaining benefices for their relatives. Ennoblement, either by the king of France at Philip's request or by the duke himself, was more sparingly used, but at least four of Philip's leading financial officers were recompensed in this way: the receivers-general of Burgundy, Jehan d'Auxonne and Joceran Frepier; the receiver-general of all finances and Dijon *maître des comptes*, Amiot Arnaut; and Hervé de Neauville, *maître de la chambre aux deniers* between 1386 and 1391.[3]

No account of the ducal civil service under Philip the Bold would be complete without some mention of its close relationship to the royal civil service. There were temporary loans of royal personnel to the ducal service for a specific task. Thus a *maître des comptes* of the Paris *chambre*, Jehan Creté, was lent to Philip in 1385 to help reorganize the financial administration of Flanders and set up a *chambre des comptes* at Lille, and again in 1386 for the same purpose in Burgundy.[4] There were a number of ducal civil servants, like Jehan de Pacy and Thomas de le Beke in the Lille *chambre*, who were recruited from the royal service;[5] and there were many who served in

---

[1] Lestocquoy, *Évêques d'Arras*, 40–2.
[2] *Registre des Parlements de Beaune*, 340, and *Inventaires mobiliers*, ii. 516 n. 5. For what follows, see, e.g., *Documents relatifs au Grand Schisme*, iii. nos. 659 and 2054.
[3] d'Arbaumont, *RNHB* (n.s.) ii (1866), 153–4; Billioud, *États*, 191; and *Songe véritable*, 410–11.
[4] Van Nieuwenhuysen, *Recette générale*, 14 and ACO B1465, f. 40b. See too *Testaments enregistrés au Parlement de Paris*, no. 20.
[5] Jehan de Pacy was a *maître des comptes* at Lille from 1386 until at least 1400; he had been clerk and royal notary at Paris, van Nieuwenhuysen, *Rec. gén.*, 17. Thomas de le Beke, who was *m. des comptes* at Lille, 1386–94,

the royal, as well as in the ducal, administration. At least eight of the secretaries in the regular employment of the duke were at the same time royal secretaries: Daniel Alarts, Jehan Blanchet, Robert Dangeul, Jehan Hue, Laurence Lamy, Jehan Lemol, Jehan Potier and Jacques du Val. However, the exact significance of this whole-sale sharing of secretaries remains doubtful, for secretaryships were commonly held in plurality: the humanist Jehan de Montreuil, provost of the chapter of St. Peter's, Lille, was secretary of the dauphin, John of Berry, Philip the Bold and Louis of Orleans.[1] Much less equivocal evidence of the close relationship of the two civil services is afforded by the careers of Nicolas de Fontenay, Pierre de Montbertaut, Hervé de Neauville and others, which were divided between them.[2] Nicolas de Fontenay, a *bourgeois* of Troyes who began his career as a royal financial official there, became royal bailiff of Troyes, a royal councillor and treasurer of France; yet he was head of the Burgundian financial administration between 1379 and 1391. Pierre de Montbertaut, *maître* of Philip's *chambre aux deniers* from 1392 to 1395 and his receiver-general of all finances from 1395 to 1397, was also his treasurer and governor of finances in 1395–9 and 1402–4. In the royal service, he was *trésorier des guerres* in 1396, *trésorier sur le fait de la justice* in 1400–3; and receiver-general of *aides* in 1402. He must have been a very busy man. Even in 1398, when he was ducal receiver-general and apparently not employed by the French crown, he spent only sixteen days in his *hôtel* at Arras: during the whole of the rest of the year he was away on ducal business. Hervé de Neauville began his career in the royal service as receiver at Gisors and Lisieux, and ended it in 1403–10 as *maître extraordinaire* in the Paris *chambre des comptes*; in the meanwhile he had served Philip as *maître de la chambre aux deniers* from 1386 to 1391.

These were by no means the only persons who served both king and duke: Pierre d'Orgemont, who became chancellor of France in 1373, was an active councillor of Philip; Jehan du Drac's career in the Paris *Parlement* did not deter him from serving Philip at the same

---

also came from Paris, and is probably to be identified with the clerk of the receiver-general of royal *aides* of that name in 1370 (AN J571/21).

[1] Coville, *Col*, 73–4.

[2] De Fontenay: *Inventaires mobiliers*, ii. 97, n. 3; Poquet, *MSHDB* v (1937), 37 and 46; van Nieuwenhuysen, *Recette générale*, 41 and 48. De Montbertaut: van Nieuwenhuysen, *Rec. gén.*, 41 and 46; ACO B1511, f. 181 and B1514, f. 79a–b. De Neauville: van Nieuwenhuysen, *Rec. gén.*, 47; *Songe véritable*, 410–11.

time as councillor and *maître des requêtes*; Philibert Paillart, after crowning his career in Philip's service by serving as chancellor in 1363-6, was thereafter, until his death in 1397, a president in the Paris *Parlement* while remaining a councillor of Philip; and, when Philip retired his *maître de la chambre aux deniers*, Jehan de Bray, on grounds of age, he used his power in France to have him transferred to the royal service as receiver of *aides* in the diocese of Amiens.[1] Quite apart from this close relationship of personnel, Philip the Bold also made use of the royal civil service for the administration of his own territories. Thus the Beaune *Parlement* was on several occasions before 1393 presided over by an official of the Paris *Parlement* or a royal councillor, and the receivers of royal *aides* in Artois and Rethel were often used to collect the ducal *aides* in these areas.[2]

Perhaps the use of the term 'civil service' with reference to Philip the Bold's Burgundy is inaccurate and misleading, for it was really little more than a collection of loosely linked groups of persons devoting themselves in varying degrees to the service of the duke. On the other hand, these councillors, *gens de finances*, bailiffs and others all owed allegiance to the duke, and the majority swore solemn oaths to him on taking office. Moreover, they were dismissible by him, and many were personally appointed by him. A significant proportion remained in his service for life, and were followed or accompanied by relatives. However loosely integrated they may have been, they formed a recognizable group which played an essential part in the formation of the Burgundian state under Philip the Bold.

[1] Mirot, *Les d'Orgemont*, 14-19; *Testaments enregistrés au Parlement de Paris*, no. 38, *Inventaires mobiliers*, ii. no. 3726 and ACO B1495, f. 47b, etc. (du Drac); *Invs. mobs.*, i. 61 n. 8 (Paillart); ACO B1511 bis, fos. 1 and 45b (de Bray).
[2] *Ordonnances du duché*, p. clxi and van Nieuwenhuysen, *Recette générale*, 77-8.

CHAPTER ELEVEN

The Finances of the Burgundian State

In examining the finances of a medieval state, the historian is seeking answers to questions which seldom or never occurred to the rulers and financial experts of those days. He wants to know what was the total income and what the expenditure, and, further, what were the different sources of income and the principal items of expenditure. While the accounts of a modern state or commercial organization are specifically designed, by means of a classified analysis and final balance, to reveal and display this information, the primary aim of the accounts, in a medieval state, was to establish the financial position *vis-à-vis* the ruler of the individual officers who made them. Thus the accounts of the Burgundian receipt-general of all finances were not public, but private, documents; they were not designed to exhibit the receipts and expenditure of the state, but simply to record the financial transactions of the receiver-general of all finances. Furthermore, since the financial administration was designed to avoid the transport of specie, neither receipts nor expenditure were centralized. Some mention has already been made of the way in which payments for one item were split up between several accounts, and of the system of assignments, in which a specific payment was assigned by one receiver to a junior colleague, the payment being entered among the receipts of the former and the expenses of the latter. The financial administration of a medieval state was, in fact, an exceedingly complex mechanism organized for purposes wholly foreign to the interests of the present-day observer in trying to ascertain in what exactly its financial resources really consisted. For this reason, as much as because of the nature of the present work, the sketch which follows is necessarily tentative and incomplete, and the figures only approximate.

Although the task of establishing, even approximately, the annual financial resources of the Burgundian state is a complex and difficult one, there are several ways of attempting it.[1] Let us first confine ourselves to the middle years of Philip the Bold's reign in all his territories, that is to say, to the years 1394–6 inclusive. One method of assessing his revenues is to add together the *receipts* recorded in the accounts of the regional receipts-general, in particular those of the two Burgundies and of Flanders and Artois, and to join to their combined total two kinds of revenue recorded in the accounts of the receipt-general of all finances but not in those of the other receipts-general: royal gifts and ducal *aides*. Using this method, the average annual income in the years 1394–6 may be set out as follows:

Source	Approx. annual income, 1394–6
Receipt-gen. of Burgundies, total receipts:	85,000 francs
Receipt-gen. of Flanders/Artois, total receipts:	197,000 ,,
Royal gifts recorded in rec.-gen. of all finances:	99,000 ,,
Ducal *aides* ditto:	57,000 ,,
TOTAL:	438,000 ,,

Since this figure excludes the ordinary revenues of the smaller receipts-general of Rethel, Nevers, and the Champagne lands, which may be estimated at 40,000 francs, it should be increased to 478,000 francs.

Alternatively, we may try to ascertain the total resources of the state by analysing the *expenditure* recorded in these accounts. To do this, it is necessary to add to the total expenses recorded by the receiver-general of all finances the moneys expended *locally* by the regional receipts-general. Very roughly, this calculation yields an annual average figure for 1394–6 of 383,000 francs, which again must

[1] This chapter is partly based on Mlle van Nieuwenhuysen's unpublished thesis, *Recette générale*, and her tables have been the basis of many of my calculations. I have also used Pocquet, *AB* x (1938), 261–89; *MSHDB* vi (1939), 113–44 and vii (1940–1), 95–129; *RHDFE* (4) xviii (1939), 388–422; Mollat, *RH* ccxix (1958), 285–321; and the series of accounts of the receipt-general of all finances and of the receipts-general of Flanders and Artois and of the two Burgundies, preserved at Lille and Dijon, as well as those of the *maître de la chambre aux deniers* at Dijon. It should be noted that discrepancies between the figures given here and those in the above-mentioned works of van Nieuwenhuysen and Mollat, as well as in Coville, *Études . . . Monod*, 405–13, are largely due to the fact that these authors studied a single series of accounts, those of the receipt-general of all finances.

be on the small side, since it excludes the sums expended locally in Nevers, Rethel and Champagne: 400,000 would be more realistic.

A third method of assessing the ducal revenues in the middle years of Philip's reign is afforded by a document drawn up at the end of 1394 or early in 1395 which constitutes the nearest approach we have

Approximate estimated revenues for the year 1395 in francs

From the ducal aides:

Flanders	134,040[1]	
Flemish clergy	10,620	
Malines and Antwerp	10,340	
Lille, Douai and Orchies	10,000	
Artois (after certain deductions)	5,000	
duchy of Burgundy	20,000	
county of Burgundy	10,000	
Rethel	6,000	
Nevers	10,000	
county of Charolais and the Champagne lands	4,000	
	TOTAL:	220,000

From the king of France:

owed to the duke	80,000	
the duke's *pension*	36,000	
	TOTAL:	116,000

From the domains and 'aides ordinaires':[2]

duchy and county of Burgundy and Charolais	74,000	
Flanders (including 7,000 f. from 'recoprement de gaiges d'officiers')	47,000	
Artois, Lille, Douai	28,000	
Nevers and the Champagne lands	22,000	
Rethel	12,000	
	TOTAL:	183,000
	TOTAL:	519,000

---

[1] This figure (printed in error by le Roulx as 134,015 f.) is described in the document as approximate 'environ', and this is no doubt true of the others. Mr Walter Prevenier has pointed out, in a letter to me, that the conversion rate of 1 noble = ± 68s. par., used in this document, does not tally with the rate used in official documents concerning the 1394 Flemish *aide*, which was 1 noble = 72s. par. Since, however, the application of this apparently more correct second rate to these figures would increase the overall total by less than 10,000 f., it has seemed better to follow the rate used in the document itself.

[2] These are the royal *aides* which had been made over to the duke. See below, p. 230.

to a budget, for its purpose was to discover approximately what moneys could be made available in the year 1395 for the duke's projected crusade.[1]

This document, which was probably meant as a rough guide only, is difficult to interpret exactly. The figure for ducal *aides* represents not the annual average from this source, but the most that could be raised from *aides* at this particular time. Moreover, the amounts of ordinary receipts from the different areas represent what might be expected to remain after the deduction of local expenses. If, to allow for these facts, we deduct 150,000 francs from the total figure from *aides*, thus reducing it to little more than the annual average, and add 75,000, which probably represents approximately the local expenses in Burgundy and Flanders, to the ordinary receipts, the total comes to 444,000 francs. All three of our estimates are thus in broad agreement:

Analysis of receipts	478,000
Analysis of expenditure	400,000
Analysis of 1395 'budget'	444,000

Probably, in the middle years of his reign, Philip the Bold could annually dispose of some 400,000–450,000 francs, a figure which may be compared with Charles VI's annual income of perhaps a million and a half.[2] France was at least three times as wealthy as Burgundy.

Before leaving the subject of the total ducal financial resources, some attempt may be made to assess their increase during Philip the Bold's reign. The revenue of the two Burgundies, which averaged about 70,000 francs p.a., shows no overall rise in this period, but that of Flanders and Artois increased from about 160,000 francs p.a. in 1385–6 to about 240,000 francs in 1400–2. The income from ducal *aides*, as recorded in the receipt-general of all finances, was about 25,000 francs p.a. in 1384–5, and only 15,000 francs p.a. in 1401–4.[3] The income from the French crown increased from about 65,000 francs p.a. in 1384–6 to about 175,500 francs p.a. after 1396. These figures, together with the estimated receipt from the smaller receipts-general, may be tabulated as follows to show the total increase in revenues during Philip's reign.

---

[1] Printed by Delaville le Roulx, *France en Orient*, ii. no. 5. See above, pp. 63–4.
[2] *Hist. des institutions françaises*, i. 266–8.
[3] Not all the ducal *aides* were paid into the receipt-general of all finances. For an assessment of the total annual revenue from this source, see below, pp. 232–3.

	1384–6	1400–3
Receipt-general of Burgundies, total receipts:	70,000	70,000
Receipt-general of Flanders, total receipts:	160,000	240,000
Ducal *aides* in rec.-gen. of all finances:	25,000	15,000
Royal gifts	65,000	175,500
Smaller receipts-general, estimated total receipts:	40,000	40,000
	360,000	540,500

This calculation, based on the analysis of receipts, is broadly borne out by that of expenditure for, while the sums expended locally by the regional receipts-general did not alter substantially, remaining at about 75,000 francs p.a., the expenses of the receipt-general of all finances increased from about 300,000 to 500,000 francs p.a. during Philip the Bold's reign.

No comprehensive analysis of Philip the Bold's different sources of revenue can be provided here, but two of them merit consideration in some detail, both because of the relative ease in investigating them, and for their intrinsic importance: they are, income from the French crown, and ducal *aides*.

Philip the Bold's systematic financial exploitation of the French crown provided him with a direct and an indirect income from this source. The direct income consisted of regular *pensions* paid to him and members of his family, and of gifts, which were often justified as rewards for services rendered or compensation for some loss sustained by the duke in the service of the crown.[1] Thus Philip persuaded the king to reimburse him to the tune of 220,000 francs for his expenses in taking over and defending his own county of Flanders in 1384–6; and, on 12 December 1402, he helped himself to 10,000 francs from the royal treasury in compensation for the fact that, on 1 January 1401, though he had given the king the traditional New Year's gift, the king had omitted on that occasion to return the compliment. Philip's indirect income from France took the form of grants of royal *aides*. These comprised all the indirect taxes theoretically belonging to the crown in the duchy of Burgundy, and half those of Artois, Rethel, Nevers and some smaller areas,[2] and the total income from this source was probably about 60,000 francs p.a. The direct exploitation of

[1] See especially Pocquet, *MSHDB* vi (1939), 113–44 and vii (1940–1), 95–129; and van Nieuwenhuysen, *Recette générale*, 73–82. Pocquet's list of royal gifts is supplemented by that in BN Coll. de Bourgogne 53, fos. 222–30b. For what follows, see above, p. 34 and for another example, p. 99.

[2] For these, see Pocquet, *AB* x (1938), 161–89.

French resources, through gifts and pensions, increased in scope during Philip's reign, until, at the end of his life, he was awarded an annual *pension* of 100,000 francs and, on average, more than this sum in gifts each year. In these circumstances it is hardly surprising that, after 1397, he became a royal creditor. Nevertheless, the accounts of the receipt-general of all finances, in which this income was recorded, show that he actually received, on average, 175,500 francs from the king in each of the last seven or eight years of his life. If we add to this sum the 60,000 francs p.a. from royal *aides*, the total of 235,000 francs constitutes nearly one half of the ducal revenues. No better example could be found of the contribution made by French resources to the formation of the Burgundian state.

The other element in the ducal income which is relatively easy to assess, though very much smaller, is that provided by the ducal *aides* or special taxes which were voted by local representative institutions in the form of lump sums. In this matter, the duchy of Burgundy; the counties of Charolais, Nevers, Burgundy, Rethel, Artois and Flanders; the towns of Malines and Antwerp; and the towns and castellanies of Lille, Douai and Orchies, as well as some smaller units, all acted separately. In the table that follows, these smaller units— Limbourg, the county of Auxonne and the Champagne lands—which occasionally voted small *aides*, have been omitted. Apart from these, an effort has been made to include all the *aides* voted to the duke. The figures for Flanders represent the sums voted, in francs, and differ from the totals arrived at for taxation purposes after their detailed apportionment, which were often rather larger. As to the proportion of these *aides* actually paid over to the ducal receivers, it is clear, at any rate in Flanders, that, though payments were often delayed, the whole was usually ultimately paid. The monthly Flemish *aides* of 1384 and 1386 are an exception, and here the figure given represents the approximate sum actually paid.[1] It should be borne in mind that, in Artois, Rethel, Nevers and the duchy of Burgundy, the taxes recorded in the table are extra sums voted to the duke over and above what these areas paid to him in royal *aides*.

Unlike the royal *aides*, which yielded a similar annual revenue of about 60,000 francs, the ducal *aides* were an irregular source of income which had the immense advantage of being capable of very large

---

[1] The figures for the Flemish *aides* are taken from Prevenier, *RBPH* xxxviii (1960), 330–65, especially 365; those for Malines and Antwerp are from van Nieuwenhuysen, *Recette générale*, 174. For delays in the payment of Flemish *aides*, see above p. 178.

Aides granted to Philip the Bold, 1384–1403

NORTHERN TERRITORIES. FIGURES IN FRANCS

	Flanders	Flemish clergy	Lille, Douai, Orchies	Malines, Antwerp	Artois	Rethel	TOTAL
1384	c.30,000						30,000
1385			?10,000		?		10,000
1386	c.10,500			8,000			18,500
1387			2,000[1]				2,000
1388	100,000			?		5,000	105,000
1389			?10,000	4,000[2]	?		14,000
1390							
1391	98,182					?	98,182
1392			?				
1393							
1394	141,818	11,509	10,000	8,727	20,000	4,000	196,054
1395							
1396							
1397	218,182	15,696	?12,000	10,600	?20,000	?5,000	281,478
1398							
1399			c.5,175				5,175
1400						4,000	4,000
1401			?4,000	c.4,800			8,800
1402					?	5,000	5,000
1403							

APPROXIMATE ANNUAL AVERAGE: 38,900   TOTAL: 778,189

increases at given times. This is particularly apparent in the years 1394 and 1397, when an effort was made to extract the maximum possible, first for the crusade, and then for the ransom, of John of Nevers. The importance of the ducal *aides* lay in this flexibility rather than in their overall contribution to the ducal finances. The sporadic nature of the income provided by them does not, however, mask its diminution towards the end of Philip's reign. Evidently the widespread and unusually large *aides* of 1394 and 1397 had to some extent exhausted the taxpayers. On the other hand, since this source of income was only about one-eighth of the ducal revenues as a whole, these remained virtually unaffected.

Material has already been provided in the foregoing pages for a rough estimate of the geographical distribution of the ducal income.

[1] Lille only.   [2] Malines only.

Aides granted to Philip the Bold, 1384–1403

SOUTHERN TERRITORIES. FIGURES IN FRANCS

	duchy of Burgundy	county of Burgundy	Charolais	Nevers	TOTAL
1384	40,000				40,000
1385	20,000				20,000
1386	60,000	?12,000		?	72,000
1387				?	
1388	40,000	?			40,000
1389	25,000				25,000
1390					
1391	30,000	?			30,000
1392				8,000	8,000
1393	40,000	12,000	4,000		56,000
1394				?10,000	10,000
1395					
1396	40,000	12,000			52,000
1397	50,000		5,000	10,000	65,000
1398					
1399					
1400	12,000		2,000		14,000
1401					
1402					
1403	16,000	10,000	2,000	6,000	34,000

APPROXIMATE ANNUAL AVERAGE: 23,300   TOTAL: 466,000

More than three-fifths of the average annual revenue from ducal *aides* was provided by the northern territories, but this figure, which excludes the income from royal *aides*, involves only a fraction of the ducal resources. More significant is a comparison of the total revenues of the two principal regional receipts-general, and of the sums they paid into the central offices of receipt-general of all finances, *chambre aux deniers*, and the like. While the Burgundian receipt varied throughout Philip's reign between 60,000 and 90,000 francs p.a., of which about 50,000 p.a. was paid to the centre, the Flemish receipt rose from about 160,000 p.a. to nearly 240,000 francs in 1400–2, when it was paying more than 150,000 francs p.a. to the central offices. Roughly speaking, then, by the middle of the reign, about two-thirds of Philip's ordinary revenues (i.e. his total income excluding royal gifts and ducal *aides*) came from the northern group of territories, and one-third from the southern. The county of Burgundy, incidentally, contributed only about one-sixth of the revenues of the receipt-general of the two Burgundies.

The analysis of expenditure, like that of receipts, and for similar reasons, is fraught with difficulties. It would be particularly interesting to ascertain what proportion of the ducal revenues was devoted to administrative purposes, but the classification of expenses in the accounts does not help in this respect, for these expenses are divided between several headings, such as '*dons*', '*pensions a volunte*', etc., most of which include also non-administrative expenses. Thus an accurate total figure could only be obtained by analysing the entire contents of all the ducal accounts, including those of the local receivers who paid the wages of the local officials. In default of this, one may hazard a guess that administrative expenses accounted for some 150,000 francs p.a. or more; one-third, at least, of the ducal revenues.

Fortunately it is possible to assess approximately the average annual expenditure on certain recurrent items, and also to establish the total spent on certain specific projects. These may be set out as follows:

Approximate average annual expenditure on recurrent items in francs (*after 1395*)

Hôtel	Ordinary expenses of household and court paid for by the *maître de la chambre aux deniers*. Figure derived from his surviving accounts:	100,000
Duchess	Expenses of her *pension*, robes, *hôtel*, etc., estimated in 1395 'budget' at 44,400 f. (Delaville le Roulx, *France en Orient*, ii. no. 5). Probable annual average:	50,000
John of Nevers	After 1399, annual payment of 24,000 f. +extras (van Nieuwenhuysen, *Rec. générale*, 119–22):	25,000
New Year's gifts	(see David, *P. le Hardi, train somptuaire*, 55–64 and 148–55):	25,000
	TOTAL:	200,000

The recurring items recorded here consist wholly of expenditure directly for or connected with the court, but they do not by any means include all the expenses of this kind. In particular, they do not include the expenditure on supplies, especially jewellery, tapestries,

Approximate total expenditure on certain specific projects

Double wedding at	77,800 f. were spent on gifts (Plancher, iii.	
Cambrai, 1385	86) and 34,000 on livery (above, p. 88).	
	Total expenses must have been at least:	150,000
Sluis castle and	(figures in van Nieuwenhuysen, *Rec. gén.*,	
Tour de Bourgogne	142–3, totalled):	160,000
Charterhouse of		
Champmol	(ditto, ibid., 138):	150,000
Ransom and return		
of John of Nevers		
after Nicopolis	(above, p. 77):	500,000

wine and horses. Since the receiver-general of all finances spent at least 60,000 francs p.a. on these, we may conclude that rather more than half the total annual revenues were normally devoted to what may broadly be described as the court, though it should be pointed out that, since the court was also the administrative centre of the state, a proportion of this expenditure could equally well be included under the heading 'administration'. Apart from the court and the civil service, other recurring items were relatively insignificant: war, for instance, probably cost Philip the Bold less than 5,000 francs p.a. On the whole, he did not fight wars, and, when he did, other people, notably the king of France and the duchess of Brabant, usually paid for them.

There is no question, in Philip's reign, of a surplus carried over from year to year. He lived and ruled very much from hand to mouth, and was evidently seldom or never in a position to draw on reserves. These simply did not exist, nor was any provision made for them in the financial administration. When, as happened from time to time, extra funds were required, these were raised either by levying *aides*, as in 1394 and 1397; by means of loans; or by melting down the ducal plate. To raise loans, Philip turned to the towns of Burgundy and Flanders, to the burgesses of Paris, and to his own knights and civil servants. He also borrowed money from the royal financial officers, from his banker and financial adviser Dino Rapondi, from Giangaleazzo Visconti of Milan, and from numerous others. Forced loans were from time to time extracted from his knights and civil servants by the simple device of temporarily reducing their wages: a procedure resorted to in 1389, when all *pensions* were to be halved for six months; in 1397, when this was done for a full year; in 1399, when 7,000 francs were borrowed from a specified group of *pensions*; and at other times.[1] The pawning of jewellery and valuables was an equally common means of raising loans; indeed such treasure was amassed partly with this in view. The melting down of plate was less usual, but a large quantity was melted down in the autumn of 1382 to help pay for the immediate expenses of the Roosebeke campaign, Philip afterwards amply recouping himself from the king of France.[2]

What conclusions can be drawn from this brief survey of the Burgundian finances under Philip the Bold? Clearly, they depended on French help for costly projects like the Charterhouse of Champmol and the Nicopolis crusade, not to mention the duke's personal extravagance and liberality. Because of this, when Philip died in 1404, his successor was faced with the choice of a large-scale retrenchment or a continued exploitation of France in the face of increasing political difficulties there. But, though nothing had been saved, and Burgundian dependence on France in the financial sphere had been perpetuated, all the available resources had been applied in the formation of the Burgundian state; for the Nicopolis crusade and Sluis castle, just as much as the court and administration, all contributed to this end.

[1] Plancher, iii. no. 130, p. 153 and no. 192. On loans, see especially van Nieuwenhuysen, *Recette générale*, 82–95 and Biver and Mirot, *BEC* ciii (1942), 324–31.
[2] *Inventaires mobiliers*, ii. 104–18.

Epilogue

The controversial nature of the theme, and even the title, of the present work, cannot be denied. It is implied that Burgundy was a state, and suggested that this state was formed under the aegis of, if not directly by, Philip the Bold, in the years 1384–1404. Although no claim is made that its formation was completed in these years (indeed the contrary is true), this theme nevertheless entails the acceptance of Philip the Bold as the founder or creator of the Burgundian state. It is thus directly opposed to the views of historians like Pirenne, who regard Philip the Good in this light, and of those who, with Huizinga, are loath to accept Burgundy as a true state until after the loss of the duchy in 1477.[1]

Although Philip the Bold's Burgundy comprised a group of scattered territories, in each of which he ruled by a different title, and all of which were part either of the Empire or of France, they shared a single ruler. It was he who appointed or dismissed the administrative personnel in all these lands, just as it was he who collected and spent their public rents and taxes. He possessed his own court; he lavished funds on his own artistic projects; he launched his own crusade; and he pursued his own dynastic and expansionist policies. But all this requires qualification, for Philip the Bold was juridically and financially dependent on France. The supreme court for all his French territories was the *Parlement* of Paris and, although the king of France had almost completely forgone his right to levy *aides* in the ducal territories, Philip still relied on the French crown for almost half his annual revenue.

---

[1] Pirenne, *AHR* xiv (1908–9), 477–502 and Huizinga, *MA* xl (1930), 171–93 and xli (1931), 11–35, 83–96. Pirenne's view is accepted by Heimpel, *GWU* iv (1953), 257–72 and by the authors of the *Algemene geschiedenis der Nederlanden*, see iii. chapter 10, J. Bartier, 'Filips de Goede en de vestiging van de Bourgondische staat'.

To what extent, in these circumstances, is the historian justified in describing Philip the Bold's Burgundy as a state? Certainly not at all if that word bears its modern connotation of a single and exclusive political, national and territorial unity. But in the later Middle Ages a state was not necessarily an exclusive and completely independent entity. The king of England did homage to the king of France for his French-speaking continental possessions, but these still formed part of his state. The provinces of Hainault, Holland and Zeeland under their Wittelsbach rulers formed a single state, even though they lacked both territorial contiguity and, since they formed part of the Empire, full independence. Nor is there any reason why the word state should not be applied to the Neapolitan kingdom of Charles of Anjou and his successors, even though it was divided between Provence and the south Italian mainland, and the latter area was a papal fief. Used in this sense of a political though not necessarily territorial or even juridical entity, under a single ruler and capable of acting in its own interests and of having its own relations with its neighbours, the word state accurately describes Philip the Bold's Burgundy. It came into existence in the years 1384–7 in a three-fold manner. In the first place, its constituent territorial units were brought together under Philip early in 1384 on the death of Louis of Male; secondly, in 1385, Jehan Canard became, not just chancellor of Burgundy or Flanders, but chancellor of the duke, with powers of direction and control, especially over the administration, which extended throughout all his territories. Finally, in 1386–7, a major reorganization of the state was carried out, based on the twin administrative capitals of Lille and Dijon, which resulted in two more or less unified administrative areas of about equal size and importance, with a central administration at Paris.[1]

The foundation of the Burgundian state took place at a moment when the political condition of Western Europe was exceedingly favourable. The great rulers of the fourteenth century had recently died: Edward III of England in 1377; the Emperor Charles IV in 1378; and Charles V of France in 1380. They were replaced in England and France by boys and, in Germany, by the drunken Wenzel.

[1] It is difficult to justify Pirenne's identification of the Burgundian state with the Low Countries, to the exclusion of the two Burgundies; *AHR* xiv (1908–9), 477. It must not be forgotten that, in Philip the Bold's reign, the latter were larger in area than his possessions in the former; they provided more personnel for the central administration; their *chambre des comptes* was senior to that at Lille; and the duke visited them and their capital just as often as he did Flanders and Lille.

All three countries now entered a period of civil strife and declining public authority which had its ecclesiastical counterpart in the papal Schism. It was in these conditions of turmoil and disorder that Burgundy appeared on the European scene. Her appearance was facilitated not only by the favourable political context, but also by the genius of her first ruler, for Philip the Bold was surpassed by few of his contemporaries in political and administrative ability. He won European fame for himself and Burgundy through two elaborate military projects, the invasion of England in 1386 and the crusade of Nicopolis ten years later. Although the first never took place and the second ended in disaster, both were mentioned or celebrated by the chroniclers of England, Germany, France, Italy and Spain. His qualities as a statesman led to his arbitration of disputes in France and in the Low Countries, and his mediation was proffered on one occasion in Italy. He was entrusted at different times with the government of Brittany, Savoy and Luxembourg, and in all his activities he was supported and aided by his wife Margaret, herself by no means unpractised or unskilled in matters of state.

While the merits of Philip the Bold as a statesman are undisputed, his outlook and aims are still a subject for controversy. A certain consensus of historical opinion attributes to him a specifically French approach to politics, but when the Belgian historian Bonenfant claims that 'il n'agit jamais qu'en prince des fleurs de lys',[1] his exact meaning remains unclear. If this claim implies that Philip the Bold acted always in the best interests of the French crown, it must be rejected, for this is exactly what the princes of the royal blood of France were *not* doing at this time. Philip the Bold, Louis of Anjou and Louis of Orleans were all three of them intent on their own schemes, in pursuing their own interests. Whether or not they identified these interests with those of France, by regarding their own private projects as redounding to the public good of France, is beside the point. Philip the Bold, like the others, was acting for himself, and for his own house. France was there to be used and exploited, and, in this use and exploitation of France, Philip excelled his rivals and relatives both in the amount of material assistance he extracted, and in the unscrupulous-

---

[1] *P. le Bon*, 9. Heimpel says of Philip: 'Auch jetzt blieb er ein französischer Prinz', *GWU* iv (1953), 257. Other historians, e.g. Steinbach, *RV* ix (1939), 62, claim that Philip was not trying to found a state, but simply to extend his own and France's influence. It is hardly surprising to find Christine de Pisan taking this 'French' view of her patron Philip: he was a prince 'de grant travail et grant volunté de l'augmentacion, bien et accroissement de la couronne de France', *Livre des fais*, i. 145–6.

ness of his means in extracting it. No doubt his motives for seizing and maintaining power in France were partly linked to his position as First Peer of the realm and uncle of the king, but we can hardly credit him with disinterest in the fact that one-sixth to one-eighth of the revenues of the French crown were annually being diverted to his own treasury. Far from being in the best interests of France, Philip the Bold's activities there were sinister, selfish and unscrupulous. His political outlook was Burgundian, not French.

When Philip died at Hal, near Brussels, on 27 April 1404, the bulk of his territories passed as a single unit to his eldest son, John of Nevers. He had by no means rested content with the lands he had acquired by marriage: in particular he had contrived to secure the succession of Brabant for his younger son Anthony. In this and other ways he had adumbrated the plan later executed by his grandson Philip the Good, of uniting the Low Countries under his house. But, while he taught his children Flemish, he married his grandchildren into the French royal family. He pointed the way towards the Low Countries with one hand, but the other was firmly engaged in France. Thus the future of the Burgundian state was left, as it were, poised delicately in the balance. Philip's son, in the face of increasing difficulties, managed to maintain this balance, and it was only under his successors, Philip the Good and Charles the Rash, that the disengagement from France was fully achieved, and finally consummated by open warfare between the two countries.

Bibliography

Full Titles of Works Referred to in the Notes

Actes concernant les rapports entre les Pays-Bas et la Grande-Bretagne de 1293 à 1468 conservés au château de Mariemont. Ed. P. Bonenfant. *BCRH* cix (1944), 53–125.

Algemene geschiedenis der Nederlanden. Ed. J. A. van Houtte *et al.* 13 vols. Utrecht, 1949–58.

Alpartils, M. de. *Chronica actitatorum* i. Ed. F. Ehrle. Quellen und Forschungen aus dem Gebiete der Geschichte, xii. Paderborn, 1906.

Ampl. coll. Veterum scriptorum . . . amplissima collectio. Ed. E. Martène and U. Durand. 9 vols. Paris, 1724–33.

Analectes belgiques, i. Ed. L. P. Gachard. Brussels, 1830.

Analectes historiques. Ed. A. le Glay. Paris, 1838.

Andt, E. *La chambre des comptes de Dijon à l'époque des ducs valois,* i. Paris, 1924.

Anglo-French negotiations at Bruges, 1374–1377. Ed. E. Perroy. Royal Historical Society, Camden Miscellany, xix. London, 1952.

Arbaumont, J. d'. 'Les anoblis de Bourgogne; période ducale (1361–1477).' *RNHB* (n.s.) ii (1866), 151–65.

——. *Armorial de la chambre des comptes de Dijon.* Dijon, 1881.

Asseldonk, G. A. van. *De Nederlanden en het Westers Schisma.* Nijmegen, 1955.

Atiya, A. S. *The Crusade of Nicopolis.* London, 1934.

——. *The Crusade in the later Middle Ages.* London, 1938.

[Aubrée, G.] *Mémoires pour servir à l'histoire de France et de Bourgogne.* 2 vols. Paris, 1729.

Avout, J. d'. *La querelle des Armagnacs et des Bourguignons.* Paris, 1943.

Bachmann, A. *Geschichte Böhmens.* Geschichte der europäischen Staaten. 2 vols. Gotha, 1899, 1905.

Bahr, K. *Handel und Verkehr der deutschen Hanse in Flandern während des vierzehnten Jahrhunderts.* Leipzig, 1911.

Barante, A. de. *Histoire des ducs de Bourgogne de la Maison de Valois.* Ed. L. P. Gachard. 2 vols. Brussels, 1838.

Bartier, J. *Charles le Téméraire.* Brussels, 1944.

——. *Légistes et gens de finances au xve siècle. Les conseillers des ducs de Bourgogne.* MARBL 1 (2). Brussels, 1952.

Bazin, J. L. 'La Bourgogne sous les ducs de la Maison de Valois, i, ii.' *MSE* (n.s.) xxix (1901), 33–67 and xxx (1902), 85–160.

——. *Histoire des évêques de Chalon-sur-Saône,* i. *MSHAC* xiv (1914).

Beaune, H. 'État des officiers de Philippe le Hardi duc de Bourgogne.' *RNHB* (n.s.) i (1865), 49–56.

Beazely, C. R. *The dawn of modern geography.* 3 vols. London, 1897–1906.

Berchen, W. van. *Gelderse kroniek.* Ed. A. J. de Mooy. Werken uitgegeven door de Vereeniging Gelre, xxiv. Arnhem, 1950.

Berthollet, J. *L'évêché d'Autun.* Autun, 1947.

Bess, B. 'Frankreich und sein Papst, 1378–1394.' *ZK* xxv (1904), 48–89.

Beuken, J. H. A. *De Hanze en Vlaanderen.* Maastricht, 1950.

Billioud, J. *Les États de Bourgogne aux xive et xve siècles. MAD* (5) iv (1922), extra number.

Biver, A. and L. Mirot. 'Prêts consentis au duc et à la duchesse de Bourgogne en Nivernais et en Donziois de 1384 à 1386.' *BEC* ciii (1942), 324–31.

Blondeau, G. 'Les origines du Parlement de Franche-Comté.' *MSED* (n.s.) iv (1924), 90–106.

——. 'Le Parlement de Franche-Comté pendant la deuxième moitié du xive siècle et les premières années du xve siècle.' *MSED* (n.s.) v (1925), 79–103.

Boldingh-Goemans, W. L. *Christine de Pizan.* Rotterdam, 1948.

Bonenfant, P. *Philippe le Bon.* 3rd ed. Brussels, 1955.

Bonet, H. *Somnium super materia scismatis.* Ed. N. Valois, under the title 'Un ouvrage inédit d'Honoré Bonet'. *ABSHF* (1890), 193–228.

——. *L'Apparicion maistre Jehan de Meun et le Somnium super materia scismatis.* Ed. I. Arnold. Publications de la Faculté des lettres de l'Université de Strasbourg, xxviii. Paris, 1926.

——. *The Tree of Battles of Honoré Bonet.* Transl. G. W. Coopland. Liverpool, 1949.

Bossuat, R. *Manuel bibliographique de la littérature française du moyen âge.* Melun, 1951, and supplements.

Boüard, M. de. *Les origines des guerres d'Italie. La France et l'Italie au temps du Grand Schisme d'Occident.* BEFAR cxxxix. Paris, 1936.

Bouault, J. 'Les justices de bailliage en Bourgogne pendant la période ducale.' *RB* xxiii (1913), 76–84.

——. 'Les bailliages du duché de Bourgogne aux xive et xve siècles'. *AB* ii (1930), 7–22.

Brabantsche Yeesten of Rymkronyk van Braband. Ed. J. F. Willems and J. H. Bormans. CRH. 3 vols. Brussels, 1839–69.

Buntinx, J. *De audientie van de graven van Vlaanderen.* Verhandelingen van de Koninklijke Vlaamse Academie. Letteren, x. Brussels, 1949.

——. 'De raad van Vlaanderen en zijn archief.' *APAE* i (1950), 4–76.

Cabaret d'Orville, J. *La chronique du bon duc Loys de Bourbon.* Ed. A. M. Chazaud. SHF. Paris, 1876.

Caeneghem, R. van. 'Les appels flamands au Parlement de Paris au moyen âge.' *Études d'histoire du droit privé offertes à Pierre Petot*, 61–8. Paris, 1959.

——. 'De appels van de Vlaamse rechtbanken naar het Parlement van Parijs.' *AFAHB* xxxvi (1956), 191–2.

Cafmeyer, M. 'Het kasteel van Male.' *ASEB* lxxxiii (1940–6), 112–32.

Calendar of State Papers. Venice, i. Ed. R. Brown. London, 1864.

Calmette, J. *Les grands ducs de Bourgogne.* 2nd ed. Paris, 1956.

Canat de Chizy, M. *Marguerite de Flandre, duchesse de Bourgogne, sa vie intime et l'état de sa maison.* Paris, 1860. Reprinted from *MAD* (2) vii (1858–9), 65–332.

Canat de Chizy, N. 'Étude sur le service des travaux publics, et spécialement sur la charge de maître des œuvres, en Bourgogne.' *BM* lxiii (1898), 245–72, 341–57 and 439–73.

Cartellieri, O. *Geschichte der Herzöge von Burgund, 1363–1477*, i, *Philipp der Kühne.* Leipzig, 1910.

Cartulaire de l'ancienne Estaple de Bruges. Ed. L. Gilliodts van Severen. 4 vols. Bruges, 1904–6.

Cartulaire des comtes de Hainaut. Ed. L. Devillers. CRH. 6 vols. Brussels, 1881–96.

Catalogue d'une partie des livres composant la bibliothèque des ducs de Bourgogne au xve siècle. Ed. G. Peignot. 2nd ed. Dijon, 1841.

Charageat, M. 'Le parc d'Hesdin. Création monumentale du xiiie siècle.' *BSHAF* (1950), 94–106.

Charmasse, A. de. 'L'église d'Autun pendant la Guerre de Cent Ans.' *MSE* (n.s.) xxvi (1898), 1–135.

Chartes de communes et d'affranchissements en Bourgogne. Ed. J. Garnier. 3 vols. Dijon, 1867–77.

Chartes et documents de l'abbaye de Saint-Pierre au Mont Blandin à Gand. Ed. A. van Lokeren. 2 vols. Ghent, 1868, 1871.

Chérest, A. *L'Archiprêtre, épisodes de la Guerre de Cent Ans au xiv⁰ siècle.* Paris, 1879.

Choix de documents luxembourgeois inédits tirés des Archives de l'État à Bruxelles. Ed. N. van Werveke. PSHIL xl. 149–252. Luxembourg, 1889.

Choix de pièces inédites relatives au règne de Charles VI. Ed. L. Douët d'Arcq. SHF. 2 vols. Paris, 1863, 1864.

Chronicon comitum Flandrensium. Ed. J. J. de Smet. CRH. Recueil des chroniques de Flandre, i. 34–257. Brussels, 1837.

Chronique des quatre premiers Valois. Ed. S. Luce. SHF. Paris, 1862.

Chronique des règnes de Jean II et de Charles V. Ed. R. Delachenal. SHF. 4 vols. Paris, 1910–20.

Chronique rimée des troubles de Flandre. Ed. E. le Glay. Lille, 1842.

——. Ed. H. Pirenne. Publication extraordinaire de la Société d'histoire et d'archéologie de Gand, i. Ghent, 1902.

Chronographia regum Francorum. Ed. H. Moranvillé. SHF. 3 vols. Paris, 1891–7.

Clerc, E. *Essai sur l'histoire de la Franche-Comté.* 2nd ed. 2 vols. Besançon, 1870.

——. *Histoire des États Généraux et des libertés publiques en Franche-Comté.* 2 vols. Besançon, 1882.

Codex diplomaticus prussicus. Ed. J. Voigt. 6 vols. Königsberg, 1836–61.

Codex Germaniae diplomaticus. Ed. J. C. Lünig. 2 vols. Frankfurt and Leipzig, 1732, 1733.

Cognasso, F. 'L'influsso francese nello stato sabaudo durante la minorità di Amedeo VIII.' *MAH* xxxv (1915), 257–326.

Colin, P. *Les ducs de Bourgogne.* Brussels, 1941.

Commerce et expéditions militaires de la France et Venise au moyen âge. Ed. L. de Mas Latrie. CDIHF. Mélanges historiques, choix de documents, iii. 1–240. Paris, 1880.

Commissioni di Rinaldo degli Albizzi per il comune di Firenze, i (*1399–1423*). Ed. C. Guasti. Documenti di storia italiana, i. Florence, 1867.

Comptes de l'argenterie des rois de France au xiv⁰ siècle. Ed. L. Douët d'Arcq. SHF. Paris, 1851.

Cordey, J. *Les comtes de Savoie et les rois de France pendant la Guerre de Cent Ans (1329–1391).* BEHE clxxxix. Paris, 1911.

Coulborn, A. P. R. 'The economic and political preliminaries of the crusade of 1383.' *BIHR* x (1932–3), 40–4.

Coussemaker, F. de. 'Thierry Gherbode.' *ACFF* xxvi (1901–2), 175–385. Reprinted separately, Lille, 1902.

Coville, A. *Les Cabochiens et l'Ordonnance de 1413.* Paris, 1888.

——. 'Les finances des ducs de Bourgogne au commencement du xve siècle.' *Études d'histoire du moyen âge dédiées à Gabriel Monod.* 405–13. Paris, 1896.

——. *Gontier et Pierre Col.* Paris, 1934.

——. *La vie intellectuelle dans les domaines d'Anjou-Provence de 1380 à 1435.* Paris, 1941.

[Creton, J.] *Translation of a French metrical history of the deposition of King Richard II . . . with a copy of the original.* Ed. and transl. J. Webb. *Archaeologia* xx (1824), 1–423.

Croniques de Franche, d'Engleterre, de Flandres, de Lile et espécialement de Tournay. Ed. A. Hocquet. Publications de la Société des bibliophiles belges, xxxviii. Mons, 1938.

Daenell, E. *Die Blütezeit der deutschen Hanse.* 2 vols. Berlin, 1905, 1906.

Daguin, A. 'Les évêques de Langres.' *MSHAL* iii (1880–1901), 1–188.

Dale, J. H. van. *Een blik op de vorming der stad Sluis.* Middelbourg, 1871.

David, H. *Philippe le Hardi, duc de Bourgogne, protecteur des arts.* Dijon, 1937.

——. *Philippe le Hardi. Le train somptuaire d'un grand Valois.* Dijon, 1947. Partly reprinted from *AB* xvi (1944).

——. *Claus Sluter.* Paris, 1951.

——. 'Jeunesse de Jean, second duc valois de Bourgogne. Le double mariage de Cambrai.' *Miscellanea Prof. Dr D. Roggen,* 57–76, Antwerp, 1957.

Debrie, E. 'Documents sur les artistes dijonnais de la fin du xive siècle.' *AB* ix (1937), 302–6.

Dehaisnes, C. *Histoire de l'art dans la Flandre, l'Artois et le Hainaut avant le xve siècle.* Lille, 1886.

Delachenal, R. *Histoire de Charles V.* 5 vols. Paris, 1909–31.

Delaville le Roulx, J. *La France en Orient au xive siècle.* BEFAR xliv and xlv. Paris, 1886.

Delisle, L. *Recherches sur la librairie de Charles V.* 2 vols. Paris, 1907.

Demuynck, R. 'De Gentse oorlog (1379–1385).' *ASHAG* (n.s.) v (1951), 305–18.

Deschamps, E. *Œuvres complètes.* Ed. Q. de Saint Hilaire and G. Raynaud. Société des anciens textes français. 11 vols. Paris, 1878–1903.

Deutsche Reichstagsakten. Ed. J. Weizsäcker *et al.* 16 vols. Munich and Gotha, 1867–1928.

Dillon, P. W. 'Remarks on the manner of the death of King Richard II.' *Archaeologia* xxviii (1840), 75–95.

Dimier, L. 'Manuel distingué de Malouel.' *BSHAF* (1929), 46–9.

——. 'Les primitifs français, ii.' *GBA* (6) xvi (1936) (2), 205–32.

Dixmude, O. van. *Merkwaerdige gebeurtenissen vooral in Vlaenderen en Brabant van 1377 tot 1443.* Ed. J. J. Lambin. Ypres, 1835.

Documenti ed estratti . . . riguardanti la storia del commercio e della marina ligure, i. *Brabante, Fiandra e Borgogna.* Ed. C. Desimoni and L. T. Belgrano. Atti della Società ligure di storia patria, v. 355–547. Genoa, 1867.

Documents et extraits divers concernant l'histoire de l'art dans la Flandre, l'Artois et le Hainaut avant le xvᵉ siècle. Ed. C. Dehaisnes. Lille, 1886.

Documents luxembourgeois à Paris concernant le gouvernement du duc Louis d'Orléans. Ed. A. de Circourt and N. van Werveke. PSHIL xl. 53–148. Luxembourg, 1889.

Documents pour servir à l'histoire de la Maison de Bourgogne en Brabant et en Limbourg. Ed. H. Laurent and F. Quicke. *BCRH* xcvii (1933), 39–188.

Documents pour servir à l'histoire des relations entre l'Angleterre et la Flandre. Le Cotton MS. Galba B 1. Ed. E. Scott and L. Gilliodts van Severen. CRH. Brussels, 1896.

Documents relatifs au Grand Schisme, iii. *Suppliques et lettres de Clément VII (1379–1394).* Ed. H. Nelis. Analecta Vaticano-Belgica, xiii. Rome, 1934.

Dortmunder Urkundenbuch. Ed. K. Rubel. 4 vols. Dortmund, 1881–1910.

Doutrepont, G. *La littérature française à la cour des ducs de Bourgogne.* Bibliothèque du xvᵉ siècle, viii. Paris, 1909.

Drouot, H. 'L'atelier de Dijon et l'exécution du tombeau de Philippe le Hardi.' *RBAHA* ii (1932), 11–39.

——. 'Études slutériennes, i. Autour de la pastorale de Claus Sluter.' *AB* xiv (1942), 7–24.

Dubosc, N. *Voyage pour négocier la paix entre les couronnes de France et d'Angleterre.* Ed. E. Martène and U. Durand. *Voyage littéraire de deux religieux bénédictins de la congrégation de Saint-Maur,* ii. 307–60. Paris, 1724.

Dubrulle, H. *Cambrai à la fin du moyen âge.* Lille, 1904.

Duhem, G. 'Le trésor des chartes et les archives du comté de Bourgogne.' *BAB* (1936), 145–63.

Dumay, G. 'Guy de Pontailler.' *MSBGH* xxiii (1907), 1–222.

Dumont, M. 'Les mentions extrasigillaires dans les lettres des ducs de Bourgogne-Valois.' *APAE* xv (1958), 33–61.

Dupin, P. *Chronique du Conte Rouge*. Ed. D. Promis. *Monumenta historiae patriae*, iv. *Scriptorum*, ii. cols. 391–592. Turin, 1839.

Dupont. *Histoire ecclésiastique et civile de la ville de Cambrai*. 3 vols. Cambrai, 1759–67.

Dupont-Ferrier, G. *Études sur les institutions financières de la France*. 2 vols. Paris, 1930, 1932.

Durrieu, P. 'MSS. de luxe exécutés pour des princes et des grands seigneurs français, iv, v.' *Le Manuscrit*, ii (1895), 82–7, etc. and 162–8, etc.

Dynter, E. de. *Chronique des ducs de Brabant*. Ed. P. de Ram. CRH. 3 vols. Brussels, 1854–7.

Ernst, S. P. *Histoire du Limbourg*. 7 vols. Liége, 1837–52.

Eulogium historiarum sive temporis. Ed. F. S. Haydon. Rolls series. 3 vols. London, 1858–63.

Extraits analytiques des anciens registres des consaux de la ville de Tournai. Ed. H. Vandenbroeck. 2 vols. Tournai, 1861, 1863.

Faussemagne, J. *L'apanage ducal de Bourgogne dans ses rapports avec la monarchie française, 1363–1477*. Lyons, 1937.

Finot, J. *Recherches sur les incursions des Anglais et des Grandes Compagnies dans le duché et le comté de Bourgogne à la fin du xive siècle*. Vesoul, 1874. Reprinted from *Bulletin de la Société d'agriculture, sciences et arts du département de la Haute-Saône* (3) v (1874), 69 ff.

——. *Les comptes et pièces comptables concernant l'administration de l'hôtel des comtes de Flandre . . . conservées aux Archives du Nord*. Lille, 1892.

——. 'Le commerce entre la France et la Flandre au moyen âge.' *ACFF* xxi (1893), pp. xxi–392. Reprinted as *Étude historique sur les relations commerciales entre la France et la Flandre au moyen âge*. Paris, 1894.

——. 'Relations commerciales et maritimes entre la Flandre et l'Espagne au moyen âge.' *ACFF* xxiv (1898), 1–353. Reprinted as *Étude historique sur les relations commerciales entre la Flandre et l'Espagne au moyen âge*. Paris, 1899.

Foedera, conventiones etc. Ed. T. Rymer. 3rd ed. 10 vols. The Hague, 1739–45.

Foucart, J. *La gouvernance du souverain-bailliage de Lille-Douai-Orchies-Mortagne et Tournaisis*. SHDPF. Bibliothèque, xii. Lille, 1937.

Fredericq, P. *Essai sur le rôle politique et social des ducs de Bourgogne dans les Pays-Bas*. Ghent, 1875.

——. 'Le vieux courtraisien de Dijon.' *BARBL* (1909), 379–90.

Fremaux, H. 'Histoire généalogique de la famille de la Tannerie.' *BSEC* xii (1908), 195–243.

Friccius, W. 'Der Wirtschaftskrieg als Mittel hansischer Politik im 14. und 15. Jahrhundert, i.' *HG* lvii (1932), 59–77.

Fris, V. *Histoire de Gand.* Brussels, 1913.

Froissart, J. *Chroniques.* Ed. Kervyn de Lettenhove. 25 vols. Brussels, 1867–77.

——. Ed. S. Luce, G. Raynaud *et al.* SHF. 13 vols. Paris, 1869–1957 (in progress).

——. *Jehan Froissart's cronyke van Vlaenderen.* Ed. N. de Pauw. Koninklijke Vlaamse Academie. 4 vols. Ghent, 1898–1909.

Gabotto, F. *Gli ultimi principi d'Acaia.* Turin, 1898.

Gace de la Buigne. *Le roman des deduis.* Ed. A. Blomquist. Studia romanica Holmiensia, iii. Karlshamn, 1951.

Gachard, L. P. *Rapport à monsieur le Ministre de l'Intérieur sur . . . les archives de Lille.* Brussels, 1841.

Gailliard, J. *Bruges et le Franc.* 5 vols. Bruges, 1857–64.

Garnier, J. *La recherche des feux en Bourgogne aux xive et xve siècles.* Dijon, 1876.

——. *L'artillerie des ducs de Bourgogne.* Paris, 1895.

Gaunt, John of. *Register.* Ed. E. C. Lodge and R. Somerville. Royal historical society, Camden third series, lvi, lvii. London, 1937.

Gedenkwaardigheden uit de geschiedenis van Gelderland. Ed. J. A. Nijhoff. 6 vols. Arnhem and The Hague, 1830–75.

Geschiedenis van Vlaanderen. Ed. R. van Roosbroeck *et al.* 6 vols. Amsterdam, 1936–49.

Giard, E. 'Jean Canard.' *PTSEC* (1902), 23–8.

Gollut, L. *Les mémoires historiques de la république séquanoise et des princes de la Franche-Comté de Bourgogne.* Ed. C. Duvernoy. Arbois, 1846.

Gras, P. 'Cherches de feux chalonnaises au xive siècle.' *AB* xv (1943), 289–92.

——. 'Un siège épiscopal au temps des papes d'Avignon et du Grand Schisme d'Occident. Les évêques de Chalon de 1302 à 1416.' *MSHDB* xv (1953), 7–50.

Handelingen van de Leden en van de Staten van Vlaanderen (1384–1405). Ed. W. Prevenier. CRH. Brussels, 1959.

Hansisches Urkundenbuch. Ed. K. Höhlbaum, C. Kunze *et al.* 11 vols. Halle, Leipzig, etc., 1876–1916.

Hartl, W. *Die österreichisch-burgundische Heirat des xiv Jahrhunderts.* Vienna, 1884.

Heimpel, H. 'Burgund, Macht und Kultur.' *GWU* iv (1953), 257–72.

Hirschauer, C. *Les États d'Artois, 1340–1640.* 2 vols. Paris, 1923.

Histoire des institutions françaises au moyen âge. Ed. F. Lot and R. Fawtier. 2 vols. Paris, 1957, 1958 (in progress).

Historia Gelriae auctore anonymo. Ed. J. G. C. Joosting. Werken uitgegeven door de Vereeniging Gelre, ii. Arnhem, 1902.

Hommel, L. *Le grand héritage.* 4th ed. Brussels, 1951.

Höpffner, E. *Eustache Deschamps. Leben und Werke.* Strasbourg, 1904.

Huguet, A. *Aspects de la Guerre de Cent Ans en Picardie maritime (1400–1450).* Mémoires de la Société des antiquaires de Picardie, xlviii, l. Amiens, 1941, 1944.

Huizinga, J. 'L'État bourguignon, ses rapports avec la France et les origines d'une nationalité néerlandaise.' *MA* xl (1930), 171–93 and xli (1931), 11–35 and 83–96.

Hulin, G. 'La bible de Philippe le Hardi historiée par les frères de Limbourc.' *BSHAG* xvi (1908), 183–8.

Humbert, F. 'Les finances municipales de Dijon du milieu du xive siècle à 1477.' *PTSEC* (1958), 51–8.

IAB. L. Gilliodts van Severen. *Inventaire des archives de la ville de Bruges*, i (1). *13e–16e siècle.* 7 vols. Bruges, 1871–8.

IAC. C. Mussely. *Inventaire des archives de la ville de Courtrai.* 2 vols. Courtrai, 1854–8.

IACOB. C. Rossignol et al. *Inventaire sommaire des archives départementales de la Côte-d'Or. Série B.* 6 vols. Paris and Dijon, 1863–94.

IACD. L. de Gouvenain et al. *Inventaire sommaire des archives communales de Dijon.* 4 vols. Dijon, 1867–1900.

IADB. J. Gauthier. *Inventaire sommaire des archives départementales du Doubs. Série B.* 3 vols. Besançon, 1883–95.

IADNB. A. le Glay et al. *Inventaire sommaire des archives départementales du Nord. Série B.* 10 vols. Lille, 1863–1906.

IAEG. C. Wyffels. *Inventaris van de oorkonden der graven van Vlaanderen.* Ghent, n.d.

IAGRCC. L. P. Gachard et al. *Inventaire des archives des chambres des comptes.* 6 vols. Brussels, 1837–1931.

IAGRCL. A. Verkooren. *Inventaire des chartes et cartulaires de Luxembourg.* 5 vols. Brussels, 1914–21.

IAGRCR. H. Nelis. *Inventaire des comptes en rouleaux des chambres des comptes de Flandre et Brabant.* Brussels, 1914.

IAM. P. J. van Doren. *Inventaire des archives de la ville de Malines.* 8 vols. Malines, 1859–94.

IAPCA. J. M. Richard. *Inventaire sommaire des archives départementales du Pas-de-Calais. Série A.* 2 vols. Arras, 1878, 1887.

IAY. I. L. A. Diegerick. *Inventaire analytique et chronologique des chartes et documents appartenant aux archives de la ville de Ypres.* 7 vols. Bruges, 1853–68.

Inventaire de la 'librairie' de Philippe le Bon (1420). Ed. G. Doutrepont. CRH. Brussels, 1906.

Inventaire de l'orfèvrerie et des joyaux de Louis I duc d'Anjou. Ed. H. Moranvillé. Paris, 1906.

Inventaire du mobilier de Charles V. Ed. J. Labarte. CDIHF (3), Archéologie. Paris, 1879.

Inventaires de Jean duc de Berry. Ed. J. Guiffrey. 2 vols. Paris, 1894, 1896.

Inventaires mobiliers et extraits des comptes des ducs de Bourgogne de la Maison de Valois (1363–1477). Ed. B. and H. Prost. 2 vols. Paris, 1902–13.

Istore et croniques de Flandres. Ed. Kervyn de Lettenhove. CRH. 2 vols. Brussels, 1879, 1880.

Itinéraires de Philippe le Hardi et de Jean sans Peur, ducs de Bourgogne (1363–1419). Ed. E. Petit. CDIHF. Paris, 1888.

Jarry, E. *La vie politique de Louis de France duc d'Orléans. 1372–1407.* Paris and Orleans, 1889.

——. 'La "voie de fait" et l'alliance franco-milanaise (1386–1395).' *BEC* liii (1892), 213–53 and 505–70. Reprinted separately, Paris, 1892.

——. *Les origines de la domination française à Gênes (1392–1402).* Paris, 1896.

Jorga, N. *Thomas III marquis de Saluces.* Saint-Denis, 1893.

——. *Philippe de Mézières, 1327–1405, et la croisade au xive siècle.* BEHE cx. Paris, 1896.

Kervyn de Lettenhove. *Histoire de Flandre.* 6 vols. Brussels, 1847–50.

Kleinclausz, A. 'Les peintres des ducs de Bourgogne.' *RAAM* xx (1906), 161–76 and 253–68.

La Chauvelays, J. de. 'Les armées des trois premiers ducs de Bourgogne de la Maison de Valois.' *MAD* (3) vi (1880), 19–335.

Lacour, R. *Le gouvernement de l'apanage de Jean duc de Berry.* Paris, 1934.

Laenen, J. *Les Archives de l'État à Vienne au point de vue de l'histoire de Belgique.* Brussels, 1924.

La Marche, O. de. *Mémoires.* Ed. H. Beaune and J. d'Arbaumont. SHF. 4 vols. Paris, 1883–8.

Lameere, E. *Le grand conseil des ducs de Bourgogne de la Maison de Valois.* Brussels, 1900.

Langlois, E. *Notices des MSS. français et provençaux de Rome antérieures au xvie siècle.* Notices et extraits des MSS. de la Bibliothèque Nationale et autres bibliothèques, xxxiii (2). Paris, 1889.

Mandements et actes divers de Charles V. Ed. L. Delisle. CDIHF (1). Histoire politique. Paris, 1874.

Marie José. *La Maison de Savoie. Les origines, le Comte Vert, le Comte Rouge*. Paris, 1956.

Mauricette, L. *Le bailliage de l'Eau de l'Écluse sous les ducs de Bourgogne*. Unpublished thesis (Diplôme d'études supérieures). University of Lille, 1955–6.

Memorieboek der stad Ghent. Ed. P. J. van der Meersch. Maetschappy der Vlaemsche bibliophilen (2) xv. 4 vols. Ghent, 1852–64.

Minerbetti, P. di G. *Cronica*. Ed. J. M. Tartini. *Rerum italicarum scriptores*, ii. cols. 79–628. Florence, 1770.

Mirot, L. 'Isabelle de France, reine d'Angleterre (1389–1409).' *RHD* xviii (1904), 544–73 and xix (1905), 60–95, 161–91 and 481–522. Reprinted separately, Paris, 1905.

——. *Les insurrections urbaines au début du règne de Charles VI (1380–1383)*. Paris, 1905.

——. *Les d'Orgemont*. Bibliothèque du xve siècle, xviii. Paris, 1913.

——. 'Une tentative d'invasion en Angleterre pendant la Guerre de Cent Ans (1385–1386).' *REH* lxxxi (1915), 249–87 and 417–66.

——. 'Études lucquoises, iii. La Société des Raponde. Dino Raponde.' *BEC* lxxxix (1928), 299–389. Reprinted in *Études lucquoises*. Nogent-le-Rotrou, 1930.

——. *La politique française en Italie de 1380 à 1422*, i. *Les préliminaires de l'alliance florentine*. Paris, 1934. Reprinted from *REH* c (1933), 493–542.

——. 'Notes pour servir à l'histoire du Nivernais et du Donziois (1360–1404).' *MSAN* xxxviii (1936), 125–53.

——. 'Les raisons de la rupture entre Philippe le Hardi et Louis d'Orléans.' *CABSS* xii (1937), 48–9.

——. 'Jean sans Peur de 1398 à 1405.' *ABSHF* (1938), 129–245. Reprinted separately, Paris, 1939.

Mirot, L. and E. Deprez. *Les ambassades anglaises pendant la Guerre de Cent Ans (1327–1450)*. Paris, 1900. Reprinted from *BEC* lix–lxi (1898–1900).

Mohr, F. *Die Schlacht bei Rosebeke*. Berlin, 1906.

Mollat, M. 'Recherches sur les finances des ducs valois de Bourgo⟨ *RH* ccxix (1958), 285–321.

Monget, C. *La Chartreuse de Dijon*. 3 vols. Montreuil-sur-M⟨ Tournai, 1898–1905.

Monier, R. *Les lois, enquêtes et jugements des pairs du cast⟨ SHDPF. Documents et travaux, iii. Lille, 1937.

Laroche, L. 'Les États particuliers du Charolais.' *MSHDB* vi
 145–94.

Laurent, H. and F. Quicke. *Les origines de l'État bourguignon. L'a*
 de la Maison de Bourgogne aux duchés de Brabant et de Limbourg
 1407). MARBL xli (1). Brussels, 1939.

Lavalleye, J. 'Le château de Courtrai.' *ASRAB* xxxv (1930), 157–

Lebeuf, J. *Mémoires concernant l'histoire ecclésiastique et civile d'Au*
 2 vols. Paris, 1743.

Leclercq, F. 'Étude du personnel de la chambre des comptes de Lille
 les ducs de Bourgogne.' *PTSEC* (1958), 87–92.

Le Fèvre, J. *Journal*, i. Ed. H. Moranvillé. Paris, 1887.

Lefranc, A. *Olivier de Clisson*. Paris, 1898.

Leman, A. 'Un traité inédit relatif au Grand Schisme d'Occident.' *R*
 xxv (1929), 239–59.

Léonard, E. G. *Les Angevins de Naples*. Paris, 1954.

Le Petit, J. F. *La grande chronique ancienne et moderne de Hollan*
 Zélande etc. jusques à la fin de l'an 1600. 2 vols. Dordrecht, 1601.

Leroux, A. *Nouvelles recherches critiques sur les relations politiques de*
 France avec l'Allemagne de 1378 à 1461. Paris, 1892.

Lestocquoy, J. *Les évêques d'Arras*. MCMP iv (1). Arras, 1942.

Lettres secrètes et curiales du pape Urbain V (1362–1370) se rapportant à
 France. Ed. P. Lecacheux and G. Mollat. BEFAR (3). Paris, 1902–5

Lichtervelde, P. de. 'Les bâtards de Louis de Mâle.' *ASEB* lxxviii (193
 48–58.

——. *Un grand commis des ducs de Bourgogne, Jacques de Lichtervel*
 Brussels, 1943.

Liebreich, A. *Claus Sluter*. Brussels, 1936.

Limburg-Stirum, T. de. *La cour des comtes de Flandre, leurs offic*
 héréditaires, i. *Le chambellan de Flandre et les sires de Ghistelles*. Ghe
 1868.

Lindner, T. *Geschichte des deutschen Reiches unter König Wenzel*. 2 v
 Brunswick, 1875, 1880.

Livre de comptes, 1395–1406. Guy de la Trémoille et Marie de Sully. Ed.
 de la Trémoille. Nantes, 1887.

Lopez de Ayala, P. *Cronicas de los reyes de Castilla*. Ed. E. de Llagu
 Amirola. Colleccion de las cronicas y memorias de los reyes de Casti
 i, ii. Madrid, 1779, 1780.

Maere d'Aertrycke, M. de. *Recherches concernant quelques questions c*
 troversées à propos des batailles de Courtrai et de Rosebecque. Annales in
 nationales d'histoire. Congrès de Paris, 1900. 1e section, 125–60. Pa
 901.

Monier, R. *Les institutions centrales du comté de Flandre de la fin du ixe siècle à 1384.* SHDPF. Bibliothèque, xiii. Lille and Paris, 1944.

——. *Les institutions financières du comté de Flandre du xie siècle à 1384.* SHDPF. Bibliothèque, xix. Paris, 1948.

Monteuuis, G. 'Le siége de Bourbourg en 1383.' *ACFF* xxii (1895), 259–313.

Monumenta spectantia historiam Slavorum meridionalium. Ed. S. Ljubić et al. Academia scientiarum et artium Slavorum meridionalium. 43 vols. Zagreb, 1868–1917.

Moranvillé, H. *Étude sur la vie de Jean le Mercier.* Paris, 1888. Reprinted from Mémoires de l'Académie des inscriptions et belles-lettres (2) vi.

——. 'Conférences entre la France et l'Angleterre (1388–1393).' *BEC* l (1889), 355–80.

Moreau, P. E. de. *Histoire de l'Église en Belgique.* 5 vols. Brussels, 1940–52 (in progress).

Morrall, J. B. *Gerson and the Great Schism.* Manchester, 1960.

Müller, T. *Frankreichs Unionversuche unter der Regentschaft des Herzogs von Burgund, 1393–1398.* Evangelisches Gymnasium zu Gütersloh. Bericht über das Schuljahr 1880–1, 3–28. Gütersloh, 1881.

Nelis, H. 'La collation des bénéfices ecclésiastiques en Belgique sous Clément VII, 1378–1394.' *RHE* xxviii (1932), 34–69.

Nieuwenhuysen, A. van. *La recette générale de Philippe le Hardi.* Unpublished thesis, University of Brussels, 1955.

——. 'Le transport et le change des espèces dans la recette générale de Philippe le Hardi.' *RBPH* xxxv (1957), 55–65.

Notes et documents relatifs à Jean, roi de France, et à sa captivité en Angleterre. Ed. H. d'Orléans. Philobiblon Society. Bibliographical and historical miscellanies, ii (6). London, 1855–6.

Nowé, H. *Les baillis comtaux de Flandre des origines à la fin du xive siècle.* MARBL xxv. Brussels, 1929.

Oorkonden in de Archives Nationales te Parijs aangaande de betrekkingen der Hollandsche graven uit het Henegouwsche en het Beiersche huis tot Frankrijk. Ed. A. Hulshof. *BMHGU* xxxii (1911), 266–405.

Ordonnances des ducs de Bourgogne sur l'administration de la justice du duché. Ed. E. Champeaux. *RB* xvii (2, 3) (1907).

Ordonnances des rois de France de la troisième race. Ed. D. F. Secousse et al. 21 vols. Paris, 1723–1849.

Ordonnances franc-comtoises sur l'administration de la justice (1343–1477). Ed. E. Champeaux. *RB* xxii (1, 2) (1912).

Oudegherst, P. d'. *Les chroniques et annales de Flandres.* Antwerp, 1571.

Owen, L. V. D. *The connection between England and Burgundy during the first half of the fifteenth century.* Oxford, 1909.

Panofsky, E. *Early Netherlandish Painting.* 2 vols. Cambridge, Mass., 1953.

Paris, A. P. *Les manuscrits françois de la Bibliothèque du Roi.* 7 vols. Paris, 1836–48.

Pellegrin, E. *La bibliothèque des Visconti et des Sforza.* Publications de l'Institut de recherche et d'histoire des textes, v. Paris, 1955.

Perier, A. *Un prévôt de Paris sous Charles V. Hugues Aubriot.* Dijon, 1908.

Perret, P. M. *Histoire des relations de la France avec Venise.* 2 vols. Paris, 1896.

Perroy, E. *L'Angleterre et le Grand Schisme d'Occident.* Paris, 1933.

——. 'Feudalism or principalities in fifteenth-century France'. *BIHR* xx (1943–5), 181–5.

——. *The Hundred Years War.* London, 1951. Translation of *La Guerre de Cent Ans.* Paris, 1945.

Petit, E. 'Campagne de Philippe le Hardi en 1372 dans le Poitou, l'Angoumois etc.' *MSBGH* ii (1885), 421–40.

——. *Entrée du roi Charles VI à Dijon . . . février 1390.* Dijon, 1885.

——. *Histoire des ducs de Bourgogne de la race capétienne.* 9 vols. Paris, 1885–1905.

——. *Ducs de Bourgogne de la Maison de Valois,* i. *Philippe le Hardi,* i. *1363–1380.* Paris, 1909.

Petot, P. 'L'accession de Philippe le Hardi au duché de Bourgogne et les actes de 1363.' *MSHDB* ii (1935), 5–13.

——. 'L'avènement de Philippe le Hardi en Bourgogne et les lettres de 2 juin 1364.' *MSHDB* iii (1936), 125–37.

Peyronnet, G. 'Les relations politiques entre la France et l'Italie, principalement au xive et dans la première moitié du xve siècles, i, ii.' *MA* lv (1949), 301–42.

Piaget, A. 'La Cour Amoureuse dite de Charles VI.' *Romania* xx (1891), 417–54.

——. 'Un manuscrit de la Cour Amoureuse de Charles VI.' *Romania* xxxi (1902), 597–603.

Picard, E. 'La vénerie et la fauconnerie des ducs de Bourgogne.' *MSE* (n.s.) ix (1880), 297–418. Reprinted separately, Paris, 1881.

——. 'L'écurie de Philippe le Hardi, duc de Bourgogne.' *MAD* (4) x (1905–6), 307–439. Reprinted separately, Paris, 1906.

——. 'La dévotion de Philippe le Hardi et de Marguerite de Flandre.' *MAD* (4) xii (1910–13), 1–116. Reprinted separately, Dijon, 1911.

Picard, E. 'Le château de Germolles et Marguerite de Flandre.' *MSE* (n.s.) xl (1912), 147–218.

——. 'Les hôtels de mgr. le duc de Bourgogne à Dijon.' 'L'ancienne chambre des comptes au Palais ducal' and 'Séjour de Philippe le Hardi ... à l'abbaye de Saint-Bénigne, 1376–1377.' *MCACO* xvii (1913–21), pp. xcv–xcvii and cccxcvii–cccciii.

Pinchart, A. 'Jean de Malines, poëte français du quatorzième siècle.' *BBB* xii (1856), 28–37.

Pinet, M. J. *Christine de Pisan. 1364–1430.* Paris, 1927.

Piquard, M. 'Étude sur la situation politique des archevêques de Besançon de 1290 à 1435.' *PTSEC* (1929), 193–200.

Pirenne, H. *Histoire de Belgique.* 7 vols. Brussels, 1902–32.

——. 'The formation and constitution of the Burgundian state.' *AHR* xiv (1908–9), 477–502. Translation of 'Die Entstehung und die Verfassung des burgundischen Reiches im 15. und 16. Jahrhundert.' *JGVV* xxxiii (3) (1909), 33–63.

Pisan, C. de. *Œuvres poétiques.* Ed. M. Roy. Société des anciens textes français. 3 vols. Paris, 1886–96.

——. *Le livre des fais et bonnes meurs du sage roy Charles V.* Ed. S. Solente. SHF. 2 vols. Paris, 1936, 1940.

Pitti, B. *Cronica.* Ed. A. Bacchi della Lega. Collezione di opere inedite o rare dei primi tre secoli della lingua. R. Commissione pe' testi di lingua nelle provincie dell' Emilia. Bologna, 1905.

Plancher, U. *Histoire générale et particulière de Bourgogne.* 4 vols. Dijon, 1739–81.

Pocquet du Haut Jussé, B.A. 'Deux féodaux: Bourgogne et Bretagne (1363–1491), i, ii.' *RCC* xxxv (2) (1933–4), 481–93 and 595–612. Reprinted separately, Paris, 1935.

——. 'Les séjours de Philippe le Hardi, duc de Bourgogne, en Bretagne. La tutelle de Jean V.' *MSHAB* xvi (1935), 1–62. Reprinted separately, Rennes and Paris, 1935.

——. 'Le retour de Nicopolis et la rançon de Jean sans Peur. Compte inédit de Maître Oudart Douay pour le duc de Bourgogne. 1397–1398.' *AB* ix (1937), 296–302.

——. 'Les chefs des finances ducales de Bourgogne.' *MSHDB* iv (1937), 5–77.

——. 'Les dons du roi aux ducs de Bourgogne Philippe le Hardi et Jean sans Peur (1363–1419).' 'Le don des aides.' *AB* x (1938), 261–89. 'Les dons ordinaires'. *MSHDB* vi (1939), 113–44. 'Les dons extraordinaires.' *MSHDB* vii (1940–1), 95–129.

Pocquet du Haut Jussé, B.A. 'Les aides en Bourgogne sous Philippe le Hardi et Jean sans Peur. 1363–1419.' *RHDFE* (4) xviii (1939), 388–422.

——. 'Les pensionnaires fieffés des ducs de Bourgogne de 1352 à 1419.' *MSHDB* viii (1942), 127–50.

Pot, J. *Histoire de Regnier Pot, conseiller des ducs de Bourgogne*. Paris, 1929.

Potvin, C. 'La charte de la Cour Amoureuse de l'année 1401.' *BARB* (3) xii (1886), 191–220.

Prevenier, W. 'Het Brugse Vrije en de Leden van Vlaanderen.' *ASEB* xcvi (1959), 5–63.

——. 'De beden in het graafschap Vlaanderen onder Filips de Stoute (1384–1404).' *RBPH* xxxviii (1960), 330–65.

——. 'Réalité et histoire. Le quatrième membre de Flandre.' *RN* xliii (1961), 5–14.

[——. *De Leden en de Staten van Vlaanderen (1384–1405)*. Verhandelingen van de Koninklijke Vlaamse Academie, Letteren. Brussels (not yet published).] See p. xiv above.

Proceedings and Ordinances of the Privy Council of England. Ed. H. Nicholas. 7 vols. London, 1834–7.

Prost, H. 'Les États du comté de Bourgogne des origines à 1477.' *PTSEC* (1905), 115–22.

Prou, M. *Étude sur les relations politiques du pape Urbain V avec les rois de France Jean II et Charles V*. BEHE lxxvi. Paris, 1888.

Quicke, F. *Les Pays-Bas à la veille de la période bourguignonne. 1356–1384*. Brussels, 1947.

Ramsay, J. H. *Genesis of Lancaster, 1307–1399*. 2 vols. Oxford, 1913.

Recesse und andere Akten der Hansetage von 1256–1430. Ed. K. Koppmann. 8 vols. Leipzig, 1870–97.

Recueil de plusieurs pièces curieuses servant à l'histoire de Bourgogne. Ed. E. Pérard. Paris, 1664.

Régestes de la cité de Liége. Ed. E. Fairon. 4 vols. Liége, 1933–40.

Registre des Parlements de Beaune et de Saint-Laurent-lès-Chalon. 1357–1380. Ed. E. Petot. Paris, 1927.

Rekeningen der stad Gent. Tijdvak van Philips van Artevelde. 1376–1389. Ed. J. Vuylsteke. Maatschapij van Nederlandsche letterkunde en geschiedenis . . . te Gent. Ghent, 1893.

Religieux de Saint-Denys. *Chronique*. Ed. L. Bellaguet. CDIHF (1). Histoire politique. 6 vols. Paris, 1839–52.

Remy, F. *Les grandes indulgences pontificales aux Pays-Bas à la fin du moyen âge (1300–1531)*. Louvain, 1928.

Riandey, P. *L'organisation financière de la Bourgogne sous Philippe le Hardi.* Dijon, 1908.

Richard, J. 'Les archives et les archivistes des ducs de Bourgogne.' *BEC* cv (1944), 123–69.

——. 'La grèneterie de Bourgogne et les mésures à grains dans le duché de Bourgogne.' *MSHDB* x (1944–5), 117–45.

——. *Les ducs de Bourgogne et la formation du duché.* Publications de l'Université de Dijon, xii. Paris, 1954.

——. 'Le gouverneur de Bourgogne au temps des ducs valois.' *MSHDB* xix (1957), 101–12.

Richebé, A. 'Note sur la comptabilité des communes et des établissements publics de la Flandre et sur le contrôle exercé par le comte sur leur gestion financière.' *ACFF* xxii (1895), 141–84.

Roggen, D. 'Hennequin de Marville en zijn atelier te Dijon.' *GBK* i (1934), 173–213.

——. 'De Kalvarieberg van Champmol.' *GBK* iii (1936), 31–85.

——. 'Klaas Sluter voor zijn vertrek naar Dijon in 1385.' *GBK* xi (1945–8), 7–40.

Rolland, P. 'Dijon, Bruxelles et Tournai'. *RBAHA* v (1935), 335–44.

Roussel, N. *Histoire ecclésiastique et civile de Verdun.* 2 vols. Bar-le-Duc, 1863, 1864.

Royal and historical letters during the reign of Henry IV, i. *1399–1404*. Ed. F. C. Hingeston. Rolls series. London, 1860.

Sagher, H. de. 'À propos du conseil de Flandre'. *ASEB* lxii (1912), 228–38.

Saint-Aubin, P. de. 'Documents inédits sur l'installation de Pierre d'Ailly à l'évêché de Cambrai en 1397.' *BEC* cxiii (1955), 111–39.

Salembier, L. *Le Cardinal Pierre d'Ailly.* Société d'études de la province de Cambrai, xxxv. Tourcoing, 1932.

Schoos, J. *Der Machtkampf zwischen Burgund und Orleans.* PSHIL lxxv. Luxembourg, 1956.

Schötter, J. *Geschichte des Luxemburger Landes.* Luxembourg, 1882.

Silberschmidt, M. *Das orientalische Problem zur Zeit der Entstehung des türkischen Reiches nach venezianischen Quellen.* Beiträge zur Kulturgeschichte des Mittelalters und Renaissance, xxvii. Berlin, 1923.

Skalweit, G. *Der Kreuzzug des Bischofs Heinrich von Norwich im Jahre 1383.* Königsberg, 1898.

Söchting, W. 'Die Beziehungen zwischen Flandern und England am Ende des 14. Jahrhunderts.' *HV* xxiv (1927–9), 182–98.

Songe véritable, Le. Ed. H. Moranvillé. *MSHP* xvii (1890), 217–438.

Steinbach, F. 'Gibt es einen lotharingischen Raum?' *RV* ix (1939), 52–65.

Sterling, C. *La peinture française; les primitifs.* Paris, 1938.

Stouff, L. *Catherine de Bourgogne et la féodalité de l'Alsace autrichienne.* *RB* xxiii (2, 3, 4) (1913). Reprinted separately, Paris, 1913.

Table chronologique des chartes et diplômes relatifs à l'histoire de l'ancien pays de Luxembourg. Règne de Wenceslas II, 1383–1419. Ed. F. X. Würth-Paquet. PSHIL iii. 1–238. Luxembourg, 1870.

Testaments enregistrés au Parlement de Paris sous le règne de Charles VI. Ed. A. Tuetey. CDIHF. Mélanges historiques, choix de documents, iii. 241–704. Paris, 1880.

Textes historiques sur Lille et le Nord de la France avant 1789. Ed. P. Thomas. SHDPF. Bibliothèque, v, x. Lille, 1931, 1936. Reprinted from *RN* xv–xxi (1929–35).

Thibault, M. *Isabeau de Bavière reine de France. La jeunesse. 1370–1405.* Paris, 1903.

Thomas, P. 'La renenghelle de Flandre aux xiiie et xive siècles.' *BCHDN* xxxiii (1930), 168–70.

Tout, T. F. *Chapters in the administrative history of medieval England.* 6 vols. Manchester, 1923–35.

Trésor des chartes du comté de Rethel. Ed. G. Saige and H. Lacaille. Collection des documents historiques publiés par ordre du Prince Albert Ier de Monaco. 4 vols. Monaco and Paris, 1902–16.

Troescher, G. *Claus Sluter und die burgundische Plastik um die Wende des xiv Jahrhunderts.* Freiburg im Breisgau, 1933.

Ulveling, J. *Invasions dans le Luxembourg de la part de Valéran, comte de St-Pol.* PSHIL xxxi, 141–6. Luxembourg, 1876.

Urkunden- und Quellenbuch zur Geschichte der altluxemburgischen Territorien. Ed. C. Wampach. 10 vols. Luxembourg, 1935–55 (in progress).

Urkunden zur Geschichte der teutschen Hanse. Ed. F. J. Mone. Anzeiger für Kunde der teutschen Vorzeit, vi. Karlsruhe, 1837.

Valois, N. *Le conseil du roi au xive, xve, et xvie siècles.* Paris, 1888.

——. *La France et le Grand Schisme d'Occident.* 4 vols. Paris, 1896–1902.

Vandenpeereboom, A. *Ypriana. Notices, études et documents sur Ypres.* 7 vols. Bruges, 1878–83.

Vansteenberghe, E. 'Gerson à Bruges.' *RHE* xxxi (1935), 5–52.

Varenbergh, E. *Histoire des relations diplomatiques entre le comté de Flandre et l'Angleterre au moyen âge.* Brussels, 1874. Reprinted from *Messager des sciences historiques* (1869–73).

Vernier, J. J. 'Traités entre le comte de Savoie Amédée VI et la Maison de Bourgogne en 1369 et 1379.' *MAS* (4) iv (1893), 493–507.

——. 'Philippe le Hardi duc de Bourgogne, son mariage, sa vie intime etc.' *MSA* lxiii (1899), 29–63.

——. 'Philippe le Hardi duc de Bourgogne, son mariage avec Marguerite de Flandre en 1369.' *BCHDN* xxii (1900), 89–133.

——. 'Le duché de Bourgogne et les compagnies dans la seconde moitié du xive siècle.' *MAD* (4) viii (1901–2), 219–320.

——. 'Une page d'histoire bourguignonne: hostilités entre les deux Bourgognes au xive siècle (1363–1365).' *RCB* i (1904), 1–23 and 183–203. Reprinted separately, Bar-sur-Aube, 1904.

Vielliard, J. and L. Mirot. 'Inventaire des lettres des rois d'Aragon à Charles VI et à la cour de France conservées aux Archives de la Couronne d'Aragon à Barcelone.' *BEC* ciii (1942), 99–150.

Walsingham, T. *Historia anglicana*. Ed. H. T. Riley. Rolls Series. 2 vols. London, 1863, 1864.

Werveke, H. van. *De Gentsche stadsfinanciën in de middeleeuwen*. MARBL xxxiv. Brussels, 1934.

Wigand of Marburg. *Chronik*. Ed. T. Hirsch. *Scriptores rerum prussicarum*, ii (6), 428–662. Leipzig, 1863.

Wrong, G. M. *The Crusade of 1383 known as that of the Bishop of Norwich*. London, 1892.

Wylie, J. H. *History of England under Henry IV*. 4 vols. London, 1884–98.

Zantfliet, C. *Chronicon*. Ed. E. Martène and U. Durand. *Veterum scriptorum . . . amplissima collectio*, v. cols. 67–504. Paris, 1729.

Index